Betwixt Development and Discontent

About the Author

Dr. Lalta Prasad (born 1940-), obtained his Ph.D. Degree from Gorakhpur University in 1977 and D. Litt. (Washington, D.C., U.S.A.) in 1999. He served as the Head of the Post Graduate Department of Sociology from 1963 – 1986 in S.M.M.P.G. College, Ballia, and as Principal in Sri Bajrang P.G. College, Dadar Ashram, Sikandarpur, Ballia from 11-8-1986 to 30-6-2001. Dr. Prasad is an Educationist par excellence endowed with an insight and a vision for the betterment of the future generation.

He has guided 20 Ph.D. Research Scholars and written two books—"Rural Sociology and Community Development" and "Growth of Small Towns". He has been Members in various prestigious and Expert Committees. He has participated and presented papers in several National and International Conferences. Presently, he is Member in N.A.A.C. [National Assessment and Accreditation Council, Bangalore (Karnataka)]. He has also been conferred various Awards, such as, Bharat Gaurav, Vikas Ratna in 1998, The Arch of India Gold Star Award, 1998 at London and Life Time Achievement Award 1999 at Chennai (Tamil Nadu).

Betwixt Development and Discontent

Dalit Adivasis on the South-Eastern Margins of Uttar Pradesh

Lalta Prasad

CONCEPT PUBLISHING COMPANY PVT. LTD.
NEW DELHI-110059

ISBN-13: 978-93-5125-220-7

First Published 2017

Published and Printed by

Since 1974 **Concept Publishing Company Pvt. Ltd.**
A/15-16, Commercial Block, Mohan Garden,
New Delhi-110059 (INDIA)
Phones : 25351460, 25351794, *Fax* : 091-11-25357109
Email : publishing@conceptpub.com
Website: www.conceptpub.com
Editorial Office: H-13, Bali Nagar, New Delhi-110 015, India.

Cataloging in Publication Data—DK Courtesy: D.K. Agencies (P) Ltd. <docinfo@dkagencies.com>

Prasad, Lalta, 1940- **author.**
Betwixt development and discontent : dalit adivasis on the south-eastern margins of Uttar Pradesh / Lalta Prasad.
pages cm
Includes bibliographical references and index.
ISBN 9789351252207 (hardback)

1. Dalits—India—Uttar Pradesh—Social conditions. 2. Adivasis—India—Uttar Pradesh—Social conditions. 3. Dalits—India—Uttar Pradesh—Economic conditions. 4. Adivasis—India—Uttar Pradesh—Economic conditions. 5. Dalits—Government policy—India—Uttar Pradesh. 6. Adivasis—Government policy—India—Uttar Pradesh. I. Title.

HT720.P73 2016 DDC 305.568809542 23

Dedicated

to

Professor Prithvish Nag

Vice Chancellor

Mahatma Gandhi Kashi Vidya Peeth

Varanasi

Preface

These scheduled tribes in India constitute 573 groups and sub-groups (according to the People of India Project) and 8.3 per cent of the country's population (2001 Census) and are distributed in different proportions in most of the States and Union Territories of the sub-continent. There is a wide variation in their social system, economic organization and political structure. But one conspicuous commonality with the scheduled tribes of India is their backwardness and underdevelopment. Extreme poverty has been reported in Madhya Pradesh, Orissa and Uttar Pradesh. Uttar Pradesh witnessed tribal poverty in the range of 30-50 per cent. The south-eastern part of Uttar Pradesh (Sonbhadra, Mirzapur, Chandauli, Allahabad and Chitrakoot) has witnessed lowest level of poverty among tribals and lowest level of employment opportunities, health and educational advancement. The tribals of this region are facing the problems related to land alienation, infiltration of non-tribals in tribal regions, involuntary migration and multiple displacements due to the developmental projects like Rihand Dam, installation of several Thermal Plants, Chemical Industries, Cement factories and Coal mines, etc. Their main sources of income had been the forest land and its produces. At present the forest department forcibly does not allow them to enter into the territory where the tribals had been the natural inhabitants in spite of Right of Forest Land Act 2006. The original and the real owners of water, forests, land and other natural resources are not only deprived of their Rights, but are also have to fight for their social and cultural identity as also for the basic needs of their daily existence. Highly polluted air and water have damaged their health conditions, several hunger deaths due to extreme poverty, malnutrition and pollution have often been flashed by the media. Torturing by feudal landlords of Chitrakoot and Allahabad by employing them as bonded labourers, indebtedness and rape crime with tribal women, have often resulted in suicide.

The whole South-Eastern Sub-Region of Uttar Pradesh has been in the news for some years now as Naxalite Activities Zone. The area is contagious with the tri-junction of the vast country's tribal region lying in Jharkhand, Chhattisgarh and Madhya Pradesh which have emerged as the main theatres of Naxal Activities and, therefore, a major problem of national concern. For sixty eight years, people living in these areas, particularly tribals have eagerly been waiting for the winds of development to touch their lives. But when the long wait tears the fabrics of patience turns into anger, they become willing pawns for exploitation by those armed groups who have no fear of law. This face of Naxalites is reflected in a montage of those areas of this region which are impoverished and hungry, face suicidal debts, unemployment, illiteracy and shortage of potable water. It is not a coincidence that Naxalism, which it triggered off with the dream of a new people's revolution is rooted deeply in areas that are lowest in the human development index. There are numerous examples of this. The death of 18 children due to disease of hunger was revealed by "People's vigilance committee on Human Rights" in Naibasti, Rope village, tehsil Robertsganj, district Sonbhadra. Children died of the disease of hunger and what else. Newspapers highlighted starvation deaths, which were investigated by a group of journalists. It was found that none of the families had the Red Ration Card meant for BPL families. This committee also discovered one 'Ghasia' tribes who has nothing to eat for their survival except the poisonous grass and wild mushrooms. The adults somehow managed to survive the ill effects of the poisonous intake, but little children were unable to tolerate the poison and prominently succumbed to death. *Dainik Jagran* January 4, 2004 highlighted that thousands of people in Patha region [Chitrakoot and Shankargarh (Allahabad)] were affected by hunger and were at the verge of starvation. 200 suicides related to hunger and debt took place in Patha region. Six *dalit adivasis* in Patha region were duped badly as loans worth Rs. 40,000 each were illegally taken in their name by feudal lords. This resulted in life long bonded labourers and suicide. Several suicides and deaths related to disappointment with public distribution system have often been flashed by the newspapers in all the five districts.

Besides all such incidences, the Naxalites have created obstructions in progress made after the implementation of Forest Rights Act (2006), meant for scheduled tribes and other traditional forest dwellers. The funds allocated for MNREGA, National Rural Health Mission (NRHM), Mid-Day Meal Scheme, Sarvashiksha Abhiyan and Pradhan Mantri Gram Sadak Yojna (PMGSY) and other welfare programmes have rarely reached the tribes. It was founds that the overall percentage of expenditure (disbursement of funds to beneficiaries) under MNREGA was 72 per cent in this region as compared to 41.04 per cent under PMGSY, 57.44 per cent under NRHM and 37.60 per cent for programmes under the Forest Rights Act in the April 2009 to January 2010 period.

The study under the heading "Betwixt Development and Discontent", which forms the central theme of this work, writer of the book has identified several parameters and pointers which have a direct bearing on the subject in question. This study describes the surmounting difficulties and unspeakable pathos faced by the *dalit adivasis* of this South-Eastern part of Uttar Pradesh (Sonbhadra, Mirzapur, Chandauli, Allahabad and Chitrakoot) after Independence due to development plans, land alienation by the Government, forest department, *maphias*, landlords, prohibition to utilize forest land and forest produce, Land grabbing by feudal landlords in the name of land distribution and forest Land Right and embezzlement of all the welfare funds by the mediators and Government officials with the help of the chapters mentioned under separate headings.

Acknowledgements

The very first idea of working on this topic entitled, "Betwixt Development and Discontent": Dalit Adivasis on the South-Eastern margins of Uttar Pradesh, came from a discussion with Former Prof. B.N. Juyal, Gandhian Institute, Rajghat, Varanasi, I take this opportunity to express my sincere and immense gratitude to him.

I am privileged to aknowledge my immense debt and gratitude to Prof. A.K. Srivastva, H.O.D. of Sociology, Lucknow University, who not only allowed me to conduct this research work in the premises of the Department of Sociology, but also enriched my knowledge by his valuable suggestions throughout.

I wish to express my sincere thanks to all Professors, Associate Professors and Asstt. Professors, of the Department of Sociology, Lucknow University, Lucknow for inspiring encouragement and interest which helped me in successful completion of my work.

I convey my sincere gratitude to Dr. Tarak Nath Tripathi, Retd. Principal, Nagrik P.G. College, Mehrawan, Jaunpur, who inspired me and helped my by his valuable suggestions during survey in Sonbhadra, Mirzapur and Chanduali tribal areas.

I have a special word of thanks for Dr. Vinod Misra, Assistant Professor, Jagatguru Ram Bhadracharya Handicapped Vishwavidyalaya, Chitrakoot, U.P. and for Dr. Vinod Shankar Singh, Head of the Deptt. of Social Work, M.G. Gramodaya Vishwavidyalaya, Chitrakoot, Satna (M.P.), who helped me in conducting the fieldwork in Manikpur Kol Tribal area by providing trained students from his department.

I take this opportunity to record my deep sense of gratitude to Sri Shyam Narayan Lal Srivastva, editor of the newspaper named '*Mahakal*', who enriched my knowledge by explaining the root causes of suffering of the tribals of Sonbhadra, Chandauli and Mirzapur districts.

I owe a great debt of gratitude to Sri Gopal Bhai, the Director, 'Akhil

Bhartiya Samaj Sewa Sansthan', Chitakoot, who enriched my knowledge regarding how the feudal landlords and dacoits of Patha region, Chitrakoot, had been tourchering Kol Tribes since long.

Dr. Udai Narayan Rai the C.O. (Police Deptt.) Varanasi, Dr. Bachcha Rai, the Physician, Sikanderpur, Ballia and his son Dr. Rohit Rai have been the moving forces in my endeavour. Their uninsted stimulation spurred me to complete this work in time. I am greatly indebted to them.

I am priviledged to acknowledge my immense debt and gratitude to my bosom and childhood friend Prof. Binod C. Agarwal, former Advisor to ISRO, Ahmedabad, who has been the encouraging force for academic work in my life. It is he who took initiative in publication of this research work.

I express my sincere gratitude to Sri Kailash Nath Singh, the Deputy Registrar and Sri Ranjeet Yadav, Deputy Registrar, Lucknow University, for giving me adequate support.

I fumble for words to express my deepest sense of gratitude to Prof. Prithvish Nag, the Vice Chancellor, M.G. Kashi Vidyapith University, Varanasi, whose inspirations have come to me in ways to numerous and personal to specify.

I am particularly grateful to Mr. Shamim Ahmed Khan, Deputy Registrar, M.G. Kashi Vidyapith University, Varanasi for his sincere cooperation.

I have a special words of thanks for Sri Ashutosh Kumar Srivastava, Senior Statistical Officer, New Delhi and Sri Abhay Nath, Senior Statistical Officer, New Delhi, for providing me support in processing and calculating the data and for making graphs etc.

I am grateful to Sri Ashok Kumar Mittal, Director, The Concept Publishing Company Pvt. Ltd., New Delhi, for being kind to understand the importance of the work and agreeing to publish this work. I am very much thankful to my spiritual brother Dr. R.N. Tripathi, Reader, Deptt. of Sociology, T.D. College, Jaunpur for the interest he took in my work.

Last but not the least, I must thank my son-in-law, Sri Karunakar, my daughter Dr. Vishva Jeotsna, my son Dr. Vishvajeet, my daughter-in-law. Dr. Jaya Srivastva my grand children Sanya and Raj could not help me better than what they actually did.

Lucknow University **Lalta Prasad**

Contents

List of Tables

List of Figures

Abbreviations

AMSKS	Adivasi Mahila Sashaktikaran Scheme
ANM	Auxiliary Nurse Midwife
BOP	Beneficiary Oriented Programme
FRA	Forest Rights Act
FRC	Forest Rights Commission
GER	Gross Enrolment Ratio
IFA	Indian Forest Act
ITDP	Integral Tribal Development Programme
ITDP	Integrated Tribal Development Projects
LAMPS	Large Scale Multipurpose Societies
MADA	Modified Development Approach
MPTB	Multi Purpose Tribal Blocks
NRRP	National Rehabilitation and Resettlement Policy
NTFDC	National Tribal Financial Development Corporation
PDS	Public Distribution System
PHC	Primary Health Centre
PRA	Participatory Rural Appraisal
PRI	Panchayati Raj Institution
PTG	Particularly Vulnerable Group
SCA	Special Central Assistance
SHC	Sub-Primary Health Centre
SHG	Self-Help Group
SMPT	Special Multi-Purpose Tribal
TAC	Tribal Advisory Committee
TDA	Tribal Development Agency
TDB	Tribal Development Blocks
TSP	Tribal Sub-Plan
VTG	Vulnerable Tribal Group

Maps

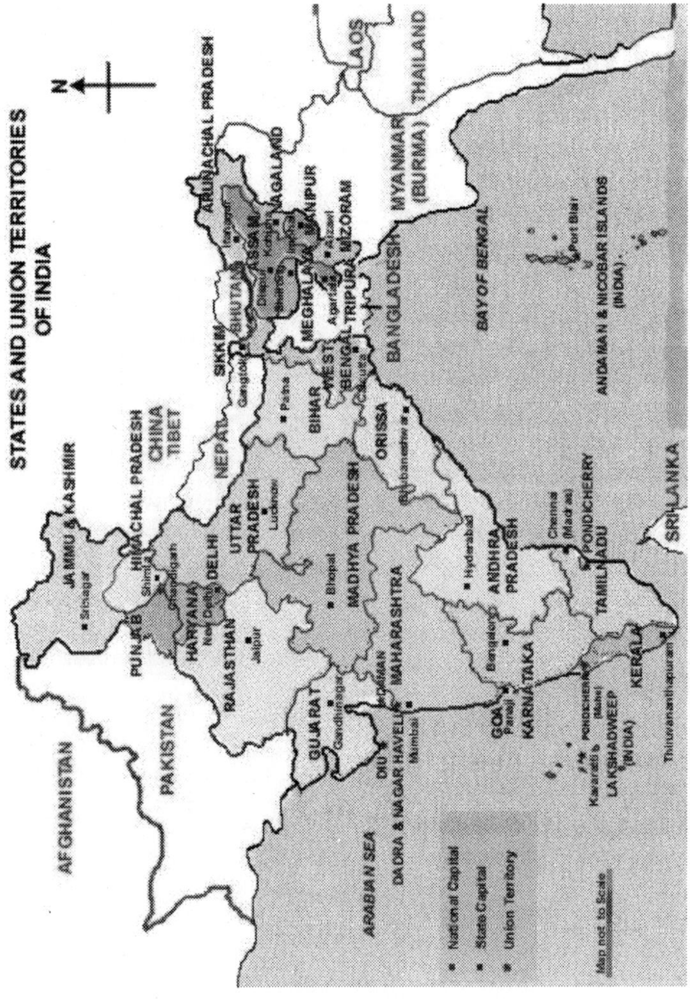
STATES AND UNION TERRITORIES OF INDIA
N
JAMMU & KASHMIR
Srinagar
HIMACHAL PRADESH
Shimla
PUNJAB
Chandigarh
HARYANA
DELHI
New Delhi
UTTAR PRADESH
Lucknow
RAJASTHAN
Jaipur
GUJARAT
Gandhinagar
MADHYA PRADESH
Bhopal
MAHARASHTRA
Mumbai
BIHAR
Patna
ORISSA
WEST BENGAL
SIKKIM
Gangtok
BHUTAN
ASSAM
ARUNACHAL PRADESH
NAGALAND
MANIPUR
MEGHALAYA
TRIPURA
MIZORAM
ANDHRA PRADESH
Hyderabad
KARNATAKA
Bangalore
GOA
Panaji
KERALA
Thiruvananthapuram
TAMIL NADU
Chennai (Madras)
PONDICHERRY
DIU
DAMAN
DADRA & NAGAR HAVELI
LAKSHADWEEP (INDIA)
Kavaratti
ANDAMAN & NICOBAR ISLANDS (INDIA)
Port Blair
AFGHANISTAN
PAKISTAN
CHINA TIBET
NEPAL
BANGLADESH
MYANMAR (BURMA)
THAILAND
LAOS
SRI LANKA
ARABIAN SEA
BAY OF BENGAL
National Capital
State Capital
Union Territory
Map not to Scale

CHHATTISGARH
Physical
UTTAR PRADESH
GB Panth Sagar
JHARKHAND
North Koel
Sonpar Hills
Akla(932)
Deogarh (1029)
Gulgupar(1164)
Jalangpet (1123)
Huandar Falls
Johilla
Son
Rihand
Deogarh Hills
Chotanagpur Plateau
Bija Pahar (1057)
Korea Hills
Barkhuar (1152)
Narmada
Burhner
Sohagpur Basin
Surguja Basin
Mand
Banjar
Pendra Plateau
Chhuri Hills
Udaipur Hills
Hasdo
MADHYA PRADESH
Maikala Range
Chhattisgarh Basin
Korba Basin
Hirakund Reservoir
Seonath
Kharun
Mahanadi
Raigarh Basin
ORISSA
www.mapsofindia.com
Mahanadi Basin
Ong
MAHARASHTRA
Tandula Tank
Kanker Basin
INDIA
Parasgaon Plateau
Kotri
Narainpur Basin
Bandia
Baster Hills
Tel
Banabadhara
Nagavati
Indravati Plateau
Indravati
Physical Altitude Scale
1350m
900
600
300
150
0 m
m=metres
Dantewara Plateau
Albaka Hills
Gollapalli Plateau
Sabari
Jalaput Reservoir
Balimela Reservoir
ANDHRA PRADESH
Sileru
Map not to Scale
Copyright © 2007 Compare Infobase Limited

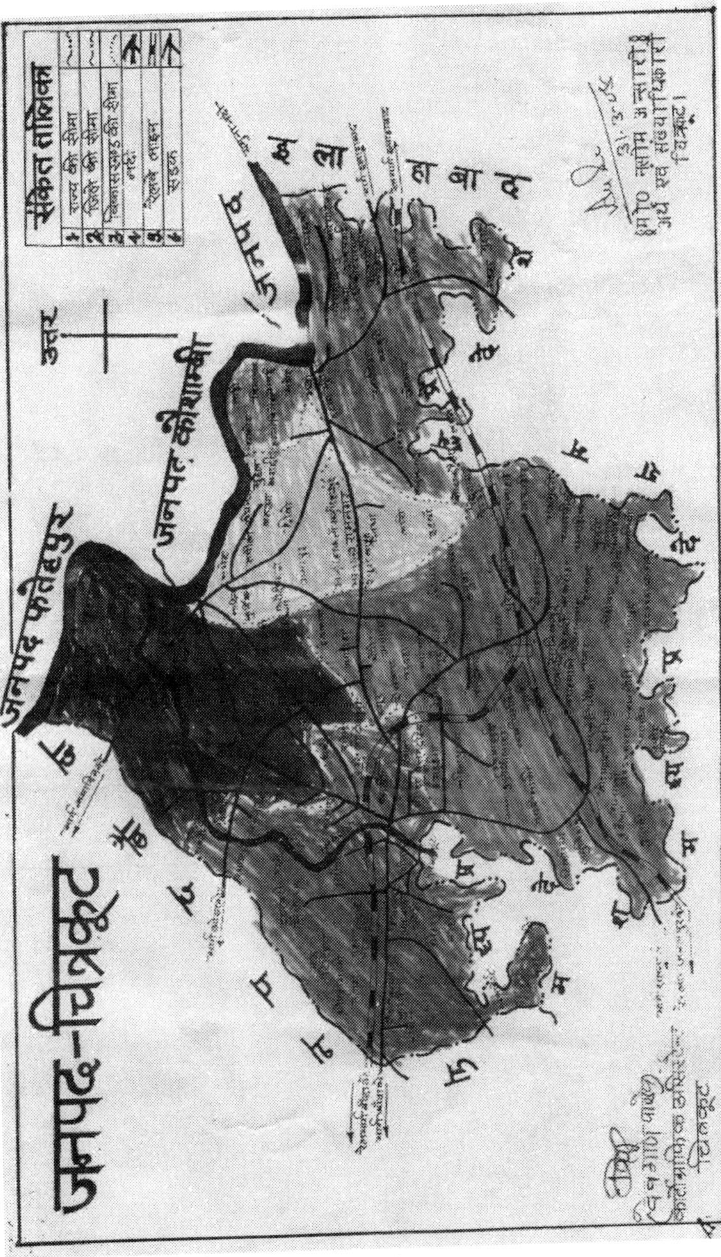
जनपद-चित्रकूट
जनपद फतेहपुर
जनपद कौशाम्बी
उत्तर
संकेत तालिका

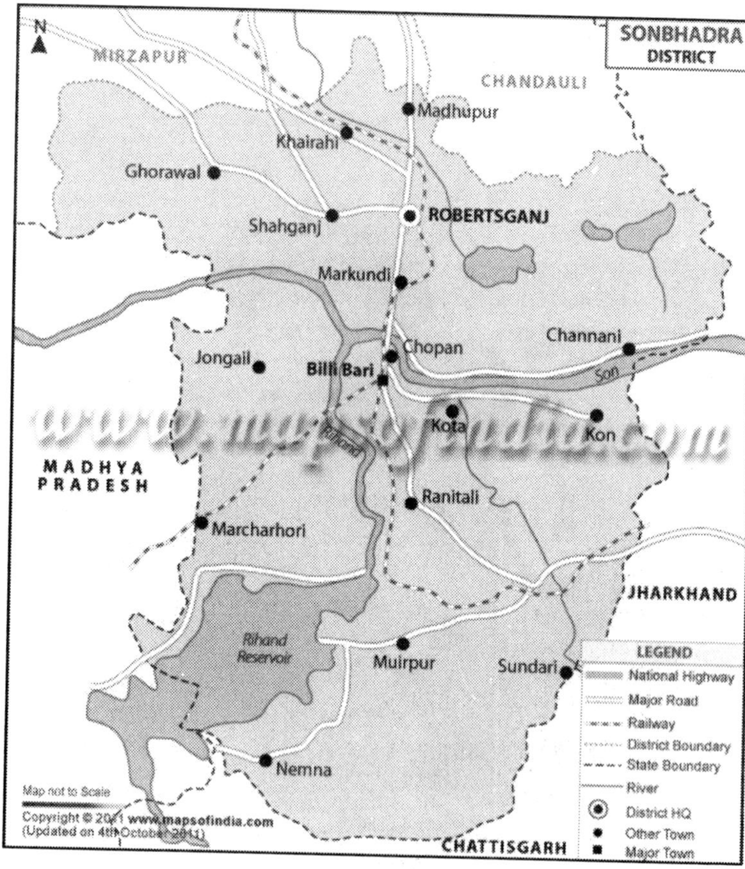

SONBHADRA
DISTRICT
N
MIRZAPUR
CHANDAULI
Madhupur
Khairahi
Ghorawal
Shahganj
ROBERTSGANJ
Markundi
Channani
Chopan
Jongail
Billi Bari
Son
Kota
Kon
Rihand
MADHYA
PRADESH
Ranitali
Marcharhori
JHARKHAND
Rihand
Reservoir
Muirpur
Sundari
Nemna
CHATTISGARH
LEGEND
National Highway
Major Road
Railway
District Boundary
State Boundary
River
District HQ
Other Town
Major Town
Map not to Scale
Copyright © 2011 www.mapsofindia.com
(Updated on 4th October 2011)

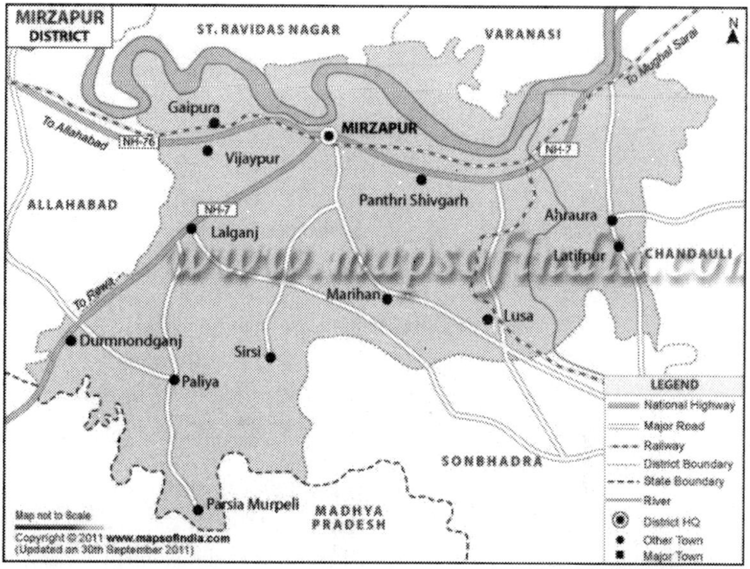
MIRZAPUR
DISTRICT
ST. RAVIDAS NAGAR
VARANASI
To Mughal Sarai
Gaipura
To Allahabad
NH-76
MIRZAPUR
Vijaypur
NH-7
ALLAHABAD
Panthri Shivgarh
NH-7
Lalganj
Ahraura
Latifpur
CHANDAULI
To Rewa
Marihan
Lusa
Durmnondganj
Sirsi
Paliya
SONBHADRA
Parsia Murpeli
MADHYA
PRADESH
LEGEND
National Highway
Major Road
Railway
District Boundary
State Boundary
River
District HQ
Other Town
Major Town
Map not to Scale
Copyright © 2011 www.mapsofindia.com
(Updated on 30th September 2011)

UTTAR PRADESH
DISTRICTS
UTTRAKHAND
INDIA
NEPAL
HARYANA
RAJASTHAN
MADHYA PRADESH
MADHYA
PRADESH
BIHAR
JHARKHAND
Saharanpur
SAHARANPUR
Muzaffarnagar
MUZAFFARNAGAR
BIJNOR
Bijnor
MEERUT
GHAZIABAD
Ghaziabad
Noida
RAMPUR
Rampur
Moradabad
MORADABAD
PILIBHIT
BAREILLY
Bareilly
BUDAUN
BULANDSHAHR
ALIGARH
Aligarh
KHERI
Lakhimpur
SHAHJAHANPUR
Shahjahanpur
MATHURA
Mathura
SITAPUR
Sitapur
SRAVASTI
BALRAMPUR
FARRUKHABAD
Hardoi
HARDOI
Agra
AGRA
FIROZABAD
MAINPURI
ETAWAH
KANNAUJ
LUCKNOW
Bara Banki
GONDA
MAHARAJGANJ
BASTI
KUSHINAGAR
UNNAO
Unnao
AURAIYA
FAIZABAD
GORAKHPUR
DEORIA
JALAUN
Orai
KANPUR
NAGAR
Raebareli
RAEBARELI
SULTANPUR
AZAMGARH
MAU
BALLIA
Ballia
JHANSI
HAMIRPUR
BANDA
Banda
FATEHPUR
PRATAPGARH
JAUNPUR
GHAZIPUR
MAHOBA
KAUSHAMBI
ST. RAVIDAS NAGAR
VARANASI
Chitrakoot
CHITRAKOOT
ALLAHABAD
MIRZAPUR
Mirzapur
CHANDAULI
Lalitpur
LALITPUR
Robertsganj
SONBHADRA
LEGEND
International Boundary
State Boundary
District Boundary
State Capital
District Headquarter
Map not to Scale
Copyright © 2011 www.mapsofindia.com
(Updated on 16th September 2011)

ALLAHABAD
DISTRICT MAP
N
Partapgarh
Jaunpur
Mau Aimma
Sevaith
Sikandra
Athrampur
NH - 2
To Fatehpur
ALLAHBAD
Sarai Mamrez
Kaushambi
Naini
Ganga
Saidabad
To Varanasi
Panasa
Sirsa
Bara
To Chitrakut
Shankargarh
Tons
Khondar
Bharatganj
Manda
NH - 27
Khiri
Koraon
MADHYA PRADESH
Barokhar
Mirzapur
LEGEND
National Highway
Major Road
Railway
District Boundary
State Boundary
River
District HQ
Other Town
Map not to Scale
Copyright © 2011 www.mapsofindia.com (Last Updated on 5th Sept. 2011)

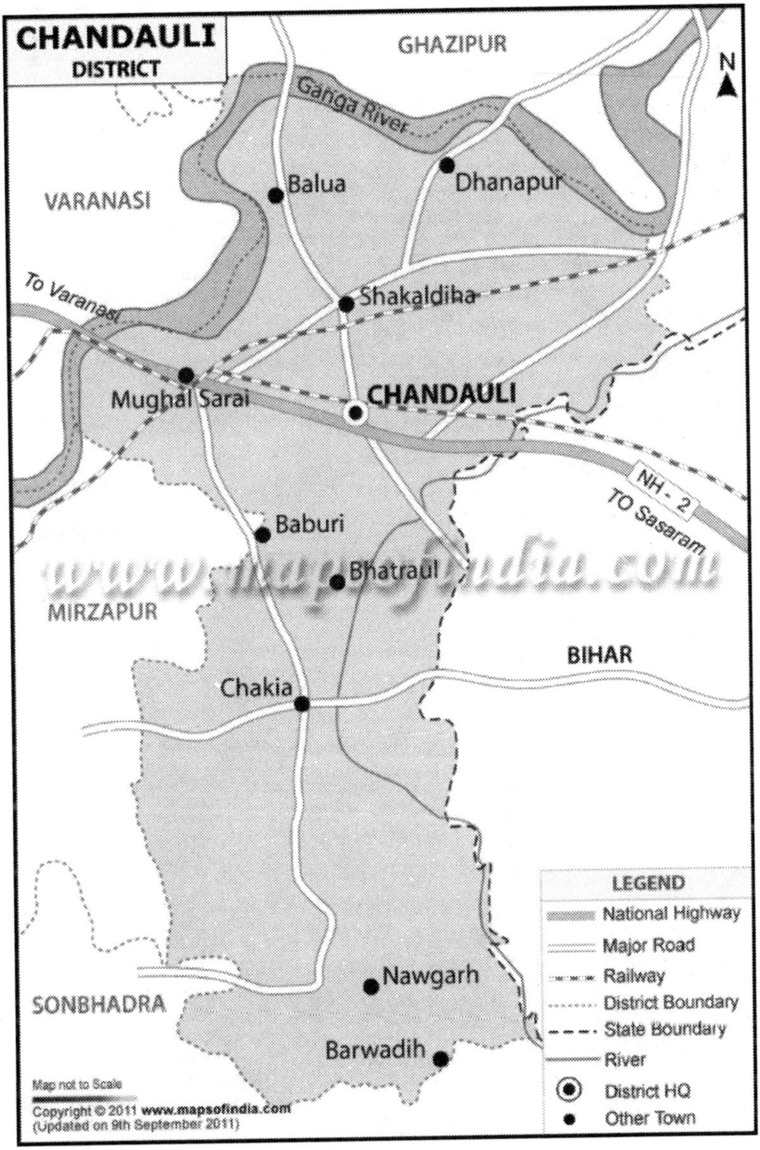
CHANDAULI
DISTRICT
GHAZIPUR
N
Ganga River
Balua
Dhanapur
VARANASI
To Varanasi
Shakaldiha
Mughal Sarai
CHANDAULI
NH - 2
TO Sasaram
Baburi
Bhatraul
www.mapsofindia.com
MIRZAPUR
BIHAR
Chakia
LEGEND
National Highway
Major Road
Railway
District Boundary
State Boundary
River
District HQ
Other Town
Nawgarh
SONBHADRA
Barwadih
Map not to Scale
Copyright © 2011 www.mapsofindia.com
(Updated on 9th September 2011)

BIHAR
District Map
N
NEPAL
UTTAR PRADESH
WEST BENGAL
JHARKHAND
PASCHIM CHAMPARAN
Bettiah
Motihari
PURBA CHAMPARAN
SITAMARHI
Sitamarhi
Shivhar
SHIVHAR
GOPALGANJ
Gopalganj
Siwan
SIWAN
MADHUBANI
Madhubani
MUZAFFARPUR
Muzaffarpur
Darbhanga
DARBHANGA
SUPAUL
Supaul
ARARIA
Araria
KISHANGANJ
Kishanganj
SARAN
Chhapra
VAISHALI
Hajipur
Samastipur
SAMASTIPUR
Saharsa
Madhepura
MADHEPURA
KOSHI
PURNIA
Purnia
KATIHAR
Katihar
Buxar
BUXAR
Ara
BHOJPUR
PATNA
BEGUSARAI
Begusarai
KHAGARIA
Khagaria
Munger
MUNGER
BHAGALPUR
Bhagalpur
BHABHUA
Bhabhua
ROHTAS
Sasaram
Arwal
ARWAL
Jahanabad
JAHANABAD
NALANDA
Bihar Sharif
Shekhupura
SHEKHPURA
Luckeesarai
LUCKEESARAI
Aurangabad
AURANGABAD
Gaya
GAYA
Nawada
NAWADA
Jamui
JAMUI
Banka
BANKA
LEGEND
International Boundary
State Boundary
District Boundary
State Capital
District Headquarter
Map not to Scale
Copyright © 2011 www.mapsofindia.com
(Updated on 4th May 2011)

Chapter 1
Introduction

Why there is a long list of adverse consequences of development of our tribal brethren residing in dense forest of Vindhya range of south-eastern sub-division of Uttar Pradesh? Why are they being described as victims of civilization? Is it not true that they have been victimised by developmental projects, industrialization, urbanization, displacement, intervention, alienation of their ancestral lands, consumer culture advancing globalization etc., depriving them from forest rights and other fundamental rights? Are we not trying to erase the presence of the tribal people by ignoring them? Do we not just want to close our eyes and wish them to vanish forever along with their vanishing habitat—the forests? Why are tribals of India and especially in south-eastern part of Uttar Pradesh seething with discontent. It seems that we have failed miserably in our tribal development efforts and managed to marginalise and ignore them as people with definite wants and needs and as a result, this region (Sonbhadra, Mirzapur, Chandauli, Allahabad and Chitrakoot) has been in the news for some years as a Naxalite activity zone.

The story of South Kaimur, Singrauli of the district is even more startling. It is now known as the "Energy Capital of India, for its highest power generation capacity. One could recall that in 1964 it was the construction of the Rihand Dam" symbol of so-called development that this entire process of displacement and alienation of the *adivasis* was triggered off. As a result, the most fertile land was submerged under water and lakhs of people lost their homes and livelihood. In fact, no record has been maintained to tell the destiny of at least 20,000 people who were forced to leave. It is tragic that viable rehabilitation plan was choked out for these people. They were only doled out plots of 40×60 yards for residential purposes. However, for the last 51 years, they have been awaiting fair compensation for their agricultural land that had been taken away from them.

The question of a sustained livelihood for these displaced people still remains unanswered. Who were benefited from the construction of the Rihand Dam? Was it for irrigation or for power generation? Even today the Uttar Pradesh Government has no answer to this question. On the contrary, it has become a dumping ground for the townships; the flyash released by the six power houses, located on the periphery of the dam is converting this reservoir into a poisonous well. The people who live around the reservoir are forced to consume the highly radioactive water and tolerate the toxic atmosphere so created. Whenever these displaced people have tried to fight for their rights they have been brutally crushed by the administration and entangled them in false criminal cases to the extent of being declared as 'Naxalites'.

Speaking at the report of 'the Coal Curse' under 'fact finding Mission' organised by the Greenpeace in September 22, 2011 in Baidhan village, Singrauli district, Ms. Priya Pillai said, "Singrauli has been scared by environmental and human rights violations. Our report uncovers the dirt and destruction in the power capital of the country. Entire communities are in the shadow of coal mines overburdened with dust everywhere. The tribals gave up their land for power, that does not reach them, and now have no reliable livelihood and their health has been ruined. This cannot be called development. We cannot continue to ignore the impacts of such large ravaging of the land and people without addressing their rights and imposing limits on the environmental degradation we are causing".

The "Patha" region of Uttar Pradesh, spread over Mau and Manikpur blocks of Chitrakoot district and Shankargarh blocks of Allahabad district, has been repeatedly in the news for both these wrongs—the terror of dacoits as well as large-scale of poverty and deprivation rooted in a high exploitative system. In recent years this region has been appearing in national level news mostly for wrong reasons. Acute drought distress including starvation deaths involving particularly the Saharia tribal community, numerous cases of acute exploitation and land grabbing from Kol tribals and the killings and abductions by the dacoit gangs 'Dadua gang', particularly the biggest one in Chitrakoot, which continues to enjoy very good political connections despite killings dozen of persons. As is often the case, the heaviest burden falls on the already overburdened shoulders of the weakest sections, i.e. tribals. These distressing headlines, however, reflect only the sporadic outburst of the deeper social malaise which the common people experience in the form of deepening distress and increasing stress in their everyday life.

This area is contagious with the tri-junction of the vast country's tribal region lying in Jharkhand, Chhattisgarh and Madhya Pradesh which have emerged as the main theatre of Naxal activities and, therefore, a major problem of national concern. Though comparatively smaller on geographic scale, this Uttar Pradesh portion is regarded as extension of the vast Naxalite affected region and so, strategically as critically important from the point of national security, as any other. As such, the relatively smaller geographic area/population do not subtract from the critically importance of the study.

From development point of view especially from the view point of improvement in their physical and social quality of life how and to what extent these interventions and exposures to outside world have impacted tribals, is a matter of debate. Because in terms of economic development, neither all are hunter and gatherer nor all are employed in secondary sector. The reality is that they are, even today, called as 'Primitive tribes'. If we examine their status from both empowerment and human rights point of view here also the picture seems significantly frustrating.

Besides being the victim of land alienation since the British days they are the victims of poverty, indebtedness, bonded labourhood, housing, quality education, alcoholism, communication, unemployment, disease, illness, malnutrition, migration, decreasing condition of local resources and their access to the resources and mega development projects. If we examine roots of poverty among these tribes, it seems that not by accident they are poor but they have been systematically deprived of their lands, homes and livelihood by the State since the British days.

Whether the transformation is good or bad, is a different question. But tribal development is a major issue as they are primary players in a consumer economy. Evidently, tribal development is a buzz word of political system. Concomitantly, lack of political will, bureaucratic apathy, public indifference choked their development process (Niranjan Pani, and Jitendra Sahoo: 1). Necessarily, tribal development is a collective affair. It is the work of Planning Commission. It is the work of Prime Minister, Chief Ministers, political leaders, specialists and administrators. Hence, development is a dynamic process. It has national and local significance, Government makes plans, innovative approaches and welfare measures. To provide in the path of tribal development, the responsibility of implementation is given to bureaucracy. They are incharge of focussing a techno-economic approach to the tribal development.

The welfare programmes are related to integrated programmes of investment in agriculture production and natural resource development, human resource development, rural development, land survey and settlement and implementation management supports. But the tribal development exacerbated partly due to the lack of a true participatory spirit in infrastructure development activities. Therefore, the lack of ownership by the tribals and partly due to the weak commitment on the part of the government in the maintenance of the structures are also handicaps to the development. Their participation in educational and skill development programmes as well as training to build awareness on issues such as environmental concerns, social conditions, trading practices, legal and land rights are very essential. But their participation has very much suffered a lot due to their inactiveness and ignorance. Thus, it can be said that the target tribal groups are no longer active partners in the development process. Therefore, their concern and priorities are not reflected adequately in the welfare programme. Another need is the degree of beneficiary participation at all stages. Tribal people are seldom involved in developing the annual programme of work and budget. This has created an atmosphere of discontent and lack of confidence towards the implementing authorities. Community and people's participation, therefore, are of utmost significance.

Our Constitution provides for a social order, free from all forms of discrimination and also a comprehensive frame for the protection and advancement of the tribal people. It has reformulated different laws to protect and promote their concerns. Such provisions are—

(1) Protective Provisions (Articles 15, 16, 19, 23, 29, 46, 164, 330, 332, 335, 338, 339, 342 and 371)
(2) Development (Articles 15, 16, 19, 46, 275 and 399.
(3) Administrative (Articles 344).
(4) Reservation (Articles 330, 332, 334, 335, 340 for reservation in Parliament/State assemblies/Government Jobs and admission).

I.R.D.P., N.R.E.P., N.R.L.E.G.P., TRYSEM, J.R.Y., S.H.G., I.A.Y., J.Y., D.P.A.P., I.W.L.D.R., N.R.Y., S.E.E.U.Y., S.J.G.S.Y., A.Y., National Old Age Pension Scheme, I.C.D.S.I.N.H.P., Literacy Mission, Watershed Mission, Sarva Shiksha Abhiyan, Pre-and Post-Matric Scholarship, Ashram School, Tendu Patta Policy, Employment Guarantee Scheme, M.N.R.E.G.A., NRHM and so on to actualize these provisions and Articles of Constitution of India. These development projects have been implemented among the tribals across the nation. But what was the outcome of all? Even after sixty five years of development planning and the implementation of special programmes both at the Centre and State, around 40 per cent of these sections SC/ST remained poor and underdeveloped. What is happening to the billions of rupees and millions of bureaucratic manpower employed to ameliorate the conditions of these people? Regrettably more number of people have been killed or committed suicide due to the failure of our system. At the same, the billionaires of our country are able to find a place in the list of the world's to most rich, year after year. Is this the mandate of the Constitution?

There are several areas of our concern—Rights, Education, Skill formation, special component Plan. And tragedy is this that *Dalit Adivasis* have been kept out of active participation in the economy. It is shameful that not even one officer in the rank of Secretary to the Government of India and not even half a dozen Joint Secretaries are from these communities, and no *Dalit Adivasi* has been allowed to reach a position of heading any public sector undertaking so far and there has been no concerned effort to make them head such position.

Conceptual Framework

Dalit

It is pertinent to point to make at the very outset that officially the State of Uttar Pradesh did not have any Scheduled Tribe population, when some groups concentrated mostly in Sonbhadra and Chitrakoot were notified as Scheduled Tribe. So long all of them were classified among the Scheduled Castes. Even at present, the second largest group among the various tribal groups after the Gonds that is the Kols, have not been recognised as Scheduled Tribes and continue to be counted among Scheduled Castes, though they are recognised as a tribe in the adjacent districts of Madhya Pradesh. As such, the term '*Dalit Adivasis*' is all the more appropriate in the context of this study, though it includes both the categories, i.e., S.C. and S.T., Moreover, after observing their social, economic, educational and political situations one can easily accept them as *Dalit. Dalit* has come to mean here persons who are cut, split, broken or torn asunder scattered or crushed and destroyed. These tribes have been reduced to nothingness or helplessness. It refers to the deplorable state of conditions, state of deprivation and oppressed. Therefore, the author has used the term '*Dalit Adivasis*' in place of *Scheduled Tribes* of these places.

The Constitution (Scheduled Tribes) (Uttar Pradesh) Order, 1967 (c.o. 78)

In exercise of the powers conferred by clause (1) of Article 342 of the Constitution of India, the President, after consultation with the Governor of the State of Uttar Pradesh, is pleased to make the following order, namely:

1. This order may be called the Constitution (Scheduled Tribes) (Uttar Pradesh) Order, 1967.
2. The tribes or tribal communities, or parts of, or groups within, tribes or tribal communites, specified in the Schedule to this Order, shall, for the purposes of the Constitution of India, be deemed to be Scheduled Tribes in relation to the State of Uttar Pradesh so far as regards members thereof resident in that State.

The Scheduled Tribes are The Constitution (Scheduled Tribes) (Uttar Pradesh) Order, 1967

1 Bhotia 8. Saharya (in the district of Lalitpur).
2 Buksa 9. Parahiya (in the district of Sonbhadra).
3 Jannsari 10. Baiga (in the district of Sonbhadra).
4 Raji 11. Pankha, Panika (in the districts of Sonbhadra and Mirzapur).
5 Tharu.
6 Gond, Dhuria, Nayak, Ojha, Pathari, Raj Gond 12. Agariya (in the district of Sonbhadra) (in the districts of Mehrajganj, (Siddharth Nagar), 13. Patari (in the district of Sonbhadra), Basti, Gorakhpur, Deoria, Mau, Azamgarh, Jaunpur, 14 Chero (in the districts of Sonbhadra and Ballia, Ghazipur, Varanasi, Mirzapur and Sonbhadra) Varanasi.
7. Kharwar, Khairwar (in the district of Deoria), 15 Bhuiya, Bhuinya (in the district of Sonbhadra).

Ballia, Ghazipur, Varanasi, Mirzapur and Sonbhadra

1. Gazette of India Extrordinary, 1967, Part II, Section 3(i).
2. Ins. By Act 10 of 2003, S. 4 and the Second Sch. 189.

Adivasis

The oldest ethnic group of India's national population are referred as '*Adivasis*' or original inhabitants of the country. The origin of *Adivasis* can be treated to such races as the Pro-Australoids, who one time believed to have practically covered the whole India. They were compelled to shift to their present habitants as they were unable to defend themselves against the invading people like the Aryans and Mangolians who came with mechanical equipment to safeguard their interests. Thus, the original people had to take the shelter in mountain ranges and dense forests, where a considerable number of them are still found, Martin, A.B. Thakkar, Herbert Risely, Lele and others have used the term 'Aborigines' for these people. Gandhiji used *adimjati* for *adivasis*. However, this *adivasis* or *adimjati* or Aborigines are found everywhere in the world. The tribe is the general term which is commonly used for such communities all over the world.

Tribe

The term tribe is defined as a group of people in a primitive or barbarian stage of development acknowledging the authority of a chief and usually regarding themselves as having a common as ancestor. Western thinkers generally mean an ethnic group, geographically isolated or semi-isolated, identified with one particular territory and having distinct social, economic context. The term has undergone several changes in the post-Independence period. Therefore, D.N. Majumdar has defined Indian tribes by keeping their social, economic and political characteristics, facts, in view as follows:

(i) A tribe must have a traditional territory.
(ii) All the members of a tribe may not be kin of each other, but within every Indian tribe kinship operates as a strong, associative, regulative and integrating principle.
(iii) Members of an Indian tribe speak a common language of their own and that of their neighbours.
(iv) The other distinguishing features of Indian tribes are their dormitory institutions, absence of institutional schooling for their children, distinctive customs, peculiarities of religious beliefs and rituals which may distinguish tribes from low caste Hindus (1961: 367).

According to R. Desai following characteristics are generally found in almost all the tribal groups:

(i) They live away from the civilized world, in mountains hills and forests and at times in unapproachable places.

(ii) They are associated with anyone of the Nigrito, Astroloid or Mongoloid racial group.
(iii) They speak a common dialect.
(iv) They believe in a primitive religion which follows the principles of animism and which has a special place for evil and ancestral or soul worship.
(v) They are engaged in tribal occupations, i.e., collection of useful natural/forest produce, huntingm etc.
(vi) Mostly they are non-vegetarians.
(vii) A few of these tribes are at the naked or semi-naked stage.
(viii) They have nomadic habits and take special interest in dancing and drinking.
(ix) Their technological knowledge is quite unrefined, economic system is simple, backward and based on the basis of geographical separation. The kinship relation is deep and full of significance.

However, the concept of tribe in modern times in India has undergone a remarkable change being a political entity consisting of a group of people identified with poverty and backwardness. Therefore, under the Constitution of India under Article 342 mostly tribes have been enlisted as the scheduled tribes for the purpose of their upliftment and for providing special facilities in terms of social, economic, political and other benefits. The main idea behind these facilities is to bring them into the mainstream of Indian nationalism, to make them capable of exercising their fundamental rights and may become capable of standing on their own feet.

The tribal communities in India constituting around 8 per cent of the total population live in roughly 15 per cent of areas of the country most of which are hills and dates, forests and plateaus. The following Table 1.1 shows the decadal population growth of general people and the tribal people sex-wise distribution.

The scheduled tribes of India constituted only 6.86 per cent of total population during 1961 Census which increased to 8.2 per cent during 2001. Thus, the growth percentage of tribal population to total population was only 1.16 per cent over a period of more than four decades.

The percentage decadal variation of total and tribal population as shown below is 24.45 between 1991-2001.

Decadal variations of total population and tribal population during the last decades between 1961-2001 is shown in Table 1.3. Remarkably there was a decreasing trend in percentage increase of total population

Table 1.1: Tribal Population of India

Census Period	Population			Tribal Population		
	Total	Male	Female	Total	Male	Female
1961	438608104	225990667	212617437	29883470 6.86	15040707 6.65	14842763 6.98
1971	533534500	276335036	257199464	36408514 6.82	18361797 6.64	18046717 7.02
1981	665287849	343930423	321357426	51628638 7.76	26038535 7.57	25590103 7.96
1991	838583988	435216358	403367630	65157838 7.77	34363271 7.90	33395109 8.28
2001	910286103	532136772	496453556	84332624 8.20	42640829 8.1	41685411 8.40

Source: Census of India 2001.

between the four decades whereas in case of tribal population. There has been an upward trend in the percentage increase only during 1971-1981 over a period of time. Thereafter, percentage increase of population showed a downward trend.

There are 573 different tribal groups most of which are divided into several sub-groups. They are settled far away from the general settlements

Table 1.2: Percentage Growth of ST Polpulation Census of India 2001

Census Period	Percentage of ST population to total Population
1961	6.86
1971	6.82
1981	7:76
1991	8.00
2001	8.20

Source: Census of India 2001.
Note: There are 573 different tribal groups.

Table 1.3: Percentage Decadal Variation of Total and Tribal Population

Census Period	Total Population	S.T. Population
1961-71	25.5	25.3
1971-1981	24.3	30.6
1981-1991	23.79	25.67
1991-2001	21.51	24.45

Source: Census of India 2001.

in remote inaccessible and backward areas without any facilities and amenities of civil life and still keep themselves immune from the national mainstream. The following Table 1.4 shows the sex ratio of the tribal population percentage of children population in 1991-2001.

Table 1.4: Sex Ratio of Tribal Population of India

Census Period	*Total Population*	*Tribal Population*
1961	941	937
1971	930	982
1981	935	983
1991	927	972
2001	933	977

Source: Census of India 2001.

It is evident from the above Table 1.4 that tribal female per thousand male population 977 is slightly higher then Indian total population 933.

Table 1.5: Percentage of Child Population

Census Period	*Total Population*	*ST Population*
1991	17.97	20.18
2001	16.03	18.43

Source: Census of India 2001. *S.T. Atlas of India.

Normally, the child population of any place is treated as non-working population. The percentage of tribal children as shown in the above Table 1.5 is higher than the general population which is 18.43 per cent and 16.03 per cent respectively as per 2001 Census. Though there was reduction in percentage of child population from 1991 Census in both the cases.

Naturally, the density of population in tribal areas will be quite low as compared to the population residing in urban and rural areas of the country. Tribals are often nomadic or temporary settled. Moreover, the ecological conditions are adverse for settlement in forest or hilly areas. The following Table 1.6 shows the comparative figure of density of population. The density per sq. km. in tribal areas is abnormally low as compared to general population. Though it has increased to 28 during 2001 from 22 in 1991. The density is much higher in general population, i.e., 266 which is increased substantially 303 during 2001.

Table 1.6: Density of Tribal Population of India

Census Period	*Total Population (Per Sq. Km.)*	*S.T. Population (Per Sq. Km)*
1991	266	22
2001	303	28

Source: Census of India 2001. S.T. Atlas of India.

So far as Uttar Pradesh State in which the study areas—1. Sonbhadra, Chandauli, Mirzapur, Allahabad and Chitrakoot are included, are concerned, the percentage of tribal population to the general population (2001 Census) is very very low, i.e., 07 per cent. The fact is that many tribals including Kol tribe has not been legally categorised and included in scheduled tribe list. Although the percentage of tribals in U.P. is quite low in comparison to other States. The percentage of tribals in Sonbhadra, Chandauli, Mirzapur, Chitrakoot and Allahabad is quite high due to Kaimur and Vindhya range hills and forests.

Development

As the present study is mainly focused on the terms 'Development and Discontent', therefore, it is very essential to explain the concept of Development, before discussing other aspects of this study. The term Development signifies all aspects of development of a collective nature, i.e., to say pertaining to society as a whole. This term has been used either with reference to the welfare aspects of development or in connection with structural transformation (George and Sree Kumar, 1993: 79-81). According to Gandhiji, 'Development' means the development of man in his entirety, making aware of himself as part of development process, raising the standard of his living and life and giving him freedom not only from foreign domination, but also from economic exploitation, economic indebtedness and intellectual servitude. It is the process of growth of man, gaining in self-confidence and becoming self-reliant and self-sufficient (Mukherjee, *et al.*, 1981: 7).

The U.N. experts defined the concept of Development "As process of improving the capabilities of a country's institutions and value system to meet increasing and different demands of social, cultural and political as well as economic character. Development involves mobilization of natural resources, augmentation of trained manpower, capital and technical know-how and their utilization for the attainment of constantly rousing national goal, higher living standards and the change over from a traditional to a modern society."

Longman terms, "Development is a change in the positive or progressive direction". But these terms 'positive' and 'progressive' are value loaded. Therefore, 'Development' is considered as 'change in the desired direction within stipulated time. When we talk about as sensitive an issue as tribal development, the question that automatically comes is: whose desires—those of the planners or of implementers or of tribal's themselves. The question becomes more relevant when we realize that in the name of Tribal development, other have tried and have imposed their will on tribes.

Garry Jacobs (1983) observed that Development is not a programme executed by government but a social movement of the entire population, initiated, guided and led by government. Developments call for information, education, training, organization and administration at the widest possible level. Effective development is, therefore, a comprehensive balanced or integrated development, it is dynamic process signifying goal oriented, guided and gradual change from something considered to be less desirable to something thought to be desirable or more desirable (Spar Kman 1961). Thus, development may be considered as a process aimed at an improvement in the living standards of people in economic, social and cultural spheres with the active participation of the people themselves. So as to be self sustaining in nature. It involves a detailed planning and formulation of specific programmes to bring about change in the desired direction.

The approach to tribal development was first laid down by Pt. Jawaharlal Nehru in the form of 'Tribal Panchsheel', the five fundamental priciples famous for international cooperation offered by Nehru at the Bandung Conference 1955. Besides other things, he advocated that the tribals should be allowed to develop according to their own genius, that should be free to possess and promote their own cultural ethos and objects that they should be integrated into the national mainstream without the loss of their identity, etc.

In the present study, the concept and programmes of development have been examined in the context of tribal development. Issues, dimensions, and strategies pertaining to tribal developments have been examined sociologically speaking functional and dysfunctional from the point of view of fulfilment of their:

(1) Basic needs,
(2) Restoration of their human rights,

(3) Attainment of the state of empowerment, and
(4) to examine the functioning of tribal development projects.

The Economic growth, Educational growth and improvement of Health have been accepted as major indicators of Development.

Discontent

The problemtique of 'development' and 'discontent' especially as it relates to the tribal people could be said to have been recognised as also the dilectics been Naxalism or militant protest officially been movement for the matter, as a law and order or development problems. Discontent is the manifestation of dissatisfaction of a person or a group of persons against what have been expected by them. It expresses the philosophical and psychological aspects of mind of a person who runs madly in search of material happiness in the world. But in case of tribals of India, the term discontent shows the extremity of their disappointment and frustrations against the lolly pop given by the government in the name of their development and welfare programmes. Now, they have started realizing that they have been befooled. Discontent arises in them when they lose their tolerance. For ages, the Indian tribals have lived a life of geographical isolation. They remained cut off from mainstream of national life resulting in their backwardness in the economic and social spheres when compared to other communities. They have continuously been exploited by the foreign rulers, by the henchmen of the alien rule, landlords and money lenders. Even after expiry of the period of 68 years of our Independence about 85 per cent of the tribal families are still living below poverty line rather suffering from chronic poverty. Literacy rate in tribals in India is 59.14 per cent (Male) and 34.75 per cent (Female). It is quite below as compared to Literacy percentage (71.40) of India. Due to unavailability of facilities for minimum required calories intake and medical facilities, tribals are not in a position to maintain their normal health. Moreover, they have been victimized by various exploitative means. The gap between the targets and the physical achievements of various tribal development schemes is widening beyond control. Thus, these are some causes of discontents, arising among tribals of India.

Naxal Movement

The Naxalite movement is essentially an ideological movement and not an ethnic or religious movement. It gets its sustenance from social evils, such as poverty, unemployment, exploitation of the poor classes, etc. It is also a movement which has drawn into its fold a large number of poor people across the tribal belt in India (B. Raman Former Distinguished Fellow Research Foundation). The Naxal movement could be termed as 'left wing communism'. It is a concomitant growth of the communist movement. Even Karl Marx and Friedrich Engels had to face the movement initiated by Mikhail Bakunin. In his time, Lenin has to deal with the Narodniks and Left Social revolutionaries in Russia. The Naxalites represent this trend in India.

The United Communist Party in India split in the early 1960s. Then in 1960s, a kind of revolt erupted in Naxal Bari village of north Bengal and caught on, giving birth to the terms 'Naxal Bari movement'. 'Naxal movement' and Naxalites, which gained popular currency in Indian political lingo. After the split in the communist movement, the trend which emerged was linked with Charu Mazumdar, who prompting a Maoist model of New Democracy. Theoretical elaboration of this trend coincided with the Naxal Bari movement. Fundamentally, the Naxalites are disassociated with mainstream politics and confront the state through the violence, treating violence as their programmatic position. Thus, in turn, they are confronted with an all too powerful and repressive machinery.

Naxalism has not been able to succeed or emerge as a national movement in its 55 years of history, but has remained regional, confined to certain States and regions of the country.

At present, the movement is active mainly in Chhattisgarh, Jharkhand, Andhra Pradesh, Orissa, Bihar, south-eastern part of Uttar Pradesh and in some other States to a certain extent. The social base of Naxalites is mainly the tribal and *dalit* in backward and remote forest areas. The main issues they raise is the all important 'Land' issue. The crucial question is: Are land reforms possible now? With globalization and neo-liberal economic policies order of the day, the government, both at the Centre and the State level, is concerned more with big industries and firms, than landless peasant and small and marginal farmers. Indeed, land reforms need to be implemented in the entire country without reversing the land ceiling acts. In several States, it is a vital, live issue. It is unfortunate that various State Governments show lack of commitment to distribute surplus land or wasteland. Unless, this is done, one cannot simply wish away movements like the Naxalite movement. There are several other reasons for the rise and growth of Naxalite movements. In the country side, money lending is a thriving business. The tribal people are trapped in the clutches of the money lenders. There are also the problems of caste and social discrimination. The serious problem, tribals are facing, is the problem of rehabilitation after displacement of the establishment of industries, power stations, factories and the construction of dams in the name of national development plans on their ancestral tribal lands. The assurance of rehabilitation and compensations by the government and by industrialists proved to be failed at the later stages. Thus, the tribal frustration is immediately blackmailed by the Naxalites. What are the conditions of tribals even after expiry of 68 years of Independence? On 21 July, 2004, the Ministry of Environment and Forests, under a directive from the Supreme Court, accepted a few hard facts mentioned as follows:

(1) Injustice committed against the tribal communities under the forest administration were age old and still continued unabated.
(2) Since the demands and rights of the tribal communities are not being respected and granted by Government, there have been atrocities.
(3) Since, the tribal do not have the documents to support their ownership of their land, the demarcation of the forests have not been formalized.
(4) After 1947, large tracts of forests were declared as being protected area, but even then the rights of the tribals were not taken care of.

Therefore, tribals, victimized by authorities, are being evicted from their lands on a regular basis; and the Naxalites may have engaged with the victims of these atrocities (Ruchir Garg: 26-31).

The south-eastern region of Uttar Pradesh comprises the regions of Mirzapur, Sonbhadra and Chandauli, Allahabad and Chitrakoot is rich in forest produces and mineral resources. Whatever be the scale development, it has been market oriented and not people friendly. The tribals living scattered here and there are still in state of chronic poverty, many of them in debt, unable to educate their children and are deprived of all necessary amenities and medical facilities. They are being trapped and exploited by the Naxalites who enter into the boundaries of these districts from Chhattisgarh, Jharkhand and Bihar.

Review of Research and Development in the Subject

Here it is dealt with the review of studies conducted on various aspects of tribal development both at the macro-level and at the micro-level. The studies on implementation and impact of development programmes, protest movements, revolt, Naxalism, displacement, rehabilitation, general living conditions of tribal health, nutritions, education, land alienation, forest and other problems among the tribal have been reviewed here to understand the different dimensions of the problems.

The studies at macro-level include those of B. Singh (1980), Roy Burman (1980), Srivastava (1980), K.P. Singh (1988), Prasad (1988), Behura (1993), Saibaba and Rajendra Naidu (1992) have focused on tribal development strategies in different States. According to them the results achieved under T.S.P. strategies were not commensurate with the expectations as well as investments made so far. There has been too much emphasis on quantitative investment rather than qualitative achievement.

Due to lack of awareness about the developmental programmes, due to negligence from administration sides, due to implementation of stereo typed programmes with inadequate funds and due to lack of attention on the felt needs of beneficiaries, several schemes for the upliftment of tribal implemented by the Government, have failed. These aspects have been covered up through the studies of Khaund (1982), Sharma (1983) conducted a study on implementation of programmes for dispersed tribal in the country, Mishra (1983) study on implementation of programmes in Orissa, Singh (1977) study on the implementation of programmes in Bihar, Gupta (1986) investigation on the impact of programmes in Birbhum district, West Bengal, Gopal Rao (1981) on the impact of programmes in Srikakulam district of Andhra Pradesh, Kripa Shankar (2009) on land alienation among tribals in Uttar Pradesh, Nehru and Elwin on tribal development by Govind Chand Rath and Somshekhar (2008) on development programmes and social change among tribal.

Thakur (1986) conducted a study on Santhal tribe of Bihar, Mahapatro (1987) investigated into the conditions of the tribal of Koraput district of Orissa, Swaroop and Bharti (1987) conducted on the Tharu tribe of Uttar Pradesh. All these studies found that most of the tribals live below the poverty line and majority of them are landless. They lack irrigation facilities and improved techniques in their agriculture. Their annual income is very low. Most of their income is being spent on food, have been discussed by D.C. in his book *Trapped in Poverty* (2008).

With regard to tribal education, Sharma (1974) studied the progress of tribal education in the country, Nair (1979) studies the working of the tribal schools in the district of Maharashtra, Sinha (1979) conducted a study on tribal education in Bihar, Vidyarthi (1979) analysed the tribal education in the country and Lakshmaiha (1979) investigated in Ranchi

(Bihar), Damina Chaudhari (2009) investigated tribal girls Aspiration, Achievements and frustration for education and there is higher dropout rate in the tribals in all the grades than that of in the general population both for the boys and girls, has been studied by A.K. Singh (1993).

As regards to displacement of tribals, several authors have dealt with this problem from their own point of views. Rao (1986) has indicated that the displaced tribals under Rengali Dam were resettled in an area where even drinking water was a luxury. He states that the resettlement colonies resemble a pre-historic place without any basic amenity. They were poor quality of land. Alvares and Billorey (1987) have also pointed out that the distribution of a part of the village pasture as land compensation to those displaced by Sardar Sarovar project led to a clash between the outsiders and local population. The centre for science and environment (1985) in its study has explained the long struggle of the people displaced by Panchet Dam. It submerged 21 villages, displacing 1200 land owning households and 200 landless families. No notice of land acquisition was given to the people. Details of compensation remained only a rumour. The studies of Barnabas (1985), Alvares and Billorey (1988), Bana (1988) and Singh (1988) have mentioned the absence of any provision of alternative land or jobs of those who were cultivating forest areas and agricultural land without legal titles. Such studies have brought out the inadequate rehabilitation measures in terms of absence of alternative sources of livelihood for those who survive on agricultural wage earning. Those cultivating families were not entitled for compensation and thus left to unbearable misery.

Economic and Political Weekly report (1968) has observed that the H.E.C. did not consider the displaced tribal's for recruitment in jobs for which they were qualified. Sarkar (1970), in his study conducted in Bokaro Steel Project Area, has mentioned the suffering of the displaced people for finding alternative jobs. Vidyarthi (1987) has also stated that due to low income, the people displaced by various industrial projects in Bihar had to dispose of their cattle, utensils, etc. Sharma (1986) has pointed out that due to lack of appropriate rehabilitation measures, the persons displaced by major dams are unable to meet their requirements.

Shatrughna (1981), Vyas (1983), Centre for Science and Environment (1985), Gandhi and Ajit Kumar (1986), Alvares and Billorey (1988) and Thukral (1988) have mentioned cases of inadequate compensation, disparities in fixation of compensation, scandal in payments especially to tribals and many instances of exploitation by land owners, money lenders and lawyers.

Sen, Rahul, Mukhopadhyay, Jha, Singh and others have studied the tribal protest movements, even revolts, rebellions and uprisings in India and their long history. The first peasant movement during the colonial rule was launched by the Paharia (Maler) of Raj Mahal Hills (now in Jharkhand) following it the Santhal Hul (1855) had really shook the foundation of the empire and forced upon them. The necessary of framing a special land for tribal against exploitation, usury/money lending, land alienation. The Chhota Nagpur region (Jharkhand) witnessed many massive movements like the Kharwar movement, Sardar Lari (Munda) movement, Birsa movement, the Kol insurrection, revolts in Andhra Pradesh (1803), (1862) and (1879), Kandh rising rebellion (1837-56) and Bhuyan and Juang rising in Keonjhar (1865-68) and (1891-93) in Orissa are some examples of tribal revolts which gave them recognition to British rulers. As a result, Britishers framed several rules for their welfare for example Government of India Act 1870, Scheduled Districts Act 1874.

After Independence the creation of Jharkhand and Chhattisgarh provinces were the outcome of tribal's revolt. The revolts for separate tribal State in Gujarat of seven districts—Dang, Baruch, Valsad, Surat, Panchmahal, Banaskantha and Sabarkantha, revolt in Rajasthan for separating Banswara and Dungarpur for creation of tribal State, four districts of Jhabua, Khargaon, Dhar and Ratlam in Madhya Pradesh and three districts of Pune, Nasik and Khandesh in Maharashtra for tribal States have often been in news for several years for demanding separate tribal State in the country.

Widespread social unrest and discontent has resulted in Naxalism in 13 States of India. The intensity affected geographic region in south-eastern part of Uttar Pradesh also. Roots and causes in Jharkhand and Dandakaranya (Chhattisgarh) have been investigated by Harivansh and Ruchir Garg respectively in their research papers presented in the workshop hosted by 'Research Foundation at Chennai on 28th and 29th January, 2005'. Butchering of 76 CRPF men in Dantewada on 6th April, 2010 by Naxalites shook the whole country. Arundhati Roy, the social activist, published article in *Outlook* in which she has explained in details of the explanation given by the Gond people during interview with them (29th March, 2010). During their interview they revealed their hearts, homes, motives and motivations. Lohandiguda (an area of Dandakaranya forest) was never a Naxal area and inhabitants were innocent, but due to endless exploitations, when Naxali came in, they raised their slogans "*Naxali Aao, Hamein Bachao*" began appearing on walls, they explained during discussions.

References

1. Hasmain Nadeem, 2007, '*Tribal India*', New Royal Book Company, Lucknow.
2. Verma, R.C., 2002, *Indian Tribes; Through the Ages*, Director, Publishing Division, New Delhi.
3. Pani, Niranjan, Sahoo, Jitendra, 2008. '*Tribal Development*', Mahamaya Publshing House, New Delhi.
4. Mahapatra, B.C. 2009, '*Interacting Factors for Social Development: Tribal Education in India*', Sarup Book Publishers Pvt. Ltd., New Delhi.

Chapter 2
Research Methodology

Statement of the Problem

The study covers a broad spectrum. It has been conceptualised as an open ended study attempting to gain a comprehensive understanding of one of the most burning issues confronting the nation, which is the widespread social unrest and discontent now affecting 13 States of the country with Naxalism as one form the violent burst. The intensity has affected geographic region cutting across several States, notably Uttar Pradesh, Bihar, Jharkhand, Chhattisgarh, Maharashtra, Andhra Pradesh and Orissa, also happens to be largely populated by the tribals and poorest of the poor, though dotted with mega development projects.

The Problematic of 'Development and Discontent' especially it relates to the tribal people could be said to have been officially recognised, as also the dialectics been Naxalism or Militants protest movement for the matter, as a law and order or development problem. This is the cover story of *Yojana*, the official organ of the Planning Commission.

There has been no scheduled tribal areas in the State of Uttar Pradesh as are demarcated in Jharkhand, Chhattisgarh, Madhya Pradesh and others, though there were certain partially excluded (on regulated) areas notified during the Colonial rule, but in its zeal for normalization of administration, the special status of these areas was summarily done away.

Ironically, if we look at the names and social background of those officially proclaimed as 'Naxalites', either those absconding or arrested or killed in police encounters over the years, we find that they are invariably the *dalits* and *adivasis* belonging to local villages: Chamar, Kol, Gond, Chero, Kharwar and others of the same category. Kol leads the first list in Navagrah (Chandauli district) and Marihan (Mirzapur). The Chamar and Kharwar do it in Robertsganj, Chero in Chopan and

Gond in Dudhi in Sonbhadra district, depending largely on the composition of the agricultural labour force in different micro-regions.

There is hardly any name of the middle class, ideology-driven cadre/ leaders or any person with landed upper caste background mentioned in connection with the Naxalite leadership in this region spherically. Thus, the geographic area and the social group selected for this study truly constitutes peripheral or marginalized entities. This revolt of the truly or traditionally oppressed people, really, is a matter of grave social concern and a serious question mark on the practice of the principle of equity and justice enshrined in the Constitution of India.

But, at the policy level the problem is being dealt with essentially as a problem of Law and Order, though it may also be articulated at times as a problem of lack of adequate amount of development. The question of appropriate people-centred Development Programme hardly ever arises at the policy of Five Year Plans.

What kind of development appears to be the most pertinent issue? There is seeming paradox inherent in the situation because, if we look at the tribals (whether scheduled or not) residing in Uttar Pradesh, we find that there is relatively more manifest unrest and rebellion in the more developed South-Eastern sector, i.e., Naugarh (Chandauli) along with Sonbhadra, than in the Western sector, i.e., Southern portion of Mirzapur, Allahabad and Chitrakoot districts.

This intra-regional comparison itself puts a question mark on the accelerated development approach. Why should there be relatively greater unrest and protest in the relatively more developed parts of this elongated geographic regions? This brings in question of what type of Mainstream Development is, when this region has witnessed since 1950s, the extensive mining, string of large scale industries. Alongside extraction of forest timber and minerals first came the cement plants (Churk, Dala, Chunar), Hydel Power Projects, then a series of thermal plants, Rihund Dam, HINDALCO, Kanodia Chemicals, etc., Simultaneously stone quarries or crushers, sand extraction and several other private industrial projects have been launched here.

In the regional geography of Uttar Pradesh, Mirzapur, it really meant the southern subdivision that now constitutes Sonbhadra, was known as the most natural resource-rich and the most tribal populated part of Uttar Pradesh. In whole of history of development, these two factors have rarely gone well together. The tribal communities were the first direct victims of national development. And here the process to exploitation of these resources began quite early after independence, with the inauguration of the national development plans. In Uttar Pradesh, almost every big industrial project was located in this part, bringing massive displacement in its train.

Thus, if we go by the normal development index, it figures out as one of the most favoured regions of the State. But for the indigenous people these development projects brought displacement and deprivation in their wake. They have been squeezed out with each major development project. There was no National/State Rehabilitation policy in place when the process of displacement started here and no thought was given for providing adequate compensation, e.g., land for land or alternate means of livelihood to them. At the same, the employment opportunities opened by the projects completely bypassed them.

Further more, with the enactment of the Zamindari Abolition and Land Reform Act, all unsettled lands were transferred to State Forest Department. And most of the land cultivated by the tribals fell in this category, in the absence of any record of rights. There are indeed no community land to be managed by the Gram Sabha and Gram Panchayat in most of the villages of Sonbhadra, Chandauli, Mirzapur, Shankargarh, Koraon of Allahabad and Manikpur, Mau and Karvi of Chitrakoot districts. Tribal areas of these districts have been most affected by the so-called normalization of administration. They had the largest concentration of the tribal groups and they continue to bear the consequences of the arbitrary administrative decisions. Thus, the first and foremost, there was no legal protection available against tribal land alienation and traditional rights of forest gathering and access to other natural resources.

The 'Patha' region, which is spread over Mau and Manikpur blocks of Chitrakoot district and Shankargarh Block of Allahabad district, became closely identified with the terror of dacoits as well as large scale poverty and deprivation rooted in a highly exploitative system. It has been a normal practice of landlords of upper castes to grab illegally the landed property of poor tribals by trick and by befooling them with the conspiracy of Lekhapal and other government officials. They have also been terrorising the tribals with the help of dacoits. (Who often belong to middle upper castes). The tragedy is that they have been rarely heard by the administration and no relief was ever been provided by the local administration.

In this manner, the prevailing special features of land ownership and management in tribal areas, however, relatively small in the vast province were completely overlooked. Unfortunately, the truth of this arbitrary decision is not sufficient realized even now.

But the roots of the problems confronting the state on the Naxalite front may actually lie here. The tragedy of the tribals in the State is that their number is almost negligible and, therefore, they could be ignored. They really have very little place in the political demography of this most populated state of the country. But at the same time, this heightened the human dimensions of the problem.

Objectives of the Study

The main objective of the study was to find an explanation for the continuing tribal unrest and violence as it manifested in the so-called 'Naxalite' and other protest actions, among the *dalit-adivasis* on the south-eastern periphery of Uttar Pradesh. As part of the main objective, the study has focused on the following:

(i) The prevailing socio-economic conditions among the main subjects of the study, i.e., the *dalit adivasis*.

(ii) The present state of village structures and the traditional forms of economic/wage exploitation and social oppression.

(iii) The impact of the various development programmes and projects implemented in the post-independence period, especially the land reform/land distribution among landless and various tribal development and *Harijan* and Social welfare.

(iv) Especially, reconstruct the performance of land and other agrarian reforms introduced in the post-era and how it affected the land owning cultivating status of various *dalit-adivasis* group/individual, including access to common property resources (CPRs) and to the forest and other natural resources available in the area.

(v) The extent of the reduction replenishment or replacement of the traditional means of livelihood.

(vi) The extent of intrusion and influence wielded by outside settlers and especially investigate the extent of *dalit-adivasis* land alienation through legal or illegal means.

(vii) The extent of development inflicted on and compensatory rehabilitation measures taken by the State/private sector development projects, in different phases.

(viii) To find and prioritize the people's grievances record the administrative response.

(ix) Perception of people regarding the causes of unrest and violent protest action, in specific term the so called 'Naxalite Movement' and its legitimacy, as well as direct relevance to the perceived causes of unrest.

Universe of the Study

Geographically, the study focuses on the outer extensions of Vindhya-Kaimur plateau region, administratively falling in the State of Uttar Pradesh, which forms its southern periphery lying below the Ganga-Yamuna Plain. The narrow of land, running from Chitrakoot to Sonbhadra also forms the main tribal tract of Uttar Pradesh. It is pertinent to mention here that the tribal population of the State, whether scheduled or unscheduled, is so fragmented and scattered that there is no tribal developmental Block or area or even a Scheduled Tribe reserve constituency in the State.

Administratively, the study area has included selected Blocks of Chitrakoot, Allahabad, Mirzapur, Chandauli and Sonbhadra, i.e., five districts in which these *dalit* tribals are concentrated. There are minor tribal pockets (Saharias) in south-western corner of the State (i.e., Jhansi, Lalitpur) but these have not been included in the study. The main *dalit-adivasi* tract in the State formally, e.g., census the two broad categories were limped together as scheduled caste until 2003 when some groups were reclassified as Scheduled Tribes in selected districts, though some, prominently, the Kol, continue to be treated as SC, lies in elongated narrow strip at the feet of Gangetic plain, and along the inter-state border with Madhya Pradesh (and now Chhattisgarh). It extends from Chitrakoot to Sonbhadra and then merges with Jharkhand and Bihar, towards the east. Thus, the universe of the study has embraced the following districts and Blocks population 2001 within them.

The study is not directly related to the 'Naxalite' (or Maoist) movement as such; it is an attempt to identify and verify through appropriate investigation, the causes of unrest in what is officially declared as the Naxalite Zone and contiguous area. As such, the universe of the study is defined by these two parameters. As an added methodological aspect of the study, it is important to mention here that it has an inherent comparative focus as well. If we divide the Eastern Part and Western Sectors with the dividing line falling in the middle of Mirzapur district, only the Eastern Sector falls in the core Naxalite Zone, (Mirzapur, Sonbhadra and Chandauli), whereas the Western Sector (Allahabad and Chitrakoot) has been kept out, as there is no manifest reasons of unrest, though the socio-economic conditions and so also the intensity of caste

Table 2.1: Mirzapur, Sonbhadra, Chandauli, Allahabad and Chitrakoot Districts, their Blocks, Total Population and SC/ST Population

Disaggregated from 2001 Census

Sl. No.	District	Block	Total Population	SC and ST Population
1.	Mirzapur	Lalganj	108430	43864
		Halia	176360	78038
		Manihan	102979	57430
		Rajgarh	171202	61533
		Kon	99908	28645
2.	Sonbhadra	Robertganj	82617	74554
		Nagwan	76454	40838
		Chopan	227022	127523
		Dudhi	12135	68779
		Babhani	79870	50056
3.	Chandauli	Sahebganj	123282	37210
		Naugarh	62848	28253
4.	Allahabad	Jasra	143231	31090
		Shankar Garh	13486	46225
		Meja	158979	35051
		Koraon	248803	74051
5.	Chitrakoot	Karvi	198871	44842
		Mau	127935	33995
		Manikpur	144395	52486

oppression of the *Dalit-Adivasis*, they are not better. Unless they consider the Dacoit gangs, a succession of them and some may legitimately claim to be forms of social banditry. But then, the gangs have often been led by the newly emergent dominant intermediate peasant castes. For comparison point of view, Sonbhadra, Mirzapur and Chandauli have been categorized as Naxal Prone area and Allahabad and Chitrakoot as Dacoit Prone area.

For this, the Principal Investigator surveyed 3,000 sample households of villages of 19 Blocks of the five districts as above mentioned. The aim was to understand accurate situation and reliable information and data on the living conditions of the problems faced by the tribals. During survey the investigator travelled extensively in tribal areas, contacted personally the tribals, organised meeting and made discussions with them. The government officials, social welfare department, several government agencies and NGO's were also contacted and were tried to collect the information from them regarding tribal development programmes, their implementation and the outcomes really reached to the people for whom they were intended.

For the present study, therefore, Normative Survey and cross-section approach have been selected. Normative Survey method is a very useful method for the investigation which aims at studying, analysing, describing and interpreting the exciting data which are concerned with conditions of relationships that exists, practices that prevail, beliefs, points of views or attitudes that are held, processes that are going on, effects that are being felt or trends that are developing.

The term 'Survey' implies the gathering of evidence relating to current conditions whereas the term 'Normative' means the determination of normal or typical conditions or practices. In fact survey research is a method for collecting and analysing data obtained from a large number of respondents, representing a specific population collected through highly structured and detailed interview schedules.

In the present study, a comparative study of tribals of south-eastern part and south-western parts of study area has been made with regard to their frustration, discontent and unrest level. For the present study as the sample was a large one that is 3,000 tribals, therefore, for such a large, sample, survey method was useful.

Research Design and Hypothesis

The present study has exploratory research design, its main purpose being to delineate the root causes of discontent among the tribals of the South-Eastern-Western margins of Uttar Pradesh even after the implementation of all the Five Year Plans, special government assistance sub-plan, Tribal Development plan and several welfare programmes. The ecological theory of the adverse conditions of forest area, no doubt, tries to formulate a law relating to the physical development but it is not necessary that it would be compatible to the Government initiated plans. Obviously, therefore, we cannot proceed with any hypothesis as regards the developmental pattern of this region. However, in respect of the developmental impact on this region, certain hypothesis can be formulated. In doing so we may depend on the studies of Hoselitz, Learner and Wirth. Hoselitz has made a distinction between what he calls parasitic and generation type of development. The generative type of developments are those which exerts a favourable influence on economic development of the areas. The parasitic, on the other hand, are those development which either do not exert any influence on the economic development of the surrounding areas or exert a negative influence. Among the other characteristics of generative development that Hoselitiz mentions, their occupational structure is the most important. If the demographic growth of that area is accompanied by a diversification of its occupational base that is if the growing population of that region gets increasingly absorbed into secondary and tertiary industries, then that region would be deemed to have a favourable impact on economic development. On the other hand, with the present population and the growth of the population of that region, there is no corresponding growth of secondary and tertiary occupations to absorb the population and the growing population remains largely engaged in primary occupations, in other words, if the existing population demographic growth of the region is not adequately backed by industrialization, it will be deemed to be parasitic and frustrating. If population is even deprived of the primary occupation, discontent resentments, etc., would naturally take birth in the minds of the population and they consequently results in revolts, insurgency, etc.

With development, Learner, has like-wise tried to link literacy and accept as indicator of development. If the growth of literacy is not commensurate with development, the development is bound to become non-developmental. Louis Wirth has, in a similar way, considered attitudes as a natural corollary of development. If the development does not result in the attitudinal changes and the people do not accept and change their way of thinking and way of life, it would be unproductive.

The World Health Organisation (WHO) has stated that Health is a state of complete physical, mental and social being and not merely the absence of diseases and infirmity. Sound health on one hand, is a by-product of socio-economic development and on the other hand, it is an important determinant of the quality of human resources of a country. Therefore, good health is a prerequisite to human productivity and development process.

If any sort of development is launched in any region, it must be associated with the improvement of the health conditions of the existing population. Instead of improving the health conditions and providing medical facilities, if the development process brings adverse health conditions by producing environmental pollution, etc., to the people of the region, that development would not be acceptable as development. Thus, the improvement of health conditions is an important indicator of development. However, while evaluating the development role and its impact as discontentment spread over in this region under study, we have the above insights in the background of analysis.

Keeping the above theoretical background in view of the following hypothesis that have been formulated.

(i) The original and the real owners of water, forests and other natural resources, are not only deprived of their rights, but are having to fight for their social and cultural identity as also the living basic needs of their daily existence.

(ii) The democratic representatives only went about the business of ruling and had no concern or responsibility for the development and welfare of the common folk.

(iii) The multiple displacement of large number of tribal people from their land, habitat and occupation has been without proper rehabilitation and without providing proper compensation.

(iv) The non-tribal immigrants have surpassed the local tribes in acquiring their fertile land, taking advantage of the ignorance, illiteracy and simplicity of the tribes.

(v) Several backdoor methods have been used to get the tribal land transferred to the non-tribals with the help of the lower rank government officials of the revenue department.

(vi) The main role of the police administration often appears to be forcibly prevent the *adivasis* from exercising their age old basic rights of their ownership of forest land and other land and their home.

(vii) By the land management committee (LMC) with the Gram Pradhan and with collusion of Lekhpal and other revenue officials the allotment of *Patta*, is done to muscles power men and to feudal landlords. Thus, they have created the land alienation among the tribals.

(viii) Even after the enforcement of Forest Land Right Act 2006, the *adivasis* are still deprived of their land rights.

(ix) The budget and funds allotted for the development programmes and welfare programmes has been embezzled by the government officials, alongwith the local maphias, the political leaders and the public representatives.

(x) After installation of several industries, power plants, mining activities, the water and air pollution has crossed its limit. Repeated displacement and living in the adverse conditions around the industrial; and mining areas have created a lot of problems. The *dalit adivasis* are facing a lot of health problems. Mostly newly born children are handicapped and diseased.

(xi) As Government welfare financial help scheme through MNREGA, JRY, NRHM, PDS, women, old age pension, mid-day meal, scholarships, etc., are not properly reaching to them, the *dalit adivasis* are suffering from cronic poverty.

Sampling Procedure

Given the geographic spread over the research universe and the methodological demand that the causative factors need to be located/related to the wider social and agrarian structure, it has to be a purposive multistage sampling; the purpose being served by the indication of intensity of the discontent/unrest manifested not necessarily only in terms of Naxalite violence, but other forms of strong protest action also, has been followed.

At the first stage, Sonbhadra, Chandauli and Mirzapur districts were chosen because these districts rank first in terms of Naxal prone tribal population. The tribals of these districts are extremely backward, illiterate and have been uprooted by the establishment of heavy industries and by the forest department. The districts of Allahabad and Chitrakoot were chosen because the tribal population living in dense forest had continuously been exploited by the landlords of higher caste people and they had been worstly victimised by dacoits hidden in the forest area. Moreover, they have also been victimised by the forest department which have uprooted from their land by demarcating the area of possession for sanctuary.

At the next stage it was decided to select blocks of these districts, village Panchayats, households and lastly to select some individuals for case studies in the following manner.

(a) *The Blocks were selected on the intensity index*: Using both the criteria, i.e., the administrative classification of the affected areas and relevant social-demographic factors. Thus, the choice of the Blocks was almost given; Naugarh (Chandauli), Robertganj, Nagwan, Kon (Chopan), Dudhi and Babhani, Ghorawal were classified on the intensity index with weightage being given to worst affected Blocks in the district Sonbhadra; Marihan, Rajgarh, Halliya in Mirzapur district; Shankargarh in district Allahabad, Karvi and Manikpur in Chitrakoot district. One hundred fifty households of tribals from each Block were selected randomly for interview. Thus, in all 750 households from Mirzapur, 750 households from Sonbhadra and 450 households from Chandauli. 600 households from Allahabad and 450 households from Chitrakoot were randomly selected for interview.

(b) *Village Panchayat Level*: Within the selected Blocks, villages were selected on the same basis of intensity index and social-demographic factors viability of the *dali: adivasi* group and thus a number of villages selected had varied from Block to Block.

(c) *Household Level*: Within the selected villages 15 per cent, i.e., 3000 *dalit adivasi* households were selected randomly, depending on the homogeneity/heterogeneity factors for household survey.

(d) *Individual Level Case Study*: Some persons were also selected who had been exploited, looted and tortured even to death by the landlords, outsiders, forest department, dacoits and by the administration. Some villages, the so called hardcore Naxal ones and the families at the centre of major conflicts were selected for in depth study.

(e) *Secondary Level*: In order to generate corroborative data for the 'objective' study made on the basis of secondary sources, regarding the existential conditions of the *dalit adivasis* and the development and deprivation experienced in the process of more than five decades of national planning were also gathered from recorded sources.

Interdisciplinary Approach

As the subject demanded an interdisciplinary approach and the choice of the methods and tools of data generation (not collection or just gathering in very precise term), it would not be within narrow disciplinary boundary of sociology, for example, Environmental destruction and degradation of the traditional *adivasis* habits approached to be the major cause of unrest and discontent among these people and study of this aspect as such had needed to be investigated from environmental and geographical perspectives also.

Again in order to put the problems being investigated in a temporal perspective, it had needed a chronological/historical method. So, also, the use of the Anthropological protocols in order to collect the vast amount of observational data, needed for the study.

Though, control was not being used in exact experimental sense, but the study had been done for the purpose comparison between 'Active' (Naxal affected) eastern and 'passive' western sections of the tribals tract, even granted that the discontent in the Western section might manifest in somewhat muted on other forms.

Tools used for Data Collection

In the background of the various methodological requirements, issued involved therein, the tools of data collection are being listed below:

(1) *Historical method (Library study and documentation)*: The study needed a great deal of longitudinal data in order to study how the colonial policies; land settlement, revenue administration, etc., forest management and the land reforms development of measures of the post-independence era have impacted on the *dalit adivasis* in the region. Apart from the written sources, which may be scattered all over, this needed recording of oral history from selected panel of knowledgeable persons.

(2) *P.R.A.s and focus group discussions and Participant observation*: The data on causative factors of discontent and unrest were generated through discussing with community leaders and local knowledgeable persons of participatory rural and appraisal (PRA) and focus group discussions. The investigator joined these groups as participant observer.

(3) *Survey*

 (a) *Community Survey*: Data were collected regarding the village/community structure, availability and control over land and other productive community assets, pattern of dominance, entrenched/emerging inter-caste relatives, past and present, history of artifacts with *dalit adivasis*, etc., labour reactions and wage system/rates, Panchayati Raj institutional structures, *dalit adivasis* representation etc.

 (b) *Household Survey*: Longitudinal data in the then and now framework on the changing socio-economic status of the family, e.g., on land ownership, success of livelihood, level of living, indebtedness, land alienation, occupational/special mobility, education status, etc., were generated through household interview schedules.

 (c) *Case Study*: In order to understand the reality of exploitation and the actual happening, incidences and suffering in the name of Naxalism and feudalism, persons were interviewed in detail.

The data collected from all the primary and secondary sources were processed and analysed using appropriate statistical tools. The analysis was done in such a manner as to throw light on variations in different aspects of tribal development and discontent among the sample villages of the districts of Mirzapur, Sonbhadra, Chandauli, Allahabad and Chitrakoot. The impact of developmental programmes on the quality of the sample households were analysed in terms of acquisition of land, household and other assets as well as generation of other income and employment, expenditure pattern, level of literacy and indebtedness.

Statistical Method

Interpretation of Data: The obtained informations were interpreted through Multivariate analysis, chi-square and 't' test. The Chi-square is a statistical test commonly used to compare observed data with data we would expect to obtain according to a specific hypothesis. The chi-square test is always testing what scientists call the null hypothesis which states that there is no significant difference between the expected and observed results. All these results were obtained by using SPSS (Statistical Analysis Software) data analysis package.

The expected frequency counts were computed separately for each level of one categorical variable at each level of the other categories. The results of the expected frequencies were obtained by using MS-Excel software.

The focus of the study had been to compare the level of conditions of tribals among the different Tribal districts of Uttar Pradesh where the scheduled tribes are not given the status of Scheduled Tribes they are treated in the list of Scheduled Castes.

Chapter 3

Profile of the Study Area, Social and Economic Characteristics of Sample Households and Respondents

Attempts have been made to describe the profile of the study area, i.e., Sonbhadra, Mirzapur, Chandauli, Allahabad and Chitrakoot, the five districts of Uttar Pradesh in terms of geographical spread of the *dalit adivasis* and some details of the universe of the study from historical, geographical, religious, demographic and other points of view. Out of the five districts, the Blocks have also been selected on the basis of intensity index, using both the criteria, i.e., the administrative classification of the affected areas and social-demographic factors. Thus, the Blocks—Naugarh, Sahebganj from Chandauli districts, Robertsganj, Nagwan, Chopan, Dudhi and Babhani, from the district Sonbhadra, Marihan, Rajgarh, Hallia, Kon and Lalganj Blocks from Mirzapur and Blocks—Jasra, Shankargarh, Meja and Koraon from Allahabad district and Blocks—Karwi, Mau and Manikpur from Chitrakoot districts have been chosen for our study.

On one side, Sonbhadra, Chandauli and Mirzapur districts have been the main hub of all sorts of development due to their natural richness, several industries, mines and power plants were installed. They were accepted as indicators of developments, but on the other side, these developments resulted in extreme exploitation of inhabitants, especially the original inhabitants, i.e., the tribals who once enjoyed the complete benefits of the natural resources and the forest. As a result, several problems came up for example problem of displacement and rehabilitation, land alienation, deprived of the rights of forest and forest produce and so many related problems.

Maoist and Naxalites are always in search of such type of situations where their ideology can flourish in those areas of the country. Naturally, they got the best place, i.e., Sonbhadra, Chandauli and Mirzapur forests as safest shelter and the tribals of these districts as the best carriers and supporters for launching their campaign. As a result, several incidents occurred during last twenty years. Though all aspects of these problems have been dealt separately, yet it is necessary to describe some incidents as example for showing the characteristics of these areas and tribal people in this chapter. Therefore, the writer had categorized Sonbhadra, Chandauli and Mirzapur as Naxal prone area of the study.

On the other side, the Chitrakoot and Allahabad districts tribals face quite a different type of problems. The tribals have been tortured since beginning by feudal landlords, and had never been treated as human being. The Patha region and Bundelkhand regions have been enlisted as the poorest regions. Several poverty related deaths including suicides and hunger deaths have been recorded in recent years. Rocky land, shortage of water, drought, abnormal weather conditions, feudal landlords who used to grab the land of the tribals, treatment as bonded labours from generation to generation, Indebtedness, displacement by the forest department, prohibited for using and collecting forest produce, loans taken fraudulently by feudal lords in the name of poor tribal people, exploitation of sex of female tribals, etc., have forced them to starve, to commit suicide and to die with several vulnerable diseases.

Over and above, the terror of dacoits who often attack in tribal villages, where they looted, tortured, raped women and brutally murdered their enemies. The big landlords and contractors of forest produce and other materials, take help from the dacoit gangs for grabbing the tribal land, snatching forest materials and other property. Their women are extremely exploited and raped by landlords, contractors and dacoits. This is their pathetic conditions which shows the act of extremity of inhumanity. Keeping all these facts in view, the author has categorised Chitrakoot and Allahabad tribal districts as Dacoit prone area.

Therefore, the profile of the tribal areas of the five districts and social and economic characteristics of the respondents and households have been highlighted in this chapter.

I. PROFILE OF MIRZAPUR DISTRICT[1, 2]

Mirzapur is located at 25°09′N 82°35′E/25.15°N 82.58°E. It has an average elevation of 80 metres (265 feet). The District of Mirzapur lies between the parallels of 23.52 and 25.32 North latitude and 82.7 and 83.33 East longitude. It forms a portion of the Varanasi Division. On the north and noth-east it is bounded by the Varanasi district; on the south bounded by district Sonbhadra, on the north-west by the district of Allahabad. The shape to the north and west is totally regular. In no direction, except for about 13 km. in the north-east where the Ganges separates the Tehsil of Chunar from the district of Varanasi, Mirzapur has a natural frontier. According to Central Statistical Organisation the district of Mirzapur has an area of 4,521 km^2. At the Census 2001, the population of the district is 16,57,140 (male 10,93,849 and females 9,80,860) of which 17,88,203 were living in rural and 2,86,506 in the urban area of the district.

Mirzapur district, an administrative district of Uttar Pradesh, few years ago formed a portion of Varanasi Division. The sovereignty of this district was formally ceded to the East India Company in 1775 by Nawab of Awadh, but the tract itself was included in the *Zamindari* of the Raja of Benares and remained in actual possession until 1794. In 1830 Mirzapur became a separate revenue jurisdiction of its towns.

Mirzapur is in the heart of North India, nearly 650 km between Delhi and Kolkata and also equidistant from Allahabad and Varanasi. Located in the State of Uttar Pradesh. It is renowned for its famous carpet and brassware industry. It is a city with several spots around it including many hills such as Rajdari, Devdari, Lakhaniyadari and Windom fall and Sirshi. It is the headquarters of Mirzapur District.

The total population of Mirzapur is 205,264 (2001) male constitutes 54 per cent and female 46 per cent. The literacy rate is 62 per cent. Mirzapur district has four Tehsils, namely Mirzapur Sadar, Chumar, Marihan and Lalganj from administrative point of view. It has 12 development Blocks. Out of 12 Blocks, Lalganj, Hallia, Marihan, Rajgarh and Kon have been selected for our investigation.

The present name of the district is derived from Goddess Lakshmi who emerged from the sea. The word "Mirza" is formed from two words; 'Mir' meaning sea and 'Za' meaning from the sea. It is also locally believed that the town was founded by Raja Nanner and was known as Girizapur.

But after the British conquest it came to be known as Mirzapur. The earliest mention of the town is found in the writings of Tieffenthaler, who drew up in his description of the country between 1760 and 1770. He mentioned it under the name of Mirzapur, especially as a great mart. In the records of Jonathan Duncan, who was a resident of Varanasi, frequent mention is made of the place as Mirzapur. Before 1 April 1989, Mirzapur was the largest district of India. Mirzapur is also a Naxalite hot spot.

As per some unofficial evidence Mirzapur is the first named as

Gangayatan Ghat, but it was an oldest stairway of Mirzapur, however, Mirzapur was established by British Ruler and its establishment was only to grow up the Business through river Ganga.

Mirzapur is the only place in India where the holy river Ganga meets with Vindhya Range. This is considered significant in Hindu mythology and has a mention in *Vedas*.

Reports suggest that Mirzapur was a commercial city, being situated on the banks of the river Ganges. These reports are backed by the Naar Ghat, a carved stone with rates of toll taxes of Ashokan times inscribed on it. Most of the city was established by English officers and so places are named after Englishmen like Wellesley Ganj (Lord Wellesley), Mukeri Bazar (Lord Mercury), Dankeen Ganj (Mr. Danseen) and a famous waterfall of the city, Windham Water Fall (Mr. Windham). The Municipal Corporation building was also built by the English Government.

Some interesting petroglyphs in the sandstone of the Vindhya range are found in Morhana Paharin Mirzapur district. The depictions of chariots, horses, weapons and people in these works have given rise varied interpretations and findings by historians.

On the outskirts of the area, there is a patch of forest that contains ancient wall paintings, called Lakhania Dari and there are small rapids at the place. This has made it a popular picnic spot among residents of nearby cities. The forest area is still inhabited by some tribes. Possibly, ten tribes are still present in the region.

The indigenous ruler Saiyyad Shah Mirza was captured by the British Government, and so the city was documented by the British as Mirzapur in the name of its ruler. Some information about an ancient city near the local Kachhawa Bazar has also been found, but is awaiting concrete proof. Near the Kachhawa Bazar an ancient temple of Lord Shiva in Larawak village. It is locally believed that this temple was built in *Treta Yuga* during *Ramawataar*. This temple is so attractive in architecture point of view and all the design of stone is just like the Khajuraho. Now this temple is protected and supervised by Archaeological Survey of India (ASI). This temple gives a lot of information about the ancient life cycle of the human being. This temple is located in the heart of the Larawak village.

The District of Mirzapur, with the exception of the villages namely Mowat, Merolatand, Mahespur, Durjanipur, Mangarahi Deohat, Katra and Bamsaur received from Allahabad in 1861, falls entirely within the tract of country once known as the province of Benares. The sovereignty of this was formally ceded to the East India Company in 1775 by the Nawab-

Virzir of Avadh; but the tract itself was included in the Zamindari of the Raja of Benares and remained in his actual possession until 1794, when Mahip Narayan Singh surrendered its control to the Governor General of India by the agreement of 27th October of that year. It is not until 1830 that Mirzapur became a separate revenue jurisdiction of its own, because until that year it had been included in Varanasi. Mirzapur was then placed under a local collector of customs, the subdivisions assigned to new collectorate being Tappas Chaurasi, Chhiyanve, Upraudh, Kon and Sakteshgarg of pargana Kantit and other paragnas. Bhagat Bhuili, Haveli, Chunar, Quriat, Sikhar, Agori, Barhar and Bijaigarh, Bhadohi, Kon and Majhwa were restored to Varanasi on the protest of Raja but were afterwards reannexed to Mirzapur. At present Agori, Barharand, Bijaigarh are in Sonbhadra District. However, Bhadohi is in Sant Ravidas Nagar District. There has been no change in the territorial limits of Mirzapur since 1833, when the revenue and judicial administrations were made to consider throughout the Benares province; but several alternations have been made in the sub-divisional boundaries since the tract came into the possession of the British. In 1801 every pargana and tappa, with a few exception had a separate Tehsildar. In 1804 it was resolved to abolish the office of Tehsildar in the Benares Province. In 1806, tahsildars were established for tappas Chaurasi, Upraudh, Chhiyanvey, Sakteshgarh and Bhagwat at Chaurasi; and for parganas Agori-Barhar and Bijaigarh (at present lies in Sonbhadra District) at Kusancha. The first of the two tahsils created in 1809 corresponds to a great extent with the present Mirzapur tehsil. Saketeshgarh and Bhagwat have been taken away from it and Kon and Majhwa were added to the tehsil which had its headquarters in 1809 at Kusancha, Singrauli and Shahganj tehsil (Now all these are in Sonbhadra District).

Chunar

About 32 km from Mirzapur there is the famous fort of Chunar. There are some rock paintings in Mirzapur district. Hasauli is the first village which was awarded by the Ex-President A.P.J. Abdul Kalam and is also famous for its handicrafts. Chunar is the fort of King Shivdautt. Before 7-8 km away from Chunar railway station, there is a village Usarahawa on NH No. 7.

Vindhyachal

Mirzapur district of Uttar Pradesh is well known for the Vindhyavasini temple in Vindhyachal. It is one of the holiest places in India and is situated exactly in the middle of two pious cities Prayag and Kashi.

A few miles away from this city, is a site of pilgrimage to Hindus known as Vindhyachal where according to the mythology a part of *Sati* (an *avatar* of Durga) fell. The river Ganges flows through this city. Other sites of pilgrimage include Kali Khoh (literally 'the cave of the Goddess Kali') where a statue of Kali has a mouth formed in the shape of a cave, hence the name. Very close to the city is a waterfall.

The city itself has many *ghats* (steps to a river). There are few cinema halls. At first look the city appears to be a confluence of town, village and city life. Electricity supply is now regular up to some extent.

Commerce

The main business in Mirzapur is carpet manufacturing. Manufacturers range very small (with less than $ 100,000 in assets) to medium sized (with around $ 10 millions in assets). Most of the carpets are sold internationally as India has a limited market for carpets. The second main business is of metal pots.

It is evident from Table 3.1 that the average household size is 7.0 in Lalganj. The sex ratio in SC and ST is 902 and 909 respectively. Proportion of SC population is 42.4 per cent in male and 42.6 per cent in female. Proportion of ST population is 0.1 per cent, in total, Literacy rate is 43.4 per cent in total, 57.6 per cent in male and 27.3 per cent in female. Illiteracy rate is 86.1 per cent in total, 71.2 per cent in male and 102.0 per cent in female. Work participation rate is 37.2 per cent in total, 46.1 per cent in male, 27.3 per cent in female. Proportion of main workers is 23.3 per cent in total, 35.9 per cent in male and 9.1 per cent in female. Proportion of marginal workers is 14.0 per cent in total, 10.2 in male and 18.2 per cent in female. Proportion of Non-workers is 62.8 per cent in total, 59.9 per cent in male and 72.7 per cent in female. Proportion of cultivators to total workers is 39.9 per cent in total, 45.3 per cent in male and 29.7 per cent in female. Proportion of agricultural labourers to total workers is 43.9 per cent in total, 34.9 in male and 61.2 per cent in female. Proportion of workers in household industries to total workers is 6.0 per cent in total, 6.4 per cent in male and 5.2 per cent in female. Percentage of other workers to total workers is 10.2 per cent in total, 13.4 per cent in male and 4.0 per cent in female.

It is evident from the Table 3.2 that the average household size is 6.0 in Halliya. The sex ratio in SC and ST is 899 per thousand male. Proportion

Table 3.1: Area Profile of Lalganj Block

Number of Households		*43,908*		*Household size*			*7.0*
				Proportion of Urban population (%)			*0.0*
	P	*M*	*F*	*Sex Ratio (females per 1000 males)*			*893*
Population-Total	287,983	152,154	135,829	Sex Ratio (0-6 Years)			928
Population-Rural	287,983	152,154	135,829	Sex Ratio (SC)			902
Population-Urban	0	0	0	Sex Ratio (ST)			909
Population (0-6)	65,547	34,002	31,545				
SC Population	122,031	64,174	57,857		*P*	*M*	*F*
ST Population	189	99	90	Proportion of SC population (%)	42.4	42.2	42.6
				Proportion of ST population (%)	0.1	0.1	0.1
Number of literates	96,536	68,033	28,503	Literacy Rate (%)	43.4	57.6	27.3
Number of illiterates	191,447	84,121	107,326	Illiteracy Rate (%)	86.1	71.2	102.9
Total workers	107,241	70,189	37,052	Work Participation Rate (%)	37.2	46.1	27.3
Main workers	67,041	54,651	12,390	Proportion of Main Workers (%)	23.3	35.9	9.1
Marginal workers	40,200	15,538	24,662	Proportion of Marginal Workers (%)	14.0	10.2	18.2
Non-workers	180,742	81,965	98,777	Proportion of Non-Workers (%)	62.8	53.9	72.7
Cultivators	42,816	31,830	10,986	Proportion of cultivators to total workers (%)	39.9	45.3	29.7
Agricultural labourers	47,129	24,468	22,661	Proportion of agricultural labourers to total workers (%)	43.9	34.9	61.2
Workers in household industries	6,395	4,479	1,916	Proportion of workers in household industries to total workers (%)	6.0	6.4	5.2
Other workers	10,901	9,412	1,489	Percentage of other workers to total workers (%)	10.2	13.4	4.0

Source: Statistical Magazine—Mirzapur District, 2009.

of SC population is 27.8 per cent in total, 27.7 per cent male and 27.9 per cent in female. Literacy rate is 54.3 per cent in total, 57.6 per cent in total, 68.0 per cent in male and 38.7 per cent in female. Illiteracy rate is 74.5 per cent in total, 60.2 per cent in male and 90.7 per cent in female. Work participation rate is 26.6 per cent in total, 43.2 per cent in male and 7.9 per cent in female. Proportion of main workers is 19.8 per cent in total, 33.8 per cent in male and 4.2 per cent in female. Proportion of marginal workers is 6.8 per cent in total, 9.4 per cent in male and 3.8 per cent in female. Proportion of Non workers is 7.34 per cent in total, 56.8 per cent in male and 92.1 per cent in female. Proportion of cultivators to total workers is 40.9 per cent in total, 44.7 per cent in male and 17.5 per

Table 3.2: Area Profile of Halliya Block

Number of Households	*930*			*Household size*			*6.0*
				Proportion of Urban population (%)			*0.0*
	P	*M*	*F*	*Sex Ratio (females per 1000 males)*			*891*
Population-Total	5,817	3,076	2,741	Sex Ratio (0-6 Years)			923
Population-Rural	5,817	3,076	2,741	Sex Ratio (SC)			899
Population-Urban	0	0	0	Sex Ratio (ST)			0
Population (0-6)	1,300	676	624				
SC Population	1,618	852	766		*P*	*M*	*F*
ST Population	0	0	0	Proportion of SC population (%)	27.8	27.7	27.9
				Proportion of ST population (%)	0.0	0.0	0.0
Number of literates	2,452	1,632	820	Literacy Rate (%)	54.3	68.0	38.7
Number of illiterates	3,365	1,444	1,921	Illiteracy Rate (%)	74.5	60.2	90.7
Total workers	1,546	1,329	217	Work Participation Rate (%)	26.6	43.2	7.9
Main workers	1,153	1,039	114	Proportion of Main Workers (%)	19.8	33.8	4.2
Marginal workers	393	290	103	Proportion of Marginal Workers (%)	6.8	9.4	3.8
Non-workers	4,271	1,747	2,524	Proportion of Non-Workers (%)	73.4	56.8	92.1
Cultivators	632	594	38	Proportion of cultivators to total workers (%)	40.9	44.7	17.5
Agricultural labourers	456	339	117	Proportion of agricultural labourers to total workers (%)	29.5	25.5	53.9
Workers in household industries	131	97	34	Proportion of workers in household industries to total workers (%)	8.5	7.3	15.7
Other workers	327	299	28	Percentage of Other workers to total workers (%)	21.2	22.5	12.9

Source: Statistical Magazine—Mirzapur District, 2009.

cent in female. Proportion of agricultural labourers to total workers is 29.5 per cent in total, 25.5 per cent in male and 53.9 per cent in female. Proportion of workers in household industries to total workers is 8.5 per cent in total, 7.3 per cent in male and 15.7 per cent in female. Percentage of other workers to total workers is 21.2 per cent in total, 22.5 per cent in male and 12.9 per cent in female.

Table 3.3 shows that the household size in Marihan is 6.0. Sex ratio in SC and ST is 922 and 1057 respectively per thousand male. The proportion of SC population is 49.3 per cent in total, 49.0 per cent in male, 49.5 per cent in female. Portion of ST population is 0.3 per cent in total, 0.3 per cent in male and 0.3 per cent in female. Literacy rate is 43.5 per cent in total, 56.9 per cent in male and 28.6 per cent in female. Illiteracy rate is 84.0 per cent in total, 69.8 per cent in male and 99.8 per cent in

Table 3.3: Area Profile of Marihan Block

Number of Households			*31,171*	*Household size*			*6.0*
				Proportion of Urban population (%)			*0.0*
	P	*M*	*F*	*Sex Ratio (females per 1000 males)*			*912*
Population-Total	189,950	99,356	90,594	Sex Ratio (0-6 Years)			957
Population-Rural	189,950	99,356	90,594	Sex Ratio (SC)			922
Population-Urban	0	0	0	Sex Ratio (ST)			1057
Population (0-6)	41,013	20,958	20,055				
SC Population	93,575	48,692	44,883		*P*	*M*	*F*
ST Population	617	300	317	Proportion of SC population (%)	49.3	49.0	49.5
				Proportion of ST population (%)	0.3	0.3	0.3
Number of literates	64,809	44,602	20,207	Literacy Rate (%)	43.5	56.9	28.6
Number of illiterates	125,141	54,754	70,387	Illiteracy Rate (%)	84.0	69.8	99.8
Total workers	78,798	48,287	30,511	Work Participation Rate (%)	41.5	48.6	33.7
Main workers	53,028	39,184	13,844	Proportion of Main Workers (%)	27.9	39.4	15.3
Marginal workers	25,770	9,103	16,667	Proportion of Marginal Workers (%)	13.6	9.2	18.4
Non-workers	111,152	51,069	60,083	Proportion of Non-Workers (%)	58.5	51.4	66.3
Cultivators	28,098	19,278	8,820	Proportion of cultivators to total workers (%)	35.7	39.9	28.9
Agricultural labourers	38,739	19,131	19,608	Proportion of agricultural labourers to total workers (%)	49.2	39.6	64.3
Workers in household industries	4,405	3,575	830	Proportion of workers in household industries to total workers (%)	5.6	7.4	2.7
Other workers	7,556	6,303	1,253	Percentage of Other workers to total workers (%)	9.6	13.1	4.1

Source: Statistical Magazine—Mirzapur District, 2009.

female. Work participation rate is 41.5 per cent in total, 48.6 per cent male and 33.7 per cent in female. Proportion of main workers is 27.9 per cent in total, 39.4 per cent in male and 15.3 per cent in female. Proportion of marginal workers is 13.6 per cent in total, 9.2 per cent in male and 18.4 per cent in female. Proportion of non-workers is 58.5 per cent in total, 51.4 per cent in male and 66.3 per cent in female. Proportion of cultivators to total workers is 35.7 per cent in total, 39.9 per cent in male and 28.9 per cent in female. Proportion of agricultural labourers to total workers is 49.2 per cent in total, 39.6 per cent in male and 64.3 per cent in female. Proportion of workers in household industries to total workers is 5.6 per cent in total, 7.4 per cent in male and 2.7 per cent in female. Percentage of other workers to total workers is 9.6 per cent in total, 13.1 per cent in male and 4.1 per cent in female.

Table 3.4: Area Profile of Rajgarh Block

Number of Households	*205*			*Household size*	*6.0*		
				Proportion of Urban population (%)	*0.0*		
	P	*M*	*F*	*Sex Ratio (females per 1000 males)*	*962*		
Population-Total	1,228	626	602	Sex Ratio (0-6 Years)	887		
Population-Rural	1,228	626	602	Sex Ratio (SC)	909		
Population-Urban	0	0	0	Sex Ratio (ST)	0		
Population (0-6)	300	159	141				
SC Population	504	264	240		*P*	*M*	*F*
ST Population	0	0	0	Proportion of SC population (%)	41.0	42.2	39.9
				Proportion of ST population (%)	0.0	0.0	0.0
Number of literates	459	315	144	Literacy Rate (%)	49.5	67.5	31.2
Number of illiterates	769	311	458	Illiteracy Rate (%)	82.9	66.6	99.3
Total workers	462	295	167	Work Participation Rate (%)	37.6	47.1	27.7
Main workers	300	254	46	Proportion of Main Workers (%)	24.4	40.6	7.6
Marginal workers	162	41	121	Proportion of Marginal Workers (%)	13.2	6.5	20.1
Non-workers	766	331	435	Proportion of Non-Workers (%)	62.4	52.9	72.3
Cultivators	194	119	75	Proportion of cultivators to total workers (%)	42.0	40.3	44.9
Agricultural labourers	176	89	87	Proportion of agricultural labourers to total workers (%)	38.1	30.2	52.1
Workers in household industries	29	26	3	Proportion of workers in household industries to total workers (%)	6.3	8.8	1.8
Other workers	63	61	2	Percentage of Other workers to total workers (%)	13.6	20.7	1.2

Source: Statistical Magazine—Mirzapur District, 2009.

Table 3.4 shows that the size of the household in Rajgarh is 6.0. Sex ratio in SC and ST is 909. The proportion of SC, ST population is 41.0 per cent in total, 42.2 per cent in male and 39.9 per cent in female. Literacy rate is 49.5 per cent in total, 67.5 per cent in male and 31.2 per cent in female. Illiteracy rate is 82.9 per cent in total, 66.3 per cent in male and 99.3 per cent in female. Work participation rate is 37.6 per cent in total, 47.1 per cent male and 27.7 per cent in female. Proportion of main workers is 24.4 per cent in total, 40.6 per cent in male and 7.6 per cent in female. Proportion of marginal workers is 13.2 per cent in total, 6.5 per cent in male and 20.1 per cent in female. Proportion of non workers is 62.4 per cent in total, 52.9 per cent in male and 72.3 per cent in female. Proportion of cultivators to total workers is 42.0 per cent in total, 40.3 per cent in male and 44.9 per cent in female. Proportion of agricultural labourers to total workers is 38.1 per cent in total, 30.2 per cent in male and 52.1 per cent in female. Proportion of workers in household industries to total workers is 6.3 per cent in total, 8.8 per cent in male and 1.8 per cent in female. Percentage of other workers to total workers is 13.6 per cent in total, 20.7 per cent in male and 1.2 per cent in female.

Table 3.5: Area Profile of Kon Block

Number of Households			*180*	*Household size*			*6.0*
				Proportion of Urban population (%)			*0.0*
	P	*M*	*F*	*Sex Ratio (females per 1000 males)*			*951*
Population-Total	1,112	570	542	Sex Ratio (0-6 Years)			1066
Population-Rural	1,112	570	542	Sex Ratio (SC)			963
Population-Urban	0	0	0	Sex Ratio (ST)			0
Population (0-6)	250	121	129				
SC Population	367	187	180		*P*	*M*	*F*
ST Population	0	0	0	Proportion of SC population (%)	33.0	32.8	33.2
				Proportion of ST population (%)	0.0	0.0	0.0
Number of literates	343	234	109	Literacy Rate (%)	39.8	52.1	26.4
Number of illiterates	769	336	433	Illiteracy Rate (%)	89.2	74.8	104.8
Total workers	346	253	93	Work Participation Rate (%)	31.1	44.4	17.2
Main workers	271	249	22	Proportion of Main Workers (%)	24.4	43.7	4.1
Marginal workers	75	4	71	Proportion of Marginal Workers (%)	6.7	0.7	13.1
Non-workers	766	317	449	Proportion of Non-Workers (%)	68.9	55.6	82.8
Cultivators	199	132	67	Proportion of cultivators to total workers (%)	57.5	52.2	72.0
Agricultural labourers	108	88	20	Proportion of agricultural labourers to total workers (%)	31.2	34.8	21.5
Workers in household industries	11	6	5	Proportion of workers in household industries to total workers (%)	3.2	2.4	5.4
Other workers	28	27	1	Percentage of Other workers to total workers (%)	8.1	10.7	1.1

Source: Statistical Magazine—Mirzapur District, 2009.

Table 3.5 shows that the size of the household in Kon is 6.0. Sex ratio in SC and ST is 963 per thousand male population. The proportion of SC and ST population is 33.0 per cent in total, 32.8 per cent in male and 33.2 per cent in female. Literacy rate is 39.8 per cent in total, 52.1 per cent in male and 26.4 per cent in female. Illiteracy rate is 89.2 per cent in total, 74.8 per cent in male and 104.8 per cent in female. Work participation rate is 31.1 per cent in total, 44.4 per cent male and 17.2 per cent in female. Proportion of main workers is 24.4 per cent in total, 43.7 per cent in male and 4.1 per cent in female. Proportion of marginal workers is 6.7 per cent in total, 0.7 per cent in male and 13.1 per cent in female. Proportion of non-workers is 68.9 per cent in total, 55.6 per cent in male and 82.8 per cent in female. Proportion of cultivators to total workers is 57.5 per cent in total, 52.2 per cent in male and 72.0 per cent in female. Proportion of agricultural labourers to total workers is 31.2 per cent in total, 34.8 per cent in male and 21.5 per cent in female. Proportion of workers in household industries to total workers is 3.2 per cent in total, 2.4 per cent in male and 5.4 per cent in female. Percentage of other workers to total workers is 8.1 per cent in total, 10.7 per cent in male and 1.1 per cent in female.

II. PROFILE OF SONBHADRA DISTRICT[3,4]

The southern part of Mirzapur, recently known as Sonbhadra was created a new district in 1989 and is located in the Vindhya ranges of Uttar Pradesh and is densely forested a century ago. The total area of the district is 6,788 sq. km. The forest land is nearly 55 per cent of the total area, i.e., 3,782.86 sq. km area of the district is covered with forest. Dense forest covers the area of 1,078 sq. km whereas open forest covers the 1,369 sq. km. Area. It is bounded on the south by Sarguja of Chhattisgarh and Siddhi of Madhya Pradesh, east by Jharkhand State. It is bounded on the west by Rewan of Madhya Pradesh and on the north by Mirzapur and Chandauli districts of Uttar Pradesh.

The district Sonbhadra lies between 23°52' N and 25°32' N latitudes and 82°72' E and 83°33' E longitudes. The total population is 15,04,860. It is the only district in India which borders four States namely Madhya Pradesh, Chhattisgarh, Jharkhand and Bihar. The density of population is 274 per square kilometre; the sex ratio is 913 females for every 1000 males. Literacy rate is 49.3 per cent (2001).

Robertsganj, Headquarters of Sonbhadra is located about 90 km from the city of Varanasi, which is also the nearest airport. Flights are available to all major Indian cities including Delhi, Mumbai, Kolkata, Lucknow, Agra, Bangalore, Chennai, Patna, Khajuraho, Hyderabad, Gaya, etc. International connections are Bangkok, Colombo, Hong Kong, Macca and Kathmandu. Robertsganj is well connected to Lucknow, Allahabad, Varanasi and Mirzapur by road. Buses are available at all hours of the day from Varanasi and it normally takes 2½ hours to cover the distance. The city is connected by rail to Delhi, Allahabad, Ranchi and Patna. Some notable trains passing through the town are Muri Express (Jammu Tawi-Delhi-Tata Nagar), Jharkhand Swarna Jayanti Express/12873 (Hatia-Kanpur-Delhi), Triveni Express (Bareilly-Lucknow-Shaktinagar) and Shaktipunj Express/11448 (Howrah-Bokaro-Chopan-Jabalpur). As of now no rail connection exists between Robertsganj and Varanasi. The easiest way, thus, to reach Sonbhadra is by train or air up to Varanasi and then by taking a bus or private taxi.

The highway connecting Varanasi and Waidhan passes through the city. Though this is not a national highway it is a very busy road because of the towns Renukot, Anpara, Shaktinagar which are sufficiently commercialized areas. National Thermal Power Corporation is in Shaktinagar and also National Coalfield different projects like Singrauli, Khadia, Jayant, Dudhichua, Amlori, Kakri, etc. These areas have several major coal mines which cater a big part of the coal need of the State. Churk a nearby town is situated around 10 km, where Jaypee group is establishing a thermal power project. One of the main reasons this road is always busy is due to daily transport of around 1,000 trucks of grits and sand.

The Son river flows through the district from east to west and its tributary the Rihand river, which rises to the south in the highlands of Surguja district of Chhattisgarh, flows north to join the Son in the centre of the district. Sonbhadra is located in the south-eastern ranges of the Vindhyachal mountain. The Govind Ballabh Pant Sagar, a reservoir on the Rihand, lies partly in the district and partly in Madhya Pradesh. The district has historic, cultural, and ecological affinities with the Bagelkhand region. Obra and NTPC Rihand are the power projects located in this city. Robertsganj is the main town. Almost 100 km from Varanasi, the cultural centre of Indian epitome of Vedic civilization, holds a prime importance as the district headquarters.

The southern region of Sonbhadra District is referred as the "Energy Capital of India"; this region has many electrical power stations around Govind Ballabh Pant Sagar. NTPC (a leading power generation company in India) has three coal-based thermal power plants at Shaktinagar (India's first NTPC), Vindhyanagar (largest capacity in India, 3,260 MW) and Bijpur (Rihandnagar). Other power stations are Anpara (UPRVUNL), Obra (UPRVUNL), Renusagar (Hindalco Pipri-Hydro (UPRVUNL). NCL (a branch of Coal India Ltd.) has its headquarters and many coal mines in this region. Hindalco has a major aluminium plant at Renukut.

This region became an industrial heaven from an area of forest and hills. Some of the hills were having limestone and lot of them were having coal. There were some small rivers running through the area and the major was the Son.

Owing to the limestone hills, initially one cement factory was established at Churk in 1956. Later another cement factory started at Dala in 1971 and ancillary unit of Dala got started at Chunar in 1980. The cement factories became the foundation on which other industries were built. A big dam constructed at Pipri in 1961, named Rihand Dam. The dam produced 300 MW of electricity. Another small dam was constructed at Obra in 1968, 40 km from Rihand dam which generated 99 MW of electricity.

The Birla group then set up an aluminium plant at Renukut, which is one of the biggest aluminium plant of Hindalco. Later, the Birla group set-up its own power plant at Renusagar in 1967. This plant has the current capacity of 887.2 MW and supplies the power to Hindalco. The Birlas also started a company in Renukut called HiTech Carbon. Another industrial group initiated a company in Renukut named Kanoria Chemicals, which produces chemicals and later it started own power plant at Renukut in 1998 which generates 50 MW of electricity.

A big thermal power plant construction was started at Obra in 1967 with support from Russian engineers and was successfully completed in 1971. This had a capacity to produce 1,550 MW of electricity. Another power plant was initiated at Anpara in 1980. It produces 1,630 MW of electricity and has proposed to extend the capacity to 2,630 MW. The thermal power plant that NTPC started in Shaktinagar, generates 2,000 MW. The plant at Bijpur generates 2,000 MW.

Three cement factories, one of the biggest aluminium plants, a carbon plant, a chemical factory and an energy hub to India, which generates 11,000 MW with plans to reach 20,000 MW. The whole country is benefiting from this region, which was once full of forests and hills, which seemed like infertile land. Last but not least, Geological Survey of India.

In 2006 the Ministry of Panchayati Raj named Sonbhadra one of the country's 250 most backward districts (out of a total of 640). It is one of the 34 districts in Uttar Pradesh currently receiving funds from the Backward Regions Grant Fund Programme (BRGF).

Table 3.6 mentioned establishments are self-evident that this region has become an industrial heaven from the area of forest and hills. Some

Table 3.6: Installation of Power and Industrial Units

Sl. No.	*Year of Establish-ment*	*Name of Industry Plant*	*Name of Place*	*Production*
1.	1956	Churk Cement Factory	Churk	800 Tonnes per day.
2.	1961	Rihand Dam	Pipri	Reservoir for power plants, 300 MW of electricity.
3.	1962	Hindalco Aluminium Plant	Renukoot	Alumina refining 1145000 TPA. Aluminium metal 424000 TPA.
4.	1965	Kanoria Chemicals	Renukoot	Acetaldehyde-10000 TPA, Formaldehyde 70000 TPA, Lindane-875 TPA, Hexamine-4000 TPA, Industrial alcohol-225 million litres/annum, Aluminium chloride-6875 TPA, Ethyl Acetate-3300 TPA, Acitic Acid-6000 TPA, Commercial Hydrogen.
5.	1967	Renu Sagar Power Plant (Hindalco)	Renukoot	887.2 MW of electricity.
6.	1968	Obra Dam	Obra	99 MW of electricity, Reservoir for Power Plant.
7.	1971	Dala Cement Factory	Dala	3600 Tonnes per day.
8.	1980	Chunar Cement Factory	Chunar (Mirzapur)	Ancillary unit of Dala Cement Factory.
9.	1980	Anpara Thermal Power Plant UPSEB	Anpara	1630 MW of electricity.
10.	1983	B.P. Construction Company	Anpara, Sonbhadra	—
11.	1984	Singrauli Thermal Power Plant NTPC	Shakti Nagar	2000 MW of Electricity.
12.	1988	Hi Tech Carbon	Renukoot	Carbon Black 160000 Metric Tonnes per annum.
13.	1989	Rihand Thermal Power Plant NTPC	Bijpur	2000 MW of electricity.
14.	1990	Finding of Gold Mine in Hills	Mirchandhuri	—
15.	1998	Konoria Chemical Power Plant	Renukoot	50 MW of electricity.

Source: Statistical Magazine—Sonbhadra District, 2009.

of the hills were having limestone and lot of them were having coal. There were some small rivers running through the area and the major was the river Son. Owing to the limestone hills, initially one cement factory was established at Churk in 1956. Later another cement factory started at Dala in 1971 and ancillary unit of Dala got started at Chunar in 1980. The cement factories became the foundation on which other industries were built. A big Dam constructed at Pipri in 1961, named as Rihand Dam. The Dam produced 300 MW of electricity. Another small dam was constructed at Obra in 1968, 40 km away from Rihand Dam which generated 99 MW of electricity. The Birla group then set up an aluminium plant at Renukoot, which is one of the biggest aluminium plant of

HINDALCO. Later, the Birla group set up its own power plant at Renusagar in 1967. This plant has the current capacity of 887.2 MW and supplies the power to Hindalco. The Birla also started a company in Renukoot named Kanoria Chemicals, which produces chemicals and later it started own power plant at Renukoot in 1998 which generates 50 MW of electricity. A big thermal power plant construction was started at Obra in 1967 with support from Russian Engineers and was successfully completed in 1971. This had a capacity to produce 1,550 MW of electricity. Another power plant was initiated at Anpara in 1980. It produces 1,630 MW of electricity and has proposed to extend the capacity to 2,630 MW, This thermal power plant that NTPC started in Shakti Nagar, generates 2,000 MW. The plant at Bijpur generates 2,000 MW. Three cement factories one of the biggest aluminium plants, a carbon plant, a chemical factory and energy hub to India, which generates 11,000 MW with plans to reach 20,000 MW. The whole country is benefited from this region, which was once full of forests and hills, which seemed like infertile land.

Following Dalit Adivasis are found in Sonbhadra

Gond, Dhuria, Nayak, Ojha, Pathari, Rajgond, Kharwar, Khairwar, Paharia, Baiga, Pankha, Panika, Agaria, Pathari, Chero and Bhuiya, Bhunia have enlisted in Scheduled Tribes by the order of the Secretary, Social Welfare Department, Uttar Pradesh Government's Order No. 111, B.S./26.03-03(7)/2003 dated 3/7/2003. The Kol still could not be included in this revised list of S.T.

Sonbhadra has been highlighted not only because of its richness of mineral and for energy capital of India, but also for its oldest and richest heritage also. The fossils which were found in Salkhan area of Sonbhadra, have been confirmed by Paleo Botanists and historians that they were 110 crore years old. Several stone arms and several stone made figures of animals had also been discovered from the Ganga-Son and Belan Valley (Sonbhadra). The remanence of animal bones and its period has been estimated 1.25 lakh years old. In addition to it, nearly fifty caves have also been discovered which had been decorated with hundreds of coloured paintings. They are possibly 5,000 to 30,000 years old. There are Vijay Garh and Rajgarh forts which were established in tenth century AD. Near Vijay Garh fort several stone statues of gods and goddesses are maintained in a museum in Mau area of Robertsganj. They were installed during tenth century A.D.

Table 3.7: Area Profile of Sonbhadra Block

Number of Households		*115,656*		*Household size*			*6.0*
				Proportion of Urban population (%)			*15.2*
	P	*M*	*F*	*Sex Ratio (females per 1000 males)*			*904*
Population-Total	686,497	360,530	325,967	Sex Ratio (0-6 Years)			959
Population-Rural	582,163	304,242	277,921	Sex Ratio (SC)			925
Population-Urban	104,334	56,288	48,046	Sex Ratio (ST)			1039
Population (0-6)	141,437	72,216	69,221				
SC Population	247,299	142,468	104,831		*P*	*M*	*F*
ST Population	261	128	133	Proportion of SC population (%)	40.0	39.5	40.4
				Proportion of ST population (%)	0.0	0.0	0.0
Number of literates	259,681	177,181	82,500	Literacy Rate (%)	47.6	61.5	32.1
Number of illiterates	426,816	183,349	243,467	Illiteracy Rate (%)	78.3	63.6	94.8
Total workers	253,703	172,030	81,673	Work Participation Rate (%)	37.0	47.7	25.1
Main workers	170,666	137,293	33,373	Proportion of Main Workers (%)	24.9	38.1	10.2
Marginal workers	83,037	34,737	48,300	Proportion of Marginal Workers (%)	12.1	9.6	14.8
Non-workers	432,794	188,500	244,294	Proportion of Non-Workers (%)	63.0	52.3	74.9
Cultivators	88,572	63,532	25,040	Proportion of cultivators to total workers (%)	34.9	36.9	30.7
Agricultural labourers	103,287	54,738	48,549	Proportion of agricultural labourers to total workers (%)	40.7	31.8	59.4
Workers in household industries	5,846	3,896	1,950	Proportion of workers in household industries to total workers (%)	2.3	2.3	2.4
Other workers	55,998	49,864	6,134	Percentage of Other workers to total workers (%)	22.1	29.0	7.5

Source: Statistical Magazine—Sonbhadra District, 2009.

It is evident from Table 3.7 that the average size of the household is 6.0. Sex ratio in SC and ST is 925 and 1039 respectively. The proportion of SC and ST population is 40.0 per cent in total. Illiteracy rate is 63.6 per cent in male and 94.8 per cent in female. Work participation rate is 37.0 per cent in total, 47.7 per cent male and 25.1 per cent in female population. As regards proportion of main workers percentage, it is 24.9 per cent in total, 38.1 per cent in male and 10.2 per cent in female. Proportion of marginal workers is 12.1 per cent whereas percentage of proportion of non-workers is 63.0 per cent. Proportion of cultivators to total workers is 34.9 per cent, proportion of agricultural labourers to total workers is 40.7 per cent.

Table 3.8: Area Profile of Nagaon Block

Number of Households	*94*			*Household size*			*5.0*
				Proportion of Urban population (%)			*0.0*
	P	*M*	*F*	*Sex Ratio (females per 1000 males)*			*826*
Population-Total	471	258	213	Sex Ratio (0-6 Years)			836
Population-Rural	471	258	213	Sex Ratio (SC)			921
Population-Urban	0	0	0	Sex Ratio (ST)			0
Population (0-6)	101	55	46				
SC Population	219	114	105		*P*	*M*	*F*
ST Population	0	0	0	Proportion of SC population (%)	46.5	44.2	49.3
				Proportion of ST population (%)	0.0	0.0	0.0
Number of literates	94	73	21	Literacy Rate (%)	25.4	36.0	12.6
Number of illiterates	377	185	192	Illiteracy Rate (%)	101.9	91.1	115.0
Total workers	272	140	132	Work Participation Rate (%)	57.7	54.3	62.0
Main workers	271	140	131	Proportion of Main Workers (%)	57.5	54.3	61.5
Marginal workers	1	0	1	Proportion of Marginal Workers (%)	0.2	0.0	0.5
Non-workers	199	118	81	Proportion of Non-Workers (%)	42.3	45.7	38.0
Cultivators	67	35	32	Proportion of cultivators to total workers (%)	24.6	25.0	24.2
Agricultural labourers	205	105	100	Proportion of agricultural labourers to total workers (%)	75.4	75.0	75.8
Workers in household industries	0	0	0	Proportion of workers in household industries to total workers (%)	0.0	0.0	0.0
Other workers	0	0	0	Percentage of Other workers to total workers (%)	0.0	0.0	0.0

Source: Statistical Magazine—Sonbhadra District, 2009.

Table 3.8 shows the following Household size is 5.0. Sex ratio in SC and ST is 921. The proportion of SC and ST population is 46.5 per cent. The literacy rate is 25.4 per cent in total, 36.0 per cent in male and 12.6 per cent in female. Illiteracy rate is 101.9 per cent in total 91.1 per cent in male and 115.0 per cent in female. Work participation rate is 57.7 per cent in total, 54.3 per cent male and 62.0 per cent in female. Proportion of main workers is 57.5 per cent, and proportion of non-workers is 42.3 per cent. Proportion of cultivators to total workers is 24.6 per cent, proportion of agricultural labourers to total workers is 75.4 per cent.

Table 3.9 shows that the size of the household in Chopan is 6.0. Sex ratio in SC and ST is 915 male per thousand of population. The proportion of SC and ST population is 4.4 per cent. Literacy rate is 35.2 per cent in total, 44.3 per cent in male and 24.8 per cent in female. Illiteracy rate is 92.2 per cent in total, 82.5 per cent in male and 103.3 per cent in female.

Table 3.9: Area Profile of Chopan Block

Number of Households			*532*	*Household size*			*6.0*
				Proportion of Urban population (%)			*0.0*
	P	*M*	*F*	*Sex Ratio (females per 1000 males)*			*881*
Population-Total	2,978	1,583	1,395	Sex Ratio (0-6 Years)			916
Population-Rural	2,978	1,583	1,395	Sex Ratio (SC)			915
Population-Urban	0	0	0	Sex Ratio (ST)			0
Population (0-6)	640	334	306				
SC Population	1,233	644	589		*P*	*M*	*F*
ST Population	0	0	0	Proportion of SC population (%)	41.4	40.7	42.2
				Proportion of ST population (%)	0.0	0.0	0.0
Number of literates	823	553	270	Literacy Rate (%)	35.2	44.3	24.8
Number of illiterates	2,155	1,030	1,125	Illiteracy Rate (%)	92.2	82.5	103.3
Total workers	875	678	197	Work Participation Rate (%)	29.4	42.8	14.1
Main workers	740	630	110	Proportion of Main Workers (%)	24.8	39.8	7.9
Marginal workers	135	48	87	Proportion of Marginal Workers (%)	4.5	3.0	6.2
Non-workers	2,103	905	1,198	Proportion of Non-Workers (%)	70.6	57.2	85.9
Cultivators	289	253	36	Proportion of cultivators to total workers (%)	33.0	37.3	18.3
Agricultural labourers	309	180	129	Proportion of agricultural labourers to total workers (%)	35.3	26.5	65.5
Workers in household industries	9	6	3	Proportion of workers in household industries to total workers (%)	1.0	0.9	1.5
Other workers	268	239	29	Percentage of Other workers to total workers (%)	30.6	35.3	14.7

Source: Statistical Magazine—Sonbhadra District, 2009.

Work participation rate is 29.4 per cent in total, 42.8 per cent male and 14.1 per cent in female. Proportion of main workers is 24.8 per cent in total, 39.8 per cent in male and 7.9 per cent in female. Proportion of marginal workers is 4.5 per cent in total, 3.0 per cent in male and 6.2 per cent in female. Proportion of non workers is 70.6 per cent in total, 57.2 per cent in male and 85.9 per cent in female. Proportion of cultivators to total workers is 33.0 per cent in total, 37.3 per cent in male and 18.3 per cent in female. Proportion of agricultural labourers to total workers is 35.3 per cent in total, 26.5 per cent in male and 65.5 per cent in female. Proportion of workers in household industries to total workers is 1.0 per cent in total, 0.9 per cent in male and 1.5 per cent in female. Percentage of other workers to total workers is 30.6 per cent in total, 35.3 per cent in male and 14.7 per cent in female.

Table 3.10 shows that the household size is 6.0. Sex ratio in SC and ST is 928 and 915 per thousand male population. The proportion of SC

Table 3.10: Area Profile of Dudhi Block

Number of Households			*100,002*	*Household size*			*6.0*
				Proportion of Urban population (%)			*29.9*
	P	*M*	*F*	*Sex Ratio (females per 1000 males)*			*884*
Population-Total	551,198	292,609	258,589	Sex Ratio (0-6 Years)			955
Population-Rural	386,574	201,591	184,983	Sex Ratio (SC)			928
Population-Urban	164,624	61,018	103,606	Sex Ratio (ST)			915
Population (0-6)	110,688	56,619	54,069				
SC Population	238,329	123,604	114,725		*P*	*M*	*F*
ST Population	224	117	107	Proportion of SC population (%)	43.2	42.2	44.4
				Proportion of ST population (%)	0.0	0.0	0.0
Number of literates	238,116	158,777	79,339	Literacy Rate (%)	54.1	67.3	38.8
Number of illiterates	313,082	133,832	179,250	Illiteracy Rate (%)	71.1	56.7	87.6
Total workers	192,210	135,484	56,726	Work Participation Rate (%)	34.9	46.3	21.9
Main workers	128,685	109,588	19,097	Proportion of Main Workers (%)	23.3	37.5	7.4
Marginal workers	63,525	25,896	37,629	Proportion of Marginal Workers (%)	11.5	8.9	14.6
Non-workers	358,988	157,125	201,863	Proportion of Non-Workers (%)	65.1	53.7	78.1
Cultivators	60,042	42,803	17,239	Proportion of cultivators to total workers (%)	31.2	31.6	30.4
Agricultural labourers	60,057	27,075	32,982	Proportion of agricultural labourers to total workers (%)	31.2	20.0	58.1
Workers in household industries	4,740	3,079	1,661	Proportion of workers in household industries to total workers (%)	2.5	2.3	2.9
Other workers	67,371	62,527	4,844	Percentage of Other workers to total workers (%)	35.1	46.2	8.5

Source: Statistical Magazine—Sonbhadra District, 2009.

and ST population is 43.2 per cent. Literacy rate is 54.1 per cent in total, 67.3 per cent in male and 38.8 per cent in female. Illiteracy rate is 71.1 per cent in total, 56.7 per cent in male and 87.6 per cent in female. Work participation rate is 34.9 per cent in total, 46.3 per cent male and 21.9 per cent in female. Proportion of main workers is 23.3 per cent in total, 37.5 per cent in male and 7.4 per cent in female. Proportion of marginal workers is 11.5 per cent in total, 8.9 per cent in male and 14.6 per cent in female. Proportion of non workers is 65.1 per cent in total, 53.7 per cent in male and 78.1 per cent in female. Proportion of cultivators to total workers is

31.2 per cent in total, 31.6 per cent in male and 30.4 per cent in female. Proportion of agricultural labourers to total workers is 31.2 per cent in total, 20.0 per cent in male and 58.1 per cent in female. Proportion of workers in household industries to total workers is 2.5 per cent in total, 2.3 per cent in male and 2.9 per cent in female. Percentage of other workers to total workers is 35.1 per cent in total, 46.2 per cent in male and 8.5 per cent in female.

It is evident from Table 3.11 shows that the household size is 5.0. Sex ratio in SC and ST is 938 per thousand male population. The proportion of SC and ST population is 31.0 per cent in total, 29.1 per

Table 3.11: Area Profile of Babhani Block

Number of Households			*19*	*Household size*			*5.0*
				Proportion of Urban population (%)			*0.0*
	P	*M*	*F*	*Sex Ratio (females per 1000 males)*			*818*
Population-Total	100	55	45	Sex Ratio (0-6 Years)			917
Population-Rural	100	55	45	Sex Ratio (SC)			938
Population-Urban	0	0	0	Sex Ratio (ST)			0
Population (0-6)	23	12	11				
SC Population	31	16	15		*P*	*M*	*F*
ST Population	0	0	0	Proportion of SC population (%)	31.0	29.1	33.3
				Proportion of ST population (%)	0.0	0.0	0.0
Number of literates	47	33	14	Literacy Rate (%)	61.0	76.7	41.2
Number of illiterates	53	22	31	Illiteracy Rate (%)	68.8	51.2	91.2
Total workers	47	30	17	Work Participation Rate (%)	47.0	54.5	37.8
Main workers	26	22	4	Proportion of Main Workers (%)	26.0	40.0	8.9
Marginal workers	21	8	13	Proportion of Marginal Workers (%)	21.0	14.5	28.9
Non-workers	53	25	28	Proportion of Non-Workers (%)	53.0	45.5	62.2
Cultivators	28	21	7	Proportion of cultivators to total workers (%)	59.6	70.0	41.2
Agricultural labourers	14	5	9	Proportion of agricultural labourers to total workers (%)	29.8	16.7	52.9
Workers in household industries	0	0	0	Proportion of workers in household industries to total workers (%)	0.0	0.0	0.0
Other workers	5	4	1	Percentage of Other workers to total workers (%)	10.6	13.3	5.9

Source: Statistical Magazine—Sonbhadra District, 2009.

cent in male and 33.3 per cent in female. Literacy rate is 61.0 per cent in total, 76.7 per cent in male and 41.2 per cent in female. Illiteracy rate is 68.8 per cent in total, 51.2 per cent in male and 91.2 per cent in female. Work participation rate is 47.0 per cent in total, 54.5 per cent male and 37.8 per cent in female. Proportion of main workers is 26.0 per cent in total, 40.0 per cent in male and 8.9 per cent in female. Proportion of marginal workers is 21.0 per cent in total, 14.6 per cent in male and 28.9 per cent in female. Proportion of non workers is 53.0 per cent in total, 45.5 per cent in male and 62.2 per cent in female. Proportion of cultivators to total workers is 59.6 per cent in total, 70.0 per cent in male and 41.2 per cent in female. Proportion of agricultural labourers to total workers is 29.8 per cent in total, 16.7 per cent in male and 52.9 per cent in female. Proportion of workers in household industries to total workers is 0.0 per cent in total. Percentage of other workers to total workers is 10.6 per cent in total, 13.3 per cent in male and 5.9 per cent in female.

III. PROFILE OF CHANDAULI DISTRICT

Chandauli district derives its name from Chandra Shah, the founder, a Barhaulia Rajput, who built the fort in the district. This district was created out of Varanasi district in 1997. A tug of war between Ex-Chief Minister Mayawati and her arch rival and Samajwadi Party Chief Mulayam Singh Yadav had resulted in separation of Chandauli from Varanasi, remerger and restoration of the district in the one decade. During her past regime, the Ex-Chief Minister Mayawati had carved out Chandauli from Varanasi as a separate district in 1997. However, SP Ex-Chief Mulayam Singh Yadav merged it again in Varanasi district after coming back to power in 2004. Finally, a High Court order helped in restoring the status of Chandauli district in July 2004. But in this tug of war, the forest natives of Chandauli lost the status of scheduled tribe and in the lack of revenue records of past 75 years, proving them to be the traditional forest dwellers also became impossible. It also jolted the bid of the Chandauli administration to utilize this act as a major weapon against Maoists.

The district is surrounded by Bihar State in the East, Mirzapur in the West, Ghazipur district and Bihar State in North, Sonbhadra district in the South. The Ganga, the Karamnasha and the Chandraprabha are the main rivers in the district. The population of the district is 16,39,777 (Census 2001). The area covers 2,541 sq. km. The rural population of the district is 89.4 per cent. It has dozens of forests all around. It is divided into parts—Chakia and Chandauli. One of the Tehsil is Naugarh.

With a population of 16,43,251, Chandauli accounts for 0.99 per cent of the population of Uttar Pradesh. 10.56 per cent of the population lives in towns and cities. The three largest towns in the district are Mughalsarai, Mughalsarai Railway Settlement and Chandauli.

Scheduled Castes and Scheduled Tribes form 3,99,427 and 24.31 per cent of the total population respectively. The three largest scheduled caste groups are Chamar, Dusadh and Musahar. The three largest scheduled tribe groups are Tharu, Generic tribes and Bhotia.

51.53 per cent of the district population is in working age group of 15-59 years. The district ranks 282 among 591 districts of India in terms of proportion of population in working age group (a higher ranks reflects a good performance). An inclusive growth process and employment generation have been accorded high priority in the Eleventh Five Year Plan. Specific action plans need to tailored for every district depending on the size of urbanization and educational attainment of the workforce.

The largely the elderly population, the greater would be the need of for social support for the elderly. 7.73 per cent of the district population is over the age of 59 years. The sex ratio in the district is 923/1000. As often used indicator to capture the extent of discrimination against the girl child is the child sex ratio. In Chandauli, the sex ratio, i.e., the girl per thousand boys, among children in the age group 0-6 years is 936. Ideally the sex ratio at birth should be between 943 and 954.

One aspect of living condition in the district is the type of dwelling that households reside in 6.1 per cent of households live in a temporary structure while 47.4 per cent of households live in semi permanent structure. The district ranks 377 among 591 districts of India in terms of per cent of household living in a temporary structure (a higher rank reflects a poor performance).

1,68,838 of households in the district have a bank account, a proxy for the extent of financial intermediation. The district ranks 216 among 591 districts of India in terms of extent of financial intermediation (a higher rank reflects a good performance).

Access to the outside world is important indicator. Improved access and connectivity can contribute to improving livelihoods. As part of a poverty reduction strategy, the Pradhanmantri Gram Sadak Yojana, aims at improving connectivity in rural habitations. This district ranks 116,352,309 among 591 districts of India in terms of percentage of villages having paved approach road, bus services, and post, telegraphs and telephone facilities.

The overall literacy rate in district is 59.72 per cent. The male and female literacy rate are respectively 7404, 44.13. This district ranks 344 and 410 among all districts of India in terms of male and female literacy (a higher rank reflects a good performance). However, the level of literacy does not reflect educational attainment.

The total number of years of schooling that an Indian boy or girl can expect to receive in school in future is only 9.8 years. Even this average is an overtime mate because of grade repetition.

With 9.3 per cent of its population completing middle school, Chandauli ranks 224 among 590 districts of India.

Central to the ability to increase the level of educational attainment is case of access to schools. Of the 1419 villages, 52.7 per cent have a primary school, 16.3 have middle schools, 3.8 per cent have a secondary school and 1.1 per cent has colleges. Chandauli ranks 328 in terms of per cent of villages having a middle school (higher rank reflects better school infrastructure in district).

The district is divided into 2 tehsils. Further, for development point of view, it has been divided into three Blocks.

The district is named after its tehsil headquarters name. The region covered by the present district was part of the ancient kingdom of Kashi. Apart from the numerous legends connected with this district, valuable evidence of antiquity has been found here and the remains of brick strewn mounds are spread all over the district.

The history of the district for the most part is unknown. There are some deserted sites, tanks and kund seen in tehsils of the district and they carry vague legends. One of the ancient site of the district, "Baluwa" is situated about 21 km. to the southern part of tehsil Sakaldiha at the banks of river Ganga where Ganga flows from east to west direction. A religious fair for Hindus takes place every year in the month of *Magha* (January) which is known as "*Pachchim Vahini Mela*" it is said that the Ganga flows east to west direction only at two places in the country—first in Allahabad and second one at Baluwa.

Village Ramgarh of tahsil Sakaldiha, known as birth place of great Aghoreshwari Saint Shree Kinaram Baba is just 6 km. away from Chahniya. He was a great follower of Vaishnava faith and also Shiva and Shakta faith, and believed in god power. He devoted his entire life for the services of mankind. This place has become holy place for Hinduism.

In one of the ancient sites in the village Hetampur of the district, there is a fort which is known as "Fort of Hetam" which is situated about 22 km. to the north-east from the district headquarters. The ruins of this fort are spread over on 22 *bighas* in area. It is said that this fort was designed and constructed between fourteenth to fifteenth centuries by Todar Mal Khatri who was the construction supervisor in the kingdom of Sher Shah Suri. After Mughal period, Hetam Khan, Talukedar and Jagirdar captured this fort. There are five famous ruined Kot, known as Bhulaini Kot, Bhitari Kot, Bichali Kot, Uttrai Kot and Dakchhani Kot, which attract the visitors. Some says that it was constructed by Hetam himself.

Being the part of Kashi Kingdom, the history of the Chandauli district is the same as of Kashi Kingdom and of Varanasi district. Before the birth of Lord Buddha, in sixth century B.C., Bharatvarsha was divided into sixteen Mahajanpadas, Kashi was one of them and its capital was Varanasi. Modern Benares with its surroundings region was called as Kashi Mahajanpada. Varanasi city is one of the ancient cities of India, as well as among the ancient towns of the world. Its name comes in *Puranas*, *Mahabharata* and *Ramayana*. It is a sacred place of Hindu as well as Buddhist and Jain also. The name of Kashi came to be known after name of King Kashi, the seventh King of this dynasty. After the seventh generation a famous King Dhanwantri, ruled over this region, whose name is famous in the field of medicine as founder of Ayurveda.

Kashi kingdom was, however, dominated by Brahmadatta dynasty of Magadha during the century preceding the *Mahabharata* war, but past *Mahabharata* period saw the rise of Brahmadatta dynasty. About hundred kings of this generation are said to have had their supremacy over this region, some of these rulers become the *Chakravarti Samrat*. King Manoj of Kashi brought the kingdom of Kaushala, Anga and Magadha in his possession and annexed their territories to his empire. In the Jain scriptures, a King of Kashi named Ashwasena was the father of 23rd *Tirthankar* Parshvanatha.

In 1775, Kashi Kingdom had come under the influence of British Empire. The last king of this generation was Bibhuti Narayan Singh who ruled for about eight years till the emergence of independence, Benares state was merged with India.

Table 3.12 shows that the household size in Sahabganj Block is 7.0. Sex ratio in SC and ST is 883 per thousand male. The proportion of SC and ST population is 25.2 per cent in total, 25.8 per cent in male and 24.6 per cent in female. Literacy rate is 57.2 per cent in total, 69.3 per cent in male and 44.3 per cent in female. Illiteracy rate is 69.1 per cent in total, 57.9 per cent in male and 81.1 per cent in female. Work participation rate

Table 3.12: Area Profile of Sahabganj Block

Number of Households			*560*	*Household size*			*7.0*
				Proportion of Urban population (%)			*0.0*
	P	*M*	*F*	*Sex Ratio (females per 1000 males)*			*926*
Population-Total	3,709	1,926	1,783	Sex Ratio (0-6 Years)			876
Population-Rural	3,709	1,926	1,783	Sex Ratio (SC)			883
Population-Urban	0	0	0	Sex Ratio (ST)			0
Population (0-6)	773	412	361				
SC Population	936	497	439		*P*	*M*	*F*
ST Population	0	0	0	Proportion of SC population (%)	25.2	25.8	24.6
				Proportion of ST population (%)	0.0	0.0	0.0
Number of literates	1,679	1,049	630	Literacy Rate (%)	57.2	69.3	44.3
Number of illiterates	2,030	877	1,153	Illiteracy Rate (%)	69.1	57.9	81.1
Total workers	1,056	825	231	Work Participation Rate (%)	28.5	42.8	13.0
Main workers	651	620	31	Proportion of Main Workers (%)	17.6	32.2	1.7
Marginal workers	405	205	200	Proportion of Marginal Workers (%)	10.9	10.6	11.2
Non-workers	2,653	1,101	1,552	Proportion of Non-Workers (%)	71.5	57.2	87.0
Cultivators	118	105	13	Proportion of cultivators to total workers (%)	11.2	12.7	5.6
Agricultural labourers	259	192	67	Proportion of agricultural labourers to total workers (%)	24.5	23.3	29.0
Workers in household industries	37	32	5	Proportion of workers in household industries to total workers (%)	3.5	3.9	2.2
Other workers	642	496	146	Percentage of Other workers to total workers (%)	60.8	60.1	63.2

Source: Statistical Magazine—Sonbhadra District.

is 28.5 per cent in total, 42.8 per cent male and 13.0 per cent in female. Proportion of main workers is 17.6 per cent in total, 32.2 per cent in male and 1.7 per cent in female. Proportion of marginal workers is 10.9 per cent in total, 10.6 per cent in male and 11.2 per cent in female. Proportion of non workers is 71.5 per cent in total, 57.2 per cent in male and 87.0 per cent in female. Proportion of cultivators to total workers is 11.2 per cent in total, 12.7 per cent in male and 5.6 per cent in female. Proportion of agricultural labourers to total workers is 24.5 per cent in total, 23.3 per cent in male and 29.0 per cent in female. Proportion of workers in household industries to total workers is 3.5 per cent in total, 3.9 per cent in male and 2.2 per cent in female. Percentage of other workers to total workers is 60.8 per cent in total, 60.1 per cent in male and 63.2 per cent in female.

It is evident from the Table 3.13 shows that the household size in

Table 3.13: Area Profile of Naugarh Block

Number of Households		*83*		*Household size*			*7.0*
				Proportion of Urban population (%)			*0.0*
	P	*M*	*F*	*Sex Ratio (females per 1000 males)*			*930*
Population-Total	577	299	278	Sex Ratio (0-6 Years)			847
Population-Rural	577	299	278	Sex Ratio (SC)			1500
Population-Urban	0	0	0	Sex Ratio (ST)			0
Population (0-6)	109	59	50				
SC Population	20	8	12		*P*	*M*	*F*
ST Population	0	0	0	Proportion of SC population (%)	3.5	2.7	4.3
				Proportion of ST population (%)	0.0	0.0	0.0
Number of literates	300	179	121	Literacy Rate (%)	64.1	74.6	53.1
Number of illiterates	277	120	157	Illiteracy Rate (%)	59.2	50.0	68.9
Total workers	155	135	20	Work Participation Rate (%)	26.9	45.2	7.2
Main workers	123	112	11	Proportion of Main Workers (%)	21.3	37.5	4.0
Marginal workers	32	23	9	Proportion of Marginal Workers (%)	5.5	7.7	3.2
Non-workers	422	164	258	Proportion of Non-Workers (%)	73.1	54.8	92.8
Cultivators	33	22	11	Proportion of cultivators to total workers (%)	21.3	16.3	55.0
Agricultural labourers	11	11	0	Proportion of agricultural labourers to total workers (%)	7.1	8.1	0.0
Workers in household industries	9	7	2	Proportion of workers in household industries to total workers (%)	5.8	5.2	10.0
Other workers	102	95	7	Percentage of Other workers to total workers (%)	65.8	70.4	35.0

Source: Statistical Magazine—Sonbhadra District.

Naugarh is 7.0. Sex ratio in SC and ST is 1500 per thousand male. Proportion of SC and ST population is 3.5 per cent in total, 2.7 per cent in male and 4.3 per cent in female. Literacy rate is 64.1 per cent in total, 74.6 per cent in male and 53.1 per cent in female. Illiteracy rate is 59.2 per cent in total, 50.0 per cent in male and 68.9 per cent in female. Work participation rate is 26.9 per cent in total, 45.2 per cent male and 7.2 per cent in female. Proportion of main workers is 21.3 per cent in total, 37.5 per cent in male and 4.0 per cent in female. Proportion of marginal workers is 5.5 per cent in total, 7.7 per cent in male and 3.2 per cent in female. Proportion of non-workers is 73.1 per cent in total, 54.8 per cent in male and 92.8 per cent in female. Proportion of cultivators to total workers is 21.3 per cent in total, 16.3 per cent in male and 55.0 per cent in female. Proportion of agricultural labourers to total workers is 7.1 per cent in total, 8.1 per cent in male and 0.0 per cent in female. Proportion of workers in household industries to total workers is 5.8 per cent in total. 5.2 per cent in male and 10.0 per cent in female. Percentage of other workers to total workers is 65.8 per cent in total, 70.4 per cent in male and 35.0 per cent in female.

IV. PROFILE OF ALLAHABAD DISTRICT[5, 6]

Allahabad is located 25°27′N, 81°50′E, 25.45° N, 81.84°E in the eastern part of the Uttar Pradesh at an elevation of 98 metres (322 ft) and stands at the confluence of the two, the Ganges and Yamuna. The region was known in antiquity as the Vats country. To its south and south-east is the Baghelkhand region. To its east is middle Ganges valley of North India, or Purvanchal. To its South-West is the Bundelkhand region to its north and north-east is the Awadh region and to its west along with Kausambi, it forms the parts of Doab, i.e., the Lower Doab region. Allahabad stands at a strategic point both geographically and culturally. An important part of the Ganges-Yamuna Doab region, it is the last point of the Yamuna river and it is the last frontier of the Indian west. The land of the Allahabad district that falls between the Ganges and Yamuna is just like the rest of Doab, fertile but not too moist, and is especially suitable for the cultivation of wheat. The non-Doabi parts of the district, which are the southern and eastern part of the district, are some what similar to those of adjoining Bundelkhand and Baghelkhand regions—dry and rocky.

Allahabad district has a population of 49,36,106 while Allahabad city has a population of 1,206 as per the 2001 Census. It lists as the 32nd most populous city in India. Allahabad literacy rate is 82 per cent. As Allahabad has an area of about 70 km and is 98 m (322 ft) above sea level. It is situated at the confluence of the Ganges and Yamuna rivers. It encompasses a large area and is an inland peninsula surrounded by rivers on three sides with only one side connected to the mainland. Because of this to handle growing traffic and connectivity demands, Allahabad has many bridges crossing rivers the Ganges and Yamuna.

Shankargarh, Jasra, Meja and Koraon development Blocks of Allahabad district cover forest parts of Allahabad. Hundreds of tribals are living since long in the forest land. There main occupation has been mining activities, stone quarrying, collection of fuel wood and other forest produce and sell them in the urban areas for their livelihood. The profile of tribal areas and characteristics of the tribal people of this district is quite similar to Chitrakoot district, therefore, the tribals of Allahabad and Chitrakoot have been covered into one category, i.e., Dacoit prone area. Sample households have been selected from Shankargarh, Jasra,

Meja and Koraon Blocks for our study. Out of these Blocks, Shankargarh possesses the true tribal characteristics of Allahabad district.

Allahabad is a name given by the Mughals to the ancient city of Prayag, by some accounts the second oldest city of India. It is in the North Indian State of Uttar Pradesh and is the administrative headquarters of the Allahabad District. Allahabad is one of the fastest growing cities in India at present. It is located 205 kilometres (127 miles) south of the State capital, Lucknow. The ancient name of the city is Prayag (Sanskrit for "place of sacrifice"), as it is believed to be the spot where Brahma offered his first sacrifice after creating the world. It is one of four sites of the mass Hindu pilgrimage *Kumbh Mela*, the other being Haridwar, Ujjain and Nasik. It has a position of importance in Hindu scriptures for it is situated at Triveni Sangam, the confluence of the holy rivers Ganga, Yamuna and the ancient Saraswati river.

In ancient times, the city was known as Prayag (place of the confluences). According to Hindu religious texts, it is believed that here Brahma the Hindu creator of the Universe, attended a sacrificial ritual.

For Hindu of India, Prayag and the district of Kaushambi were important parts of their territory. The area became a part of the Mauryan and Gupta empire of the east and the Kushan empire of the west before becoming part of the Kannauj empire.

The founder of Sikh Religion Guru Nanak Dev Ji visited Allahabad then known as Prayag and the Ninth Sikh Guru Tegh Bahadur visited Allahabad in 1666 and Sikh religion was preached in this city.

Allahabad became a part of the Mughal Empire after their invasion of India in 1526. The Mughal Emperor Akbar built a magnificent fort in Allahabad. The city was the scene of Maratha incursion before colonial rule was imposed over India.

In 1765, the British established a garrison at Fort Allahabad. In 1857, Allahabad was active in the Indian Mutiny.

The annual convention of the Indian National Congress was held on the extensive grounds of Darbhanga Castle, Allahabad in 1888 and 1892.

In 1931, at Alfred Park in Allahabad, the revolutionary Chandrashekhar Azad killed himself when surrounded by the British Police. In the years of the struggle for Indian independence, the Nehru family homes of Anand Bhavan and Swaraj Bhavan, both in Allahabad, were the centre of the political activities of the Indian National Congress. Thousands of *satyagrahis* (non-violent resistors) went to jail. The first Prime Minister of India, Jawaharlal Nehru, was from Allahabad.

Hindi, Urdu and English are spoken in Allahabad. The dialect of Hindi spoken in Allahabad is Awadhi, although *Khariboli* is most commonly used in the city area. In the eastern non-Doabi part of Allahabad district Bagheli dialect is more common. Bengali and Punjabi are also spoken in some quarters. All major religions are practised in Allahabad. Hindus comprise 86.81 per cent and Muslims 12.72 per cent. There are small groups of Christians, Sikhs and Buddhists with 0.18 per cent, 0.13 per cent, and 0.04 per cent of population, respectively.

The Sangam

Every year thousands gather at Allahabad to take part in a festival on the banks of the Ganges, the *Magh Mela*. The same festival is organised in a larger scale every twelfth year and attracts millions of people and is called the *Kumbha Mela*. *Kumbh Mela* (especially the *Maha Kumbh Mela*) is the most sacred of all the pilgrimages. Thousands of holy men and women (monks, saints and *sadhus*) attend, and the auspiciousness of the festival is in part attributable to this. The *sadhus* are seen clad in saffron clothes with plenty of ashes and powder dabbed on their skin as required by ancient traditions. Some called *nanga sannyasis* or *Digambars* may often be seen without any clothes even in severe winter, generally considered to live an extreme lifestyle. This tends to attract a lot of western attention as it is seemingly in contrast to a generally conservative social modesty practised in the country.

Allahabad attracts students and learners from all over the country. Allahabad has one Central University, three Deemed Universities, an Open University, Research and Technical Institutions and colleges known for providing higher education in vast range of disciplines. Few of the reputed ones can be listed as following:

- Motilal Nehru National Institute of Technology (MNNIT) Allahabad is one of the twenty National Institutes of Technology and an Institute of National Importance of India. The college is always ranked among the top 15 Technical Colleges of India.
- Allahabad University founded in 1887 is the fourth oldest University of India.
- Motilal Nehru Medical College it is one of the seven medical colleges in Uttar Pradesh, and has a hospital attached.
- Prayag Sangeet Samiti offers education in Hindustani Classical Music.

- J.K. Institute of Applied Physics and Technology, University of Allahabad is one of the oldest Engineering Institutes of India offering B.Tech., M.Tech. and higher courses in the field of Electronics and Telecommunications.
- Uttar Pradesh Rajarshi Tandon Open University is the lone open university of Uttar Pradesh.
- Allahabad Agricultural Institute, established in 1910, is the oldest such Institute in South Asia.
- Harish Chandra Research Institute is an institute funded by Department of Atomic Energy, Government of India, dedicated to research in Mathematics and Physics.
- Indian Institute of Information Technology, Allahabad [IIIT-A] is one of the top engineering colleges in India which offers undergraduate and postgraduate courses in computer science and allied areas. It was established by MHRD as a centre of excellence in IT. It is State's lone Indian Institute of Information Technology, better known as IIT.

It is the first IIT of the country to get the status of "Institute of National Importance" by Government of India.

- Institute of Engineering and Rural Technology, Allahabad, was established to provide diploma courses in various engineering disciplines, and now offers degree courses also from Uttar Pradesh Technical University.
- Ewing Christian College, founded in 1902, is the only Autonomous Minority Co-Educational College of the Allahabad University. The College was established by The American Presbyterians visiting India on Christian Mission.
- Birla Institute of Technology of Allahabad is an extension centre of Birla Institute of Technology of Mesra
  - buildings.
  - Ewing Christian College-American and Victorian era architecture; the College was established by American Presbyterians in 1902 by banks of the river Yamuna. and
  - Sachcha Baba Ashram, Arail, Naini.

Many government offices of both Central and State Government are present in the city, such as the Allahabad High Court, the Principal Accountant General Office (AG Office), the Uttar Pradesh Public Service

Commission Office, Uttar Pradesh Police Headquarters (PHQ), headquarters of the North Central Railway, the regional office of the Central Board of Secondary Education and the Uttar Pradesh Board of High School and Intermediate Education, Uttar Pradesh Madhyamik Shiksha Seva Chayan Board, Allahabad, Principal Controller of Defence Accounts (Pensions) Allahabad, etc. Allahabad is also home of India's fourth oldest University, AU and UP's single National Institutes of Technology.

Some Places of Interest in Allahabad are:

- Sangam and surroundings, particularly in December to February, when *Kumbh Mela, Magh Mela* is underway.
- Anand Bhavan and Jawahar Planetarium.
- New Yamuna Bridge, Yamuna Bank Road.
- Company Bagh, Alfred Park and Allahabad Museum.
- Allahabad High Court building.
- All Saints Cathedral was built in the Gothic style in the nineteenth century. Also commonly known as Patthar Girja Ghar, it stands at a prominent location of the city in lush green premises. It is among the finest cathedrals of India. Though it was consecrated in 1887, it took another 40 years for it to be completed.
- Allahabad University, established on 23 September, 1887, is the fourth oldest University of India after Calcutta, Bombay and Madras. Many people consider it to be the Oxford of India. Its sprawling 320 acres (1.3 km^2) campus in the middle of the city has many old buildings.

Allahabad is one of the regional divisions of CBSE and head office of UP Board of High School and Intermediate Education. English is the medium of instructions in most private schools while Government aided schools and colleges offer both Hindi and English medium education. To cater needs of vocational, technical and professional education in rural areas of Allahabad and nearby districts, the Ministry of HRD, Government of India has recently started another University named Nehru Gram Bharti Vishwavidyalaya at Dubawal village of Allahabad. The university currently offers academic programmes at graduate and post-graduate levels in various disciplines including Arts, Commerce, Science, Education (as subject), Law, Management, Rural Development, Master of Social Works, Computer Applications, Journalism, etc

National Highway No. 2 runs through the middle of the city. It is also proposed as one of the routes of Golden Quadrilateral Highway, Delhi-Kolkata section. It runs out of the city through newly constructed bypass. NH No. 96 connects to NH No. 28 at Faizabad. Another is NH No. 27 which is 93 km (58 miles) long and starts from Allahabad and ends at Mangawan in Madhya Pradesh connecting to National Highway No. 7. A four lane access controlled bypass road of 84.7 km aided by World Bank is completed.

There are other State highways that link Allahabad to all other parts of the country. A number of road bridges on rivers Ganges and Yamuna have been built to connect Allahabad with its suburb towns like Naini, Jhusi, etc. A new eight lane access controlled expressway—Ganga Expressway is also proposed to pass through Allahabad. A 8 laned outer ring road is proposed in the Allahabad district.

Allahabad city is one of the largest commercial centres in the State. It is also one of the most prominent industrial towns, with 18 medium and large industrial units, and more than 3,000 small scale industries operating there. The Third All India Census for Small Scale Industries shows that there are more than 10,000 unregistered small scale industry units in the district, employing thousands of people.

Allahabad has glass, wire based industries. The main industrial area of Allahabad is Naini and Phulpur, where several public and private sector companies have their units, offices and factories. These include AREVA T&D India (a division of multinational Areva Group), Bharat Pumps and Compressors (BPC) which is a Miniratna now, Indian Telephone Industries Limited [ITI] was set-up in Naini in the year 1971 for the manufacture of transmission equipment. The major products are optic fibre systems of both PDH and SDH and telephone instruments of various types, Reliance Industries—Allahabad Manufacturing Division, Hindustan Cables also called as HCL which has now been taken over by Defence for its revival, Triveni Structurals Limited (TSL, a subsidiary of Bharat Yantra Nigam), GEEP battery factory, etc. Indian Farmers Fertilizer Co-Operative is in Phulpur. IFFCO's Phulpur complex has two Urea production units and once was world's largest fertiliser complex based on naphtha as feedstock. But owing to environmental concerns, it has been switched to Natural Gas based Plant Baidyanath Ayurved has its unit in Naini, Allahabad which has a State of the Art manufacturing facility spread over 30 acres. This unit was the largest manufacturing facility of its kind in the whole world. This unit boasts of manufacturing not only over 800 formulations, it also is capable of of manufacturing the bulk drugs required for these formulations, it also got recognition when the Managing Director of Shree Baidyanth Ayurved, Shri Ram Awtar Sharma was awarded The Nagarjuna Award for Quality, by Ex-President Smt. Pratibha Patil.

In the new projects, three mega thermal power projects are coming up at Meja, Bara and Karchna tehsils of the district being constructed by Jaypee Group and National Thermal Power Corporation, they are expected to be over by 2016.

BPCL (Bharat Petroleum Corporation Limited), one of India's largest oil marketing companies, the State-owned petroleum firm is setting up a seven million tonnes per annum (MTPA) capacity refinery with an estimated investment of 62 billion at Lohgara, Allahabad to meet the growing demand for petroleum products in the northern region, especially in Uttar Pradesh.

Shankargarh is a town in Allahabad district in the Indian State of Uttar Pradesh. As of 2001 the Census of India, Shankargarh had a population of 13,116. Males constitute 53 per cent of the population and female 47 per cent. Shankargarh has an average literacy rate of 61 per cent higher than the national average of 59 per cent male literacy is 70 per cent and female literacy is 52 per cent. In Shankargarh 17 per cent of the population is under 6 years of age.

The main occupation of local population is mining activity, stone quarrying as the land is not much fertile. The Raja of Shankargarh has mining rights over 46 villages covering an area of 150 km in perpetuity and gives the rights to contractors who in term hire local labours to extract minerals.

It is famous for its silica mines. The majority of villages are inhabited by tribals. They are landless and bonded labourers and they are employed at extremely exploitative rates. Since three-fourth of Shankargarh is rocky and unfit for cultivation, the local population has no other source of income than mining.

The majority of the landless labourers are tribals at the bottom of the social heap. This area is characterised by rigid castes and class hierarchies expressed in terms of hostility towards the lower castes and frequently violence, threats, robberies and assaults on women.

Patha region of Uttar Pradesh, which is spread over Mau and Manikpur Blocks of Chitrakoot district and Shankargarh Block of Allahabad district, has been repeatedly in the news for many wrong reasons mentioned below:

> Terror of dacoits as well as large scale poverty and deprivation rooted in a highly exploitative system, e.g., (i) Bonded labour, (ii) Loan taken by influential people in the name of poor peoples. (iii) land grabbing, (iv) atrocities on weaker sections-especially Kol tribes, and (v) Indebtedness and deaths by hunger; and all these have brought this area into the public gaze at various times. In fact this region provides a glaring example of how, despite all manner of egalitarian legislation—such as land ceiling laws and bonded labour abolition laws—a few rich men can keep a large number of poor households mainly Kols and Harijans in their grip. Although a large scale land distribution effort has been initiated in this area, the economically dominant landlords class of upper castes have been able to convert even this initiatives to their own advantage. They have often also maneuvered procedures to actually gain land at the expense of the very beneficiaries of these land distribution efforts.

Many a time the actual beneficiaries are not even aware of which land exactly has been allotted to them. In the mean time, the landlords amass wealth from the very same plot. And often there is often the bizarre incidence to the real allottees working as other people's labourers on their own. Convening these disadvantaged people is not a very difficult task for the landlords. With both muscle power and a wide net work of links with corrupt local bureaucrats at their disposal, hoodwinking or plain, browbeating the poor becomes that much easier.

Rapacious landlords are not the only hurdles in the very way for equitable land distribution schemes. Conniving forest officials are equally pernicious factor. Many a family has suffered due to the arbitrary methods of these officials whose decisions are often crucial for any land related activities in the rural areas. After the forest corporation was created, tribals looked up it for bringing relief from the oppressor contractors, but the corporation also functioned frequently on narrow commercial lines.

Acute drought distress including starvation deaths involving particularly the Saharia community, numerous cases of acute exploitation and land grabbing from Kol tribals and the killing and abductions by the Dacoit gangs particularly the biggest one in Chitrakoot, which continue to enjoy very good political, connections despite killing dozens of persons. Life for most people of all sections appear to have more tension and stress. These distressing headlines, however, reflect only the sporadic outburst of the deeper social malaise which the common people experience

Table 3.14: Area Profile of Jasra Block

Number of Households		*697*		*Household size*			*7.0*
				Proportion of Urban population (%)			*0.0*
	P	*M*	*F*	*Sex Ratio (females per 1000 males)*			*903*
Population-Total	4,591	2,413	2,178	Sex Ratio (0-6 Years)			988
Population-Rural	4,591	2,413	2,178	Sex Ratio (SC)			968
Population-Urban	0	0	0	Sex Ratio (ST)			0
Population (0-6)	817	411	406				
SC Population	913	464	449		*P*	*M*	*F*
ST Population	0	0	0	Proportion of SC population (%)	19.9	19.2	20.6
				Proportion of ST population (%)	0.0	0.0	0.0
Number of literates	2,715	1,631	1,084	Literacy Rate (%)	71.9	81.5	61.2
Number of illiterates	1,876	782	1,094	Illiteracy Rate (%)	49.7	39.1	61.7
Total workers	1,542	1,196	346	Work Participation Rate (%)	33.6	49.6	15.9
Main workers	1,317	1,089	228	Proportion of Main Workers (%)	28.7	45.1	10.5
Marginal workers	225	107	118	Proportion of Marginal Workers (%)	4.9	4.4	5.4
Non-workers	3,049	1,217	1,832	Proportion of Non-Workers (%)	66.4	50.4	84.1
Cultivators	129	89	40	Proportion of cultivators to total workers (%)	8.4	7.4	11.6
Agricultural labourers	288	124	164	Proportion of agricultural labourers to total workers (%)	18.7	10.4	47.4
Workers in household industries	247	160	87	Proportion of workers in household industries to total workers (%)	16.0	13.4	25.1
Other workers	878	823	55	Percentage of Other workers to total workers (%)	56.9	68.8	15.9

Source: Statistical Magazine—Allahabad District, 2009.

in the form of deepening distress and increasing stress in their everyday life. As is often the case, the heaviest burden falls on the already overburdened shoulders of the weaker sections.

Table 3.14 shows that in Jasra Block of Allahabad the household size is 7.0. The sex ratio in SC and ST is 968. Proportion of SC and ST is 19.9 per cent. Literacy rate is 71.9 per cent and illiteracy rate is 49.7 per cent. The work participation rate is 33.6 per cent, proportion of main workers is 28.7 per cent, Proportion of marginal workers is 4.9 per cent and proportion of non-workers is 66.4 per cent. Proportion of cultivators to total workers is 8.4 per cent, proportion of agricultural labourers to total workers is 18.7 per cent, proportion of workers in household industries to total workers is 16.0 per cent and percentage of other workers to total workers is 56.9 per cent.

Table 3.15 shows that in Shankargarh Block of Allahabad the household size is 6.0. Sex ratio in SC and ST is 904 and 741 per thousand male in scheduled tribes. Proportion of SC is 21.6 per cent and proportion of ST population is 0.4 per cent. The literacy rate is 72.2 per cent and

Table 3.15: Area Profile of Shankargarh Block

Number of Households	*2,181*			*Household size*			*6.0*
				Proportion of Urban population (%)			*100.0*
	P	*M*	*F*	*Sex Ratio (females per 1000 males)*			*881*
Population-Total	13,102	6,964	6,138	Sex Ratio (0-6 Years)			924
Population-Rural	0	0	0	Sex Ratio (SC)			904
Population-Urban	13,102	6,964	6,138	Sex Ratio (ST)			741
Population (0-6)	2,341	1,217	1,124				
SC Population	2,825	1,484	1,341		*P*	*M*	*F*
ST Population	47	27	20	Proportion of SC population (%)	21.6	21.3	21.8
				Proportion of ST population (%)	0.4	0.4	0.3
Number of literates	7,770	4,673	3,097	Literacy Rate (%)	72.2	81.3	61.8
Number of illiterates	5,332	2,291	3,041	Illiteracy Rate (%)	49.5	39.9	60.7
Total workers	3,850	2,996	854	Work Participation Rate (%)	13.9	43.0	13.9
Main workers	3,175	2,746	429	Proportion of Main Workers (%)	24.2	39.4	7.0
Marginal workers	675	250	425	Proportion of Marginal Workers (%)	5.2	3.6	6.9
Non-workers	9,252	3,968	5,284	Proportion of Non-Workers (%)	70.6	57.0	86.1
Cultivators	183	144	39	Proportion of cultivators to total workers (%)	4.8	4.8	4.6
Agricultural labourers	73	41	32	Proportion of agricultural labourers to total workers (%)	1.9	1.4	3.7
Workers in household industries	482	198	284	Proportion of workers in household industries to total workers (%)	12.5	6.6	33.3
Other workers	3,112	2,613	499	Percentage of Other workers to total workers (%)	80.8	87.2	58.4

Source: Statistical Magazine—Allahabad. District, 2009.

illiteracy rate is 49.5 per cent. The illiteracy rate is higher in female by 60.7 per cent. Working participation rate is 13.9 per cent, proportion of main workers is 24.2 per cent, proportion of marginal workers is 5.2 per cent and proportion of non workers is 70.6 per cent in total, 57.0 per cent in male and 86.1 per cent in female. Proportion of cultivators to total workers is 4.8 per cent, proportion of agricultural labourers to total workers is 1.9 per cent, proportion of workers in household industries is 12.5 per cent in total, 6.6 per cent in male and 33.3 per cent in female. The percentage of other workers to total workers is 80.8 per cent in total, 87.2 per cent in male and 58.4 per cent in female.

As regards in Meja Block of Allahabad, the household size is 7.0. Sex ratio in SC is 890 and in Scheduled Tribes is 775 per thousand male. The proportion of SC population is 21.2 per cent and ST population is

0.1 per cent. The literacy rate is 58.8 per cent in total, 77.1 per cent in male and 38.4 per cent in female. Illiteracy rate is 67.6 per cent in total, 48.9 per cent in male and 88.6 per cent in female. Work participation rate is 34.7 per cent in total, 42.9 per cent male and 25.6 per cent in female. The proportion of main workers is 20.3 per cent in total, 31.0 per cent in male and 8.5 per cent in female. Proportion of marginal workers is 14.4 per cent in total, 11.9 per cent in male and 17.1 per cent in female. Proportion of non-workers is 66.3 per cent in total, 57.1 per cent in male and 74.4 per cent in female. Proportion of cultivators to total workers is 36.1 per cent in total, 38.1 per cent in male and 31.3 per cent in female.

Table 3.16: Area Profile of Meja Block

Number of Households	*63,970*			*Household size*			*7.0*
				Proportion of Urban population (%)			*5.7*
	P	*M*	*F*	*Sex Ratio (females per 1000 males)*			*895*
Population-Total	471,851	249,023	222,828	Sex Ratio (0-6 Years)			922
Population-Rural	445,115	234,896	210,219	Sex Ratio (SC)			890
Population-Urban	26,736	14,127	12,609	Sex Ratio (ST)			775
Population (0-6)	98,917	51,454	47,463				
SC Population	100,047	52,946	47,101		*P*	*M*	*F*
ST Population	504	284	220	Proportion of SC population (%)	21.2	21.3	21.1
				Proportion of ST population (%)	0.1	0.1	0.1
Number of literates	219,741	152,327	67,414	Literacy Rate (%)	58.9	77.1	38.4
Number of illiterates	252,110	96,696	155,414	Illiteracy Rate (%)	67.6	48.9	88.6
Total workers	163,895	106,856	57,039	Work Participation Rate (%)	34.7	42.9	25.6
Main workers	96,016	77,109	18,907	Proportion of Main Workers (%)	20.3	31.0	8.5
Marginal workers	67,879	29,747	38,132	Proportion of Marginal Workers (%)	14.4	11.9	17.1
Non-workers	307,956	142,167	165,789	Proportion of Non-Workers (%)	65.3	57.1	74.4
Cultivators	59,175	41,333	17,842	Proportion of cultivators to total workers (%)	36.1	38.7	31.3
Agricultural labourers	54,295	27,482	26,813	Proportion of agricultural labourers to total workers (%)	33.1	25.7	47.0
Workers in household industries	17,042	9,397	7,645	Proportion of workers in household industries to total workers (%)	10.4	8.8	13.4
Other workers	33,383	28,644	4,739	Percentage of Other workers to total workers (%)	20.4	26.8	8.3

Source: Statistical Magazine—Allahabad. District, 2009.

Proportion of agricultural labourers to total workers is 33.1 per cent in total, 25.7 per cent in male and 47.0 per cent in female. Proportion of workers in household industries to total workers is 10.4 per cent in total. 8.8 per cent in male and 13.4 per cent in female. Percentage of other workers to total workers is 20.4 per cent in total, 26.8 per cent in male and 8.3 per cent in female.

Table 3.17 shows that in Koraon Block of Allahabad district, the size of the household is 7.0. The sex ratio in SC and ST are 898 and 877 per thousand male population. The proportion of SC and ST population is 29.4 per cent in total, 29.4 per cent in male and 29.5 per cent in female. Proportion of Scheduled Tribes population is 4.0 per cent in total. Literacy rate is 49.9 per cent in total, 66.2 per cent in male and 31.6 per cent in

Table 3.17: Area Profile of Koraon Block

Number of Households	*44,818*			*Household size*	*7.0*		
				Proportion of Urban population (%)	*4.1*		
	P	*M*	*F*	*Sex Ratio (females per 1000 males)*	*895*		
Population-Total	299,125	157,858	141,267	Sex Ratio (0-6 Years)	930		
Population-Rural	286,983	151,397	135,586	Sex Ratio (SC)	898		
Population-Urban	12,142	6,461	5,681	Sex Ratio (ST)	877		
Population (0-6)	65,798	34,087	31,711				
SC Population	88,008	46,370	41,638		*P*	*M*	*F*
ST Population	1,295	690	605	Proportion of SC population (%)	29.4	29.4	29.5
				Proportion of ST population (%)	0.4	0.4	0.4
Number of literates	116,510	81,881	34,629	Literacy Rate (%)	49.9	66.2	31.6
Number of illiterates	182,615	75,977	106,638	Illiteracy Rate (%)	78.3	61.4	97.3
Total workers	125,278	75,574	49,704	Work Participation Rate (%)	41.9	47.9	35.2
Main workers	82,684	59,862	22,822	Proportion of Main Workers (%)	27.6	37.9	16.2
Marginal workers	42,594	15,712	26,882	Proportion of Marginal Workers (%)	14.2	10.0	19.0
Non-workers	173,847	82,284	91,563	Proportion of Non-Workers (%)	58.1	52.1	64.8
Cultivators	62,251	39,070	23,181	Proportion of cultivators to total workers (%)	49.7	51.7	46.6
Agricultural labourers	45,170	23,926	21,244	Proportion of agricultural labourers to total workers (%)	36.1	31.7	42.7
Workers in household industries	7,370	4,277	3,093	Proportion of workers in household industries to total workers (%)	5.9	5.7	6.2
Other workers	10,487	8,301	2,186	Percentage of Other workers to total workers (%)	8.4	11.0	4.4

Source: Statistical Magazine—Allahabad District, 2009.

female. Illiteracy rate is 78.3 per cent in total, 61.4 per cent in male and 97.4 per cent in female. Work participation rate is 41.9 per cent in total, 47.9 per cent male and 35.2 per cent in female. Proportion of main workers is 27.6 per cent in total, 37.9 per cent in male and 16.2 per cent in female. Proportion of marginal workers is 14.2 per cent in total, 10.0 per cent in male and 19.0 per cent in female. Proportion of non workers is 58.1 per cent in total, 52.1 per cent in male and 64.8 per cent in female. Proportion of cultivators to total workers is 49.7 per cent in total, 51.7 per cent in male and 46.6 per cent in female. Proportion of agricultural labourers to total workers is 36.1 per cent in total, 31.1 per cent in male and 42.7 per cent in female. Proportion of workers in household industries to total workers is 5.9 per cent in total, 5.7 per cent in male and 6.0 per cent in female. Percentage of other workers to total workers is 8.4 per cent in total, 11.0 per cent in male and 4.4 per cent in female.

V. PROFILE OF CHITRAKOOT DISTRICT[7, 8]

Chitrakoot means the 'Hills of many wonders'. It falls in the northern Vindhya range of mountains spread over the State of Uttar Pradesh. Chitrakoot district in Uttar Pradesh was created on 4th September, 1998. The population of the district is 8,02,000. The Scheduled Castes and Scheduled Tribes form 2,01,840 and 26.34 per cent of the population.

East side is bounded by Allahabad (Prayag Raj), west side is bounded by Banda, North side is bounded by Kausambi and south is bounded by Satna and Rewa (M.P.). Main rivers of Chitrakoot are Yamuna river, Mandakini river, Gunta river, Begein river, Ohan river, Balmiki river and Bardaha river. Main mountains are Madya Pahar, Chitrakoot Parwat, Mala and Balmiki Pahar.

The geographically area covers 3,164 sq km. It has been classified into 5 development Blocks namely Pahari, Karvi, Manikpur, Ram Nagar and Mau. Since most of the scheduled tribes have been included in scheduled castes, therefore, the number of population 201.840 thousand includes both the scheduled castes and scheduled tribes population.

Density population in Manikpur Block was 138 per sq. km, in Karvi 248 per sq. km., and in Mau Block it was 282 per sq. km.(2001). As regards, density of population of SC/ST in the district Chitrakoot it was 22.5 per cent in Manikpur, 26.5 per cent in Karvi and 36.3 per cent in Mau out of total density of population of the density.

Most of the area is unfertile because of significant stretches of plateaus and stoney hilly land.

Celebrated in the entire Indian literature and sacred books, the abode of Lord Ram, his spouse Sitaji and his brother Lakshman during their exile for about eleven years and a half; capable of purifying the human heart and of attracting the tourists by its charms of nature Chitrakoot is a holy place famous both for its natural scenery and its spiritual altitude. A tourist is as much thrilled by sighting its beautiful waterfalls, playful young dear and dancing peacocks as a pilgrim is overwhelmed by taking a dip in the Payaswani/Mandakini and by immersing himself in the dust of the Kamadgiri. From time immemorial, the Chitrakoot area has been a live centre of inspiration for cosmic consciousness. Thousands of mendicants, hermits, sages and saints have attained higher and higher spiritual status and have exerted a beneficial impact on the world through their penance, *sadhana*, *yoga*, *tapasya* and various arduous spiritual endeavours. Arti, Anasuya, Dattatreya, Maharshi Markandeya, Sarbhang, Sutikshna and various other sages, seers devotees and thinkers have lived in this area through all the ages; and knowledgeable people say that many such figures are still engaged in *tapasya* here in various caves and little known places. This lends the area a spiritual aroma which permeates its entire atmosphere and makes it spiritually alive to this day.

Since prehistoric period it has been a place of religious activities. Chitrakoot chain of famous hills includes 'Kamad Giri' where Lord Ram did penance for 13 years during his exile period of fourteen years, Hanuman Dhara, Janki Kund, Lakshman Pahari, Ansuiya Ashram, Devangana and others. Saint Tulsi Das wrote here the most famous religious holy book *Ram Charit Manas* here in Chitakoot at the bank of the famous river Ganga. Many people gather here on each *amavasya*, *Deepawali*, *Sharad Purnima*, *Makar Sankranti* and *Ram Navami* are special occasions for gatherings and celebrations.

But on the other side, there is a very gloomy picture of this region. Six out of seven districts of Bundelkhand region of Uttar Pradesh have been included in the list of poorest districts, several hundred poverty related deaths, including suicides and hunger deaths, have been reported in recent years.

'Patha' region which is spread over Mau, Karvi and Manikpur Blocks of Chitrakoot and Shankargarh Block of Allahabad district. This region has been repeatedly in the news for these wrong reasons (1) The terror of dacoits as well as large scale poverty and deprivation rooted in a highly exploitative system. This total region stretches in south-east part of Uttar Pradesh. In addition, there is a small intrusion into Satna district of Madhya Pradesh (Majhgava Block). From the forests and villages, hills and plains of Patha plateau there have been several reports about the terror of dacoits, the distress suffered by bonded labourers and weaker sections particularly the Kol tribals.

The three largest scheduled castes groups are Chamar, Kol and Kori. The three largest scheduled tribe groups are Raji.

49.55 per cent of the district population is in the working age group of 15-59 years. The district ranks 469 among 591 districts of India in terms of proportion of population in working age group. An inclusive growth process and employment generation have been accorded high priority in the Eleventh Five Year Plan. Specific action plans need to be tailored for every district depending on the size, level of urbanisation and educational attainment of the workforce. 7.49 per cent of the district's population is over the age of 59 years. The larger the elderly population the greater would be the need for social support for the elderly. As often used indicator to capture the extent of discrimination against the girl child is the child sex ratio.

In the district, the sex ratio, i.e., the number of girls per 1000 boys among children in the age group 0-6 years is 928. Ideally, the sex ratio at birth should be between 943-954. Addressing the issue of sex ratio selective abortion and female infanticide needs to be given high priority in districts with a sex ratio far from the norm of 943 girls per 1000 boys.

One aspect of living conditions in the districts is the type of dwelling that households reside in 1.7 per cent of households live in temporary structures, while 73.7 per cent of households live in semi permanent structures. The district ranks 551 among 591 districts in India in terms of percentage of households living in temporary structures (a higher rank reflects a poor performance) 72.2 per cent of households do not have radio, television, telephone, bicycle, scooter, car and bank account.

Another indicator is an access to the outside world is important. Improved access and connectivity can contribute to improving households. As part of poverty reduction strategy, the Pradhan Mantri Gram Sadak Yojana aims at improving connectivity in rural habitation. The district ranks 458,535 among 591 districts of India in terms of percentage of villages having paved approach road, bus services, post, telegraph and telephone facility.

District level estimation of incidence of high percentage of poverty. We can examine outcomes along the following non-income dimensions of well-being, education and health. It is not necessary that with a decline in incidence of poverty there would be an automatic improvement along these dimensions. The reason for this is that poverty line derived from personal consumption patterns and levels do not take into account items of social consumption such as basic education and health, drinking water supply, sanitation, environment standards, etc., in terms of normative requirement or effective access. The overall illiteracy rate in the district is 55 per cent. However, the literacy rate does not reflect education attainment.

The district Chitrakoot has been divided into two Tehsils namely (1) Karvi, and (2) Chitrakoot. Further, it has been divided into 5 development Blocks namely: (1) Pahari, (2) Karvi, (3) Manikpur, (4) Ram Nagar, and (5) Mau.

Our study covers only three Blocks namely Manikpur, Karvi and Mau where tribal population is in large number.

Table 3.18: Area Profile of Karwi Block

Number of Households	*86,264*			*Household size*	*6.0*		
				Proportion of Urban population (%)	*11.8*		
	P	*M*	*F*	*Sex Ratio (females per 1000 males)*	*865*		
Population-Total	540,553	289,894	250,659	Sex Ratio (0-6 Years)	930		
Population-Rural	476,745	255,733	221,012	Sex Ratio (SC)	884		
Population-Urban	63,808	34,161	29,647	Sex Ratio (ST)	0		
Population (0-6)	111,495	57,773	53,722				
SC Population	142,247	75,495	66,752		*P*	*M*	*F*
ST Population	1	1	0	Proportion of SC population (%)	26.3	26.0	26.6
				Proportion of ST population (%)	0.0	0.0	0.0
Number of literates	277,797	180,214	97,583	Literacy Rate (%)	64.7	77.6	49.6
Number of illiterates	262,756	109,680	153,076	Illiteracy Rate (%)	61.2	47.3	77.7
Total workers	227,035	138,140	88,895	Work Participation Rate (%)	42.0	47.7	35.5
Main workers	151,155	116,230	34,925	Proportion of Main Workers (%)	28.0	40.1	13.9
Marginal workers	75,880	21,910	53,970	Proportion of Marginal Workers (%)	14.0	7.6	21.5
Non-workers	313,518	151,754	161,764	Proportion of Non-Workers (%)	58.0	52.3	64.5
Cultivators	122,244	76,102	46,142	Proportion of cultivators to total workers (%)	53.8	55.1	51.9
Agricultural labourers	62,038	28,202	33,836	Proportion of agricultural labourers to total workers (%)	27.3	20.4	38.1
Workers in household industries	6,261	3,756	2,505	Proportion of workers in household industries to total workers (%)	2.8	2.7	2.8
Other workers	36,492	30,080	6,412	Percentage of Other workers to total workers (%)	16.1	21.8	7.2

Source: Statistical Magazine—Chitrakoot District, 2009.

Table 3.18 shows the average household size is 6.0 in Karwi Block of Chitrakoot. The sex ratio in SC and ST are 884. Proportion of SC and ST population is 26.3 per cent in total, 26.0 per cent in male and 26.0 per cent in female. Literacy rate is 64.7 per cent in total, 77.6 per cent in male and 49.6 per cent in female. Illiteracy rate is 61.2 per cent in total, 47.3 per cent in male and 77.3 per cent in female. Work participation rate is 42.0 per cent in total, 47.7 per cent male and 35.5 per cent in female. Proportion of main workers is 28.0 per cent in total, 40.1 per cent in male and 13.9 per cent in female. Proportion of marginal workers is 14.0 per cent in total, 7.6 per cent in male and 21.5 per cent in female. Proportion of non workers is 58.0 per cent in total, 52.3 per cent in male and 64.5 per cent in female. Proportion of cultivators to total workers is 53.8 per cent in total, 55.1 per cent in male and 51.9 per cent in female. Proportion of agricultural labourers to total workers is 27.3 per cent in total, 20.4 per cent in male and 38.1 per cent in female. Proportion of workers in household industries to total workers is 2.8 per cent in total, 2.7 per cent in male and 2.8 per cent in female. Percentage of other workers to total workers is 16.1 per cent in total, 21.8 per cent in male and 7.2 per cent in female.

It is evident from Table 3.19 that the average household size is 6.0 in Mau Block of Chitrakoot. The sex ratio in SC and ST are 903. Proportion of SC and ST population is 26.4 per cent in total, 26.3 per cent in male and 26.6 per cent in female. The literacy rate is 65.8 per cent in total, 77.8 per cent in male and 52.1 per cent in female. The illiteracy rate is 63.1 per cent in total, 50.4 per cent in male and 77.4 per cent in female. Work participation rate is 42.9 per cent in total, 47.8 per cent male and 37.5 per cent in female. Proportion of main workers is 32.5 per cent in total, 42.5 per cent in male and 21.8 per cent in female. Proportion of marginal workers is 10.5 per cent in total, 5.6 per cent in male and 15.9 per cent in female. Proportion of non workers is 57.1 per cent in total, 52.2 per cent in male and 62.5 per cent in female. Proportion of cultivators to total workers is 56.4 per cent in total, 55.3 per cent in male and 55.0 per cent in female. Proportion of agricultural labourers to total workers is 25.2 per cent in total, 20.4 per cent in male and 32.1 per cent in female. Proportion of workers in household industries to total workers is 3.6 per cent in total, 4.1 per cent in male and 2.9 per cent in female. Percentage of other workers to total workers is 14.8 per cent in total, 20.2 per cent in male and 7.0 per cent in female.

Table 3.20 shows that the per household size is 7.0 in Manikpur Block of Chitrakoot. The sex ratio in SC/ST is 1000 per thousand male population. The proportion of SC and ST population is 4.2 per cent in

Table 3.19: Area Profile of Mau Block

Number of Households	*35,563*			*Household size*	*6.0*		
				Proportion of Urban population (%)	*5.7*		
	P	*M*	*F*	*Sex Ratio (females per 1000 males)*	*892*		
Population-Total	225,672	119,284	106,388	Sex Ratio (0-6 Years)	925		
Population-Rural	212,920	112,567	100,353	Sex Ratio (SC)	903		
Population-Urban	12,752	6,717	6,035	Sex Ratio (ST)	0		
Population (0-6)	50,473	26,217	24,256				
SC Population	59,592	31,316	28,276		*P*	*M*	*F*
ST Population	0	0	0	Proportion of SC population (%)	26.4	26.3	26.6
				Proportion of ST population (%)	0.0	0.0	0.0
Number of literates	115,200	72,419	42,781	Literacy Rate (%)	65.8	77.8	52.1
Number of illiterates	110,472	46,865	63,607	Illiteracy Rate (%)	63.1	50.4	77.4
Total workers	96,921	57,061	39,860	Work Participation Rate (%)	42.9	47.8	37.5
Main workers	73,274	50,339	22,935	Proportion of Main Workers (%)	32.5	42.2	21.6
Marginal workers	23,647	6,722	16,925	Proportion of Marginal Workers (%)	10.5	5.6	15.9
Non-workers	128,751	62,223	66,528	Proportion of Non-Workers (%)	57.1	52.2	62.5
Cultivators	54,682	31,580	23,102	Proportion of cultivators to total workers (%)	56.4	55.3	58.0
Agricultural labourers	24,435	11,624	12,811	Proportion of agricultural labourers to total workers (%)	25.2	20.4	32.1
Workers in household industries	3,491	2,324	1,167	Proportion of workers in household industries to total workers (%)	3.6	4.1	2.9
Other workers	14,313	11,533	2,780	Percentage of Other workers to total workers (%)	14.8	20.2	7.0

Source: Statistical Magazine—Chitrakoot. District, 2009.

total, 4.2 per cent in male and 4.9 per cent in female. Literacy rate is 59.8 per cent in total, 80.9 per cent in male and 34.9 per cent in female. Illiteracy rate is 66.5 per cent in total, 44.7 per cent in male and 92.2 per cent in female. Work participation rate is 38.3 per cent in total, 43.5 per cent male and 32.3 per cent in female. Proportion of main workers is 27.3 per cent in total, 42.4 per cent in male and 9.8 per cent in female. Proportion of marginal workers is 11.0 per cent in total, 1.0 per cent in male and 22.6 per cent in female. The proportion of non workers is 61.7 per cent in total, 56.7 per cent in male and 67.7 per cent in female. Proportion of cultivators to total workers is 33.1 per cent in total, 34.9 per cent in male

Table 3.20: Area Profile of Manikpur Block[28]

Number of Households	*54*			*Household size*			*7.0*
				Proportion of Urban population (%)			*0.0*
	P	*M*	*F*	*Sex Ratio (females per 1000 males)*			*859*
Population-Total	355	191	164	Sex Ratio (0-6 Years)			897
Population-Rural	355	191	164	Sex Ratio (SC)			1000
Population-Urban	0	0	0	Sex Ratio (ST)			0
Population (0-6)	74	39	35				
SC Population	16	8	8		*P*	*M*	*F*
ST Population	0	0	0	Proportion of SC population (%)	4.5	4.2	4.9
				Proportion of ST population (%)	0.0	0.0	0.0
Number of literates	168	123	45	Literacy Rate (%)	59.8	80.9	34.9
Number of illiterates	187	68	119	Illiteracy Rate (%)	66.5	44.7	92.2
Total workers	136	83	53	Work Participation Rate (%)	38.3	43.5	32.3
Main workers	97	81	16	Proportion of Main Workers (%)	27.3	42.4	9.8
Marginal workers	39	2	37	Proportion of Marginal Workers (%)	11.0	1.0	22.6
Non-workers	219	108	111	Proportion of Non-Workers (%)	61.7	56.5	67.7
Cultivators	45	29	16	Proportion of cultivators to total workers (%)	33.1	34.9	30.2
Agricultural labourers	6	2	4	Proportion of agricultural labourers to total workers (%)	4.4	2.4	7.5
Workers in household industries	0	0	0	Proportion of workers in household industries to total workers (%)	0.0	0.0	0.0
Other workers	85	52	33	Percentage of Other workers to total workers (%)	62.5	62.7	62.3

Source: Statistical Magazine—Chitrakoot, District, 2009.

and 30.2 per cent in female. Proportion of agricultural labourers to total workers is 4.4 per cent in total, 2.4 per cent in male and 7.5 per cent in female. Proportion of workers in household industries to total workers is 0.0 per cent in all. Percentage of other workers to total workers is 62.5 per cent in total, 62.7 per cent in male and 62.3 per cent in female.

Social and Economic Characteristics of the Respondent Households and Respondents

Lalganj, Hallia, Marihan, Rajgarh and Kon development Blocks of Mirzapur, Robertsganj, Nagwan, Chopan, Dudhi and Babhani of

Sonbhadra, Sahebganj and Naugarh of Chandauli, Jasra, Shankargarh, Meja, Koraon of Allahabad and Karvi, Mau and Manikpur development Blocks of Chitrakoot were chosen for the study. Makari Bari, Laua, Mathhawan, Silthem, Myorepur, Chaga Khudari, Aarang Pani, Basauli Amauli, Jura, Dhankhor, Semara, Umbha, Dewatan, Majhgawan, Bairkhad, Jorukhar of Sonbhadra districts, 27 villages of Chitrakoot, 15 villages of Mirzapur, 18 villages of Allahabad and 7 villages of Chandauli districts were covered up during survey. It was found that almost all the villages were quite remote from the district headquarters, tehsil and Block headquarters. Out of 94 villages of all the 19 development Blocks selected from the five districts, 7 villages were quite near to the district headquarters, 2 villages were within 2 km, 13 villages within 3 km, 16 villages were within 5 km and rest 63 villages were located 5 km away from the district headquarters. For example the following Table 3.21 of the five districts shows the distribution of all the villages to average distance from the various facilities.

It is evident from Table 3.21 that most of facilities which are very essential for village development are located not less than 5 km of distance. Hospital, Mother Child Care Centre, Post Offices, Telephone Offices, PCOs, bus stations, Commercial Banks and other necessary facilities should be available at the shorter distances but the fact is different. Especially in the tribal villages means of transportation and communication facilities are very less. Consequently, the villages are ill equipped with essential commodities and they suffer a lot due to lack of these facilities.

It is evident from Table 3.22 that there were 50.8 per cent males and 49.2 per cent females were in 750 households of Mirzapur. The male and female percentage in Sonbhadra sample households (750) were 53.6 and 46.4 per cent respectively. In Chandauli it was 52.0 per cent male and 48.0 per cent female. 60.8 per cent male and 39.2 per cent female in Allahabad showed the maximum difference between the male-female ratio. Similarly in Chitrakoot the male-female ratio also showed the variation (57.8 male and 42.2% female). Fall in percentage of female sex may be due to the male migration in search of jobs. But it is also owing to the higher mortality rate of females in their young and early middle ages.

People's settlement whether it is temporary or of permanent nature, require several things necessarily to meet out their requirements. The government under development plans in tribal villages, has established Primary Schools, Primary Health Centres, Panchayat Ghar, Post Office, Bank, Telephone, bus stops and Dust proof roads, etc., to cater to the

Table 3.21: Average Distance from Tribal Villages of the Districts—Mirzapur, Sonbhadra, Chandauli, Allahabad and Chitrakoot for Various existing Infrastructural Facilities

Facility	*0 km*	*1 to 2 km*	*2.1 to 3.0 km*	*3.1-5.0 km*	*> 5 km*	*Total villages*
District HQ	7	2	43	83	1243	1378
Village development officer office	496	2	442	183	255	1378
PDS	594	14	531	168	71	1378
Source of drinking water	1378	0	0	0	0	1378
Krishi Seva Kendra	28	2	137	189	1022	1378
Village Market	44	1	178	232	923	1378
Krishi Mandi	0	0	44	82	1252	1378
Cold storage	0	0	0	0	1378	1378
Beej Vikraya Kendra	30	0	104	158	1086	1378
Animal Hospital	20	2	91	141	1124	1378
D Grade Animal Hospital	3	0	14	27	1334	1378
Pashu Seva Kendra	20	0	94	140	1124	1378
Artificial Insemination Centre	10	1	92	141	1134	1378
Cooperative milk collection centre	14	0	16	24	1324	1378
Primary agri. Loaning Society	58	1	140	208	971	1378
Cooperative Society	5	5	115	168	1085	1378
Govt. purchase centre	41	0	96	162	1079	1378
Primary School	933	12	337	70	26	1378
Middle School for Boys	214	3	426	358	377	1378
Middle School for Girls	90	2	388	362	536	1378
High School for Boys	40	1	135	276	926	1378
High School for Girls	12	1	135	267	963	1378
Aurvedic Hospital	21	1	78	155	1123	1378
Unani Hospital	0	0	34	77	1267	1378
Homoeopathic Hospital	21	1	72	152	1132	1378
Family Welfare Centre	148	2	196	323	709	1378
Mother Child Care Centre	165	0	198	322	693	1378
Metal Road	523	17	428	202	208	1378
Post Office	120	3	334	388	533	1378
Letter Box	204	1	424	426	323	1378
Telegraph Office	5	1	62	104	1206	1378
PCO	164	4	299	222	689	1378
Railway Station	9	0	31	62	1276	1378
Bus Station	97	13	231	275	762	1378
Village Development Bank	0	0	17	69	1292	1378
Commercial Banks	40	1	151	220	966	1378

Source: Statistical Magazine—1. Mirzapur, 2. Sonbhadra, 3. Chandauli, 4. Allahabad, 5. Chitrakoot Districts, 2009.

needs of the tribal people. During survey it was found that the facility of education, i.e., schools for their children at primary level was available almost in all the villages although some of them schools were without

Table 3.22: Distribution of Households by Sex and Facilities available from their Villages

Sl. No.	Item	Mirzapur	%	Sonbhadra	%	Chandauli	%	Allahabad	%	Chitrakoot	%
1.	No. of households	750	—	750	—	450	—	600	—	450	—
2.	Population:										
	Male	1986	50.8	2002	53.6	1183	52.0	2066	60.8	1588	57.8
	Female	1926	49.2	1733	46.4	1091	48.0	1330	39.2	1160	42.2
	Total	3912	100.0	3735	100.0	2274	100.0	3396	100.0	2748	100.0
3.	Primary School	Yes	—	Yes	—	Yes	—	Yes	—	Yes	—
4.	Distance of Upper School (km)	3	—	5.5	—	6	—	5	—	7	—
5.	Distance of PHC (km)	5	—	4.5	—	6.5	—	3.5	—	4	—
6.	Distance of Panchayat Headquarters (km)	6	—	7	—	5.5	—	4.5	—	6	—
7.	Distance of Mandal Headquarters (km)	8	—	10	—	9	—	11—	—	12	—
8.	Distance of Single Window Co-oprative Society/Regional Rural Bank	4	—	4.5	—	6	—	5.5	—	7	—
9.	Post Office (km)	6	—	8	—	5	—	10	—	11	—
10.	Telephone (km)	12	—	14	—	7	—	14	—	15	—
11.	Distance to Dust-proof road (kms)	4	—	3.5	—	5	—	6	—	5.5	—
12.	Nearest Bus Stop (km)	7	—	5	—	6	—	6	—	7	—

Source: Statistical Magazine— Mirzapur, Sonbhadra, Chandauli, Allahabad, and Chitrakoot Districts, 2009.

building. In Sonbhadra Upper Primary Schools were found located at the average distance of 5.5 km. There were no high school, Intermediate and degree colleges were not near to their villages. In Chandauli, Allahabad and Chitrakoot respondents have also the same problems of distance to cover up for their children in going to Upper Primary Schools.

The Primary Health Centres should always be quite near to the villages. If any emergency arises, the patient must get immediate relief. Under this facility also, we find that in Mirzapur, Sonbhadra, Chandauli, Allahabad and Chitrakoot tribal villages Primary Health Centres were located at an average distance of 5 km, 4.5 km, 6.5 km, 3.5 km and 4 km respectively. The distance is not so long to be covered if the condition of the approach road is good and means of transportation are easily available. Normally, villages are not located on the side of the main roads. Approach roads to the tribal villages are not plain. Even cycling and motorcycling is very very tough and risky. Therefore, even first-aid relief and treatment is very difficult to an emergency patient due to the distance shown from villages to PHC, CHC.

Others like Post Office, Panchayat Ghar, PHC, CHC, AHC, telephone booth, main road and bus stops are located at distance exceeding 4 to 8 km. In some specific cases, this distance ranges from 9 km to 43 km.

Since Sonbhadra, Chandauli, Mirzapur tribal areas have been turned into the hub of several power plants, industries and mines, the tribals have been displaced several times. Therefore, due to extreme poverty in multiple displacement in Naxal areas and in dacoit prone areas have forced the tribals to live in very very wretched conditions of housing. Mostly houses were found made of forest grass and garbage. Table 3.23 shows the housing particulars.

Table 3.23 shows that out of 750 households, 610 in Mirzapur and 595 houses in Sonbhadra districts were constructed with thatched walls and thatched roofs. In Chandauli there were 275 houses out of 450 households, 480 houses out of 600 in Allahabad and 395 houses out of 450 households were thatched houses. Similarly 140 out of 750 households in Mirzapur and 155 houses in Sonbhadra were made of mud walls and thatched roofs. 175 out of 450 households in Chandauli, 120 out of 600 in Allahabad and 55 houses out of 450 in Chitrakoot were constructed with mud walls and thatched roofs.

Brick walls and tiles roof and Brick walls and RCC or stone slab roof were completely absent in their localities.

As regards to ownership of houses, all of them were residing in their own houses. The period of acquisition indicates the temporary or

Table 3.23: Housing Particulars of the Sample Households

Sl. No.	*Item*	*Mirzapur*	*%*	*Sonbhadra*	*%*	*Chandauli*	*%*	*Allahabad*	*%*	*Chitrakoot*	*%*
Type of House											
1.	Thatched walls and Thatched roof	610	81.3	595	79.3	275	61.1	480	80.0	395	87.8
2.	Mud Walls and Thatched roof	140	18.7	155	20.7	175	38.9	120	20.0	55	12.2
3.	Brick walls and Tiled roof	0	0.0	0	0.0	0	0.0	0	0.0	0	0.0
4.	Brick walls and RCC/stone roof	0	0.0	0	0.0	0	0.0	0	0.0	0	0.0
	Total	750	100.0	750	100.0	450	100.0	600	100.0	450	100.0
Period of Acquisition											
1.	5-10 years	45	6.0	65	8.7	30	6.7	100	16.7	95	21.1
2.	3-5 years	30	4.0	80	10.7	65	14.4	410	68.3	299	66.4
3.	1-3 years	595	79.3	545	72.7	335	74.4	75	12.5	40	8.9
4.	Below 1 year	80	10.7	50	6.7	20	4.4	10	1.7	16	3.6
5	By inheritance	0	0.0	10	1.3	0	0.0	5	0.8	0	0.0
	Total	750	100.0	750	100.0	450	100.0	600	100.0	450	100.0
Source of Acquisition											
1.	Agriculture Income	744	—	739	—	440	—	591	—	439	—
2.	Income Generation from IRDP Scheme	5	—	8	—	10	—	7	—	11	—
3.	Service	1	—	3	—	0	—	2	—	0	—
4.	Business	0	—	0	—	0	—	0	—	0	—
	Total	750	—	750	—	450	—	600	—	450	—

permanent settlement nature of the tribals. The period of acquisition by inheritance indicates that these tribals have not been displaced since long. Only 1.3 per cent households in Sonbhadra, 0.8 per cent in Allahabad were found permanently settled. Below the period of one year of acquisition the percentage of houses were 10.7 in Mirzapur, 6.7 in Sonbhadra, 4.4 in Chandauli, 7.1 in Allahabad and 3.6 houses in Chitrakoot. The highest percentages of acquisition of houses were found within a period of 1-3 years. 79.3 per cent in Mirzapur, 72.7 per cent in Sonbhadra, 74.4 per cent in Chandauli. But in case of Allahabad and Chitrakoot the maximum percentage 68.3 per cent and 66.4 per cent respectively in a period of 3-5 years. Thus, this trend shows that the tribals belonging to Sonbhadra, Mirzapur and Chandauli have repeatedly displaced. As a result, the settlement of their houses was within a period of 1-3 years.

As regards to the source of acquisition of houses, a majority of the household respondents told that they could acquire their houses out of savings from agricultural income. The Government has launched Integrated Rural Development Plan and Integrated Tribal Development Plan Schemes for overall upliftment of the rural and tribal people in which housing grant facility is available. It is well known fact, that major portion of grants is embezzled by the officials and Gram Pradhan of that village.

Therefore, a very little amount of the grant is distributed to the tribals for this purpose. Only 5 respondents from Mirzapur, 8 respondents from Sonbhadra, 10 respondents from Chandauli, 7 from Allahabad and 11 respondents from Chitrakoot accepted that they received this grant under IRDP, ITDP schemes and have utilized in constructing their houses.

The number of employed in service were few. Only one respondent in Mirzapur, 3 in Sonbhadra, 2 in Allahabad told that they are employed and income out of this service they have utilised in constructing their houses. As the percentage of poor tribals is high, they don't have enough money for starting any sort of business. Therefore, the number of respondents who invested money for business was nil.

Any living house includes some basic facilities such as number of living rooms, separate kitchen, bathroom, toilet, electricity, drinking water sources, public bore well or own bore well. The Table 3.24 depicts the real picture of tribal houses. We found everywhere a multiuse covered area having only one room in all the districts of tribal areas. Thinking and talking of a separate kitchen, bathroom, toilet, electricity and private bore well in tribal families are out of question. Open field is available for toilet and bath. There were some small ponds, small rivers and some small waterfalls are the sources for their water need. Normally, the tribal women regularly go to these places for collecting water in their earthen pitchers. The Jal Nigam corporation has bored hand pumps in some villages. A few number of well was also found in some villages. The stagnant water of ponds and well and even public bore well water were found polluted and culminated with several poisonous minerals. The main pollutant was arsenic normally found everywhere in tribal areas. The regular intake of arsenic polluted water may cause several abnormalities in the human bodies. The skin abnormalities, cancer of bladder, kidney and lungs and stomach cancer are some effects of the regular intake of arsenic mixed water. Patients of cancer, stomach problems, malaria, fialeria, etc., were found during survey of these tribal areas. The Table 3.24 shows the basic facilities in the houses of sample households.

Status of the Household

The joint family system which is characterised by jointness of residence, kitchen, property and rests on the sanctity of customs and traditions are normally found in traditional society. In India the highest percentage of joint family structure is still prevailing in agrarian part of the country. But it is getting weaker day-by-day and all of its characteristics and complexities are vanishing in a natural way. The joint family is defined as two or more related married couples living in the same house having common property, common kitchen and common worship place in the same house. It is presumed that the joint family system should also be common in tribal society in any part of the country due to their agrarian background. But surprisingly, the joint family percentage in the study area has of late undergone a considerable change. It is getting weaker day-by-day and all its complexities are disappearing due to several unavoidable factors suddenly arose in their peaceful life. The following Table 3.25 shows the maximum percentage of nuclear families in respondent house.

It is evident from Table 3.25 that only 12.5 per cent joint family in Mirzapur, 30.8 per cent joint family in Sonbhadra and 22.9 per cent joint family in Chandauli were found in tribal families. Only 22.9 per cent in Naxal prone area are maintaining joint family. Similarly, this down trend of joint family was also seen in Dacoit prone area covering Allahabad and Chitrakoot districts. Respondents 17.3 per cent in Allahabad and 15.0 per cent in Chitrakoot and average of the two districts was 20.1 per cent of joint family families.

Table 3.24: Basic Facilities in the Houses of Sample Households

Sl. No.	*Item*	*Mirzapur*	%	*Sonbhadra*	%	*Chandauli*	%	*Allahabad*	%	*Chitrakoot*	%
1.	No. of living rooms										
	1	750	100	750	100	450	100	600	100	450	100
	2	0	0	0	0	0	0	0	0	0	0
	3	0	0	0	0	0	0	0	0	0	0
	4	0	0	0	0	0	0	0	0	0	0
2.	Separate Kitchen	0	0	0	0	0	0	0	0	0	0
3.	Bathroom	0	0	0	0	0	0	0	0	0	0
4.	Electricity	0	0	0	0	0	0	0	0	0	0
	Drinking water source										
(a)	Public bore-well	750	100	750	100	450	100	600	100	450	100
(b)	Own bore-well	0	0	0	0	0	0	0	0	0	0

Table 3.25: Status of Household Families

District	*Total households*	*Joint*	*%*	*Nuclear*	*%*
Mirzapur	750	94	12.5	656	87.5
Sonbhadra	750	231	30.8	519	69.2
Chandauli	450	122	27.1	328	72.9
Naxal Total	1950	447	22.9	1503	77.1
Allahabad	600	104	17.3	506	84.3
Chitrakoot	450	53	11.8	397	88.2
Dacoit Total	1050	157	15.0	903	86.0
Total of five Districts	3000	604	20.1	2406	80.2

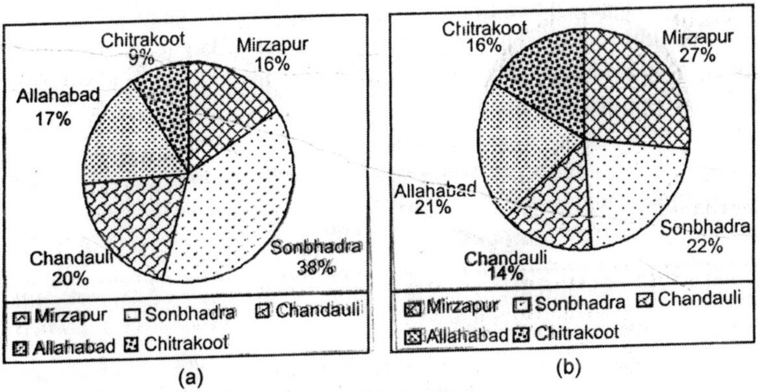

Fig. 3.1 (a) Joint family, and (b) Nuclear family.

Percentage of Joint families shown in the graph is out of 604 joint families of all the five districts and percentage of Nuclear families shown in the graph is out 2,406 nuclear famil... of all the five districts.

If we think of the reasons behind the sudden rise of percentage of nuclear family would clearly focus on the two factors. The first one is that the tribal people have lost their agrarian function because of alienation of their agricultural land and the second factor is repeatedly displacement from their living places. At present they are not at all maintaining stable life because they have no permanent land for agriculture. Due to this displacement process they stand no where at least for earning their livelihood. It appears as if they have again been thrown out to in nomadic life. Due to the activities either from government officials side or from feudal landlords or maphias or contractors etc., they have reached to the chronic poverty stage. All the government's welfare programmes and development programmes appear only on paper for filling up the statistical data. Thus, these are the reasons which have forced them to break their joint family system, Somehow the social and blood related relations are being maintained by the nuclear family system.

Table 3.26 shows the distribution of respondents in the sample households by marital status. 92.9 per cent of married respondents in Naxal prone area and 88.2 per cent married respondents in dacoit prone area indicates that the marriage either of male or female is not a social or economic problem, as it is found in urban and civilized society. There are several norms and requirements which have to be fulfilled before the settlement of marriage. The social, economic status, job position, dowry, caste, *gotra*, horoscope, etc., are some examples of impediments which have to be removed before the settlement of the marriage in Indian Hindu and Muslim society. Therefore, the percentage of late marriage and the per cent of bachelor males females are higher in modern urban society in India. If we analyse the marriage institution of tribals we find that the system of settlements, performance, etc., are very simple and does not require heavy amount of expenditure. Early childhood marriage custom is common and prevalent in the tribal society. These are the causes which make marriage performance easy in tribal society. 3.9 per cent of widow/widower in Naxal prone area and 4.0 per cent in Dacoit prone area also indicate that the remarriage among tribal men and women is also common. Marital separation per cent is very low.

Table 3.27 shows that only 41.6 per cent respondents of Mirzapur and 35.6 per cent of Sonbhadra are permanent residents. Similarly, 48.7 per cent of Chandauli district belong to the place where they are residing at present. The percentage of migrant respondents are high in all the three districts, i.e., Mirzapur, Sonbhadra and Chandauli (58.4%, 64.8% and 51.3% respectively). It clearly indicates the maximum number of tribals have been forced to leave their permanent ancestral places either by the Forest Department or by power plant units and industrial units or Mines units. There are possibilities that some maphias and musclemen could have ousted them for possession of their land. Thus, the percentage 64.4 per cent of migrants respondents of Mirzapur, Sonbhadra and Chandauli showed that they had changed their places not in search of jobs or for other reasons but only due to displacement.

Table 3.26: Distribution of Respondents on Marital Status

District	*Total households*	*Married*	*%*	*Unmarried*	*%*	*Widow/ Widower*	*%*	*Separated*	*%*
Mirzapur	750	667	88.9	13	1.7	70	9.3	0	0.0
Sonbhadra	750	707	94.3	11	1.5	29	3.9	3	0.4
Chandauli	450	438	97.3	0	0.0	12	2.7	0	0.0
Naxal Total	1950	1812	92.9	24	1.2	111	5.7	3	0.2
Allahabad	600	516	86.0	63	10.5	21	3.5	0	0.0
Chitrakoot	450	410	91.1	19	4.2	21	4.7	0	0.0
Dacoit Total	1050	926	88.2	82	7.8	42	4.0	0	0.0
Total of five Districts	3000	2738	91.3	106	3.5	153	5.1	3	0.1

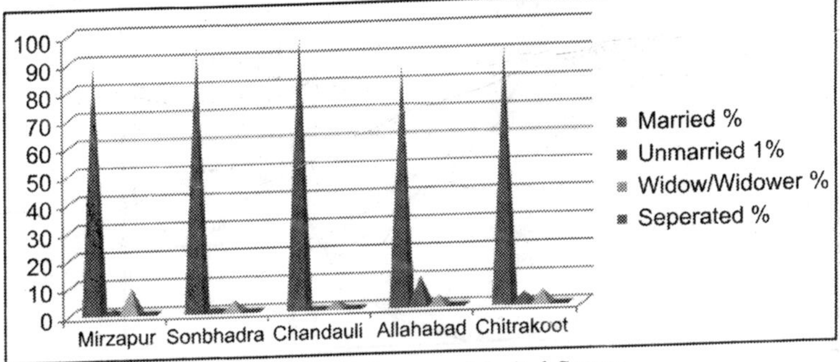

Fig. 3.2: Distribution of Respondents on Marital Status

Table 3.27: Status of Respondents—Permanent Resident or Migrated from Other Place

District	*Total households*	*Permanent*	*%*	*Migrated*	*%*
Mirzapur	750	312	41.6	438	58.4
Sonbhadra	750	267	35.6	483	64.4
Chandauli	450	219	48.7	231	51.3
Naxal Total	1950	798	40.9	1152	59.1
Allahabad	600	560	93.3	104	17.3
Chitrakoot	450	450	100.0	0	0.0
Dacoit Total	1050	1010	96.2	104	9.9
Total of five Districts	3000	1808	60.3	1256	41.9

Caste-wise Distribution of the Respondents

In order to understand the Indian social system, we have to study the traditional caste system of India. Ascribed role and status of an individual in the society is defined by the hierarchy of the castes. Since, the dawn of the civilization and since the Vedic period till date the caste system has been dominant factor in Hindu social system. One has to perform his duties within the framework of the caste system. This caste system is also prevalent in tribal society. The concept of *gotra*, clan, *kul*, etc., are the deciding factors in tribal society also. None of the members can go beyond the traditional system of their society. All these traditions were maintained when the tribals were permanently residing in their original home place, i.e., the forest. But as soon as the Government started launching development programmes in the forest, they were scattered and displaced to different places in the name of rehabilitation. As consequent, their caste hierarchy was also disturbed and they could not maintain properly their oldest caste system. The following Table 3.29 shows the concentration of some tribal caste people in the study districts. There are some tribals whose caste names are Kol, Dharkar, Chamar, Gond, Ghasia, Kharwar, Chero, Bhuiya, Agariya, Harijan, Mushar, Waiga, Pathari, Dhangar, Waiswar, Thakur found in different development Blocks of Sonbhadra, Mirzapur, Chandauli, Allahabad and Chitrakoot districts. The per cent of these caste respondents in all the five districts have been analysed on the caste basis.

Table 3.29 shows that the maximum percentage of Chamar and Kol concentration was found in Naxal prone area, i.e., 24.3 and 23.0 per cent respectively. Then after Gond comes on third and Charo on fourth. The percentage of Ghasia, Kharwar, Bhuiya, Agaria, Mushar, Waiga, Pathari, Dhangar, Waiswar and Thakur are also present in some areas of the districts but their percentage is negligible. But in dacoit prone area which includes Allahabad and Chitrakoot the percentage of Kol tribes is dominant everywhere by its highest percentage, i.e., 98.7 per cent. All other castes percentages show almost zero. Though the Kol tribe has not yet been categorised as Scheduled Tribes.

Table 3.30 shows that mostly tribal respondents of all the five districts are engaged as agricultural labour, 69.3 per cent in Mirzapur, 57.3 per cent in Sonbhadra, 60.2 per cent in Chandauli, 80.7 per cent in Allahabad and 66.7 per cent in Chitrakoot, respondents livelihood is depended on agricultural labour. In Chitrakoot area, during survey it was found that mostly tribals were engaged as bonded labour. Even now the forest

Table 3.29: Caste-wise Distribution of the Respondents

District	*Kol*	*Kol %*	*Dharkar*	*Dharkar %*	*Chamar*	*Chamar %*	*Gond*	*Gond %*	*Ghasiya*	*Ghasiya %*
Mirzapur	243	32.4	10	1.3	151	20.1	1	0.1	0	0.0
Sonbhadra	101	13.5	1	0.1	89	11.9	323	43.1	5	0.7
Chandauli	104	23.1	0	0.0	234	52.0	0	0.0	0	0.0
Naxalite area	448	23.0	11	0.6	474	24.3	324	16.6	5	0.3
Allahabad	600	100.0	0	0.0	0	0.0	0	0.0	0	0.0
Chitrakoot	444	98.7	0	0.0	0	0.0	0	0.0	0	0.0
Dacoit Area	1044	99.4	0	0.0	0	0.0	0	0.0	0	0.0

District	*Kharwar*	*Kharwar %*	*Charo*	*Charo %*	*Bhuiya*	*Bhuiya %*	*Agariya*	*Agariya %*
Mirzapur	28	3.7	199	26.5	118	15.7	0	0.0
Sonbhadra	83	11.1	23	3.1	8	1.1	6	0.8
Chandauli	5	1.1	0	0.0	0	0.0	0	0.0
Naxalite area	116	5.9	222	11.4	126	6.5	6	0.3
Allahabad	0	0.0	0	0.0	0	0.0	0	0.0
Chitrakoot	0	0.0	0	0.0	0	0.0	0	0.0
Dacoit Area	0	0.0	0	0.0	0	0.0	0	0.0

Table 3.30: Distribution of the Respondents by Occupation

Sl. No.	*Item*	*Mirzapur*	*%*	*Sonbhadra*	*%*	*Chandauli*	*%*	*Allahabad*	*%*	*Chitrakoot*	*%*
1.	Agriculture	137	18.3	237	31.6	116	25.8	107	17.8	140	31.1
2.	Agricultural Labour	520	69.3	430	57.3	271	60.2	484	80.7	300	66.7
3.	Service	44	5.9	24	3.2	11	2.4	4	0.7	6	1.3
4.	Business	49	6.5	59	7.9	52	11.6	5	0.8	4	0.9
Total		750	100	750	100	450	100	600	100	450	100

Department has not yet released the forest land in favour of SC/ST and it has not been properly executed in the favour of tribals. 18.3 per cent in Mirzapur, 31.6 per cent in Sonbhadra, 25.8 per cent in Chandauli, 17.8 per cent in Allahabad and 31.1 per cent respondents in Chitrakoot are engaged directly in agriculture on their own land which would have been allotted in their favour. If we look at the States of India figures of restored land, we can confirm our findings that practically the tribal claims, in spite of Forest Right Act and Land Abolition and Land Reform Act, have not been followed properly.

Table 3.31: Literacy Status of the Respondents

District	*Household*	*Literate*	*Literate %*	*Illiterate*	*Illiterate %*
Mirzapur	750	251	33.5	499	66.5
Sonbhadra	750	239	31.9	511	68.1
Chandauli	450	173	38.4	277	61.6
Naxalite area	1950	663	34.0	1287	66.0
Allahabad	600	205	34.2	395	65.8
Chitrakoot	450	147	32.7	303	67.3
Dacoit Area	1050	352	33.5	698	66.5
Total of five districts	3000	1015	33.8	1985	66.2

Table 3.31 indicates that the tribals of all the five districts are almost illiterate. The average illiteracy percentage is 66.2 per cent and literacy percentage has been recorded 33.8 per cent. Inaccessibility to schools, their poverty and their ignorance of the importance of schooling may be some reasons behind the high percentage of illiteracy.

The Table 3.32 shows the distribution of the respondent households by educational status. The illiteracy rate of tribals in all the respondents of the five districts is quite high, i.e., 66.5 per cent in Mirzapur, 68.1 per cent in Sonbhadra, 61.6 per cent in Chandauli, 65.8 per cent in Allahabad and 67.3 per cent in Chitrakoot. 22.5 per cent in Mirzapur, 15.6 per cent in Sonbhadra, 19.8 per cent in Chitrakoot districts and tribals are anyhow have found completed their Primary education. The percentage is much lower than the rural and urban people of the districts and state. Upper Primary school, Higher Secondary school and college education percentages are very-very low. There are significant reasons behind their lagging in educational race. The Chronic poverty and practically unavailability of educational facilities are the main reasons. Their prime

Table 3.32: Distribution of the Respondent Households by Educational Status

Sl. No.	*Item*	*Mirzapur*	*%*	*Sonbhadra*	*%*	*Chandauli*	*%*	*Allahabad*	*%*	*Chitrakoot*	*%*
1.	Illiterate	499	66.5	511	68.1	277	61.6	395	65.8	303	67.3
2.	Primary	169	22.5	117	15.6	89	19.8	44	7.3	75	16.7
3.	Upper Primary	60	8.0	59	7.9	34	7.6	62	10.3	40	8.9
4.	Higher Secondary	18	2.4	37	4.9	41	9.1	61	10.2	19	4.2
5.	College	4	0.5	26	3.5	9	2.0	38	6.3	13	2.9
Total		750	100.0	750	100.0	450	100.0	600	100.0	450	100.0

priority of their lives is how to survive and for that the entire family leaves no stones unturned to get something to be done for their families.

Notes

1. District Gazetteer—Mirzapur.
2. Profile of Mirzapur available on its Website.
3. Distict Gazetteer — Sonbhadra.
4. Profile of Sonbhadra available on its Website.
5. Distict Gazetteer — Allahabad.
6. Profile of Allahabad available on its Website.
7. Distict Gazetteer — Chitrakoot.
8. Profile of Chitrakoot available on its Website.

References

1. District Gazetteer—Mirzapur.
2. Profile of Mirzapur available on Website.
3. Statistical Magazine — Mirzapur District, 2009.
4. Distict Gazetteer — Sonbhadra.
5. Profile of Sonbhadra — available on Website.
6. Statistical Magazine — Sonbhadra District, 2009.
7. Distict Gazetteer — Allahabad.
8. Profile of Sonbhadra — available on Website.
9. Statistical Magazine — Allahabad, 2009.
10. Distict Gazetteer — Varanasi.
11. Profile of Chandauli available on Website.
12. Statistical Magazine — Chandauli District, 2009.
13. Distict Gazetteer — Chitrakoot.
14. Profile of Chitrakoot available on Website.
15. The Constitution (Scheduled Tribes) (Uttar Pradesh) Order 1967.

Chapter 4

Development: Constitutional Provisions, Five-Year Plans and Social Welfare Programmes

Development and Constitutional Provisions

An eminent development economist, Michael Jodaro has envisaged the following three main objectives of Development:

1. The ability to provide the basic necessities of life;
2. To be a person with full-esteem; and
3. Freedom of choice.

We have been spectators of the past 68 years of Indian 'Development'. While no doubt, we have also seen villages of forested south-eastern-western part of Uttar Pradesh (Mirzapur, Sonbhadra, Chandauli, Allahabad and Chitrakoot) change and their inhabitants embrace some of the modern amenities like electricity, telephone, television, yet we can say that their mindset and state of living remain completely unchanged, rather changed to the worst in the name of tribal development, For example roads were constructed and those "roads of development" turned out to be "roads of exploitation to exploitation". Through these roads moneylenders, forest contractors, Government officials and others forcibly entered into the tribal world to snatch their share claiming as if they were realizing their own legal share from tribal resources. This bitter truth was proved when Late Prime Minister Rajeev Gandhi admitted, each rupee spent on development, hardly six paise reaches to tribals of India. Several studies have shown that 80-85 per cent of all funds meant for tribal development

2. Safeguards relating to development – Articles 275(1), 339(2) of the Constitution (R.C. Verma: 2002 – 121).

The scheduled tribes are economically backward and unsophisticated class of people who are liable to be easily deceived by shrewd and disabling them from alienating even their own properties except under special conditions. Article 19(5) provides safeguard to the tribal interest in property. Provisions relating to economic development of scheduled tribes are mainly mentioned in Articles 275(1) and 339(2). The Article 275(1), first provision envisages provision for grants-in-aid for meeting the cost of such schemes of development as may be undertaken by a State with the approval of the Government of India for the purpose of promoting the welfare of its scheduled tribes or raising the level of administration of the scheduled areas their-in of the administration of the rest of the areas of the State. In pursuance of this article, provision of special central assistance has been made to the States having tribal population. As per the provision, the grant is to be made against such specific schemes as are necessary for the welfare of scheduled tribes and are undertaken with the prior approval of the Union Government. But practically this has not to be done. The grants are released without specific schemes. Articles 339(2) goes further and empowers the Union Executive to issue directive to a State as to the drawing up and execution of schemes specified in the directive to be essential for the welfare of the scheduled tribes in the State. Despite poor performance by State Governments the powers vested in these provisions have not been utilized so far and no directive has been issued.

Tribal Development Strategies during Planning Era

The development strategies adopted by the Five-Year Plans was aimed at the transformation of the tribal economy with a view to bring them at par with other population in the country. According to the Indian Planning Commission, people below the poverty line among the scheduled tribes are 80-85 per cent. Therefore, these plans adopted the strategies of achieving the development of tribals through increasing their income and employment opportunites and to provide sufficient and adequate social facilities for education, health, housing, communication, developing infrastructure, etc. In this matter, four phases of pianning have been identified. Firstly, the priority was given to provide immediate relief to the general mass of population who were denied of amenities of life during British Rule.

Secondly, the emphasis was given on resource mobilization and provision of social service infrastructure in the countryside. Thirdly, the emphasis should be given to reduce disparity and growth with justice. Fourthly, should be participatory development with a focus on self management harnessing the productive forces for meeting the basic needs as well as for contributing to the national objective of self-reliant growth is gaining momentum (Roy, Burman : 10).

Since, the dawn of tribal development plans institutions came forward with assurance to shoulder the responsibility of their development with full sincerity. The first one is the Central Government, the second is the State Government, the third is the constitutional provisions, the fourth is the political parties, and the fifth is Non-Governmental Organisations (NGOs). The tragedy is this that instead of fulfilling their promises their attention and objects were mainly concentrated on their exploitation in the name of the development plans. It is an amazing fact that bureaucracy is apathetic, to the tribal groups. Therefore, Human Rights of the tribals have been trampled underfoot. However, all the steps taken towards tribal development under each Five Year Plan, has been discussed below (Niranjan Pani, Jitendra Sahoo, 72):

During the First Five Year Plan (1951-56) Rs. 12 crores was provided by the Central Government with the main objective of developing the economy in tribal areas and Rs. 11 crores was set apart in the State sector for the development of tribal areas. During this Plan, more emphasis was given to categories and areas to bring overall changes through the instrumentality of outside agencies, i.e., Community Development Programme launched in 1952 which tried to induce the visualized process of change in most backward, isolated and inaccessible tribal areas. Since, the tribal areas were beset with peculiar problems and needs, a different administrative system was required to cater to the peculiar conditions of these areas (K. Somasekhar: 29).

In additin to that, Special Multi-Purpose Tribal (SMPT) Development Blocks were also started in some selected tribal areas in the country in 1954 to supplement the general development programmes. These Blocks were intended to evolve a satisfying concept of development to be made applicable to the tribal areas in the country (G.O.I., 1956: 163). Special provision was also made for setting-up of cooperative societies to assist the tribals in the marketing of minor forest produce and agricultural produce. Further, cooperative credit system was strengthened in the tribal areas to meet the credit needs of these people. The provision of health facilities in tribal and scheduled areas was also undertaken during this Plan period. Medical aid was given to the tribal people in the shape of starting of primary health centres, distribution of medicines and so on. Since, water supply is a crucial problem in most of the tribal concentrated areas, provisions were made in the Plan for water and irrigation (G.O.I. 1952: 636). But, as the Community Development Programme was multi-sectoral, it suffered failure in tribal areas. The situation was reviewed in 1956 by Elvin Committee which recommended a cautious approach in the introduction of multiplicity of schemes in tribal areas.

On review, the projects were substituted by a less intensive model of tribal development intensive model of tribal development Blocks in 1957. The norms of Tribal Development were confined to an area of 150 to 200 sq. miles and a population of about 25,000. The Blocks were supposed to work for tribal population under Intensive Development Programme. They were to concentrate on economic development, education, health and communication and were to have specific targets.

The Second Five Year Plan (1956) allocated a total amount of Rs. 47 crores for the scheduled tribes and scheduled areas. Rs. 27.5 crores for scheduled castes and 4 crores for former criminal tribes. Special attention was given on the settlement of the tribals. Several important development programmes were taken up and they were: Schemes for eradicating diseases, the incidence of which were particularly high such as malaria, tuberculosis, leprosy and yaws, for making available medical and public health facilities and for supply of pure drinking water. Development of communication in accessible areas especially the provision of improved villages roads, hill and forest paths, minor bridges, etc., and other schemes which will secure speedy improvement in economic conditions.

During Second Five Year Plan period the concept of Multipurpose Tribal Blocks was evolved in areas with predominantly tribal population. The budget allocated for each MPTB during the plan was 27 lakhs. 43 MPTB development Blocks were formed all over the country with a view to bring rapid improvement in the economic demand, social conditions of the scheduled tribes by concentrating specially on underdevelopment, but compact areas for multi-sided development. The tribal scenario was subjected to comprehensive review by the scheduled areas and Scheduled Tribes Commission, generally called Dhebar Commission, in April 1960, and it submitted its report in October 1961. The Commission came to conclusion that the pace of development in the tribal areas was slow. Investment and other protective measures were also inadequate and needed urgent attention of the Government. It called for comprehensive legislation to cover all tribals living within the Scheduled Area and outside, and a simple administrative system for tribal areas. It recommended a scheme of tribal development Blocks for all areas with more than 50 per cent tribal population (R.C. Verma: 190).

The recommendations of the Commission were accepted and the Block approach was continued. The Third Five Year Plan (1961-66) was directed for strengthening the agricultural, economic, developing industry, power and transport, and hastening the process of industrial and technological change achieving marked progress towards equality of opportunity and socialistic pattern of society and providing employment for the entire addition to the labour force. The main programmes undertaken during the Third Five Year Plan for the welfare of the tribals were in respect of land improvement, land reclamation and soil conservation, minor irrigation of land improvement, land reclamation and soil conservation, minor irrigation supply of improved seeds, manures, implements and bullocks, provision of facilities for training, demonstration of improved practices, development of cattle, fisheries, piggery and sheep breeding, organisation of training-*cum*-production centres and financial assistance and advice to village artisans engage in cottage industries (G.O.I.: 705).

In the Third Five Year Plan the conceptual name of Multipurpose Tribal Blocks was changed to other conceptual name, i.e., Tribal Development Blocks (TDBs) which is continuing till date. The scheme of Multipurpose Tribal Blocks had been made flexible by extending it not only to Scheduled Areas, but also by these Blocks in which the tribal population constitutes predominant section of the population. This Plan provided for the creation of 300 Tribal Development Blocks following the recommendation of Elvin Committee. Even though the Tribal Development Blocks strategy was an improvement over the general development approach, it did not serve as an effective instrument of tribal development because the administrative and protective aspects in tribal economy remained largely unattended. Elvin pointed out that there was no proper involvement of tribals in the management of development programmes by the end of Third Five Year Plan, the scheme was implemented in about 500 Blocks covering about 40 per cent of the total tribal population from the development programmes. The tribal situation, so far as protective measures and developmental programmes are concerned, remained unchanged.

In 1969, a committee under the chairmanship of Shilu AO was appointed to review the tribal development programmes. It observed that most of the recommendations of the UN Dhebar Commission had remained unimplemented and urged that they should be implemented without any further delay. This Commission also disapproved the Block approach as inadequate. That Commission also pointed out that the main problems of the tribals related to indebtedness, land alienation, economic backwardness and inadequate communication and suggested that those should be tackled on priority basis by formulating a comprehensive programme of development (R.C. Verma: 191).

In the Fourth Year Plan, six Tribal Development Agency (TDA) strategies was introduced as an additive programme focusing on specific target groups in Madhya Pradesh, Bihar, Orissa and Andhra Pradesh. Each agency covered a group of Blocks and was expected to take up various programmes and protective measures on integrated basis by pooling up the resources. In this Plan about 44 crore rupees were allotted to these agencies. The allocations were in addition to the normal outlays. Even this strategy was only a partial success as these agencies concentrated on some economic programmes like agricultural development and higher investment in arterial roads. By the end of the Fourth Five Year Plan, 504 Tribal Development Blocks were established in the country, Programmes of land allotment, grant of subsidies for purchase of ploughs and bullocks and improved seeds for development of agriculture and animal husbandry, land colonization, minor irrigation and organisation and development of cooperative were some of the programmes implemented for the economic upliftment of tribal development during this Plan period. Besides, importance was given for the modernization and diversification of the occupational pattern for the land labourers (K. Somashekhar: 31).

In actual practice, however, the agency approach practically remained in agricultural development programme and failed to achieve the desired results. This approach was not extended to other areas and the Blocks continued to be the unit of development.

The tribal situation was again reviewed on the eve of the Fifth Five Year Plan by a task force on the 'Development of Tribal Areas' constituted by the Planning Commission. It opened that the deficiency and shortcomings pointed out by the earlier commissions and committees had generally remained unattended. It observed that one of the important factors for the failure of the development programmes is that the scheduled tribes and tribal areas have been looked as a 'welfare' problem as distinguished from 'Development' (Verma: 192) problem. The general notion that the fruits of development would automatically percolate down the poor, was belied. As there was no separate budgetary head for tribal development, the money was siphoned out for other activities for other sections of the society. There was an absolute lack of coordination between different Government departments and between different States. Besides, the share of tribal development as a per cent of the Plan outlays was regularly decreasing though, in actual numbers, there was a gradual increase in every plan.

Fifth Five Year Plan was famous for the concepts of Tribal Sub Plan (TSP) and Integrated Tribal Development Projects (ITDP). A comprehensive view of the tribal problem was taken up on the eve of this plan, by launching Sub-Plan strategy in tribal areas. The emphasis was mainly on developmental as well as protective aspects with the focus not only area concept, but also on tribal population. From the point of view of tribal development, three distinct categories were identified: (1) those residing in areas tribal concentration, (2) dispersed tribals residing in plain areas, and (3) Primitive tribe groups. While area development approach was followed for the first category, family oriented approach was adopted for the second group and special projects were taken up for the third category. The objectives of Tribal Sub Plan (TSP) strategy were (A) to bring about socio-economic development of scheduled tribes and to ensure protection of tribals against exploitations (Somashekhar: 33).

During the Sixth Five Year Plan 'The Modified Area Development Approach' (MADA) was launched for intensive, integrated development of tribals by covering smaller areas of tribal concentration having a population of 10,000 and of which the tribal population constituted not less than 50 per cent. The Sub Plan approach for tribal development was continued during this Plan Period. Poverty elevation was the main object of the Plan Period. The main thrust of the policy for development of the scheduled tribes during the Plan Period was four fold, viz., (a) Integration of services at the delivery point to the beneficiaries with a view to develop self-reliance in them; (b) development of services from the bottom-upwards instead of top-downwards; (c) development of skill to diversify the occupation; and (d) introduction of latest technology based on local materials and local skills to reduce the stigma attached to their present profession. Nevertheless, the impact of tribal development programmes appears to be limited. The studies conducted by the Planning Commission on ITDPs in several States revealed that there was no well established programmes were only notional. Further, no significant dent was made on illiteracy, increasing indebtedness, insignificant role of cooperatives and high incidence of land alienation (Somashekhar: 34).

In the Seventh Five Year Plan "Modified Area Development

Approach (MADA) was extended to the pockets with a population of 5000, whereby at least half of them ought to be scheduled tribes. During Sixth and Seventh Plan period, 249 MADA pockets were identified. The Seventh Five Year Plan (85-90) laid emphasis on improving the socio-economic conditions of the tribal areas. Special attention was given towards Beneficiary Oriented Programmes. Special economic development scheme for scheduled tribes women were taken up for removing their backwardness and to improve their position. During this Plan period the ITDPs and MADA had covered only 75 per cent of the total tribal population in the country. To cover the remaining 25 per cent of the tribal population, the cluster approach was advocated for small areas with a total population of 5,000 and with more than 50 per cent scheduled tribe population (Somashekhar: 35).

The Commissioner for SC and ST after enquiry submitted his report which showed that the progress made under the ITDPs was not at all satisfactory. He commented that there was no proper follow-up of the development programmes. The Commissioner in his another report (1987) observed that absence of regular elections to Gram Panchayats, became a hindrance for the promotion of tribal leadership which might have led to improper planning and implementation of different programmes (Somashekhar: 35).

The objectives and strategy as envisaged in Sixth Plan period and continued in the Seventh Plan, was being followed onwards in Seventh Plan, but a special emphasis on the vulnerable groups. Top priority was to be given to education. A special emphasis was given to the rehabilitation of the tribals displaced under various development projects.

During Eighth Plan an attempt was made to reach the development benefits to forest villages, in a manner suited to the situation for the all-round development of tribes residing there. The legal and administrative measures and programmes were to aim at elimination of exploitation in matters relating to land, forest money lending, trade and labour. During the Eighth Five Year Plan period the functioning of cooperative institutions including the 'Large Scale Multipurpose Societies' (LAMPS) in tribal areas was reviewed with a view to meet the genuine needs of tribal people in matters of credit, marketing of minor forest produce and supply of essential commodities. Under National Policy on Education 1986, priority was to be given to the opening of primary schools in tribal areas. Anganbaris, non-formal and adult education centres were to be established in tribal areas on the priority basis. The curriculum at all stages of education was to be designed to create an awareness of the rich cultural identity of the tribal people as also of their enormous creative talent. For the primitive tribal groups, detailed plans were prepared for their economic development, as far as possible, with the family as the unit.

The working Group for Eighth Five Year Plan (1992-97) has commented that after the adoption of the TSP strategy, Central and State Governments have enacted protective laws to check exploitation of tribals by non-tribals, especially the money lenders and private traders. But the sectoral allocations under strategy had not reflected the felt needs of the tribals and hence could not create the desired impact. Protective laws formulated to provide protection from all forms of oppression has been accorded high priority, States have no doubt, enacted protective laws to provide protection to tribals from exploitation by non-tribals. But in actual implementation, this has not received priority. There are instances reported by States of tribal lands passing into the hands of non-tribals despite the existence of these laws. Moneylenders and private traders have continued to exploit the tribals.

During the Ninth Five Year Plan (1997-2002) a separate Ministry of Tribal Affairs was constituted to give more focused attention to the development of Scheduled Tribes. This new Ministry was the nodal Ministry for overall policy planning and coordination of programmes and schemes for the development of Schedules tribes. The main strategy of this was "(1) Due to introduction of New Economic policy, the rights and privileges of the tribals are encroached upon. Therefore, there was an urgent need to formulate a Tribal policy with a special focus on the rehabilitation aspects during the Ninth Plan based on the strategies advocated by "Nehru's Panchsheel" for Tribal Development; (2) The tribal community should be involved in the planning process under TSP approach. The four-tier system recommended by the Bhuria Committee should be the best suited vehicle for self management of tribal development; (3) The Indian Forest Act 1927 should be revised in consonance with the provisions of the forest policy resolution of 1988; (4) The Government will pay special attention towards tribals economy, as it stands today, can neither enter into the market created by the new economic policy nor it can withstand the competition created; (5) The traditional Panchayat systems should be utilized for planning process at the ground level. A special focus on health, education and nutrition of Primitive Tribal groups should be given highest priority in this Plan Period; (6) Extensive employment-*cum*-vocational training programmes to rehabilitate the displaced tribals with alternative sources of income on suitable basis should be provided on priority basis; (7) There is a need for recognition of Indian System of Medicines and participation of knowledgeable persons in planning health services for tribals. Special incentive should be given to the paramedical and medical staff to work in the remote and far flung tribal areas; and (8) There is a special for intensification of primary health care services in tribal areas because of the high incidence of leprosy and other infectious diseases amongst the tribal societies" (Nadeem Hasnain: 333-334).

During this plan special Central Assistance was given to all the States in order to supplement their efforts in tribal development. This assistance was basically meant for family oriented income generating schemes in the sectors of agriculture, horticulture, minor irrigation, soil conservation, animal husbandry, forests, education, cooperatives, fisheries, village and small scale industries and minimum needs programmes. During 2000-01 an amount of Rs. 500.30 crore was released to the States. An amount of 300 crore was sanctioned during 2001-02 to meet the costs of projects for tribal development (Nadeem Hasnain: 335). Part of the funds were also to be utilized for setting-up to residential schools for providing quality education to tribal students. Rs. 14.18 crore was sanctioned to all the States for the development scheme for primitive tribal groups for the establishment of 14 Tribal Research Institutes. Rs. 270 lakh was released during this Plan period. During 2001-02 an amount of Rs. 16.07 crore was released for the construction of 43 boys and 68 girls hostels. Rs. 9.97 crore was released for construction of 106 Ashram Schools during 2001-02. During 2000-01 an amount of Rs. 3 crore was released for 32 vocational training centres. During 2001-02 Rs. 3.99 crore was released for 37 complexes of 48 literacy centres where the literacy rate among the tribal girls is below 2 per cent. Rs. 99.75 crore was released as share of the Government for running the Tribal Cooperative Marketing Development Federation of India. An amount of Rs. 12.81 crore was released for encouragement of minor forest produce operation.

The Village Grain Bank Scheme was started in 1996-97 as preventive measures against deaths of children by providing a safeguard against fall in nutritional standards of scheduled tribes living in remote rural areas. 645 Grain Banks were set-up and for that Rs. 2.20 crore was released during 2001-02.

The National Tribes Financial Development Corporation (NTFDC) was set-up by the Government of India in April 2001 by bifurcating the National Scheduled Castes and Scheduled Tribes. Financial Development Corporation was a Government of India undertaking with an authorized share capital of Rs. 500 crore. The corporation extended financial assistance to scheduled tribes al concessional rate for income generating schemes costing up to rupees 10 per unit, provided grants for skill development for ST and fill the critical gaps by providing backward and forward linkage for activities undertaken by the target group.

Adivasi Mahila Sashakti Karan Yojana (AMSK) scheme was also introduced from 2002-03. Tribal women below poverty line were to be assisted for small economic activities to augment their income with a loan of up to Rs. 50,000 at an interest of 4 per cent.

To encourage the SC/ST students the Government also started Post-Matric Scholarship Scheme. Rs. 66.78 crores were released as 100 per cent financial assistance to the SC/ST students (Nadeem Hasnain: 335).

From the Tenth Five Year Plan period (2003-08) the objective and scope of special Central Assistance to Tribal Sub Plan was expanded to cover the employment-*cum*-income generation activities and infrastructural incidental thereto. Besides family based activities, other activities run by the Self-Help Group (SHG)/Community can also be taken. The ultimate objective of extending Special Central Assistance to Tribal Sub Plan was to boost the demand based income-generation programmes and this raise the economic and social status of tribals. The Special Central Assistance (SCA) fund was provided 100 per cent grants-in-aid to the States for economic development in the following areas and for the following population. The main features of guidelines were.

1. TDP area (192 Nos.) which were generally contiguous areas of the size of at least tehsil or Block or more in which the scheduled tribe population was 50 per cent or more of the total population.
2. MADA pockets (259 Nos.), which were identified pockets having 50 per cent or more ST population with a minimum total population of 10,000.
3. Clusters (83 Nos.), which were identified pockets having 50 per cent ST population with a minimum population of 5000.
4. Particularly Vulnerable Tribal Groups (VTG) characterized by a low rate of growth of population, pre-agricultural level of technology and extremely low level of literacy.

The funding support was given to the tribal population below the poverty line. 70 per cent of the Special Central Assistance (SCA) was to be used for primary schemes supporting family/Self Help Group (SHG)/Community-based employment and income generation in sector such as Agriculture/Horticulture, Land Reforms, WaterShed Development,

Animal Husbandry, Ecology and Environment, Development of forest and forest villages, Development of entrepreneurship in SSI, etc., and 30 per cent for development of infrastructural incidental thereto. Priority to be accorded to the neglected tribals living in forest villages and synchronization of the programmes with Joint Forest Magistrate. Preparation of long-term area specific micro-plans was for ITDAs/ITDPs. 30 per cent beneficiaries were to be women. Adherence was to the provisions of the Panchayats (Extensions to Scheduled Areas) Act 1996, SCA had to be an integral part of the Annual Plan of the State. 10 per cent of the overall outlay/allocation in a year was earmarked for providing incentive to those States which qualify for the same by way of effective implementation of the TSP in letter and spirit funds were to be earmarked ITDP-wise.

Criteria for allocation of funds to the States were (1) of the total annual allocation under SCA to TSP, an amount of 10 per cent was reserved for incentive grants and was released to selected States who fulfilled the criteria indicated below. Adoption of the TSP approach in letter and spirit by ensuring that the entire TSP funds at least in equal proportion to population of tribals in the State, are placed in one Budget Head under the administrative control of the Tribal Development Department of the State Government for a more integrated and focused planning and implementation of projects/schemes. Thereafter, at least on an average 75 per cent of the approved tribal Sub-Plan funds were actually utilized/ released to the implementing agencies in the preceding three financial years through the budget head of the Tribal Development Department of the State and funds awarded, as incentive to the State should be utilized only for employment and income generating activities benefiting the tribals. The remaining 90 per cent of the total annual outlay under SCA is then allocated amongst the State on the basis of the share of the programmes under the broad strategy of the Tribal Sub Plan, namely Integrated Tribal Development Project (ITDP), Modified Area Development Approach Pockets (MADA), Clusters and Primitive Tribal Groups (PTGs) and was calculated in proportion to the scheduled tribe population under each area/programme.

The allocation of fund for the year 2008-09 was Rs. 750.00 crore. which was in addition to Rs. 150.00 crore for development of forest villages, a programme meant for providing infrastructural development in identified forest villages for which funding was provided from the Head for SCA to TSP.

During Tenth Five Year Plan, one other scheme for Development of Particularly Vulnerable Tribal Groups was implemented (PTGs). Among scheduled tribes, there are certain tribal communities, who have declining or stagnant population, low level of illiteracy, pre-agricultural level of technology and are economically backward. 75 such groups in 17 States and Union Territory of A&N Islands were identified and categorized as Particularly Vulnerable Tribal Groups (PTGs), State/UT-wise. Most of these groups are small in number, have not attained any significant level of social and economic progress and generally inhabit remote localities having poor infrastructure and administrative support. Therefore, they became the most vulnerable sections among the scheduled tribes. Priority are, therefore, required to be accorded for their protection and development, and checking the declining trend of their population. In 1998-99 a separate 100 per cent Central Sector Scheme for exclusive development of PTGs was started. The Schemes covers only the 75 identified particularly Vulnerable Tribal Groups among scheduled tribes. Activities under it may include housing, land distribution, land development, agricultural development, cattle development, construction of link roads, installation on non-conventional sources of energy for lighting purpose, social security including Janshree Beema Yojana or any other innovative activity meant for the comprehensive socio-economic development of PTGs, more particularly for the PTGs who are nomadic in nature.

With an aim to tackle the problem of Naxals in Uttar Pradesh, the State Government has started to focus on comprehensive development of those districts of South-Eastern region of Uttar Pradesh. As a result, the State Social Welfare Department has decided to introduce Integral Tribal Development Programme (ITDP) in the Naxal-hit Sonbhadra, Mirzapur, Chandauli and Dacoit hit Allahabad and Chitrakoot districts. The programmes were not just ensure that the districts get support for infrastructure, but also welfare schemes to ensure its overall development, Incidentally most of the tortured and suffered belong to the Kol community, the department felt that a development approach would go a long way in curbing the problem. With this programme the State Social Welfare Department focused on creating infrastructure like roads, drinking water supply, schools, Anganbari centres for children, Mini Primary Health Centres in all villages and the Community Health centres at Block levels. The Welfare Department claimed that they would ensure employment generation through various Government sponsored welfare schemes like MNREGA and Swarnjayanti Gram Swarojgar Yojana (SGSY). For this the State has agreed to 50-50 funding with centre.

Whether the development programmes implemented so far have led to any significant improvement on the quality of life of *Dalit Adivasis* of south-eastern region of Uttar Pradesh?

What is the accessibility of development programmes to all the tribal communities?

To what extent the development programmes are responsive to the felt needs of tribal people and what is the nature and extent of participation of *Dalit Adivasis* in the development programmes?

What discontents are developing in the minds of *Dalit Adivasis* as a result of developmental programmes and in what direction are they going ahead? These are the most serious questions and problems to be thought of and to be resolved by the Government of India.

Attempt has been made to examine these questions and analyse the facts in greater details in order to properly assess the success and effectiveness both in positive and reverse direction of the tribal development programmes.

In addition to Five Year Plans the following Social and Wefare Programmes were also launched to help and uplift the downtrodden *Dalit Adivasis* and Tribals, social, economic, health, educational and other aspects of requirements (See Tables 4.2, 4.3 and 4.4).

The following departments (Table 4.5) have been authorised to implement the development programmes mentioned in the columns :

A. In addition to all the above mentioned Welfare Programmes the Union and State Governments have been sanctioned Sansad Asthaniya Kshetriya Vikas Nidhi/Vidhayak Nidhi Samagra Gram Vikas Yojana:
   The BPL families can be benefited and developments can be done by Rs. 2 crore of Sansad Nidhi and 75 lakh of Vidhayak Nidhi simultaneously in Parliamentary area and Vidhan Sabha Area.
   Other infrastructural and facilities are also available on subsidized rates. They are the following.
B. *Natural Bio-gas Plants*: A grant of Rs. 23000 for this project is sanctioned.
C. *Rashtriya Unnat Chulha*: A grant of Rs. 158 and Rs. 218.
D. *Solar Power Pack*: A grant of Rs. 1500.
E. *Solar Pump*: A grant of Rs. 70140.
F. *Community Toilet and Biogas Plant* is for 100 families.
G. *Gramin Peya Jal Yojana*: This is for SC/ST. 10 per cent

Table 4.2: Social Welfare Programmes for Scheduled Castes and Scheduled Tribes

Supply Department PDS	BPL Programme	Villagers are provided 700 gm of sugar at the rate of Rs. 13.50 per unit, 23 kg of wheat at the rate of Rs. 4.65, 12 kg of rice at the rate of Rs. 6.15, 5 ltrs of kerosene oil @ 9.85. The annual income must be below Rs. 9000. White coloured ration cards are issued.
	Annapurna Yojana	Green card is issued to old persons above 65 years of age and if there is no body to look after them. They would be provided 10 kg grain without any charge.
	Mid-Day Meal	Children getting education in primary schools would be provided 3 kg grain (cooked) per month. The menu and serials would be provided as per norms.
	Antyodaya Yojana	25 kg per month Wheat @ Rs. 2 per kg, Rice Rs. 3 per kg. to BPL. Red colour card is issued to holders.
Social Welfare Department:	Old Age National Pension/Kisan Pension Yojana:	*Eligibility*—Above 60 years, Income below 1000 per month, Land should be less than 3.5 acres, who has no son/grandson even after expiry of 20 years not employed, Handicapped, having no shelter or support from other family members. Pension amount is 150/- per month.
	National Family Benefit Yojana	Family should be BPL and the earning head of member of the family (Age 18 to 65) suddenly die, the dependent would be benefited by Rs. 1000/- at one time.
	Scheduled Tribe Children Scholarship	Class 1 to 5— Rs. 25 per month for 12 months. Class 6 to 8—Rs. 40 per month for 12 months. Class 9 to 10—Rs. 60 per month for 12 months. Above 10th—Rs. 500 at one time.
	Grant available to SC/ST for their daughter's marriage	Annual income 11000 per year Payment amount – 10000 at one time.
	Grant available to victimized/Tortured S.C./S.T.	Ordinary injury – 25000 Serious injury – 50000 Rape – 50,000 Murder – 2,00,000
Women Welfare Programme	National maternity benefit yojana:	BPL pregnant woman would be benefited Rs. 500 upto two children.
	Helpless Widow grant	Age 18-60, who could not earn more than Rs. 1000 per month for her livelihood would get Rs. 150 per month.
	Balika Samriddhi Yojana	BPL family Rs. 500 would be awarded if a baby girl is born. Class 1-3—300 per year. During Schooling Upto 4—500 per year. During Schooling Upto 6—600 per year. During Schooling 6 to 7—700 per year. During Schooling Upto 8—1000 per year. During Schooling

Table 4.3: Child Development Pusthahar Yojana

Samekit Bal Vikas Pariyojana:	Through Angan Bari Kendra Workers balanced diet is provided to 0-6 year children and to pregnant women. Children are provided informal education. Pregnant women are assisted by the Anganbari Workers for their balance diets, regular medical checkup and A.N.M. provides every medical help to pregnant women at the time of delivery and to newly born baby. Anganbari is established on 1000 population. 101 persons would be benefited by each Anganbari. Pushtahar quantity-150 gms, Panjiri—24 gms, biscuits to pregnant women. 75 gms weening food to 7 months to 6 years children. 70 gms panjiri and 24 biscuits to 3 to 6 years children. Just double quantity of these food items will be given to malnutrition children. Standard pushtahar-100 gms contain 12 gms protein, 300 calories. Care pushtahar = 135 gms proteins and 450 calories.
Vaccination	Essential medicines and vaccines are administered to pregnant women and newly born baby and mother as per instructions of the doctors. Regular health examination is also done by doctors with the help of A.N.M.
Handicapped Welfare Yojana	Persons of age group 18-60 will be entitled. Income should not be more than 1000 per month. Physically disabled to do any work. Blind, deaf and dumb, mentally retarded, physically disabled. Grant 127 per month. They may be provided Rs. 35,000 grant for artificial organ of the body.
Handicapped Students Scholarship Yojana.	Age 6-40 years. Guardian income should not be more than 2000 per month. 40% Physically disabled Class 1-5 — Rs. 25 Class 6-8 — Rs. 40 9 to Inter — Rs. 85 Graduation — Rs. 125 P.G. — Rs. 170

Table 4.4: Rural Development Programme

Indra Awas Yojana:	Started in the year 1985.	This is meant for BPL to ST/SC who have been victimized by landlords, higher caste people and by natural calamities. Rs. 20000 is sanctioned for construction of one room 17000, 3000 for kitchen and toilet.
Under Jawahar Gram Samriddhi Yojana		22.5% of the total grant is released for Indira Awas Yojana.
Pradhan Mantri Gramodaya Awas Yojana		Rs. 20000 is granted. Eligibility same as above.
Sampurna Gramin Yojana	Started on 25th September 2001.	Previously launched programmes 1. Sunischit Rojgar Yojana. 2. Jawahar Gram Samriddhi Yojana was merged into Sampurna Gramin Yojana.
		75.25% grant is released by the Central and State Government. Gram Panchayat will have to spend 50% grant on employment to SC/ST. Rs. 58 wage per day-5 kg rice (35) and Rs. 23 cash by employing them as labourer.
		The work would be taken for soil and water conservation, watershed development work, development of traditional sources of water, forestation and gram development for example—School building, Veterinary Hospital, dispensary, market development, roads and approach lanes, Panchayat Ghar etc.
Pradhan Mantri Gram Sadak Yojana:		40% of the villages have no approach road. Till 2003 villages having population of 1000 will be interconnected and till 2007 villages of 500 population will be interconnected. For this work SC/ST people will be provided employment on daily wages.
Swarn Jayanti Gram Swarojgar Yojana:		This is loan-cum-grant Yojana for BPL rural people. Through if person or group of persons may establish cottage industry, Small scale industry.
Dr. Ambedkar Gram Vikas Yojana		Under this Yojana BPL people of SC/ST will be provided all the mentioned facilities by the departments.

Table 4.5: Programme and Department

Sl. No	*Programme*	*Department*
1.	Approach Roads	Public Welfare Department
2.	Electrification	Electricity Department
3.	Drinking Water	Jal Nigam
4.	Free Boring	Laghu Sinchayi Department
5.	Indira Awas	Gram Vikas
6.	Swarn Jayanti Rojgar Yojana	Gram Vikas
7.	Drain Kharanja Road	Panchayat Raj
8.	Clean Toilets	Panchayat Raj
9.	Primary School Building	Basic Siksha Vibhag
10.	Widow Pension	Mahila Kalyan Department
11.	Old Age Pension	Samaj Kalyan Department

contribution from the users, 90 per cent from the State help in installing Mark-II Hand Pumps.

H. *Rina Sahayata Anudan and Awas Karyakrama*:
It is meant for released bonded labourers, BPL SC/ST people who have not more than 32,000 annual income per year.

I. *Samagra Gram Vikas Yojana*: The grant is released to the Gram Panchayat by the Government to provide infrastructural facilities to the villages and fulfil the basic requirements of the villagers and also to ensure the funds have properly been utilized.

J. 1. Clean water, 2. Indira Awas, 3. Clean Toilet, 4. Family Planning, 5. Vaccination, 6. Construction of inter-connecting roads, 7. Electrification, 8. Construction of Drains and Kharanja Roads, 9. Primary School building, 10. To establish senior, primary schools and construction, 11. Launching Employment oriented programme, 12. Free water pipe boring, 13. Agricultural land Ceiling, 14. To locate residential places, 15. Fishery, 16. To locate place for earthen pot makers, 17. To verify and certify the possession of land given to villagers on *Patta*, and 18. To ensure and implement the facilities provided to old age, widow and physically handicapped persons (including artificial limbs, etc.)

K. Medical facilities, Care of Health and implementation of family planning programmes are implemented by the concerning departments of the State Government.

A. 1. Development is related to population of that place. In order to control the birth rate, medical care and death rate, following measures are being taken by the Government.

2. *To Control birth temporary steps*: To provide condoms, Oral pills, Copper T.
3. *Permanent Step Vasectomy male and female.*
4. *Removal of pregnancy conditions*:
   (i) Health does not allow to conceive.
   (ii) Indication of birth of handicapped baby.
   (iii) Social reasons, mean pregnancy due to rape.
   (iv) Fear of defective birth of baby due to misuse of contraceptive devices.

B. *U.P. Population Policy*:
1. Marriage age of girls 19.5 years.
2. To reduce the birth rate from 4.3 to 2.1 before 2016.
3. To reduce mother's death rate from 707 per year to 250 per year (Death rate is 707 per lacs mothers).
4. To reduce death rate of newly born baby from 85 per thousand to 61 per thousand before 2016.
5. To make aware the men and women about the consequences of AIDS and teach them to take precautions and to save them from this disease.

C. *Safe Motherhood*: To provide all instructions and medicines to pregnant women before delivery and post-delivery. For all such facilities A.N.M., Dai's, health workers and female doctors are appointed. A.N.M. and health workers are responsible for their care and they have to do the following:
1. To take them regularly to PHC for check-up.
2. To administer Iron folic acid medicine (100) and two tines TT vaccine in a gap of one month.
3. To encourage the pregnant women to be admitted in the hospital at the time of delivery for her safety and baby.

D. Motherhood benefit yojana:
Rs. 500 are given to BPL pregnant women. Those who are above 19 years of age and not more than two children alive.

E. Taking care of babies:
1. Weight should not be less than 2.5 kg. To watch that weight is gradually increasing.
2. Special care should be taken if the babies are twin.
3. To ensure the mother is capable of breast feeding.
4. To provide vaccine of TT, Phenomena, Khasara, malnutrition and for deficiency of water in the body.
5. To ensure that the mother's feeding continue upto six

months. In case this does not continue dry milk is to be provided.

6. BCG vaccine within a year, DPT vaccine within six weeks to one year,

F. To educate the people how to protect them from contagious diseases, epidemics: diarrhoea, dysentery, jaundice, malaria, filaria, encephalitis, T.B., leprosy, tetanus, polio and other diseases and to provide medical facilities.

G. Disposal of garbage:

1. Disposal of dirty water, disposal of night soil and urine and solid matters.

H. To provide clean drinking water:

1. India Mark-II hand pump provide pure drinking water. Boring of such type of hand pumps.
2. Typhoid, dysentery, jaundice and other diseases are spread through dirty water. Therefore, the villagers should be made aware and to provide them medicines for all such diseases. Chlorine, bleaching powder, etc., should be given. They should be taught how to store drinking water.

I. To provide free legal services and assistance to SC/ST BPL. Eligibility-BPL SC/ST having not more than income Rs. 12000 per year. It is available to those who are victims of torture, human misbehaviour, physically, mentally, handicapped, victim of caste violence, beggar, bonded labour, victimized by flood, drought, earthquake, agricultural loss, etc.
They will be given free services by-lawyers in court cases.

J. Siksha Guarantee Yojana to

1. Where 6-11 year old children are available and where there is no primary school within a distance of 1 km. This programme will be started by the Gram Panchayat and one teacher "*Acharya Ji*" will be appointed on Rs. 1000 honorarium. Drinking water and toilet facilities will be available. Books will be available free of cost.
2. *Siksha Mitra Yojana*: Siksha Mitra will be appointed in the primary schools where teachers-student ratio is 1:40. The ratio of permanent teacher and Siksha Mitra should be 3:2. Payment Rs. 2,250 per month would be done for a year only. It can be extended next year.

K. *Irrigation Yojana*: Free boring facilities available to marginal farmers of SC/ST. Rs. 6,000 grant for installing pumping set loan is available.

L. *Bhumi evam Jal Sanrakshana Yojana*:
   (i) Construction of pond, repairing, drainage, check dams to preserve water, reservoir.
   (ii) Barren land is developed into fertile land.
   (iii) Kisan Credit Card is available to farmer through which they can get loan from banks for their farming.

M. Fisheries facilities and animal husbandry facilities yojana.

Through the Table 4.6 we have tried to explain the sources of information regarding getting the knowledge of all the programmes launched by the Government. It is well known fact that the tribal villages which are located in remote hilly and in dense forest area are almost completely unaware of the happenings of the district, the State and the country as well. Due to illiteracy poverty and lack of means of communications they are incapable of enjoying the information provided by the print media and the electronic media. Therefore, only sources of information left are friends, relatives, local leaders, Gram Pradhan and the persons who often visit courts, market and for other work in urban areas. As we are aware every area of a district comes under the development Blocks. Therefore, it is the official duty of BDO and other officials to supply all informations and Acts to the tribal people through loudspeaker, hand bills and through organizing meetings and cultural programmes. The religious gathering will be the best occasion to broadcast all such types of news information among the tribals.

It is evident from the Table 4.6 that Mass Media source of information is zero in all the districts. This finding clearly indicates that newspaper, transistor, radio and T.V. sources of information are completely absent in these tribal areas.

The Gram Pradhan should always be the best source of information because he is an elected body and he is expected to perform all such type of duties in the public interest. But the fact is just reverse. 30 per cent respondents in Mirzapur, 25 per cent respondents in Sonbhadra, 35 per cent respondents in Chandauli, 29 per cent in Allahabad and 62 per cent in Chitrakoot clearly shows that the Pradhans of these tribal villages do not want to convey any such plans to the the tribals the *Dalit Adivasis* of this region because he is afraid that if they are aware, they may start raising their claims. At this State of their ignorance Gram Pradhan may embezzle the grants by fraudulent means by concealing the facts.

As regards local leaders, the percentage in Mirzapur, Sonbhadra,

Chandauli, Allahabad and Chitrakoot are almost same and it is very low. The local leaders emerge out of the tribal community. They can raise their voice, may launch agitation and demonstrate for their demands. Since, they are illiterate and ignorant of the development programmes, they can't enlighten the mind of their tribal colleagues about the developmental programmes. Thus, as informer they are also helpless to act as the best source for tribals.

The Block Development Officer is the immediate officer responsible for all sorts of development programmes. The Government has appointed them for this very purpose. The low percentages 10 per cent, 19 per cent, 15 per cent, 19 per cent and 20 per cent in Mirzapur, Sonbhadra, Chandauli, Allahabad and Chitrakoot indicate that they do not perform their official duties with sincerity. They are also busy in making foul money out of their grants.

As regards, friends/relatives as informer or source, the percentage is high in comparison to other sources of information, 35 per cent, 38 per cent in Sonbhadra, 30 per cent in Chandauli, 35 per cent in Allahabad and 37 per cent in Chitrakoot clearly indicates that the friends and relatives are more sincere informer. During interview with the respondents it was asked that how friends and relatives could become capable as the best informers. On this point the respondents explained that these friends and relatives were not of their villages. They were of some other villages where they somehow could get the news and the details of the plans. As soon as they knew, they conveyed to their friends and relatives residing in other villages. Thus, the Gram Pradhan, B.D.O. including local leaders who were supposed to be the most important source of information for the people about developmental programmes, were not intentionally doing good to the *dalit adivasis*.

During survey the author organised group discussions in several tribal villages on different issues and their problems. During discussions, we felt that they had resentments and dissatisfactions over all these welfare programmes. Firstly, all the development and welfare programmes implemented by the Governments were not brought to their knowledge. Thereafter, they were asked their opinion about their satisfaction and dissatisfaction. In case, those are not satisfied then, what were the reasons behind them. 8.8 per cent respondents of Mirzapur tribal areas, 3.2 per cent respondents of Sonbhadra, 0.9 per cent of Chandauli, 0.0 per cent of Allahabad and 0.0 per cent respondents of Chitrakoot tribals expressed their opinion that they were fully satisfied, whereas on the other side, 34.4 per cent respondents of Mirzapur, 34.9 per cent in Sonbhadra, 5.8 per cent

Table 4.6: Source of Information about the Development Programmes

Sl. No	*Source*	*Mirzapur*	*%*	*Sonbhadra*	*%*	*Chandauli*	*%*	*Allahabad*	*%*	*Chitrakoot*	*%*
1.	Mass Media	0	0.0	0	0.0	0	0.0	0	0.0	0	0.0
2.	Sarpanch	30	30.0	25	25.0	35	35.0	29	29.0	62	62.0
3.	Local Leaders	25	25.0	18	18.0	20	20.0	17	17.0	11	11.0
4.	B.D.O.	10	10.0	19	19.0	15	15.0	19	19.0	10	10.0
5.	Friends/Relatives	35	35.0	38	38.0	30	30.0	35	35.0	17	17.0
Total		100	100.0	100	100.0	100	100.0	100	100.0	100	100.0

Table 4.7: Opinion of the Respondent on Satisfaction over the Social Welfare Programmes run by the Government if not then What are the Reasons

District	*Total Households*	*Fully*	%	*Some-what*	%	*Bribery*	%	*Reasons*			
								Obstacles in work	%	*Bungling and Black Marketing*	%
Mirzapur	750	66	8.8	258	34.4	126	16.8	108	14.4	192	25.6
Sonbhadra	750	24	3.2	262	34.9	194	25.9	128	17.1	142	18.9
Chandauli	450	4	0.9	26	5.8	150	33.3	133	29.6	137	30.4
Naxal Area	1950	94	4.8	546	28.0	470	24.1	369	18.9	471	24.2
Allahabad	600	0	0.0	135	22.5	331	55.2	0	0.0	134	22.3
Chitrakoot	450	0	0.0	114	25.3	311	69.1	0	0.0	25	5.6
Dacoit Area	1050	0	0.0	249	23.7	642	61.1	0	0.0	159	15.1
Total of five Districts	3000	94	3.1	795	26.5	1112	37.1	369	12.3	630	21.0

in Chandauli, 22.5 per cent in Allahabad and 23.7 per cent respondents of Chitrakoot tribal area expressed their views that they were satisfied to some extent with the welfare programmes. If we see the fully satisfied percentage in total area of study, it was only 3.1 per cent. It clearly indicates that the maximum percentage was of dissatisfaction (Table 4.7).

We further enquired from them their opinion on the reasons. They focused on the three main reasons, Bribery, Obstacles in Work and Bungling. 24.1 per cent respondents from Naxal prone area and 37.1 per cent respondents from Dacoit prone area, had opinion that they could not be benefited with all such welfare programmes if they had no money to pay as bribe to the concerning officials. Bribery is must in expediting the work. No bribe money no work done.

18.9 per cent respondents in Naxal area and 0.0 per cent respondents in Dacoit prone area had opinion that there were several obstacles and complications in the process which could not be solved by them. As result, they were unable to receive the facilities of the welfare programmes.

As regards on bungling and black marketing points the average per cent 21.0 respondents of all the households had opinion that due to bungling and black marketing, normally, persons are not getting advantage of these welfare programmes.

Objectives

To find out the difference of opinion on "what type of help was received from Government welfare programmes". To prove statistically the benefits of the welfare programmes in the five tribal districts of U.P., i.e., Mirzapur, Sonbhadra, Chandauli, Allahabad and Chitrakoot has been applied.

The analysis of the data yields results in terms of mean, S.D. and Significance Value. The obtained results have been summarized in the Table 4.8.

Table 4.8: Statistical Analysis

Sl. No.	*Subject*	*N*	*Mean*	*S.D.*	*D.F*	*Sign.*
1.	Agri. equipment	3000	1.98	.154	4	0.000
2.	Hy-seed	3000	2.00	.095		
3.	Financial	3000	2.00	.071		
4.	For Cattle	3000	1.99	.085		
5.	Piggery & Poultry	3000	2.00	.052		
6.	Cottage Industry	3000	1.99	.089		
7.	Agri. Improvement	3000	1.99	.089		

Since, the significance value is less than the significant level at 0.05. Therefore, the common opinions show that the benefits are not obtained by the households in the five tribal districts of U.P., i.e., Mirzapur, Sonbhadra, Chandauli, Allahabad and Chitrakoot.

Table 4.9: Respondent Households who were Benefited by Facilities Provided by the Government

Facility	*Naxal Area*	*Per cent*	*Dacoit Area*	*Per cent*
Not Benefited	1154	59.18	592	56.38
Benefited	796	40.82	458	43.62
Total	1950	100	1050	100

Theoretically, hundred per cent respondent household tribals should be benefited by all the welfare schemes of the Government. Why a fraction of tribal communities avail the opportunity, is a matter of investigation. Table 4.9 shows that 59.18 per cent from Naxal prone area and 56.38 per cent from Dacoit prone area tribal respondent households could not get opportunity to be benefited of the BPL Government plans. The rest percentage 40.82 and 43.62 respondent households were benefited of the Government facilities. Why more than 50 per cent respondent households were left without availing such benefit? Who should be held responsible for embezzlement of their share?

Handicapped Welfare Yojana

The State Government has launched the "Handicapped Welfare Yojana" under which any person who is deaf and dumb or blind or without hands or legs or paralysed, dependent on anybody and having less than Rs. 1000 per month income, will be entitled to receive Rs. 127 per month from the social welfare department. He or she must be between 18 to 60 years of age. In the presence of District Handicapped Welfare Officer, the list of handicapped persons is to be finalized and the scholarship of Rs. 127 per month will be disbursed per individual. In the following Table 4.10 the actual recipients of such scholarship has been analysed.

During survey the author met with some handicapped persons of the above mentioned category of disabilities. The number of handicapped persons was comparatively very high in Naxal prone area, especially in Sonbhadra, Mirzapur and Chandauli, where hundreds of rehabilitated tribal families around Churk Cement Factory, Rihand Dam, HINDALCO,

Table 4.10: Benefited by Handicapped Welfare Yojana

Handicapped Scholarship Rs. 127 per month	*No. of Respondent Household*	*Naxal Area Per cent*	*No. of respondent Households*	*Dacoit Area Per cent*
Benefited	225	11.54	115	10.95
Not Benefited	1725	88.46	935	89.05
Total	1950	100	1050	100

Aluminium Plant—Renukut, Kanoria Chemical, Renu Sagar Plant, Obra Dam, Dala Cement, Chunar Cement Factories, Anpara Thermal Power—Anpara, Singrauli Thermal Power Plant and Coal mines and other mines like Gold mine in hills, are settled in *Jhuggi-Jhopadi*. In dozens of resettled colonies for the displaced people, there was no clean water or no proper health care. Pushed to the edge of the Khadia coal mine—a ravaged landscape of dug out mount side stripped of any vegetation, residents daily battle with dust and disease. Every afternoon, dynamite blasts without the care of the overhead hills, in the hunt of coal, sending gusts of gray dust blowing into their huts. Homes flood during the monsoons when mud sludge flows down the mined hills, creating breading grounds for several diseases. Accumulation and dumped fly ash and chemicals discharged as garbage are mixed with the Rihand river and other rivers water, make the water extremely dangerous for health. But the displaced tribals have no option except to drink that polluted water. These are some examples to expose the human sufferings and environmental destruction and degradation. Consequently, most of the tribals are investigated as victims of starvation and malnutrition. Moreover, due to regular inhailing of polluted (Coal ash, Chemical mixed) air and unavailability of food, they themselves have been victimised by blindness, paralysis, deaf and dumb and their offsprings are born handicapped. The sufferings of the weaker sections in many parts of the Patha region appear to be increasing due to partly the deteriorating environmental conditions and partly the increasing dominance of criminals and dacoits. Deterioration of environment in the form particularly of farmland, pastures, forests, water resources and air and continuous drought conditions are some causes for severe malnutrition and starvation problems in tribal people. They are the main causes of being victimised by several diseases resulting in handicappedness.

In addition to all these curses, their relief fund in the name of handicapped welfare *yojana*, seems to be bungled by the concerning officials.

Table 4.10 shows that of all the five districts of our study, only 11.54 per cent in Naxal prone area and 10.95 per cent handicapped from Dacoit area, were lucky enough to receive the relief amount of Rs. 127 per head per month. The largest percentage, i.e., 88.46 per cent and 89.05 per cent in Naxal area and Dacoit prone area, were non-recipient of this facility. If clearly indicate that the huge amount would have been embezzled by the Government officials with collusion with Gram Pradhans and other related persons.

Old Age Pension Yojana

Any old person who is above 60 years, his income is below Rs. 1000 per month, having less than 3.5 acres of land and has no employed son/ grandson of more than 20 years of age, will be entitled for Rs. 125 per month from the Social Welfare Department.

Table 4.11: Benefited by Old Age National Pension Yojana for Rural Tribal

Facility	*Naxal Area*	*Per cent*	*Dacoit Area*	*Per cent*
Benefited	270	13.85	329	31.33
Not Benefited	1680	86.15	721	68.67
Total	1950	100	1050	100

Table 4.11 shows that only 13.85 per cent old persons in Naxal prone area and 31.33 per cent old persons in Dacoit prone area were found benefited by this welfare scheme. Because of Illiteracy, extreme poverty, no knowledge of the schemes and lack of source of information, the older persons are not capable of getting the Old Age Pension. Their share money is embezzled and distributed among the officials.

Awas Yojanas—Indira Awas Yojana and Pradhan Mantri Awas Yojana

Another important concern is poor housing condition. In the name of a comfortable house, the *dalit adivasis* of these areas used to construct with local available materials. Sometimes, local material is not available because of depleted forest resources. In some cases the relevant species have been replaced by commercial species and tribes has no longer free access to forest, Housing condition has, as a result, deteriorated. Housing facilities, therefore, should be provided to tribals in their areas. As per provisional estimates made available by 2001 Census and reported by the Commission, the housing shortage in the rural and tribal areas was about 149 lakh as compared to 137 lakh housing shortage as per 1991. Census, under the Indira Awas Yojana, during the last three years, on an average, about 14-15 lakh houses are being constructed every year whereas the annual requirement is about 30 lakh houses per annum as per the 2001 Census. In addition to this, it is estimated that about 10 lakh shelterless households are being added every year. Thus, against the total requirement of about 40 lakh houses, only 14-15 lakh houses are being constructed leaving a gap of about 25 lakh houses every year in the rural and tribal areas.

The Central Government of India under rural development programme launched in 1985 the Indira Housing Plan for the rural tribal SC/ST people passing their lives below poverty line. Under this plan, total amount of Rs. 20,000 is released in three instalments to BPL card holders. Only the female member of the family will be entitled for this grant, with the condition that the total area of the house be 20 sq mt and the construction upto plinth area was to be completed. The map of the house will be approved only when one living room, kitchen and toilet rooms are included in the drawing of the map. Rs. 17,000 for one room, Rs. 3,000 for construction of kitchen and latrine will be released.

22.5 per cent of the grant released for Jawahar Gram Samriddhi plan will be utilized for Indira Awas Yojana in Ambedkar villages. BPL women have to apply to the either to Gram Panchayat Adhikari or to BDO. Their applications will be put up in Gram Sabha meeting and recommendations will be done by the Gram Sabha. Thereafter, the grant will be sanctioned from the office of the Gram Panchayat Office and BDO to the Gram Panchayat.

Under this plan Rs. 1000 is also sanctioned to those who want to upgrade their hatched and earthen houses.

Like Indira Awas Yojana there is another Yojana named Pradhan Mantri Gramodaya Awas Yojana. The amount and rules are the same as applicable in Indira Awas Yojana.

During survey the respondents were also asked about availing of the Indira Awas Yojana and Pradhan Mantri Awas Yojana housing facilities. The following Table 4.12 shows the percentage of persons who availed this facility.

It is evident from Table 4.12 that only 34.51 per cent in Naxal prone area, i.e., in Sonbhadra, Chandauli and Mirzapur tribals could enjoy the Indira Awas facility. The Dacoit prone—Allahabad and Chitrakoot

Table 4.12: Respondent Households who availed Indira Awas Yojana Facility

Facility	*Naxal Area*	*%*	*Dacoit Area*	*%*
Benefited	673	34.51	252	24.00
Not Benefited	1277	65.49	798	76.00
Total	1950	100	1050	100

respondents percentage was very low, i.e., only 24 per cent who were benefited. 65.49 per cent in Naxal prone area and 76.00 per cent in Dacoit prone areas were deprived of this facility. It is well-known fact that nearly hundred per cent tribals in both the areas are below poverty line. Why a large per cent of tribals are not benefited, is a matter of great concern.

Table 4.13: Pradhan Mantri Gramodaya Awas Yojana

Facility	*Naxal Area*	*%*	*Dacoit Area*	*%*
Benefited	252	12.9	158	15
Not Benefited	1698	87.1	893	85
Total	1950	100	1050	100

As regards Pradhan Mantri Gramodaya Awas Yojana, it has also not benefited maximum percentage of tribal people. Only 12.9 per cent in Naxal area and 15.00 per cent in Dacoit area respondents could avail this facility (Table 4.13).

Reasons behind this drama is quite different in both the cases. During investigation and during group discussions some facts were disclosed. The concerning Gram Panchayat officials, Block Development officials and the Gram Pradhan had fraudulently prepared the forged documents for utilizing the whole amount on the papers. It can easily be concluded that the tribals remained houseless and the mostly Awas has been constructed on papers only. This is the naked truth of the corruption in which every official is involved. The wretched conditions of the tribals remained the same as it was since long. The corrupt officials should be taken to task.

Through Table 4.14, efforts have been made to know the views of the respondents regarding assurance and depth of interest taken by the Government officials when they met with their problems. Only 7.9 per cent respondents from Naxal area and only 3.0 per cent respondents from Dacoit area respondents were confident that their problems were heard

Table 4.14: Views of the Respondents on Assurance and Interest taken by Government Officials when they Met with Problem

District	*Total House-holds*	*Full help*	*%*	*Satis-factory*	*%*	*Not much satisfied*	*%*	*Dis-appoint-ed*	*%*
Mirzapur	750	116	15.5	328	43.7	171	22.8	135	18.0
Sonbhadra	750	36	4.8	363	48.4	166	22.1	185	24.7
Chandauli	450	2	0.4	55	12.2	53	11.8	340	75.6
Naxal Area	1950	154	7.9	746	38.3	390	20.0	660	33.8
Allahabad	600	21	3.5	166	27.7	288	48.0	125	20.8
Chitrakoot	450	10	2.2	186	41.3	97	21.6	157	34.9
Dacoit Area	1050	31	3.0	352	33.5	385	36.7	282	26.9
Total of five Districts	3000	185	6.2	1098	36.6	775	25.8	942	31.4

properly and assurance with full interest, has been given by the officials. They expected with confidence that their work would be done. 36.6 per cent of the respondents of the whole area expressed their views that they were satisfied with their assurance. Their problems have been heard by them.

Discouraging part of it is that 31.4 per cent of the total area respondents were completely disappointed with their attitude and were discouraged with their problems. They will not be solved at any cost 25.8 per cent respondents were not much satisfied.

Objective

To find out the difference of opinion on assurance and interest taken by Government officials when they met with problems. The tribes don't have any opinion about the assurance and interest taken by the Government officials in solving the problems of the tribals in the five tribal districts of U.P., i.e., Mirzapur, Sonbhadra, Chandauli, Allahabad and Chitrakoot.

Table 4.15: Statistical Analysis

Sl. No.	*Subject*	*N*	*Mean*	*S.D.*	*D.F*	*Sig.*
1.	Mirzapur	750	2.40	0.976	4	0.000
2.	Sonbhadra	750	3.10	0.845		
3.	Chandauli	450	3.62	0.711		
4.	Allahabad	600	2.86	0.778		
5.	Chitrakoot	450	2.89	0.916		

The analysis of the data yields results in terms of mean, S.D. and Significance Value. The obtained results have been summarized in the Table 4.15.

The significance value is less than the significant level at 0.05. Therefore, it shows that the tribals are not satisfied by the response of the Government officials in solving their problems of these peoples in the five tribal districts of U.P., i.e., Mirzapur, Sonbhadra, Chandauli, Allahabad and Chitrakoot.

Table 4.16: Experiences of the Respondents regarding Government Officer's Attitude during Meeting with Problems

District	*Total Respondents*	*Fair*	*%*	*Partiality discouraging*	*%*	*Neglected*	*%*	*Financial Exploitation*	*%*
Mirzapur	750	213	28.4	329	43.9	95	12.7	113	15.1
Sonbhadra	750	106	14.1	341	45.5	175	23.3	128	17.1
Chandauli	450	4	0.9	86	19.1	110	24.4	250	55.6
Naxal Area	1950	323	16.6	756	38.8	380	19.5	491	25.2
Allahabad	600	103	17.2	249	41.5	104	17.3	144	24.0
Chitrakoot	450	178	39.6	229	50.9	19	4.2	24	5.3
Dacoit Area	1050	281	26.8	478	45.5	123	11.7	168	16.0
Total of five Districts	3000	604	20.1	1234	41.1	503	16.8	659	22.0

Objective

To find out the difference of opinion on behaviour of Government officer's during meeting with problems. The attitude of Government officials with the persons of the five tribal districts of U.P., i.e., Mirzapur, Sonbhadra, Chandauli, Allahabad and Chitrakoot.

The analysis of the data yields results in terms of mean, S.D. and Significance Value. The obtained results have been summarized in Table 4.17.

Table 4.17: Statistical Analysis

Sl. No.	*Subject*	*N*	*Mean*	*S.D.*	*D.F.*	*Sig.*
1.	Mirzapur	750	1.78	0.747	4	0.000
2.	Sonbhadra	750	2.42	0.799		
3.	Chandauli	450	3.35	0.814		
4.	Allahabad	600	2.34	1.024		
5.	Chitrakoot	450	1.75	0.786		

The significance value is less than the significant level at 0.05. Therefore, the response of the household are against the behaviour of the officials in the five tribal districts of U.P., i.e., Mirzapur, Sonbhadra, Chandauli, Allahabad and Chitrakoot.

A person is disappointed, frustrated, discontented and revolted when he is not paid due attention or neglected and tortured mentally. Through media and friends the tribal people know that the Government is doing a lot for their upliftment. For this purpose, billions of rupees are sanctioned for tribal development and welfare. But on the other side they know that they are continuously facing a lot of problems related to their livelihood. Suddenly, land alienation problem is due to grabbing nature of feudal landlords and maphias, displacement due to installation of industrial plants and depriving them from forest produce right by the forest department arose before them. In the present democratic set-up they were advised to contact the Government concerning officers like SDM, ADM and DM, etc. for getting relief from exploitation and corrupt practices of lower cadre officials. They often contact police administration and pray them for providing relief from their problems. Mostly the tendency of the Government officers and the police administration has often been negative and discouraging due to the pressure of local ruling party leaders and maphias.

In the above mentioned Table 4.16 the Principal Investigator tried to gather the experiences of the respondents during meeting with the Government officers and the police administration. 16.6 per cent respondents from Naxal prone area, expressed their opinion that the Government officers were quite fair in their dealing. But on the other side, 38.8 per cent respondents and 45.5 per cent in Naxal area and Dacoit area respectively told their experiences with officers, were quite discouraging and instead of giving justice they were all the time inactive and bias in their behaviour and decision.

19.5 per cent in Naxal area and 11.7 per cent respondents from Dacoit area were found discouraged because the Government officers had paid no attention, i.e., they had always been neglected by the Government officials during hearing their problems.

25.2 per cent of Naxal area and 16.0 per cent of Dacoit prone area respondents told that without paying bribe in cash, their problems would not be heard and solved. The overall analysis of the above figures clarifies that their grievances and problems are neither heard nor solved by the officers concerned without accepting foul money. Moreover, due to political leaders and maphias pressure the Government officers often disfavour the tribals in spite of their genuine demands.

The tribal people have now gradually developed much understanding and the evaluation capacity to assess the Government work. Whether it is done in real sense honestly or on paper or done by corrupt way, is known to them.

It is evident from table 4.18 that 34.4 per cent respondents in Mirzapur, 3.9 per cent respondents in Sonbhadra, 4.2 per cent in Chandauli, 0.0 per cent respondents in Allahabad and 15.1 per cent respondents of Chitrakoot believed that the Government officials in their district have worked with full honesty.

Table 4.18: Opinion of the Respondents on the Operation of the Government Work

District	Total Respon-dents	Honesty	%	Just on Paper	%	Corrup-tion	%	Not Known	%
Mirzapur	750	258	34.4	308	41.1	166	22.1	18	2.4
Sonbhadra	750	29	3.9	379	50.5	342	45.6	0	0.0
Chandauli	450	19	4.2	76	16.9	347	77.1	8	1.8
Naxal Total	1950	306	15.7	763	39.1	855	43.8	26	1.3
Allahabad	600	0	0.0	438	73.0	162	27.0	0	0.0
Chitrakoot	450	68	15.1	158	35.1	184	40.9	40	8.9
Dacoit Total	1050	68	6.5	596	56.8	346	33.0	40	3.8
Total of five Districts	3000	374	12.5	1359	45.3	1201	40.0	66	2.2

On the other side, 39.1 per cent respondents of Naxal prone area and 56.8 per cent of Dacoit prone area had opinion that most of the Government works were done on papers only. 40.0 per cent respondents of the total respondents believed that only due to economic corruption, Government officials showed their work only on papers. Fact is this that a very few work has been done in the name of development and welfare of the tribals.

Objective

To find of the difference of opinion on how development work done in the region. To prove statistically the corruption in the development programmes in the five tribal districts of U.P., i.e., Mirzapur, Sonbhadra, Chandauli, Allahabad and Chitrakoot.

The analysis of the data yields results in terms of mean, S.D. and Significance Value. The obtained results have been summarized in the Table 4.19.

Table 4.19: Statistical Analysis

Sl. No.	*Subject*	*N*	*Mean*	*S.D.*	*D.F*	*Sign.*
1.	Mirzapur	750	1.85	0.772	4	0.00
2.	Sonbhadra	750	2.58	0.603		
3.	Chandauli	450	2.76	0.548		
4.	Allahabad	600	2.31	0.462		
5.	Chitrakoot	450	2.35	0.727		

Since, the significance value is less than the significant level at 0.05. Therefore, it show the involvement in corruption in the development programmes run by the Government in the five tribal districts of U.P., i.e. Mirzapur, Sonbhadra, Chandauli, Allahabad and Chitrakoot.

All the community development and welfare programmes are participatory programmes. Effective participation of tribals in decision making, development process and welfare process, under Acts, is essential in their interest. No doubt, it is an acknowledged fact that the people's participation is crucial to the success and sustainability of welfare initiatives of the Government. Tribals participation is must in educational and skill development programmes as well as training to build awareness on issues such as environmental concern, social conditions, trading practice and legal and land rights. The knowledge with regard to agricultural practices land and water management, agro-and food processing, medicinal matters, prevailing culture and others are essential. True, they have their own knowledge about the prevailing culture. Their know-how has developed and refined over years. That has also been transmitted through generations of people. Therefore, their knowledge and experiences need to be protected suitably further, there is need to mix their knowledge with modern practice. But that assimilation should be acceptable to tribal community and beneficial at large. The other need is the degree of beneficiary participation at all stages.

During survey and discussions with the tribal people, we could investigate the facts that these people were never involved in developing the annual programmes of work and budget. There has been no effective participation of the tribals in decision making and developmental process affecting them and administration of their own affairs. The policies and programmes have been formulated without consulting them. It has resulted in fixation of wrong priorities and failure in achieving the desired result. Consequently, it has created an atmosphere of discontent and lack of confidence towards the implementing authorities.

Table 4.20: Participation of Tribals in Government Development and Welfare Programmes

District	*Total Households*	*Regu-larly*	*%*	*Never*	*%*	*Rarely*	*%*
Mirzapur	750	128	17.1	580	77.3	42	5.6
Sonbhadra	750	119	15.9	475	63.3	156	20.8
Chandauli	450	39	8.7	284	63.1	127	28.2
Naxal Total	1950	286	14.7	1339	68.7	325	16.7
Allahabad	600	62	10.3	434	72.3	104	17.3
Chitrakoot	450	45	10.0	341	75.8	64	14.2
Dacoit Total	1050	107	10.2	775	73.8	168	16.0
Total of five Districts	3000	393	13.1	2114	70.5	493	16.4

In Table 4.20, opinion on participation in Government development and welfare programmes has been analysed. Only 17.1 per cent respondents of Mirzapur, 15.9 per cent respondents of Sonbhadra, 8.7 per cent respondents of Chandauli, 10.3 per cent of Allahabad and 10.0 per cent respondents of Chitrakoot expressed their views that they had participated in those programmes. There is a possibility that such respondents would have been the members of Gram Panchayats and local leaders who replied regarding their active participation.

The maximum percentage of respondents replied that the tribals were never asked to participate in forming and implementing the programmes. 77.3 per cent respondents of Mirzapur, 63.3 per cent respondents of Sonbhadra, 63.1 per cent of Chandauli, 72.3 per cent of Allahabad and 75.8 per cent respondents of Chitrakoot expressed their grievances that the programmes implementers had never preferred to seek participation of the tribal people, although all the programmes were meant for them.

Only 16.7 per cent respondents of Naxal area and 16.0 per cent respondents of Dacoit area told that they were rarely asked to participate.

Objective

To find the difference of opinion on participation of head of household in the village development work launched in the village by the Government. To prove statistically the role of the household in the participation in development programmes in the five tribal districts of U.P., i.e., Mirzapur, Sonbhadra, Chandauli, Allahabad and Chitrakoot.

The analysis of the data yields results in terms of mean, S.D. and

Significance Value. The obtained results have been summarized in Table 4.21.

Table 4.21: Statistical Analysis

Sl. No.	Subject	N	Mean	S.D.	D.F.	Sign.
1.	Mirzapur	750	1.89	0.470	4	0.000
2.	Sonbhadra	750	2.07	0.485		
3.	Chandauli	450	2.29	0.555		
4.	Allahabad	600	2.07	0.521		
5.	Chitrakoot	450	2.04	0.490		

Since, the significance value is less than the significant level at 0.05. Therefore, it shows the tribal participation is negative in the development programmes in the five tribal districts of U.P., i.e. Mirzapur, Sonbhadra, Chandauli, Allahabad and Chitrakoot.

In the absence of effective participation of the tribals in decision making and in implementation process, the Government experts who are outsider and ignorant of tribal priorities, agricultural practices, land and water management, medicinal matters, environmental issues, prevailing cultural traits, etc., can't succeed in their mission of work. As result, all the time they will take arbitrary, decisions with *malafide* intentions that is why tribal concerns and priorities regarding development and results of welfare programmes are not reflected adequately in the tribal areas and among the tribes.

Opinion of the respondents had also been sought on the works done by the Government agencies in their area. The Table 4.22 shows that 68.5

Table 4.22: Opinion of the Respondents on Government Work done

District	Total Respon-dents	Satisfied	%	Not satis-factory	%	No work	%
Mirzapur	750	40	5.3	196	26.1	514	68.5
Sonbhadra	750	40.5	5.4	27	3.6	624	83.2
Chandauli	450	105	23.3	85	18.9	105	86.7
Naxal Total	1950	185.5	9.5	308	15.8	1243	63.7
Allahabad	600	41	6.8	21	3.5	538	89.7
Chitrakoot	450	34	7.6	52	11.6	364	80.9
Dacoit Total	1050	75	7.1	73	7.0	902	85.9
Total of five Districts	3000	260.5	8.7	381	12.7	2145	71.5

per cent respondents of Mirzapur, 83.2 per cent of respondents of Sonbhadra, 86.7 per cent of Chandauli, 89.7 per cent of Allahabad and 80.9 per cent respondents of Chitrakoot flatly rejected this hypothesis that works were done by the Government. 71.5 per cent of the total respondents of all the five districts were firm on their opinion on the Government works. They completely denied that the work was done in their area.

Only 15.8 per cent respondents of Naxal prone area and 7.1 per cent respondents of Dacoit prone area replied that the Government has done some work and their opinion was satisfactory to some extent on this point.

Objective

To find the difference of opinion on amount of Government development work done in their region. To prove statistically the level of work done in between the five tribal districts of U.P., i.e., Mirzapur, Sonbhadra, Chandauli, Allahabad and Chitrakoot.

The analysis of the data yields results in terms of mean, S.D. and Significance Value. The obtained results have been summarized in Table 4.23.

Table 4.23: Statistical Analysis

Sl. No.	*Subject*	*N*	*Mean*	*S.D.*	*D.F.*	*Sign.*
1.	Mirzapur	750	1.77	0.506	4	0.00
2.	Sonbhadra	750	1.96	0.377		
3.	Chandauli	450	2.04	0.648		
4.	Allahabad	600	2.03	0.320		
5.	Chitrakoot	450	1.96	0.435		

Since, the significance value is less than the significant level at 0.05. Therefore, it proves that the level of work done was not of the level of requirement in the five tribal districts of U.P., i.e. Mirzapur, Sonbhadra, Chandauli, Allahabad and Chitrakoot.

As regards the ideology of Government policies regarding development and welfare programmes of the Indian tribes, they are undoubtedly, fair and without having any other intention except to remove the century old injustice perpetrated against the tribal communities. The greatest challenge that the Government of India has been facing since independence is the proper provisions of social justice to the tribes by ameliorating their social economic conditions. Tribals have also been subject to an inextricable nexus of exploitation and engaged in low yield agriculture. The draft of national tribal policy focus on strategies in India, however, it ignores the cultural perspectives of the tribal communities.

What is wrong and where is wrong with the implementation of the Government policies, really, is a serious matter and challenge to the Government of India and its development and welfare policies. What are our missions at the policy level and the implementation level. The present scenario in tribal areas has belied their hopes. The Government remained complacent with the formal compliance of the outcomes reflected in its performance. It was satisfied with the expenditure mode according to the outlay provided. The failures on the tribals front have been largely administrative. The inocent tribals has been befooled and deceived by the numerous departments and agencies working for their development in various sectors. Administrative and development personnel have not been selected from persons who have knowledge and empathy for tribal people. These are some aspects of discontent of the tribal people of the five districts of our study. Therefore, we also tried to know their attitude towards the government policies for development and welfare which have not yet brought fruitful results.

Table 4.24: Attitude of the Respondents Towards Government Policies Regarding their Overall Development

District	*Total HH.*	*Positive*	*%*	*Negative*	*%*
Mirzapur	750	222	29.6	528	70.4
Sonbhadra	750	293	39.1	457	60.9
Chandauli	450	164	36.4	286	63.6
Naxal Total	1950	679	34.8	1271	65.2
Allahabad	600	275	45.8	290	48.3
Chitrakoot	450	178	39.6	272	60.4
Dacoit Total	1050	453	43.1	562	53.5
Total of five Districts	3000	1132	37.7	1833	61.1

Table 4.24 shows that 70.4 per cent respondents of Mirzapur, 60.9 per cent respondents of Sonbhadra and 36.4 per cent respondents of Chandauli have shown their negative attitude towards the government policies. Similarly, 45.8 per cent respondents of Allahabad and 60.4 per cent respondents of Chitrakoot had negative attitude towards the Government policies.

Only 34.8 per cent respondents of Naxal prone area and 43.1 per cent of Dacoit area had shown positive attitude towards Government policies.

Objective

To find out the difference of opinion and attitude of the head of the household towards Government plans for eradication of poverty. To prove statistically about the opinion and attitude of the head of household about Government plans for eradication of poverty among the five tribal districts of U.P., i.e., Mirzapur, Sonbhadra, Chandauli, Allahabad and Chitrakoot.

The analysis of the data yields results in terms of mean, S.D. and Significance Value. The obtained results have been summarized in Table 4.25.

Table 4.25: Statistical Analysis

Sl. No.	*Subject*	*N*	*Mean*	*S.D.*	*D.F.*	*Sign.*
1.	Mirzapur	750	1.22	0.416	4	0.000
2.	Sonbhadra	750	1.69	0.463		
3.	Chandauli	450	1.64	0.481		
4.	Allahabad	600	1.45	0.497		
5.	Chitrakoot	450	1.40	0.489		

Since, the significance value is less than the significant level at 0.05. Therefore, this proves that the Government plans for eradication of poverty in the five tribal districts of U.P., i.e., Mirzapur, Sonbhadra, Chandauli, Allahabad and Chitrakoot is not up to the mark of people.

It is true that all the Government officials posted in tribal areas hail from different places and of different backgrounds. Though they are posted for the noble and welfare cause of tribal people yet they do not have any sympathy for them. In many cases, posting in tribal areas is regarded as a punishment. As such, the bulk of the staff are disinterested in carrying their responsibilities. Paid employees cannot sacrifice their own and family life at the cost of tribal welfare services. Therefore, their aims are focused mainly on the exploitation of the allotted tribal funds and really they do accordingly.

During survey we could know that the tribals were not at all pleased with officials dealing. It is evident from Table 4.26 that only 16.6 per cent respondents of Naxal area and 25.3 per cent respondents of Dacoit areas reply was in the government officials favour. They told that their dealing was quite fare.

Table 4.26: Behaviour of Government Officials

District	*Total Respondents*	*Fair*	*%*	*Partiality*	*%*	*Neglected*	*%*	*Financial Exploitation*	*%*
Mirzapur	750	213	28.4	287	38.3	93	12.4	157	20.9
Sonbhadra	750	106	14.1	312	41.6	175	23.3	157	20.9
Chandauli	450	4	0.9	86	19.1	110	24.4	250	55.6
Naxal Area	1950	323	16.6	685	35.1	378	19.4	564	28.9
Allahabad	600	103	17.2	236	39.3	117	19.5	144	24.0
Chitrakoot	450	163	36.2	216	48.0	19	4.2	52	11.6
Dacoit Area	1050	266	25.3	452	43.0	136	13.0	196	18.7
Total of five Districts	3000	589	19.6	1137	37.9	514	17.1	760	25.3

35.1 per cent respondents of Naxal area and 43.0 per cent respondents of Dacoit area expressed their views that the Government officials were biased and partial in their dealing.

19.4 per cent respondents of Naxal area and 13.0 per cent of Dacoit area were irritated with their behaviour. They told that they had all the time neglected them because of their poverty and backwardness.

28.9 per cent respondents of Naxal prone area and 18.7 per cent respondents of Dacoit area told us that they listened us and paid us attention only when their palm was greased.

Objective

To find of the difference of opinion on behaviour of Government officer's during meeting with problems. The attitude of Government officials with the persons of the five tribal districts of U.P., i.e., Mirzapur, Sonbhadra, Chandauli, Allahabad and Chitrakoot.

The analysis of the data yields results in terms of mean, S.D. and Significance Value. The obtained results have been summarized in Table 4.27.

Table 4.27: Statistical Analysis

Sl. No.	*Subject*	*N*	*Mean*	*S.D.*	*D.F.*	*Sig.*
1.	Mirzapur	750	1.78	0.747	4	0.000
2.	Sonbhadra	750	2.42	0.799		
3.	Chandauli	450	3.35	0.814		
4.	Allahabad	600	2.34	1.024		
5.	Chitrakoot	450	1.75	0.786		

Since, the significance value is less than the significant level at 0.05. Therefore, the response of the respondents are against the behaviour of the officials in the five tribal districts of U.P., i.e., Mirzapur, Sonbhadra, Chandauli, Allahabad and Chitrakoot.

Several schemes are being run by the Union Government and the State Government of Uttar Pradesh for upliftment of the tribal people. Distribution of land to landless people, housing grant, loans for starting cottage industries (by I.R.D.P. and Scheduled Castes Finance Corporation and other financial sources), job, Pension for widows/widowers living under BPL and Scholarship facilities for education and other facilities are some examples. The respondents were also enquired about the benefits of these programmes.

Table 4.28: Benefits of Uplifting Programmes of the Government Received by the Respondent Households

District	*Total Respon- dents*	*Agri. Land*	*%*	*Resid. Land*	*%*	*Indira Awas*	*%*	*Scholar ship*	*%*
Mirzapur	750	21	2.8	0	0.0	244	32.5	9	1.2
Sonbhadra	750	218	29.1	0	0.0	213	28.4	183	24.4
Chandauli	450	26	5.8	0	0.0	216	48.0	218	48.4
Naxal Total	1950	265	13.6	0	0.0	673	34.5	410	21.0
Allahabad	600	267	44.5	0	0.0	186	31.0	104	17.3
Chitrakoot	450	155	34.4	0	0.0	66	14.7	67	14.9
Dacoit Total	1050	422	40.2	0	0.0	252	24.0	171	16.3
Total of five Districts	3000	687	22.9	0	0.0	925	30.8	581	19.4

District	*Total Respon- dents*	*Pension*	*%*	*Job*	*%*	*Business*	*%*
Mirzapur	750	13	1.7	0	0.0	0	0
Sonbhadra	750	177	23.6	0	0.0	0	0
Chandauli	450	80	17.8	0	0.0	0	0
Naxal Total	1950	270	13.8	0	0.0	0	0
Allahabad	600	249	41.5	0	0.0	0	0
Chitrakoot	450	80	17.8	82	18.2	0	0
Dacoit Total	1050	329	31.3	82	7.8	0	0
Total of five Districts	3000	599	20.0	82	2.7	0	0

It is evident from table 4.28 that according to their statements out of the respondents belonging to Naxal prone area, 13.6 per cent received allotment of agricultural land, 0.0 per cent residential land, 34.5 per cent Indira Awas grants, 27.0 per cent Scholarship, 13.8 per cent pension grants, 0.0 per cent job opportunity and 0.00 per cent loan for starting any sort of business. Almost the same trend is also observed in case of Dacoit prone area respondents.

There, also 40.2 per cent respondents enjoyed the benefit of agricultural land distribution, 24.0 per cent respondent got Indira Awas grants, 16.3 per cent respondents were benefited by Scholarship, 31.3 per cent respondents received old age and handicapped Pensions and 7.8

per cent respondents were blessed with some jobs, loan for business was not released to any respondents by the loaning agencies in Dacoit prone area.

The tribals and scheduled castes of all the five districts named as "*Dalit Adivasis*", deserve 100 per cent for receiving all types of benefits, facilities and grants released by the Governments because in real sense they extremely poor, landless and have been exploited since long by several agencies. During survey we realized that they were completely ignorant of all such developments and welfare programmes. Moreover, due to their ignorance, they have been befooled by the concerning authorities and mediators. That is why the percentage of recipients of the above facilities were very low.

Objective

To find out the difference of Benefits received by the household through uplifting and development programmes by the Government. To prove statistically that whether any benefits received by the households through upliftment and development programmes of government between the five tribal districts of U.P., i.e., Mirzapur, Sonbhadra, Chandauli, Allahabad and Chitrakoot.

The analysis of the data yields results in terms of mean, S.D. and Significance Value. The obtained results have been summarized in Table 4.29.

Table 4.29: Statistical Analysis

Sl. No.	*Subject*	*N*	*Mean*	*S.D.*	*D.F.*	*Sign.*
1.	Mirzapur	750	2.90	0.409	4	0.000
2.	Sonbhadra	750	2.34	0.815		
3.	Chandauli	450	2.50	0.605		
4.	Allahabad	600	2.10	0.995		
5.	Chitrakoot	450	2.31	0.951		

Since, the significance value is less than the significant level at 0.05. Therefore no such benefits is received by the respondents by the uplifting and development programmes of Government, in the five tribal districts of U.P., i.e., Mirzapur, Sonbhadra, Chandauli, Allahabad and Chitrakoot.

The Union Government has launched its development programmes to benefit in three ways; one way is to establish industrial units, power

Table 4.30: Opinion on who are being Benefited during Operation of Government Development Work

District	Total Respondents	Political persons	%	Political powerful elected from ruling party	%	Contractor	%	Mediator	%
Mirzapur	750	155	20.7	447	59.6	41	5.5	45	6.0
Sonbhadra	750	198	26.4	283	37.7	133	17.7	75	10.0
Chandauli	450	22	4.9	195	43.3	128	28.4	55	12.2
Naxal Area	1950	375	19.2	925	47.4	302	15.5	175	9.0
Allahabad	600	103	17.2	372	62.0	63	10.5	41	6.8
Chitrakoot	450	58	12.9	170	37.8	187	41.6	3	0.7
Dacoit Area	1050	161	15.3	542	51.6	250	23.8	44	4.2
Total of five Districts	3000	536	17.9	1467	48.9	552	18.4	219	7.3

District	Total Respondents	Every one	%	powerful, selected, mediator and persons having relation with officers	%	No one	%
Mirzapur	750	26	3.5	36	4.8	0	0.0
Sonbhadra	750	0	0.0	61	8.1	0	0.0
Chandauli	450	8	1.8	38	8.4	4	0.9
Naxal Area	1950	34	1.7	135	6.9	4	0.2
Allahabad	600	0	0.0	21	3.5	0	0.0
Chitrakoot	450	0	0.0	21	4.7	11	2.4
Dacoit Area	1050	0	0.0	42	4.0	11	1.0
Total of five Districts	3000	34	1.1	177	5.9	15	0.5

plants, mining, etc., which have indirect impact on the development of that tribal areas, the second way of development is to develop infrastructure in tribal areas for example construction of approachable roads, culverts, dams, facilities for water for drinking and agriculture purpose, means of communication, hospitals both for men and animals, educational institutions, etc. The third way of development is directly related to the tribal people's total welfare programmes like PDS facilities, BPL food programmes, Annapurna Yojana, Mid-day Meals Yojana, Antyodaya Yojana, Old Age Pension Yojana, National Family Benefit Yojana, SC/ST Children Scholarship, Women Welfare Programmes, Health Programmes, Handicapped Welfare Programme, Rural Development Programme like Indira Awas Yojana, Jawahar Gram Samriddhi Yojana, MNREGA and other related welfare programmes for the total upliftment of tribal people.

Undoubtedly, the Government both the Union and the State of Uttar Pradesh as well, have released billions and billions of rupees as grants for such noble cause, i.e., tribal upliftment. But where has the money gone? Why the wretched conditions of tribal people have not yet been changed? Why more than 85 per cent of the tribals are below poverty line and suffering from the extreme chronic poverty even after the expiry of 68 years of Independence in the south-eastern part of Uttar Pradesh.

Keeping all these facts in view, we also wanted to know the opinion of the tribal respondents of these five districts. If tribals are not benefited then who are, is a matter of investigation.

It is evident from Table 4.30 that the Politically (Ruling Party) powerful persons and political persons of the district have some how managed to grab the lion's share of the grant released in the name of development. The elected MLA's and MP's have upper hands in district administration. The District Magistrate and his subordinate officers are dictated terms and conditions by the MLA's and MP's and by the local leaders especially those who are in ruling party. This is naked truth and open facts that the major portion of the allotted budget is distributed among the ruling party leaders and the concerning Government officers as if their legal share. A very little portion of the budget is spent in the name of development. The economic corruption has crossed it limits. Paper formalities are shown completed by fraudulent methods. 47.4 per cent respondents in Naxal prone area and 51.6 per cent respondents in Dacoit prone area opine that ruling powerful political leaders (elected persons) have looted their development funds. The other political elected leaders and other local leaders are also involved in this affair, the respondents opinion was 19.2 per cent in Naxal prone area and 15.3 per cent in Dacoit prone area for the other leaders. There are other actors involved in this episode. They are contractors and mediators. The contractors who are in direct touch with the concerning departments get opportunity to make their share. The role of mediators can't be ignored. There are several persons who are in regular touch with the welfare departments. The concerning officers cannot deal the terms and conditions of the utilization of the allotted budget due to the fear of anticorruption and intelligence department. Therefore, they are always in search of such persons who may mediate without disclosing anything. These mediators also make money out of the budget. 18.4 per cent respondents of the total area are of the opinion that the contractors are also benefited. 7.3 per cent respondents of the total area believe that mediators are not behind in this race. 5.9 per cent respondents of the total also believed that powerful selected mediators and persons having relations with concerning officers are benefited.

Only 1.1 per cent respondents perhaps totally ignorant, have opinion that everyone is benefited. They mean that the entire tribal community is benefited. On the other hand, only 0.5 per cent respondents of the total area believe that no one has been benefited.

Objective

To find out the difference of opinion on who are being benefited during the operation of Government development work. To prove statistically the persons who are benefited in the operation of Government development work in the five tribal districts of U.P., i.e., Mirzapur, Sonbhadra, Chandauli, Allahabad and Chitrakoot.

The analysis of the data yields results in terms of mean, S.D. and Significance Value. The obtained results have been summarized in the Table 4.31.

Table 4.31: Statistical Analysis

Sl. No.	*Subject*	*N*	*Mean*	*S.D.*	*D.F.*	*Sign.*
1.	Mirzapur	750	2.28	1.264	4	0.00
2.	Sonbhadra	750	3.32	2.077		
3.	Chandauli	450	2.99	1.501		
4.	Allahabad	600	2.24	1.168		
5.	Chitrakoot	450	2.66	1.385		

Since the significance value is less than the significant level at 0.05. Therefore, it shows common opinion about the political leaders are benefited in the operation of Government development work in the five tribal districts of U.P., i.e., Mirzapur, Sonbhadra, Chandauli, Allahabad and Chitrakoot.

The Role of Gram Panchayat

The Panchayati Raj System was enforced by the late Rajeev Gandhi, the then P.M. of India. This three tier system of Indian Democracy begins from a village. Under this democratic setup villagers of a village will elect their leader known as Gram Pradhan. The Gram Pradhan Constitutes his cabinet of ministers for administration, justice and all sorts of development in his village. Therefore, Gram Panchayat is the most responsible constitutional institution which shoulders all type of responsibilities for the village development. The Union Government as well as State Government provides all financial grants related to infrastructural development, educational, health, eradication of diseases, employment and all types social welfare programmes. People's (Villagers) participation is essential in chalking out the rural programmes and making budget of the grant. In order of priority every programme should be launched with the consent and with the consultation of the villagers.

During survey and discussions with the PRI groups and with the tribals, analysis of priorities of the community work undertaken by the Panchayat, it was revealed that there were serious mismatch between need of the community and programmes undertaken by the Panchayat. Principal causes for mismatch, between the demand of the tribal community and supply programmes by the Panchayat, are poor representation of tribals in the PRIs, their lack of participation in decision making and lack of accountability of elected representatives. What is worth noting in the fact that the corruption is rampant at all levels, public as well as private level of Panchayat system.

During investigation in both the areas of tribals, i.e., Naxal Area and Dacoit Area, all the 3000 respondents were asked their opinion regarding the sincere contribution of their Gram Panchayat to which the Governments have trusted all the social, economic and political development programmes to be implemented for overall upliftment of the tribals. The 'No faith in Gram Panchayat', the percentage 47.9 per cent of respondents of Naxal area and 67.8 per cent of dacoit area, clearly indicates that Gram Panchayat's function was against the tribal

Table 4.32: Opinion of Respondents Regarding Role of Gram Panchayat in Providing Benefits

District	*Total Households*	<25%	%	25%< 50%	%	50% <75	%	>75% = 100%	%	*No faith*	%
Mirzapur	750	54	7.2	146	19.5	168	22.4	82	10.9	300	40.0
Sonbhadra	750	30	4.0	261	34.8	53	7.1	41	5.5	365	48.7
Chandauli	450	46	10.2	51	11.3	81	18.0	2	0.4	270	60.0
Naxal Area	1950	130	6.7	458	23.5	302	15.5	125	6.4	935	47.9
Allahabad	600	0	0.0	145	24.2	62	10.3	0	0.0	393	65.5
Chitrakoot	450	0	0.0	93	20.7	38	8.4	0	0.0	319	70.9
Dacoit Area	1050	0	0.0	238	22.7	100	9.5	0	0.0	712	67.8
Total of five Districts	3000	130	4.3	696	23.2	402	13.4	125	4.2	1647	54.9

development. All the funds, instead of distributing among the weaker sections of the village, it goes in the pocket of Gram Pradhan who is mostly dominant landlords of the village.

However, 7.2 per cent in Mirzapur, 4.0 per cent in Sonbhadra, 10.2 per cent in Chandauli, 0.0 per cent in Allahabad and 0.0 per cent respondents in Chitrakoot were of the opinion that less than 25 per cent inhabitants could enjoy the benefits through Gram Panchayat. Only 10.9 per cent in Mirzapur, 5.5 per cent in Sonbhadra, 0.4 per cent in Chandauli, 0.0 per cent in Allahabad and 0.0 per cent in Chitrakoot tribal areas community believe, 75 to 100 per cent benefits are being provided by the Panchayat. Inhabitants of tribal areas are unaware of when and where public works programmes would be taken up by the Gram Panchayat. Decision is never taken openly in Gram Sabha. It is always taken by the Sarpanch of that very village secretly. The following Table 4.33 shows the mismatch between community needs and the supply by the Panchayat.

Table 4.33: Mismatch between Community Needs and the Supply by Gram Panchayat

Work Undertaken	*Community Needs*				*Total*
	Infra Structure	*Service*	*Agriculture development*	*Employment*	
Infrastructure	11%	16%	4%	10%	41%
Service	2%	2%	1%	0%	5%
Agriculture development	21%	17%	6%	10%	54%
Employment	0%	0%	0%	0%	0%
Total	34%	35%	11%	20%	100%

It is evident from Table 4.33 that only in the name of agriculture development the 54 per cent appears to be very high. The other percentage in the infrastructure is 41 per cent and in employment percentage is 0 per cent is quite low. The only employment the tribals get is from deforestation and that too mainly for seedling transplanting. The other complaints of the respondents were that employment and agricultural programmes have benefited the landlords and other mafias of that area.

Besides, all the development and social welfare programmes, there are several social, religious, economic and personal problems with which the tribal community in their everyday life face. Family problems, marriage problems, loan clearance problems, etc., need to be solved through mediating by the Gram Panchayat, Pradhan of that village. The Gram Pradhan having the sovereign power in the village is capable of solving their problems and to maintain peace, law and order among the village community.

What was the role of Panchayat of the respondents community has also been analysed through Table 4.34.

After analysing the data, the results came that 4.9 per cent respondents in Naxal area tribals and 0.0 per cent in Dacoit area expressed their opinion that the Gram Panchayat has played active role in solving the problems related to land. The loan problem is very acute among tribals. They often take loan either to fulfil their basic needs or for performance of social and religious customs. As they are suffering from chronic poverty they find themselves incapable of repayment of loans. In the case of defaulter they have to face a lot of problems. Therefore, in this worst condition they seek help from the Gram Panchayat and the Gram Pradhan. The zero per cent response from the Gram Panchayat and the Pradhan reflects the extreme negligence and cruelty from the side of Gram Panchayat. Only the percentage in solving their family problems is very high. 49 per cent in Naxal area tribals and 27.6 per cent in Dacoit area tribals accepted that the Gram Panchayat has played vital role in solving their family problems. On the other side, the frustration arose of the tribals when we see that 44.5 per cent respondent of Naxal area and 72.4 per cent in Dacoit area tribal respondents replied that their Gram Panchayat was completely neutral in resolving even their problems related to their families. Thus, conclusion can be drawn that the Gram Panchayat is not at all fare for the development of the tribals.

In addition to Government programmes, there are other agencies also by which development and welfare programmes are being run parallel to the Government. During survey, several Non-Government Organizations (NGO's) were found engaged in overall development and welfare of the tribals. Several religious and human service agencies were also found engaged in welfare activities of the down trodden tribal communities. Some foreign agencies were also found involved in the welfare programmes in these districts.

Sri Gopal Bhai is very renowned social activist, who sacrificed for the welfare of the Kol tribal communities is worth appreciable. He is Director of a voluntary organization named 'Akhil Bhartiya Samaj Sewak Sansthan (ABSSS)', Chitrakoot. This NGO started working during middle eighties. According to the ABSSS estimates, its efforts during the last 20 years have led to the availability of 4,000 acres of land to nearly 1,400

Table 4.34: Role of Gram Panchayat in Solving the Problems of the Community of the Respondents (Sample 3,000)

District	*Total Househod*	*Land*	*Land %*	*Loan Clearance*	*Loan Clearance %*	*Family problems*	*Family problems %*	*All*	*All %*	*No help*	*No help %*
Mirzapur	750	78	10.4	29	3.86	416	55.46	0	0.0	227	30.26
Sonbhadra	750	101	13.4	0	0.0	315	42.0	0	0.0	334	44.5
Chandauli	450	0	0	0	0.0	450	100.0	0	0.0	0	0.0
Naxalite area	1950	179	9.1	29	1.4	1181	60.5	0	0.0	561	28.7
Allahabad	600	0	0	0	0.0	40	6.7	0	0.0	560	93.3
Chitrakoot	450	0	0	0	0.0	250	55.6	0	0.0	200	44.4
Dacoit Area	1050	0	0	0	0	290	27.6	0	0.0	760	72.4
Total of five Districts	3000	179	5.9	29	0.96	1471	49.00	0	0	1321	44.93

Kol families. The land was previously grabbed by the influential persons (known as Dadus). ABSSS has helped to check the practice of bonded labour by helping in official and non-official surveys of this practice which helped to establish the large scale existence of the system of bonded labour in Patha region. It was not only help to landless persons to get some land, but it was also in many cases crucial to make available some irrigation facilities also. ABSSS tried to do this by constructing several check dams, tanks and wells. In Tikuniya village a check dam made by ABSSS, made it possible to grow good crops on land which was entirely barren earlier.

Next to agriculture, forestry is the second most important source of livelihood for tribal people, ABSSS also helped to get a higher income from the seasonal work of plucking *tendu* leaves and this organization agitated several times for the payment of dues of *tendu* leaves collection. It also intervened in the marketing of *mahua* in such a way that several families could get a significant benefit. ABSSS brought to light several glaring cases of misappropriating of funds, including cases in which the supposed beneficiaries of Government schemes suffered a deterioration in their living conditions. Many villages of Patha region suffer from the acute water scarcity. ABSSS has been careful to stress low cost self-reliant methods ABSSS efforts over the last two decades, have also made available education to children from poor families which could ultimately prove to be of greater significance in changing the power structure in Patha region and improving the working and living conditions of Kol tribals and other weaker sections. As result of this effort, many Kol leaders male-female both occupied the post of Gram Pradhan. ABSSS tried to create conditions in which Kol tribals and other weaker sections can vote more freely in various elections.

There is another social activist named Sri Shyam Narayan Lal Srivastava in Robertsganj, Sonbhadra. He is editor of a newspaper *Mahakol Samachar Vivaran* Sonbhadra. He is an advocate by profession. Previously he was District Government Standing Council and discharged his legal duties for several years and resigned on 21-12-2001 on humanitarian ground. He has strong feeling that the great injustice is being done to the tribals of Sonbhadra, Mirzapur and Chandauli district. He felt that they had been deprived of their ancestral land and forest produce which were once their main sources of livelihood. Due to construction of Rihand Dam, several power plants, Chemical factories, coal mines and for making places as Ash dams, nearly 4233.72 acres of their land has been occupied by the Government and the concerning agencies. Tribals

Table 4.35: Agencies which Took Initiative for Development Programmes and Welfare Programmes in Tribal Areas

District	*Total Households*	*Govt.*	*%*	*NGO*	*%*	*No Idea*	*%*
Mirzapur	750	421	56.1	304	40.5	25	3.3
Sonbhadra	750	426	56.8	190	25.3	134	17.9
Chandauli	450	240	53.3	177	39.3	33	7.3
Naxal Total	1950	1087	55.7	671	34.4	192	9.8
Allahabad	600	360	60.0	240	40.0	0	0.0
Chitrakoot	450	251	55.8	199	44.2	0	0.0
Dacoit Total	1050	611	58.2	439	41.8	0	0.0
Total of five Districts	3000	1698	56.6	1110	37.0	192	6.4

were displaced without providing appropriate compensation to them. Their multiple displacement, no proper rehabilitation and the air, water and soil pollution produced by these power plants, industries, mines have brought them at the verge of malnutrition, starvation, ill health and death. The forest produce was the main source of their livelihood has been taken away by the forest department. Under land reform movement, the land distributed in their names was grabbed by the maphias. Even after the enforcement of the Forest Right Act 2006, they have not been given justice in this regard. For all these causes of rights of the tribal people of Naxal prone area, Sri Shyam Narayan Lal Srivastava has been fighting by filing applications to concerning authorities and later on filing several writ petitions in the Hon'ble High Court of Allahabad and the Hon'ble Supreme Court, New Delhi. In spite of the orders of the Hon'ble courts, no proper relief has yet been granted to the tribals. The power plant authorities, industrial units and coal mines authorities have not yet searched any other means to minimize the water, air and the soil pollution problems of their regions.

There is one lady named Roma post-graduate from Delhi a member of Steering Committee, National Forum of Forests people and forests workers has been working here in Sonbhadra for the past two decades and she is the only woman in Uttar Pradesh to have been booked under the National Security. She was arrested along with three others for leading an agitation in August 2007 demanding land ownership rights for tribals as per the new Forest Act 2006. She believed that tribals of this south-eastern region of Uttar Pradesh are peace loving people, that is the reason why Maoists and Naxals have not been able to establish their bases in the tribal belt. But any attempt to force tribals out of their land would push them towards ultras.

One question was put-up before the respondents about their knowledge of agencies by whom their development and welfare works were going on. The above Table shows 65.7 per cent respondents of Naxal prone area replied that the development and welfare programmes were being run by the State Government whereas 46.2 per cent respondents also favoured to Non-Government Organisations. They expressed their feelings that their problems had been dealt by the NGOs in very informal ways as if they were their members of the family. Similarly, in Dacoit prone areas 55.9 per cent respondents believed that the State Government was doing their development and welfare work and 44.1 per cent respondents also believed that the NGOs were enhancing their development and welfare work. Only 7.2 per cent in Naxal prone areas and 0.0 per cent in Dacoit areas expressed their views of ignorance of all these affairs.

Note

1. Niranjan Pani and Jitendra Shahoo, *Tribal Development.*

References

1. Hasnain, Nadeem, 2007, *Tribal India*, New Royal Book Compnay, Lucknow.
2. Somashekhar, K., 2008, *Developmental Programmes and Social Change among the Tribals*, Serial Publications, New Delhi.
3. Verma, R.C., 2002, *Indian Tribes, Through the Ages*, Director, Publications Division, New Delhi.
4. Pani, Niranjan, Sahoo, Jitendra, 2008, *Tribal Development*, Mahamaya Publishing House, New Delhi.
5. Census of India 2001.
6. Government of India (1958), *Report of the Commissioner for Scheduled Castes and Scheduled Tribes*. Ministry of Home Affairs, Manager of Government Publications, New Delhi.
7. Government of India (1960), *Report of the Committee on Special Multi Purpose Tribal Blocks (Elwin Committee Report)*, Ministry of Home Affairs, New Delhi.

8. Government of India (1975), *Tribal Development in the Fifth Plan: Some basic Policy Papers*, Ministry of Home Affairs, New Delhi.
9. Government of India (1980), *Report of the Working Group on Tribal Development during Sixth Plan*, Ministry of Home Affairs, New Delhi.
10. Government of India (1985), *Report of the Working Group on Development of Scheduled Tribes during Seven Plan*, Ministry of Home Affairs, New Delhi.
11. Government of India (1991), *Census of India, Ministry of Home Affairs. Final Population*, Vol. II, Series I, New Delhi.
12. Government of India (1992), *Eighth Five Year Plan*, Vol. II, Planning Commission, New Delhi.
13. Hasnain, Nadeem (1991), *Tribal India Today*, Harnam Publications, Delhi.

Chapter 5
Indicators of Development

I. ECONOMIC GROWTH AS AN IMPORTANT INDICATOR OF DEVELOPMENT

Economic growth is an important indicator of Development. It is true that the *adivasis* were completely unfamiliar with the money economy, but their deep understanding of life sciences is evident from the fact that they know that ownership and control of the basic resources of land is the solution to the problems of livelihood of all agrarian people. Urban intellectuals and economists fail to look at the implementing agrarian reforms. The life experience of the common people has led them to believe that no dose from the Government or other agencies will ever solve the problem of hunger. It is they themselves who have to organise themselves and fight to recapture their lost land.

The tribal communities in South-Eastern and Western part of U.P. may be generally classified into five groups on the economic levels:

1. food gathering,
2. passtoralism,
3. settled cultivation,
4. artisan, and
5. mining and industrial labour.

The tribal belt of Sonbhadra, Mirzapur, Chandauli, Allahabad and Chitrakoot is characterized by resource poor, technologically stagnant and remote from State and markets where depletion of resources like land, forest and water has been a history. In this situation, the livelihood struggles and coping with resourcelessness contribute to high incidence of poverty. The livelihood struggles end up creating a vicious circle of multidimensional unfreedom; livelihood struggles under shocks prompt a social process of mortgage and asset losses, borrowing and inability to service, debt, hunger and migration.

This livelihood mechanism does provide sustenance but at the cost of freedom in a multiple way to the households. They live in inhuman conditions at the destination, their access to education not served, their opportunity to develop skills adversely affected and health services and situation made poor by any standard, above all, they often have to face abuses. Disturbing it may appear but the process is difficult to break without massive drive to create new opportunities in the economy.

The forest was an important source of fuel, fodder, food, timber and medicines. The collection of minor forest produce such as mahua, chiraunjee, tendu, amla, lakh, etc. allow them to earn some money seasonally. The forests in this region abounds in numerous species of trees each having multiple uses in the lives of tribal people. In times of famines, forest provided food security. Maize, wheat, paddy and coarse grains such as koddo, sawan, etc. were the main cereals of this South-Eastern part of Uttar Pradesh.

Agriculture has been the main source of livelihood of the tribal people and it was the mainstay with cattle forming the backbone of the local economy. Though landholdings were not large, the people could nevertheless, by sheer hard work and industry, produced enough for the family's consumption. The surplus was sold locally to buy necessities such as salt, kerosene, clothes, etc. Almost every family owned much and other cattle and there was plenty of milk.

Agriculture is rainfed wells serve less than 15 per cent of the cropped area during *Rabi* for wheat. In Chitrakoot and Allahabad tribal belt for land productivity is poor and monsoon failures are frequent, livestock and migration constitute major coping mechanisms. Yardsticks of wealth is the number of cattle, goats and hens that a family possesses. Goats are important assets that can be converted into liquid money. Moreover, pressures amongst the tribals have resulted in rapid fragmentation of agricultural land. The fragmentation of land has become a source of poverty in tribal people. Thus, seasonal migration becomes necessary for monetary supplement of the limited production base.

But the severe crisis in tribal economy started and their poverty level turned into chronic poverty level with the installation of power plants, with the process of displacement without any appropriate rehabilitation, with forest department claiming its control over forest land and uprooting the original inhabitants and with grabbing of allotted *Patta* land by mafias and feudal landlords by fraudulent methods in the South-Eastern part of

Uttar Pradesh. As per report of the National Sample Survey Organisation 86 per cent of *dalit* households (160 million or 19% of SCs) are landless or nearly landless. Those who own land either own too little or lack adequate capital for purchasing resources for cultivation like seed, fertilizers and/or hiring farm implements. Lack of access or inadequate access to agricultural land and capital leaves them no option but to resort to manual labour since 60 per cent rural tribal and SCs working as manual wage labourers. Landless agricultural labourers work for a few kilograms of rice or Rs. 15 to Rs. 35 per day much below the status prescribed minimum wage rate. Many labourers owe debts to their employers or other moneylenders. As a result of it, the vast majority of bonded labourers are from *dalit adivasis* and almost bonded children are from *dalit adivasis*.

The unemployment and underemployment rate is highest among the *dalit adivasis* in comparison to other castes. The level of employment and wage rates further determines their earnings. Obviously, they would suffer from low income and consumption and resultant greater level of poverty. Their income level is much less than the below poverty line. According to the National Sample Survey Organisation, the total calories per head had fallen from 2,211 calories in 1983 to 2,149 calories in the year 2000—a decline of 72 calories per head, which is much lower than Brazil, China, Kenya and Tanzania. Consequently, often several cases of malnutrition, starvation and suicidal cases have been flashed in the newspapers of the tribal people belonging to this region. Recently one public institution named *Hungam* (Hunger and Malnutrition) has surveyed one hundred districts of India in which one lakh children below five years of age, were studied. The findings were very alarming. 42 per cent children were found weak and of retarded height. They were acute sufferer of malnutrition. Every third child is malnourished. It is very strange that the percentage of malnutrition cases in India is twice in comparison to the children of African countries. It is all because of extreme poverty conditions prevailing in India. Table 5.1 show the High Poverty Region (41-60%), very high Poverty Region (above 60%) and official estimates of rural head count ratio of poverty in India.

Table 5.1: High Poverty Region (41-60%)

Assam Plain Western	49.9
Assam Hill	41.3
Bihar Northern	58.7

(Contd.)

Table 5.1 (*Contd.*)

Bihar Central	54.0
M.P. Chhattisgarh	44.0
MP Central	50.1
MP South	46.1
Maharashtra Inland Northern	47.2
Maharashtra Inland Central	50.0
Maharashtra Inland Eastern	49.1
Orissa Coastal	45.4
Orissa Northern	45.6
Rajasthan Southern	45.9
TN Coastal Northern	43.6
Uttar Pradesh Central	52.2
Uttar Pradesh Eastern	48.6
West Bengal Eastern	45.0
Arunachal Pradesh	45.0
Manipur	45.0
Meghalaya	45.0
Mizoram	45.0
Nagaland	45.0
Sikkim	45.0
Tripura	45.0
Dadra & Nagar Haveli	51.9

Source: NIRD (1999); Deator and Dreze (2002).

Table 5.2: Very High Poverty Region (Above 60%)

Bihar Southern	62.40
MP Southern-Western	68.20
Orissa Southern	69.00
Uttar Pradesh Southern	66.70

Table 5.3 presents official estimates of income poverty in major Indian States between 1973-74 to 1999-2000. While significant reduction in poverty has been achieved in Jammu & Kashmir, Punjab and Haryana, Himachal Pradesh, Kerala and Andhra Pradesh, Orissa, Bihar and Madhya Pradesh and Uttar Pradesh continue to remain most poor States of the country.

Table 5.3: Official Estimates of Rural Head Count Ratio of Poverty in India

State	1973-74	1977-73	1983-00	1987-88	1993-94	1994-2000
Andhra Pradesh	48.40	38.10	26.50	20.90	15.90	10.50
Assam	52.70	59.80	42.60	39.30	45.00	40.30
Bihar	68.00	63.20	64.40	52.60	58.20	44.00
Gujarat	46.30	41.80	29.80	28.70	22.20	12.40
Haryana	34.20	27.70	20.60	16.20	28.00	7.40
Himachal Pradesh	27.40	33.50	17.00	16.30	30.30	7.50
Jammu & Kashmir	45.50	42.90	26.00	25.70	30.30	4.70
Karnataka	55.10	48.20	36.30	32.80	29.90	16.80
Kerala	59.20	51.50	39.00	29.10	25.80	9.40
Madhya Pradesh	62.70	62.50	48.90	41.90	40.60	37.20
Maharashtra	57.70	64.00	45.20	40.80	37.90	23.20
Orissa	77.30	72.40	67.50	57.60	49.70	47.80
Punjab	28.20	16.40	13.20	12.60	12.00	6.00
Rajasthan	44.80	35.90	33.50	33.20	26.50	13.50
Tamil Nadu	57.40	57.70	54.00	45.80	32.50	20.00
Uttar Pradesh	56.50	47.60	46.40	41.10	42.30	31.10
West Bengal	73.20	68.30	63.00	48.30	40.80	31.70
India	56.40	53.10	46.60	39.10	37.30	26.80

Source: NIRD (1999) Deator and Dreze (2002).

Analysing the variations in income poverty across regions, the National Institute of Rural Development has shown that except Bihar, there is heterogeneity in each State (1999). Different regions of Bihar are uniformly poor as it is evident from the above Table 5.3, whereas all other States demonstrate variations in the incidence of poverty across regions. Delhi, Goa, Daman & Diu, northern Punjab and coastal of Karnataka have low incidence of poverty. On the other hand, Southern Orissa, South-Western Madhya Pradesh, South-Eastern Uttar Pradesh and South Bihar are the most poor regions of the country.

Opinion of the Sample Households towards Government Development and Welfare Programmes for Eradicating Poverty

Poverty is a complex interaction of resourcelessness, livelihood struggles and dishonest use of public funds. The nexus of political elites, bureaucracy and contractors, disconnects the poor from development affairs of the tribals. Access failure to health care and education services to the marginalized section perpetually keeps them poor in terms of human capabilities. Chronic poverty is also a manifestation of a symmetrical command of resource and decision of their use in tribal places. Decentralised governance has failed to influence poverty owing to the nefarious nexus that encourages corruption and wasteful use of resources. Chronic poor, owing to their inability to bridge, have failed to get economic benefits. Keeping all these naked truths in view, the opinion of the respondent households have been obtained through the following Table 5.4 regarding the government plans for eradicating poverty from their lives (D.C. Sah, Ashis Bhatt: 24).

Table 5.4: Opinion of the Sample Households towards Government Development and Welfare Programmes for Eradicating Poverty

District	*Total Households*	*Positive*	*%*	*Negative*	*%*
Mirzapur	750	222	29.6	528	70.4
Sonbhadra	750	293	39.1	457	60.9
Chandauli	450	164	36.4	286	63.6
Naxal Total	1950	679	34.8	1271	65.2
Allahabad	600	275	45.8	290	48.3
Chitrakoot	450	178	39.6	272	60.4
Dacoit Total	1050	453	43.1	562	53.5
Total of five Districts	3000	1132	37.7	1833	61.1

It is evident from Table 5.4 that 70.4 per cent in Mirzapur, 60.9 per cent in Sonbhadra, 63.6 per cent in Chandauli, 48.3 per cent in Allahabad and 60.4 per cent in Chitrakoot respondents of the households expressed their opinion that whatsoever have been done by the Government on development plans and welfare programmes, they have not benefited the tribal mass. Instead, the grant received in the name of plans and welfare programme, have been looted by the Government officials, contractors and Panchayat leaders. They have distributed their share among them. As consequent, their poverty had gone down to chronic poverty. The percentage of those who had positive opinion regarding these plans and programmes were very less.

The most of the tribals of South-Eastern part of Uttar Pradesh are much below the poverty line. Their main sources of their livelihood have been agricultural production, forest produce, wages earned from agricultural labourhood, some other household cottage industries and cattle business. Due to grabbing practice of their land by outsider and ban on using forest produce, have made them chronic poor. But any how they have to meet out their minimum daily requirements. In spite of their dedication towards work and hard work, they receive a very less amount

Table 5.5: Average Monthly Income per Household from all Sources of Income

District	Total households	Size of Household	Average Income/ household	Per Head
Mirzapur	750	7.5	1794	239.00
Sonbhadra	750	5.8	1783	307.00
Chandauli	450	7.0	1610	230.00
Naxal Total	1950	6.8	1729	254.00
Allahabad	600	6.7	1488	222.00
Chitrakoot	450	6.3	1493	237.00
Dacoit Total	1050	6.5	1491	229.00
Total of five Districts	3000	6.7	1610	240.00

in return. After analyzing the Table 5.5, the result shows that the per head average income comes to Rs. 322 per month. It is much below the national below poverty level amount of Rs. 368 per month per head. The average size of the family found was 5 in each household. The average income in Mirzapur was Rs. 1,794 per month, Rs. 1,783 in Sonbhadra, Rs. 1,610 in Chandauli, Rs. 1,488 in Allahabad and Rs. 1,491 per month in Chitrakoot per household. Maximum households were found poor in Allahabad and Chitrakoot. The average total income, Rs. 1610 in all the five districts shows that these tribals are really suffering from chronic poverty.

Table 5.6: Availability of Two Times Meals Regularly throughout the Year in Sample Households

District	Total House-holds	No. of families with Food throughout year	Regular Food %	No. of families without food throughout the year	No food for year %
Mirzapur	750	150	20.0	600	80.0
Sonbhadra	750	156	20.8	596	79.5
Chandauli	450	172	38.2	278	61.8
Naxalite Area	1950	478	24.5	1474	75.6
Allahabad	600	229	38.2	371	61.8
Chitrakoot	450	185	41.1	265	58.9
Dacoit Area	1050	414	39.4	636	60.6
Total of five districts	3000	892	29.7	2110	70.3

Table 5.6 shows that in Mirzapur and Sonbhadra districts, the availability of regular meals for both the times in households were 20.0

per cent and 20.8 per cent respectively. 80.0 per cent in Mirzapur and 79.5 per cent in Sonbhadra tribals were not in a position to meet out two times meal throughout the year.

In Chandauli the per cent 61.8 was less as compared to Mirzapur and Sonbhadra. In case of Chitrakoot and Allahabad the unavailability of two times meal percentage were 58.9 and 61.8 respectively.

Objective

To find out the difference of information on No-food days. Some of the months are hard for the household for getting food twice in a day in five tribal districts of U.P., i.e., Mirzapur, Sonbhadra, Chandauli, Allahabad and Chitrakoot.

The analysis of the data yields results in terms of mean, S.D. and critical ratio. The obtained results have been summarized in the Table 5.7.

Table 5.7: Statistical Analysis

Sl. No.	*Subject*	*N*	*Mean*	*S.D.*	*D.F.*	*Sig.*
1.	Mirzapur	750	1.85	0.356	4	0.00
2.	Sonbhadra	750	1.46	0.507		
3.	Chandauli	450	1.62	0.486		
4.	Allahabad	600	1.62	0.486		
5.	Chitrakoot	450	1.59	0.493		

Since, the significance value is less than the significant level at 0.05. Therefore, it shows that mostly the household don't get food twice in a day in some months of the year in the five tribal districts of U.P., i.e., Mirzapur, Sonbhadra, Chandauli, Allahabad and Chitrakoot.

The percentage shown in the graphs given below is based on the 892 households of regular food and 2,110 households with no food all the year.

Agriculture produce, forest produce, job as agricultural labour, some cottage production, cattle, etc., have been the main sources of income in tribal society. Due to upper hands of forest department and maphias, contractors and feudal landlords, their sources of income have been reduced. Consequently, they have gone down much below the poverty line. It is not at all sure that they would get their meal in the next morning. Mushar and Ghasia tribes due to their extreme poverty eat bread made of grass. Chamar in tribal areas accept dead animal flesh as their main food.

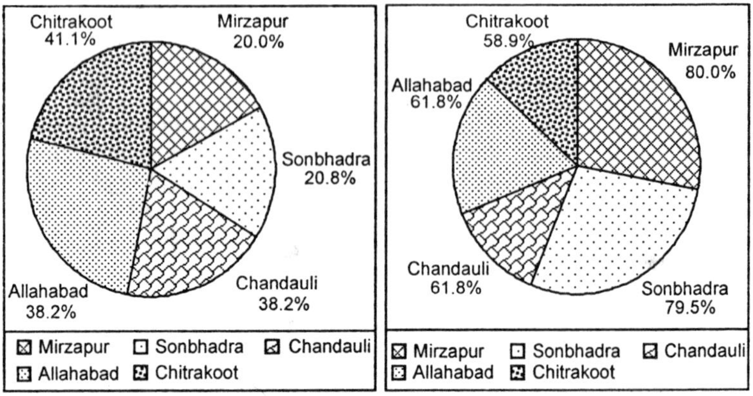

Fig. 5.1: (a) Regular Food, (b) No Food All the Year

It is beyond imagination for urban people that how they make themselves alive in the scarcity of food items in their forest villages.

Therefore, this sort of question was put-up before the respondents in order to know their real economic conditions.

Table 5.6 shows that 20.0 per cent in Mirzapur, 20.8 per cent in Sonbhadra, 38.2 per cent in Chandauli, 38.2 per cent in Allahabad and 41.1 per cent in Chitrakoot respondents were somehow in a position to meet out their food both the times throughout the year. But there is no guarantee of availability of money by which they could manage food for their families.

It can be concluded that the tribals belonging to Sonbhadra and Mirzapur are relatively more poor than Chandauli, Allahabad and Chitrakoot tribals. Thus, 70.3 per cent households are not capable of meeting out two time meals in a day throughout the year. It shows a clear indication of their extreme poverty. There is no guarantee of regular sources of income by which they could manage for their families.

Most of the families are born in debt, live in debt and die in debt. The tribals are improvident in their habits and always need money to fulfil social obligations and rituals which result in exploitation by money lenders. Small amount of money is borrowed at high rate of interest from time-to-time and that is fradulently multiplied into a sum beyond their capacity to repay. Therefore, their indebtedness and exploitation are the harrowing features of the tribal economy. At the household level it is minimum consumption requirements as well as lack of resources for carrying on gainful activity and unemployment. According to sample survey to the Planning Commission nearly 85 per cent tribal families are affected by indebtedness. The tribals borrow money from both the organised or institutionalized sources represented by private money lenders, shopkeepers, friends and relatives. More than 70 per cent tribals take loan by private money lenders. Cheating and intimidations and freely used by the traders and local non-tribal merchants, land alienation by the non-tribal immigrants and dominant groups is also a regular feature. Money economy has been gradually substituted by barter system. The innocent tribals could not fathom the evil designs of the money lenders who not only disturbed their economy but also snatched away the smiles from their innocent faces.

During survey in the present study we found in all the five districts of tribal areas that nearly 99 per cent tribal households were somehow involved in endless process of money lending. Causes for indebtedness were several in number. In the Table 5.8 some causes have been explained by the respondents of their indebtedness.

It is evident from Table 5.3 that the respondents have received loans for their abject poverty, for repayment of their previous loan, for treatment during illness, for child education, for their agricultural enhancement, for marriage function, for food, clothes, for cattle and poultry, for litigation, business and others.

Table 5.8 shows that in the Naxal affected area 2.4 per cent respondents took loan due to their abject poverty, 0.10 per cent for loan repayment, 25.0 per cent for treatment during illness, 0.9 per cent for child education, 5.5 per cent for their agricultural enhancement, 5.8 per cent for marriage function, 6.4 per cent for food and clothes, 0.0 per cent for poultry, 0.0 per cent litigation, 0.2 per cent for animal husbandry and 0.7 per cent for business.

If we analyse the total data of all the five districts, we find maximum percentage of loan, i.e., 21.0 has been taken by the tribal during their illness, the second maximum percentage of loan for arrangement of food and clothes for their family, the third maximum percentage, i.e., 7.3 per cent loan has been taken on the occasion of marriage ceremony. The percentage for agricultural development was 7.3. The loan taken in the condition of abject poverty comes the next. As regards child education, is only 0.6 per cent respondents took loan for their children education. Thus, the conclusion can be drawn that the tribals here in all the five districts are least interested in educating their children. The main causes of their indebtedness were illness, marriage, and agricultural activities. We can draw conclusions that the main reasons for indebtedness in tribal are lack of awareness about sources of institutional finances and existing

Table 5.8: Reasons of Taking Loan

District	*Total Households*	*No Income*	*%*	*Loan for Land*	*%*	*Illness*	*%*	*Child. Edu.*	*%*	*Agri.*	*%*
Mirzapur	750	4	0.5	1	0.1	266	35.5	12	1.6	70	9.3
Sonbhadra	750	42	5.6	0	0.0	117	15.6	0	0.0	32	4.3
Chandauli	450	0	0.0	0	0.0	105	23.3	5	1.1	6	1.3
Naxal Total	1950	46	2.4	1	0.1	488	25.0	17	0.9	108	5.5
Allahabad	600	40	6.7	0	0.0	95	15.8	0	0.0	18	3.0
Chitrakoot	450	0	0.0	0	0.0	48	10.7	0	0.0	12	2.7
Dacoit Total	1050	40	3.8	0	0.0	143	13.6	0	0.0	30	2.9
Total of five Districts	3000	86	2.9	1	0.0	631	21.0	17	0.6	138	4.6

District	*Total Households*	*Marriage*	*%*	*Food & Cloth*	*%*	*Poultry*	*%*	*Legal Exp.*	*%*	*Animal Husbandry*	*%*	*Business*	*%*
Mirzapur	750	28	3.7	40	5.3	0	0.0	0	0.0	0	0.0	0	0.0
Sonbhadra	750	58	7.7	49	6.5	0	0.0	0	0.0	4	0.5	12	1.6
Chandauli	450	28	6.2	36	8.0	0	0.0	0	0.0	0	0.0	2	0.4
Naxal Total	1950	114	5.8	125	6.4	0	0.0	0	0.0	4	0.2	14	0.7
Allahabad	600	69	11.5	11	1.8	0	0.0	0	0.0	0	0.0	0	0.0
Chitrakoot	450	37	8.2	85	18.9	0	0.0	0	0.0	0	0.0	3	0.7
Dacoit Total	1050	106	10.1	96	9.1	0	0.0	0	0.0	0	0.0	3	0.3
Total of five Districts	3000	220	7.3	221	7.4	0	0.0	0	0.0	4	0.1	17	0.6

protection, inability to follow complicated procedure to obtain loan and consumer credit from institutional sources, indifferent attitude of Government and bank officials, private money lenders willingness to advance money to the tribals without any security, the money lenders repose full trust in the word of mouth of the tribals, absence of alternative credit facility has compelled the tribals to compromise their fate with the money lenders and accept indebtedness as almost an inescapable aspect of their existence, lack of supply of essential commodities and agricultural inputs of fair price and lack of employment opportunities.

Due to the hedonistic type of world view, the tribals have very little savings. Naturally, when they are in need of money, they are forced to depend on others particularly on the non-tribal money lenders. Under this system, a person who takes a loan from land owner is required to serve him just like a slave according to the terms and conditions of the loan. Quite often, if he is unable to repay the loan, slavery in terms of bonded labour descends to his son or even to generation to generation.

Table 5.9: Labour Conditions of Respondent Households

Labour Conditions	*Naxal Area*	*%*	*Dacoit Area*	*%*
Bonded	1716	88	399	88
Non-Bonded	234	12	651	62
Total	1950	100	1050	100

According to the survey conducted by the National Sample Survey Organisation, the number of bonded labourers in the country was estimated to be about 3.54 lakh. According to an estimate of the programme evaluation organization of the Planning Commission about 83 per cent of the total number of bonded labourers belonged to scheduled castes and scheduled tribes. Such labourers are more in the places with feudal background. Chitrakoot and Allahabad, i.e., the 'Patha' Area of the State has the maximum percentage of bonded labourers. The feudal landlordship has been prevailing dominantly since Muslim period. Indebtedness and exploitation have been the harrowing features of the tribal economy. The tribals appear to accept indebtedness as an inevitable and inescapable aspects of their existence. Therefore, the bonded labourhood is the result of indebtedness which has been prevailing for a long time among certain economically exploited and weaker sections of the society.

Table 5.9 shows that 88 per cent respondents were working as bonded labourers in the feudal landlords families in Dacoit prone area whereas in Naxal prone area the per cent of bonded labourers was 38 per cent. The maximum percentage of landlords had been of upper caste people in Chitrakoot and Allahabad. In agrarian society all types of power are vested in feudal landlords. The dominant caste is capable of taking any arbitrary decision in their own favour. Therefore, the feudal landlords of Patha region exploited the tribal people by keeping them as their slaves. And these slaves has no right to express their views because they have been obliged by giving loan to them. Due to their poverty and ignorance they will never be free from their debt even after his generation.

As a consequence, they will remain bonded labourers from generation to generation. In case they show their resentment, they are tortured, their women are raped, ousted from the villages or are killed by the landlords. In Sonbhadra, Chandauli and Mirzapur, there has never been a long history of feudal landlordship. Therefore, the percentage of bonded labour is comparatively less in these areas. The main problem was that they were facing land alienation problems due to the Government plan and entrance of outsiders as maphias and contractors who grabbed their land.

During survey it was found that the tribals who have repeatedly been displaced by installation of different Government projects and industries, were almost hand to mouth. The number of families living below the poverty line has actually gone up. Majority of the tribal households both in Naxal prone area and dacoit prone area were in absolute poverty. Frequent displacement, land alienation and establishments of industries are the main causes of poverty in Sonbhadra, Mirzapur and Chandauli, whereas grabbing of land, indebtedness and bonded labour customs are the main causes of poverty in Chitrakoot and Allahabad tribal areas. Owing to failing monsoon and indifferent agricultural performance, the dacoit area, i.e., Bundelkhand zone in which Chitrakoot comes, the rural masses have been marginalized. Due to poor resources and inhabitation in remote area in forest they are almost cut off from the headquarters, market, health centre and bank, etc. Therefore, the livelihood struggles and coping with resourcelessness contribute to high incidence of chronic poverty. Chronic poverty is not a product created by shocks and resourcelessness. The following Table 5.10 shows the condition proving the chronic poverty in three districts in Naxal prone area and the two districts in dacoit prone area.

It is evident from Table 5.10 that the average size of the house in Sonbhadra, Chandauli and Mirzapur was 5 and also in Chitrakoot and Allahabad. The average monthly income per family was Rs. 1,729 and Rs. 1,491 in Naxal prone area and dacoit area respectively. If we calculate the monthly income per head in one household comes to Rs. 349.32 and

Table 5.10: Conditions Proving the Chronic Poverty among Sample Households

Sl. No.	*Item*	*Naxal Area*	*Dacoit Area*
1.	Average number of days work to Male (Days)	107.6	148.1
2.	Average number of days work to Female (Days)	61.9	81.6
3.	Average monthly income per family (Rs.)	1729	1491
4.a	Average family size (No.)	5	5
4.b.	Average monthly income per member (Rs.)	288.16	248.5
5.a	Average annual income from crop (Rs.)	4403	6298
5.b	Average monthly income from crop/household (Rs.)	366.92	524.83
6.	Total average income from all sources	2095.92	2015.83
7.	Average monthly income per member (Rs.) from all sources	349.32	335.97

Rs. 335.97 respectively in both the areas. As per Census of India (2005-2006), Rs. 368.50 per head in rural areas/tribal areas has been accepted as norm for below poverty lines. If we compare with Census figure Rs. 368.00, the figure of Rs. 349.32 and Rs. 335.97 are much below the poverty line. Really they are suffering from chronic poverty.

As regards the average days of work per month male comes to 107.6 days in Naxal area and 148.1 days in Dacoit area. For female, the average days of work is very less in number, i.e., 61.9 and 81.6 days per month in Naxal and Dacoit area respectively.

The number of landless tribal labourers is very high. They are forced to offer their services to landlords since morning till late night. Out of their services they receive very less amount. Mostly they are paid in kind. The average annual income from production of crop has also been calculated per house as Rs. 4,403 in Naxal area and Rs. 6,298 in Dacoit area. In selling of forest produce and wage for collecting Tendu leaves

Table 5.11: Average Annual Income of a Household from Crop

District	*Total households*	*Average Income/household*
Mirzapur	750	4486
Sonbhadra	750	3432
Chandauli	450	5291
Naxal Total	1950	4403
Allahabad	600	7748
Chitrakoot	450	4847
Dacoit Total	1050	6298
Total of five Districts	3000	5350

are included in this income. Per household income comes to Rs. 366.92 and Rs. 524.83 in Naxal and Dacoit area. In the following Table 5.11 average income from crop per household has been calculated.

In Mirzapur average per household income per annum was Rs. 4,486, in Sonbhadra it was Rs. 3,432, in Chandauli is 5,291, in Allahabad Rs. 7,748 and in Chitrakoot the average per household per annum was Rs. 6,298. In all the five districts the average income per annum was Rs. 5,350 per household. These figures present the extremity of their poverty. We have all heard of Kalahandi (Odisha), but the images of malnutrition and starvation death are not very rare in Sonbhadra, Chandauli, Mirzapur, Chitrakoot and Allahabad tribal belt.

Newspapers had highlighted starvation deaths in village Kuberdhi in Nawgarh Block of Sonbhadra district. It was found that none of the tribal families had Antyodaya Ration Card meant for BPL families. Even those who had never got the due ration. Those who got only 1/3 of their rightful amount and that too at higher cost while they were made to place their thumb print against full ration. Whenever we visited the Naxal prone villages and the Dacoit prone villages we found most of the children were mere skeletons, as if their body and flesh had been sapped away. It was obvious that they were being dragged into the cruel clutches of death. The following Table 5.12 indicates the crises of food in Naxal and Dacoit affected tribal belt of the five districts.

Table 5.12: Availability of Food Items from PDS in Naxal and Dacoit Tribal Belt to Sample Households

Sl. No.	*Item*	*Naxal Area*	*%*	*Dacoit Area*	*%*
1.	No. of households getting food-grains from PDS	478	24.51	414	39.43
2.	No. of households not getting food	1472	75.49	636	60.57
	Grains from PDS	1950	100.00	1050	100.00

It is evident from Table 5.12 that 24.51 per cent in Naxal and 39.43 per cent households in Dacoit tribal belt, receive food throughout the year from PDS, while 75.49 per cent per cent households in Naxal prone area and 60.57 per cent in Dacoit area complained that they did not get food materials from PDS. As per implementation of the PDS programme all the essential foodgrains, sugar, edible oils and kerosene oil, etc., are provided to those who have been issued Antyodaya Ration Card. After analysis of our data we have come to the conclusion that 59.18 per cent households in Naxal belt and 56.38 per cent in Dacoit tribal belt households have not been issued Red Ration Card. As a result, they are not enjoying facilities provided under PDS programmes.

Table 5.13: Work Opportunity to Households in NREGA Scheme

District	*Total Households*	*Yes*	*%*	*No*	*%*
Mirzapur	750	672	89.6	78	10.4
Sonbhadra	750	594	79.2	156	20.8
Chandauli	450	368	81.8	82	18.2
Naxal Total	1950	1634	83.8	316	16.2
Allahabad	600	393	65.5	207	34.5
Chitrakoot	450	387	86.0	63	14.0
Dacoit Total	1050	780	74.3	270	25.7
Total of five Districts	3000	2414	80.5	586	19.5

"हर हाथ को काम दो, काम का पूरा दाम दो।"

The right to work is mentioned in the "Directive Principles" of the Constitution. "The state shall direct its policy towards securing that the citizen, men and women equally have the right to an adequate means of livelihood (Article 39A). The state shall make effective provision for securing the right to work (Art. 41). The right to work is a fundamental right. The right to life is a fundamental right of all citizens under Art. 21 of the Constitution of India. Right to life includes the right to live with human dignity, it would include all these aspects which would make life meaningful, complete and living (Supreme Court)."

Objective

To find out the difference of information of tribal men/women who got opportunity to work in NAREGA. The tribes don't get work in NAREGA

Table 5.14: Statistical Analysis

Sl. No.	*Subject*	*N*	*Mean*	*S.D.*	*D.F.*	*Sig.*
1.	Mirzapur	750	1.08	0.267	4	0.000
2.	Sonbhadra	750	1.14	0.388		
3.	Chandauli	450	1.16	0.398		
4.	Allahabad	600	1.27	0.444		
5.	Chitrakoot	450	1.05	0.372		

in the five tribal districts of U.P., i.e., Mirzapur, Sonbhadra, Chandauli, Allahabad and Chitrakoot.

The analysis of the data yields results in terms of mean, S.D. and Significance Value. The obtained results have been summarized in the Table 5.14.

Since the significance value is less than the significant level at 0.05. Therefore, it shows that the tribes of these area get no work in NREGA in the five tribal districts of U.P., i.e., Mirzapur, Sonbhadra, Chandauli, Allahabad and Chitrakoot.

Following all these Constitutional provisions, the Union Government in 2005 passed an Act named National Rural Employment Guarantee Act 2005. It is a law whereby any adult who is willing to do unskilled manual work at the minimum wage is entitled to being employed on local public works within 15 days of applying. If the employment is not provided within 15 days, the application is entitled to an unemployment allowance at least one-fourth of the minimum wage for the first 30 days and at least one half of the minimum wage thereafter.

The "NREGA" which was named as "MNREGA" after adding the name of Mahatma Gandhi. Under this plan every household is treated as unit of household for registration. There are four implementing agencies (1) Gram Panchayat, (2) Other Panchayati Raj Institutions (PRI), (3) Line Departments (PWD, Forest Department), and (4) NGO's. Private contractors are banned.

After registration, the Gram Panchayat issues a "Job Card" to each applicant household. Special meeting of Gram Sabha is held to invite applications. The job is provided upto the limit of 100 days to each household. The labourers will be entitled to the statutory minimum wage for agricultural labourers in the State was Rs. 60/day later on it has been enhanced to Rs. 100/day. The payment of the wages will be done weekly or in any case not later than a fortnight directly to the person concerned in front of the community the days of work and amount will be entered into the job card.

Equal wages for men and women will be paid. There will be no discrimination of any kind in gender. Priority will be given to women in the allocation of work at least 33 per cent of labourers should be women. Block is the basic unit of implementation. In each Block, there will be a programme officer to coordinate the implementation of the programme. Gram Panchayat is the main implementing agency and the accountability will be fixed on Gram Sabha. Under MNREGA permissible works are minor irrigation, water conservation, drought proofing, distilling of tanks, flood control, construction of rural roads, etc.

"हमारा पैसा हमारा हिसाब"

All MNREGA related documents are available for public scrutiny. Copy of documents will be made available at nominal cost. Muster Rolls will be pro-activity displayed at Panchayat Bhawan. Documents can be also obtained under the Right to Information Act. Under Social Audits provision, Gram Sabha is authorized to conduct social audit of all works taken up within Gram Panchayat. All relevant documents will be provided to the Gram Sabha by the Gram Panchayat and other implementing agencies.

Thus, the Mahatma Gandhi National Rural Employment Guarantee Act (NREGA 2005), passed on August 23, 2005 is a landmark in the history of social security legislation in India. Really it is a type of Renaissance in the history of Independent India in which 100 per cent employment guarantee has been assured to the downtrodden people of rural India. Scheduled Castes and Scheduled Tribes who are living in the remote corners of the hilly places, plateaus and in dense forest areas may minimize their extreme poverty level through getting employed in MNREGA.

The respondents were asked about the jobs provided under NREGA plan implemented in all the villages of the study area. Table 5.13 shows that 89.6 per cent respondents in Mirzapur, 79.2 per cent respondents in Sonbhadra, 81.8 per cent in Chandauli, 65.5 per cent in Allahabad and 86.0 per cent in Chitrakoot agreed that their family members had got opportunity to work in NREGA. Only 19.5 per cent respondents of all the five districts told that they did not get job opportunity in NREGA.

Table 5.15: Opinion of the Respondents Regarding Corruption in MNREGA

District	*Total Households*	*Govt. Servant*	*%*	*Gram Pradhan*	*%*	*Mediator*	*%*
Mirzapur	750	236	31.5	266	35.5	170	22.7
Sonbhadra	750	193	25.7	351	46.8	50	6.7
Chandauli	450	165	36.7	203	45.1	0	0.0
Naxal Total	1950	594	30.5	820	42.1	220	11.3
Allahabad	600	251	41.8	142	23.7	0	0.0
Chitrakoot	450	87	19.3	249	55.3	51	11.3
Dacoit Total	1050	338	32.2	391	37.2	51	4.9
Total of five Districts	3000	932	31.1	1211	40.4	271	9.0

Table 5.15 shows that 80.5 per cent respondents of all the districts replied that there is corruption in NREGA.

When the respondents were asked that who were involved in the foul game, they replied that the Government servants, mediators and Gram Pradhan are involved in corruption. Average percentage of opinion of respondents for Government servants were 31.1 per cent, 40.4 per cent for Gram Pradhan and 9.0 per cent for Mediators.

Objective

To find of the difference of opinion of the head of the household on corruption in NAREGA. To prove statistically that there is corruption in NAREGA in five tribal districts of U.P., i.e., Mirzapur, Sonbhadra, Chandauli, Allahabad and Chitrakoot.

The analysis of the data yields results in terms of mean, S.D. and Significance Value. The obtained results have been summarized in Table 5.16.

Table 5.16: Statistical Analysis: Mean, S.D. and C.R. Value between the Five Tribal Districts of Uttar Pradesh, i.e., Mirzapur, Sonbhadra

Sl. No.	*Subject*	*N*	*Mean*	*S.D.*	*D.F.*	*Sig.*
1.	Mirzapur	750	1.06	0.835	4	0.00
2.	Sonbhadra	750	1.18	0.850		
3.	Chandauli	450	0.60	0.809		
4.	Allahabad	600	0.90	0.603		
5.	Chitrakoot	450	1.07	0.675		

Since, the significance value is less than the significant level at 0.05. Therefore, it shows that there is corruption in NAREGA in five tribal districts of U.P., i.e., Mirzapur, Sonbhadra, Chandauli, Allahabad and Chitrakoot.

The norms decided by the Union Government of India for Below Poverty Line people is Rs. 368.50 per month.

During survey we observed that all the scheduled caste and scheduled tribe families were extremely poor. Therefore, the BPL norm is applicable to all the tribals of the South-Eastern region of Uttar Pradesh. They are entitled to receive all the benefits provided under BPL norms.

Table 5.17 shows only 52.3 per cent respondents in Mirzapur, 63.5 per cent respondents in Sonbhadra, 63.6 per cent respondents in

Table 5.17: BPL Listed Respondent Households

District	*Total Households*	*Listed*	*%*	*Not listed*	*%*
Mirzapur	750	392	52.3	358	47.7
Sonbhadra	750	476	63.5	274	36.5
Chandauli	450	286	63.6	164	36.4
Naxal Total	1950	1154	59.2	796	40.8
Allahabad	600	434	72.3	166	27.7
Chitrakoot	450	158	35.1	292	64.9
Dacoit Total	1050	592	56.4	458	43.6
Total of five Districts	3000	1746	58.2	1254	41.8

Chandauli, 72.3 per cent in Allahabad and 35.1 per cent respondents were included in BPL list. Why 41.8 per cent respondents of all the five districts have not been included in BPL list, is a matter of great concern. The Union Government, under welfare programmes has provided several concessional facilities to the rural families which come under BPL category. Implementing the Right to Food Act, the Government issues Red Cards to the BPL families. Rice at the rate of rupees 3 and wheat at the rate of rupees 2 per kilo will be available to the Red Card holders. Similarly, the medical treatment upto the limit of Rs. 30,000 per patient will be reimbursed to the smart card holders. This card is issued only to the BPL men and women.

Objective

To find out the difference of information from the head of household for inclusion of name in BPL list. To prove statistically for inclusion of name in the BPL list in the five tribal districts of U.P., i.e., Mirzapur, Sonbhadra, Chandauli, Allahabad and Chitrakoot.

The analysis of the data yields results in terms of mean, S.D. and Significance Value. The obtained results have been summarized in Table 5.18.

Table 5.18: Statistical Analysis

Sl. No.	*Subject*	*N*	*Mean*	*S.D.*	*D.F.*	*Sign.*
1.	Mirzapur	750	1.49	0.500	4	0.00
2.	Sonbhadra	750	1.42	0.493		
3.	Chandauli	450	1.36	0.482		
4.	Allahabad	600	1.28	0.448		
5.	Chitrakoot	450	1.65	0.478		

Table 5.19: Reasons for not enlisting Respondent Households in BPL List

District	*Total Households*	*Local Problem*	%	*Bribery*	%	*Negligence*	%	*No Idea*	%
Mirzapur	750	108	30.2	206	57.5	12	3.4	32	8.9
Sonbhadra	750	48	17.5	162	59.1	38	13.9	26	9.5
Chandauli	450	40	24.4	104	63.4	12	7.3	8	4.9
Naxal Total	1950	196	24.6	472	59.3	62	7.8	66	8.3
Allahabad	600	57	34.3	84	50.6	14	8.4	11	6.6
Chitrakoot	450	19	6.5	198	67.8	30	10.3	45	15.4
Dacoit Total	1050	76	16.6	282	61.6	44	9.6	56	12.2
Total of five Districts	3000	272	21.7	754	60.1	106	8.5	122	9.7

Since, the significance value is less than the significant level at 0.05. Therefore, it shows that there is no common response about the inclusion of name in the BPL list of the five tribal districts of U.P., i.e., Mirzapur, Sonbhadra, Chandauli, Allahabad and Chitrakoot.

In Table 5.19 some reasons for not enlisted the tribal people have been analysed.

Several news related to cases of malnutrition, starvation, hunger deaths, suicides have been flashed by the print and electronic media during past few years in Mirzapur, Sonbhadra, Chandauli, Allahabad and Chritrakoot tribal people. Due to multiple displacement, due to land grabbing by feudal lords, maphias, the Government, the forest department and ban on collecting forest produce, the tribals have lost all there resources of their livelihood. How will they survive, is a big question to be solved by the Union and State Governments. Hence, under right to food and right to health, the Governments have launched several welfare programmes by including them in BPL list. Without raising any doubt, we can firmly say that cent-per-cent tribals are victims of extreme and chronic poverty. Therefore, the number of Red Card Holders, Smart Card Holders and Job Card Holders should be hundred per cent in number in this tribal region. Then why 41.8 per cent of the respondent households were left and could not avail the welfare facilities of being BPL persons. In Table 5.19 some reasons have been analysed.

Personal enmity, jealous, political reasons, bribery, forgery, negligence and others may be some reasons behind this 'action'. Under Panchayati Raj system the local politics is one of the dominant factors. Due to vote politics the village has been divided into several group of the village. The Panchayat members take revenge with their opposite groups by depriving their legal rights. The Gram Pradhan tries to oblige his supporters by snatching others share. 30.2 per cent in Mirzapur, 17.6 per cent in Sonbhadra, 24.4 per cent in Chandauli, 34.3 per cent in Allahabad and 6.5 per cent in Chitrakoot respondents were victimised by their local politics. As a result, their names have not been included in BPL list.

The second reason is bribery. The economic corruption has spread all over India and has taken in its grip the whole system of the country. No work can be done unless the palm is greased. 57.5 per cent in Mirzapur, 59.1 per cent in Sonbhadra, 63.4 per cent in Chandauli, 50.6 per cent in Allahabad and 67.8 per cent respondent household of Chitrakoot replied that the Gram Pradhan and the concerning officials cannot include their names unless they realize the bribe amount. Only average 8.5 per cent respondents in all the five districts replied that due to negligence of the concerning authorities their cards had not been issued. 9.7 per cent respondents of the study area showed their ignorance. Thus, it is clear that the local politics is one of the main reasons for including or not including the names of *dalit adivasis* in BPL list.

Objective

To find out the difference of reasons why the names have not been enlisted in BPL list. To prove statistically about the reasons of non enlisting in the BPL list the five tribal districts of U.P., i.e., Mirzapur, Sonbhadra, Chandauli, Allahabad and Chitrakoot.

The analysis of the data yields results in terms of mean, S.D. and Significance Value. The obtained results have been summarized in Table 5.20.

Table 5.20: Statistical Analysis

Sl. No.	*Subject*	*N*	*Mean*	*S.D.*	*D.F.*	*Sign.*
1.	Mirzapur	750	0.51	0.745	4	0.00
2.	Sonbhadra	750	0.59	0.934		
3.	Chandauli	450	0.44	0.717		
4.	Allahabad	600	0.59	1.128		
5.	Chitrakoot	450	2.07	1.747		

Since, the significance value is less than the significant level at 0.05. It proves statistically that the households which are not enlisted have common responses about the reason of non-enlisting in the BPL list between the five tribal districts of U.P., i.e., Mirzapur, Sonbhadra, Chandauli, Allahabad and Chitrakoot. It proves the harassment of the household.

Due to shortage of income resources, the tribals of the five districts are passing very hard days in their life. To manage two times meal is even very-very tuff. Therefore, in case of emergency conditions they have no option except to borrow money from the money lenders. As there is no security assets to the tribal respondents, they have no option before them except to keep their ownselves at security money before the money lenders. The money lenders employ them as bonded labourers and this chain never ended and continued from generation to generation.

On this point 71.6 per cent respondents of Mirzapur, 83.5 per cent of Allahabad and 66.8 per cent respondents in Chitrakoot agreed that they

Table 5.21: Worked as Bonded Labourer at Low Wages to Money Lenders Place

District	*Total Households*	*Yes*	*%*	*No*	*%*
Mirzapur	750	326	71.6	129	28.4
Sonbhadra	750	197	83.5	39	16.5
Chandauli	450	125	66.8	62	33.2
Naxal Total	1950	648	73.8	230	26.2
Allahabad	600	194	75.8	62	24.2
Chitrakoot	450	167	90.3	18	9.7
Dacoit Total	1050	361	81.9	80	18.1
Total of five Districts	3000	1009	76.5	310	23.5

had no option to repay the loan except to accept this slavery as bonded labour at the place of money lenders and landlords (*see* Table 5.21).

Only 26.2 per cent respondents of Naxal prone area and 18.1 per cent respondents of dacoit prone area, tried their best to repay the loan instead of becoming slave-bonded labour for generation to generation.

As there is no permanent sources of income, tribal people adopt several means of their livelihood. They get seasonal employment as agricultural labourers during *Rabi* and *Kharif* agricultural seasons. Besides agricultural work, they search some part time employment in private/Government construction work, in MNREGA plan, work with contractors, like in crushers, mines, etc., and some other work like collection and selling of forest produce, firewood, honey, Tendu leaf, fruits, milk, cattle, herbal medicines etc.

The Table 5.22 shows that an average a male respondent in Mirzapur got employment for 11.1 days during *Kharif*, 10.2 days during *Rabi* season, 0.4 days for collection of forest produce, 0.2 days in Government construction work, 60.7 days in MNREGA schemes and 1.8 days in contractors work. The total days of working as part time employment come up to 84.4 days per year.

In Sonbhadra a male respondent got employment for 8.9 days during *Kharif*, 7.3 days during *Rabi* season, 29.4 days for collection of forest produce, 0.4 days in government construction work, 23.1 days in MNREGA schemes and 16.6 days in contractors work. The total days of working part time employment come up to 85.7 days per year.

In Chandauli a male respondent got employment for 13.9 days during *Kharif*, 5.8 days during *Rabi* season, 51.3 days for collection of forest

Table 5.22: Average Days of Work obtained by Male Workers during Different Seasons/Schemes

District	*Total households*	*Male worker*	*During kharif (No. of days)*	*Average days/worker*	*Rabi (No. of days)*	*Average days/worker*	*Other (No. of days)*	*Average days/worker*
Mirzapur	750	964	10666	11.1	9806	10.2	385	0.4
Sonbhadra	750	839	7492	8.9	6083	7.3	24636	29.4
Chandauli	450	489	6791	13.9	2852	5.8	25100	51.3
Naxal Total	1950	2292	24949	10.9	18741	8.2	50121	21.9
Allahabad	600	868	23640	27.2	22055	25.4	9480	10.9
Chitrakoot	450	581	27266	46.9	19763	34.0	5102	8.8
Dacoit Total	1050	1449	50906	35.1	41818	28.9	14582	10.1
Total of five Districts	3000	3741	75855	20.3	60559	16.2	64703	17.3

District	*Total house-holds*	*Male worker*	*Govt. Const. (No. of days)*	*Average days/ worker*	*Narega (No. of days)*	*Average days/ worker*	*Contract (No. of days)*	*Average/ worker*	*Average days per year*
Mirzapur	750	964	180	0.2	58553	60.7	1710	1.8	84.4
Sonbhadra	750	839	376	0.4	19362	23.1	13934	16.6	85.7
Chandauli	450	489	20	0.0	16541	33.8	1320	2.7	107.5
Naxal Total	1950	2292	576	0.3	94456	41.2	16964	7.4	89.9
Allahabad	600	868	7275	8.4	29700	34.2	18330	21.1	127.2
Chitrakoot	450	581	1170	2.0	22835	39.3	9885	17.0	148.0
Dacoit Total	1050	1449	8445	5.8	52535	36.3	28215	19.5	135.7
Total of five Districts	3000	3741	9021	2.4	146991	39.3	45179	12.1	107.6

produce, 0.0 days in Government construction work, 33.8 days in MNREGA schemes and 2.7 days in contractors work. The total days of working part time employment come up to 107.5 days per year.

In Allahabad an average tribal male workers got employment for 27.2 days during *Kharif*, 25.4 days during *Rabi* season, 10.9 days for collection of forest produce, 8.4 days in Government construction work, 34.2 days in MNREGA schemes and 21.1 days in contractors work. The total days of working part time employment come up to 127.1 days per year.

In Chitrakoot an average tribal male workers got employment for 46.9 days during *Kharif*, 34.0 days during *Rabi* season, 8.8 days for collection of forest produce, 2.0 days in Government construction work, 39.3 days in MNREGA schemes and 17.0 days in contractors work. The total days of working part time employment come up to 148.0 days per year.

It clearly indicates that an average tribal man gets employment for his livelihood only for much less than half a year.

In the Table 5.23 the working days per year available to female tribal has been calculated. It is evident from Table 5.23 that a tribal women of Mirzapur got work for average 87.8 days per year. In Sonbhadra the average days of work available was 44.2 days per year. 54.8 days per year was available in Chandauli. The average days available for work in Naxal prone area was 61.9 days per year.

77.2 days of work was available to Allahabad tribal woman and 89.1 days in a year was available to Chitrakoot. Thus, average 81.6 days of working days in a year comes to Dacoit prone area.

The little number of working days of employment in such work on low wages cannot meet out their minimum requirements of their lives. Their total income comes much below the poverty line defined by the Government. Consequently, tribals of all the five districts are extremely poor and they are suffering from malnutrition and starvation.

The income of a family can be assessed by the number of crops produced and by the quantity of the produced crops. Therefore, in order to assess the income level of the respondent households such question was put up before them.

Table 5.24 shows that 79.7 per cent respondent households of Mirzapur, 66.4 per cent in Sonbhadra, 77.5 per cent in Chandauli, 68.4 per cent in Allahabad and 69.5 per cent respondent household in Chitrakoot could manage any how to produce only single crop in a year. Due to shortage of irrigation facility, unavailability of fertilizers, seeds

Table 5.23: Work Obtained by Female Workers during Different Seasons/Schemes

District	*Total households*	*Female workers*	*During Kharif*	*Average/ worker*	*Rabi*	*Average/ worker*	*Other*	*Average/ worker*
Mirzapur	750	628	9431	15.0	9225	14.7	120	0.2
Sonbhadra	750	740	8197	11.1	6613	8.9	3531	4.8
Chandauli	450	430	6192	14.4	3004	7.0	7265	16.9
Naxal Total	1950	1798	23820	13.2	18842	10.5	10916	6.1
Allahabad	600	329	5495	16.7	4310	13.1	2760	8.4
Chitrakoot	450	190	4796	25.2	3216	16.9	2151	11.3
Dacoit Total	1050	519	10291	19.8	7526	14.5	4911	9.5
Total of five Districts	3000	2317	34111	14.7	26368	11.4	15827	6.8

District	*Total households*	*Female workers*	*Govt. Const.*	*Average/ worker*	*NAREGA*	*Average/ worker*	*Contract*	*Average/ worker*	*Average days per year*
Mirzapur	750	628	1420	2.3	34887	55.6	10	0.0	51.8
Sonbhadra	750	740	900	1.2	12203	16.5	1272	1.7	44.2
Chandauli	450	430	0	0.0	7081	16.5	0	0.0	54.8
Naxal Total	1950	1798	2320	1.3	54171	30.1	1282	0.7	61.9
Allahabad	600	329	0	0.0	8436	25.6	4400	13.4	77.2
Chitrakoot	450	190	0	0.0	6525	34.3	270	1.4	89.2
Dacoit Total	1050	519	0	0.0	14961	28.8	4670	9.0	81.6
Total of five Districts	3000	2317	2320	1.0	69132	29.8	5952	2.6	71.7

Table 5.24: Number of Crops Grown in a Year

District	Total Households	Single	Single %	Double	Double %
Mirzapur	750	533	79.7	136	20.3
Sonbhadra	750	326	66.4	165	33.6
Chandauli	450	237	77.5	69	22.5
Naxal Area	1950	1096	74.8	370	25.2
Allahabad	600	355	68.4	164	31.6
Chitrakoot	450	230	69.5	101	30.5
Dacoit Area	1050	585	68.8	265	31.2
Total of five Districts	3000	1681	72.6	635	27.4

and allotted unfertile land, they were unable to produce more than one crop a year.

20.3 per cent respondents households of Mirzapur, 33.6 per cent of Sonbhadra, 22.5 per cent of Chandauli, 31.6 per cent respondent households of Allahabad and 30.5 per cent respondent households of Chitrakoot managed to produce both the crops, *Rabi* and *Kharif.* On this ground the economic status of these tribal people can easily be assessed. Because they have no sources of irrigation, do not have sufficient money to buy fertilizers, seeds, etc.

Table 5.25 shows average output of crop production per household in tribal areas of this region. Per house Paddy production was 7.5 quintals, Maize production was 0.8 quintals, 0.0 quintal in Bazri, 0.3 quintal production of Pulse, 4.6 quintal production of wheat, 0.1 quintal of (Sarso) mustard and 0.6 quintal production of other crops come an average share to a household in Naxal prone area.

In Dacoit prone area an average production of paddy was 8.0 quintal, 0.3 quintal of maize, 0.2 quintal of Bazri, 0.6 quintal of pulse, 10.2 quintal of wheat, 0.8 quintal of Sarso (Mustard) and 0.8 quintal of other crops come as share per household.

The total weight of all these production per household is so little that they cannot afford their families by this little quantity of crops.

The tribal people especially in all the five districts are extremely poor because their means of livelihood, earnings and land and their main stay and other allied sources of income have been taken away by the outsiders. Their economy is primarily agro-based land has been the only tangible asset of a tribal family. Now, they have been deprived of land, forest and resources of water on which they were once holding full authority before Independence.

Table 5.25: Average Crop Production per Household

District	*Total households*	*Paddy*	*Average/ household*	*Maize*	*Average/ household*	*Bazri*	*Average/ household*	*Pulses*	*Average/ household*
Mirzapur	750	5340.4	7.1	552	0.7	0	0.0	178.03	0.2
Sonbhadra	750	5605.85	7.5	1012.51	1.4	10	0.0	355.97	0.5
Chandauli	450	3602	8.0	53	0.1	5	0.0	68.5	0.2
Naxal Total	1950	14548.25	7.5	1617.51	0.8	15	0.0	602.5	0.3
Allahabad	600	5371	9.0	350	0.6	210	0.4	486	0.8
Chitrakoot	450	2986	6.6	15	0.0	0	0.0	101.75	0.2
Dacoit Total	1050	8357	8.0	365	0.3	210	0.2	587.75	0.6
Total of five Districts	3000	22905.25	7.6	1982.51	0.7	225	0.1	1190.25	0.4

District	*Total households*	*Wheat*	*Average/ household*	*Sarso*	*Average/ household*	*Others*	*Average/ household*
Mirzapur	750	2926.5	3.9	0	0.0	61	0.1
Sonbhadra	750	3416.85	4.6	39.13	0.1	477.25	0.6
Chandauli	450	2480	5.5	528	1.2	52	0.1
Naxal Total	1950	8823.35	4.6	567.13	0.1	590.25	0.6
Allahabad	600	6725.5	11.2	615	1.0	105	0.2
Chitrakoot	450	3999	8.9	175	0.4	712.5	1.6
Dacoit Total	1050	10724.5	10.2	790	0.8	817.5	0.8
Total of five Districts	3000	19547.85	6.5	1357.13	0.5	1407.75	0.5

Table 5.26: Utilization of Income from Agricultural Produce

District	*Total house-holds*	*For Liveli-hood*	*%*	*Paying Loans*	*%*	*Health & Clothes*	*%*
Mirzapur	750	623	93.0	32	4.8	15	2.2
Sonbhadra	750	539	86.8	58	9.3	24	3.9
Chandauli	450	283	91.6	26	8.4	0	0.0
Naxal Total	1950	1445	90.3	116	7.3	39	2.4
Allahabad	600	499	89.3	40	7.2	20	3.6
Chitrakoot	450	310	92.8	13	3.9	11	3.3
Dacoit Total	1050	809	90.6	53	5.9	31	3.5
Total of five Districts	3000	2254	90.4	169	6.8	70	2.8

Where their survival is at stake, how can they think of fulfilling secondary and tertiary needs of their life. Earnings from agricultural produce is so little that it is tough to manage two times meal for their family. Keeping these facts in view the respondents were also asked in what heads they utilize their income earned from agricultural produce. 93.0 per cent respondents of Mirzapur, 86.8 per cent of Sonbhadra, 91.6 per cent of Chandauli, 89.3 per cent of Allahabad and 92.8 per cent respondents of Chitrakoot told that the major portion of their income was utilized in meeting out their two times meal.

As this income is not at all sufficient for their livelihood, therefore, they are bound to take loan in emergency from the money lenders, 4.8 per cent respondents in Mirzapur, 9.3 per cent in Sonbhadra, 8.4 per cent in Chandauli, 7.2 per cent in Allahabad and 3.9 per cent in Chitrakoot respondents tried to spare some amount to repay the loan in instalment.

Only 2.2 per cent respondents of Mirzapur, 3.9 per cent in Sonbhadra, 0.0 per cent in Chandauli, 3.6 per cent in Allahabad, and 3.3 per cent in Chitrakoot respondents thought to spend some of the amount on secondary and tertiary needs like education, health and clothes. This negligible percentage clearly indicates the extremity of their poverty.

The South-Eastern part of Uttar Pradesh includes Mirzapur, Sonbhadra, Chandauli, Allahabad and Chitrakoot (Patha region). It is located in the Vindhya ranges of Uttar Pradesh and it was densely forested a century ago. There were several tribes but the Kol tribe was dominant from population point of view. They enjoyed full liberty to use forest produce and abundantly cultivated crops like "Kodo" and oilseeds and pulses for their own consumption. Their diet was not only contained the required calories but was balanced with ample, milk, flesh, fruits, etc.

Table 5.27: Other Sources of Income when the Crop Production is not Sufficient for Food

District	*Total Households*	*Labour*	*Labour %*	*On credit*	*On credit %*	*Forest resource*	*Forest resource %*	*Beggar*	*Beggar %*	*Cultural Activity*	*Cultural Activity %*
Mirzapur	750	301	40.1	106	14.1	75	10.0	113	15.1	155	20.7
Sonbhadra	750	201	26.8	233	31.1	60	8.0	83	11.1	173	23.1
Chandauli	450	300	66.7	84	18.7	23	5.1	30	6.7	13	2.9
Naxalite Area	1950	802	41.1	423	21.7	158	8.1	226	11.6	341	17.5
Allahabad	600	228	38.0	180	30.0	72	12.0	54	9.0	66	11.0
Chitrakoot	450	187	41.6	180	40.0	19	4.2	54	12.0	10	2.2
Dacoit Area	1050	415	39.5	360	34.3	91	8.7	108	10.3	76	7.2
Total of five districts	3000	1217	40.6	783	26.1	249	8.3	334	11.1	417	13.9

The main occupation of tribal people of this region of Uttar Pradesh has been agricultural and food gathering. Especially in case of Sonbhadra, Mirzapur and Chandauli, Allahabad and Chitrakoot, change in situation, started very rapidly after independence when several developmental plans were launched and non-tribal people—contractors, maphias and landlords started encroaching there ancestral land on which they have been producing grains for their livelihood. As a result, the area of their agricultural land either it was completely taken away or if left it was very very insufficient in area to produce the crop to fulfil their minimum needs.

Naturally, when their problem of two times meal is not solved with agricultural produce they will search some other means of livelihood to supplement their income for livelihood.

It is evident from Table 5.27 that 40.1 per cent respondents of Mirzapur, 26.8 per cent of Sonbhadra, 66.6 per cent of Chandauli, 38.0 per cent of Allahabad and 41.3 per cent respondents of Chitrakoot replied that the other means of livelihood they adopted was doing agricultural labour work on other's agricultural fields. Some of them accepted any other kind of unskilled labour work in their villages or outside villages.

14.1 per cent respondents of Mirzapur, 31.1 per cent of Sonbhadra, 18.7 per cent of Chandauli, 30.0 per cent of Allahabad and 40.0 per cent respondents of Chitrakoot took loan on interest from lenders to supplement their income.

10.0 per cent respondents of Mirzapur, 8.0 per cent of Sonbhadra, 5.1 per cent of Chandauli, 12 per cent of Allahabad and 4.2 per cent respondents of Chitrakoot got opportunities to collect forest produce like fire woods, amla, honey, chiraunjee, herbal medicines, mahua, tendu leafs, etc. They enhanced their income by selling these forest produces.

15.1 per cent respondents in Mirzapur, 11.1 per cent in Sonbhadra, 6.7 per cent in Chandauli, 9.0 per cent in Allahabad and 12.0 per cent respondents of Chitrakoot were found in their worst conditions. They added their income through begging.

Since, beginning tribal people have developed their own cultural activities. They are also different from other communities and clans. Folk dances and folk songs—*Karma, Koldahki, Natua, Domkatch, Shaila, Kalaiya, Farri, Binwat, Gondana, Pujan* and other dances, music instruments and songs are worth appreciating. They are often invited by several cultural organisations to display. They are paid for their cultural display.

20.7 per cent respondents of Mirzapur, 23.1 per cent respondents of Sonbhadra, 2.9 per cent of Chandauli, 11.0 per cent of Allahabad and 7.2

Table 5.28: Generation when Profession and Living Standard Changed in Upward Direction

District	*Total Households*	*Grand Father*	*%*	*Father*	*%*	*Self*	*%*	*Adult Son*	*%*	*Change in Worst*	*%*
Mirzapur	750	135	18.0	42	5.6	63	8.4	15	2.0	495	66.0
Sonbhadra	750	127	16.9	42	5.6	50	6.7	42	5.6	489	65.2
Chandauli	450	79	17.6	1	0.2	22	4.9	41	9.1	307	68.2
Naxal Total	1950	341	17.5	85	4.4	135	6.9	98	5.0	1291	66.2
Allahabad	600	0	0.0	0	0.0	63	10.5	21	3.5	516	86.0
Chitrakoot	450	0	0.0	4	0.9	17	3.8	3	0.7	426	94.7
Dacoit Total	1050	0	0.0	4	0.4	80	7.6	24	2.3	942	89.7
Total of five Districts	3000	341	11.4	89	3.0	215	7.2	122	4.1	2233	74.4

per cent respondents of Chitrakoot replied that they used to earn by showing, displaying and singing their tribal community dances, music and songs before the urban people.

Thus, it is clearly evident from these responses that their income from agricultural production is not at all sufficient. Therefore, they have to adopt other sources to enhance their income to meet out their primary needs.

After Independence, time has moved on, and the societies and the country have moved towards betterment. Now, we may easily declare that India is prosperous country where every material happiness goods is available to every citizen of India. In the race of advancement and development in technologies, production and material production, India has left behind several countries. Even USA, Russia, China like advance countries quote and admire the unbelievable development and achievements of India before the whole world. But why India is inhabited by poor and why some sections of our country is worstly suffering from extreme poverty. Indian tribals having 8 crores of population have not remained only where they were, but have gone worst in their every walk of life. In fact, they and their lives continue to be untouched and unconcerned by all the overwhelming forces of change that are making everything into new.

The degree of disappointment, frustration and reactions could easily be assessed when we asked them their views of their achievements and change in their professional and living standard.

The maximum percentage of respondents reply regarding "change in worst" clearly indicates their extremity of frustration. Before Independence, there was a little chance of comparison when there was no intrusion of outsiders and was no social mobility. But when the intruders started coming and encroaching their land and other sources of livelihood, they started comparing their living and professional standard with them.

Table 5.28 shows that 66.0 per cent respondents of Mirzapur, 65.2 per cent of Sonbhadra, 68.2 per cent of Chandauli, 86.0 per cent of Allahabad and 94.7 per cent respondents of Chitrakoot replied that the changes in their profession and in standard of living are the worst. They have brought only miseries in place of any relief to this present generation.

17.5 per cent respondents of Naxal prone area told that their economic standard, profession and living standard were much better and higher at the time of their grand-father period. There was no binding and restrictions on their forest land and forest produce. They had sufficient cattle with them. There was no scarcity of milk and meat, fishes during their grand-father's period.

But in case of dacoit prone area, their reply was just reverse. They remembered their grand-father's period of exploitation. It was at the extreme by the feudal landlords. By employing them as bonded labourers, they gave no relief except torture. They narrated several incidences of torturing, beating during illness, death and suicidal cases of members of their families. 0.00 per cent respondents expressed their views that their living standards of life was worst than beast during grand-father's generation.

Gradually, after the interference of several NGOs and civil society, their exploitation, however, was controlled. As a result, 3.0 per cent respondents of the total area felt change in better sense during father's generation. 7.2 per cent respondents of the total areas told that due to their awareness much better position could be achieved during their own selve's period. Present generation is spending much better life as compared to their previous generation.

Objective

To find out the difference of opinion of the head of the household on changing trend in professional standard. It is to prove statistically that is there any change in professional standard in five tribal districts of U.P., i.e., Mirzapur, Sonbhadra, Chandauli, Allahabad and Chitrakoot.

The analysis of the data yields results in terms of mean, S.D. and Significance Value. The obtained results have been summarized in the Table 5.29.

Table 5.29: Statistical Analysis

Sl. No	*Subject*	*N*	*Mean*	*S.D.*	*D.F.*	*Sign.*
1.	Mirzapur	750	1.75	0.439	4	0.00
2.	Sonbhadra	750	1.72	0.466		
3.	Chandauli	450	1.20	0.402		
4.	Allahabad	600	1.79	0.408		
5.	Chitrakoot	450	1.58	1.494		

Since, the significance value is less than the significant level at 0.05. Therefore, it shows that there is no change in the professional standard. It proves that there is no significant difference in the five tribal districts of U.P., i.e., Mirzapur, Sonbhadra, Chandauli, Allahabad and Chitrakoot.

II. EDUCATIONAL GROWTH AS AN IMPORTANT INDICATOR FOR DEVELOPMENT

There have consistently been two difficulties in real development of the tribals; one is existing inside and the other outside. Because of their superstitions, conservative, traditional way of life and concept of magic oriented notions, the tribals have often resisted any reformation, education and transculturisation, purely on a feeling that any such type of thought would be a challenge to their existence. Whenever, the leaders amongst the tribals stood up, their demands have been purely political, either to maintain their existence or with a sense of thrill and sensation. Hardly, there has been any attempt to work for social and educational upliftment. The demand for free schooling of the tribals and good institutions for proper learning are rarely found. In this vicious circle, the whole notions among the tribals which are definitely impediments towards their real development are persisting. On account of lack of education and their illiteracy have made tribals unfit in the present modern set-up of the society. Educationally, the tribal people are at different level of development, but on the whole, formal education has made very little impact on tribal groups.

The educational growth therefore, is the most important indicator for development and upliftment of tribal society. Educational development is also linked up with social and economic development as it helps in removing illiteracy and ignorance. The aim of tribal education should not be only the spreading literacy among the tribals, but it should develop awareness and also enable these people to solve their social-economic problems and improve their health condition. The Government of India has been planning and implementing various schemes and programmes for the development of the tribal people. Integrated Tribal Development Project (ITDP) is one of the major efforts towards this direction. There is a provision of sub-plan in the State plans. Tribal people are being given special consideration in the selection of beneficiaries under the ITDP. Since education is probably the most effective instrument for ensuring equality of opportunity, the tribal people are lagging behind their more fortunate fellow countrymen due to lack of education which develop awareness. Education is regarded as one of the most effective instrument for tribal social transformation.

Despite these numerous efforts for the development of tribal people in tribal areas by the government, unsatisfactory results are reported. One of the obvious reasons for this, has been the ignorance or little information about the developmental programmes by the tribals owing to illiteracy or very low educational status. Despite their desire, they do not get adequate opportunity for responding to these developmental programmes due to illiteracy. Thus, education is an unique process through which tribals may learn about physical, mental, moral and spiritual development in all respects. It determines psycho-physical traits of a person towards a certain desired goal of life. Education, therefore, contributes to the moral and spiritual development to a certain extent. According to the International Commission on the Development of Education set-up by UNESCO, "the objective of education should be to develop the complete Man". Under Article 46 of the Constitution of India, promotion of educational interest of scheduled tribes is a special responsibility of the Central and State Governments as well. The Government is, therefore, extending various facilities for the promotion of education among scheduled tribes. Due to ignorance arising out of illiteracy, the tribals have been exploited since beginning and at present they are not able to take advantage of new economic, social and political opportunities. Education is a cordial basic social input for economic development of tribals. Education is more than a mere asset for some tribal communities investment in education is, in a way, crucial for their existence. Kaun-Tsu very aptly pointed out "By sowing seed you will harvest once. By planting a tree, you will harvest tenfold. By educating the people you will harvest on hundred fold".

Studies find that educational achievement is very low among tribes. Absenteeism among tribals from school is very common because of their socio-economic-religious ethnocentric attitude. Economic problems are main reasons for them to show lack of interest in education. For the poverty ridden parents, education of their children is considered as luxury which they can hardly afford. Since, most of the tribal people are living in abject poverty under subsistence economy, it is not easy for most of them to send their children to schools. Varrier Elwin has explained this adverse situation by saying "For a tribal family, to send its grown up girl or boy to school, is essentially a matter of economic and entails dislocations in the traditional pattern of division of labour—many parents cannot just afford to send their children to School". Grown up children generally look after the younger ones when the parents go out for work. If the child is taken away from his normal economic work to attend school, the family is deprived of the little income which he brings. Instead, the parents have to feed the child out of their earning which further reduces the economic stability of the family. There are several causes for avoiding schooling to their children, is (i) the curriculum and contents of the education. They do not suit to their existing socio-cultural milieu of the tribal society. The naked truth is that there; (ii) is hardly any school building equipped with educational materials in tribal areas. If there is any school; (iii) the problem of absenteeism of the teachers is one of the important factors affecting the educational development; (iv) due to the fear of wild animals, Naxalites and Dacoits; (v) due to lack of transportation facilities, a very few teachers dare go to the forest village for administering education to their students; (vi) lack of administrative policy regarding the educational institutions in tribal areas adversely affect the education of the tribes. In spite of the recommendations and suggestions of various committees; and (vii) commissions, either by the Government of India or State Government, no specific policy for the tribal areas has ever been evolved. It is not yet decided whether the schools would run under Education Department or under the Social Welfare Department. In principle, every step towards the development of education appears to be the best and ideal but on practical platform, the picture of this mission is no true.

As a result of it, even after expiry of 68 years of Independence of India and implementation of Eleven Five Years Plans the literacy conditions is quite in the worst situation. The literacy rate among the tribals is 24 per cent which is much lower than the general population 52 per cent and also than the scheduled castes (30%). The female literacy in tribals is 15 per cent as compared to 39 per cent in general population and 19 per cent in scheduled castes. It is clearly evident that the results achieved under STP strategy are not commensurate with the expectations as well as investments made so far. Table 5.30 presents literacy rate of

Table 5.30: General Population and Tribal Population Literacy Rate of India (1961-2001)

	Year	Persons	Males	Females
General	1961	24.0	34.4	13.0
	1971	29.5	39.5	13.7
	1981	36.2	46.9	24.8
	1991	52.11	64.13	39.29
	2001	64.83	75.62	53.67
Tribes	1961	8.5	13.8	3.2
	1971	11.3	17.6	4.9
	1981	16.4	24.5	8.0
	1991	29.60	40.65	18.19
	2001	47.08	59.14	34.75

general population and scheduled tribes (male, female, total population) for the last five Census periods.

According to the latest definition of Census of India, persons of aged 7 years and above, who can both read and write with understanding in any language is considered as literate. Table 5.30 shows that the literacy rate of general population increased from 24.0 per cent to 64.83 per cent within 40 years whereas the tribal literacy rate increased from 8.5 per cent to 47.08 per cent within the same period. It is an increase of 39 per cent.

Gap of approximately 18 per cent in the literacy rate of tribals and the general population in 2001 Census is quite alarming. In case of female population there is a big gap of around 19 per cent but in male population it is nearly 16 per cent.

There has always been difference of opinion regarding the definition of literacy. According to UNESCO's definition "A person is literate who can with understanding both read and write a short simple statement on his everyday life". The definition given in Census of India was almost similar to the UNESCO's definition. The test of literacy for the Census was satisfied if a person above the age of four could with understanding both read and write. Thus, literacy shows only the ability of reading and writing only.

Table 5.31: Literacy Rate of World, Asia, India, UP, Mirzapur, Sonbhadra, Chandauli, Allahabad and Chitrakoot Districts 2001

	Literate %	*Illiterate %*
World	40.0	60.0
Asia	20.0	80.0
India	71.40	29.60
Uttar Pradesh	64.0	36.0
Mirzapur	62.0	38.0
Sonbhadra	49.3	50.7
Chandauli	59.0	41.0
Allahabad	82.0	18.0
Chitrakoot	55.0	45.0

Table 5.31 shows the general position of literacy rate in the World, in India, in U.P. and in our study districts where tribals are residing.

Between 1991 and 2001, literacy rates have increased for girls as well as overall numbers of Scheduled Caste and Scheduled Tribe groups due to higher school participation (Government of India, 2006). The total literacy rate of Scheduled Caste groups during that time increased from

37.41 per cent to 54.69 per cent, and for Scheduled Tribes it increased from 29.6 per cent to 47.1 per cent. The literacy rate, therefore, increased by 17.28 per cent among Scheduled Castes and by 17.5 per cent in Scheduled Tribes (Table 5.32).

Table 5.32: Literacy Rates and Gross Enrolment Rates for Scheduled Castes and Scheduled Tribes in India and States

State/UT	*Literacy Rate*		*GER Grade I-VII (%)*	
	SC	*ST*	*SC Students*	*ST Students*
India	54.69	47.10	83.35	86.06
Jammu & Kashmir	59.03	37.46	81.25	62.05
Himachal Pradesh	70.31	65.50	100.26	111.70
Punjab	56.22	—	97.72	—
Chandigarh	67.66	—	63.59	—
Uttranchal	63.40	63.23	105.11	91.53
Haryana	55.45	—	81.19	—
Delhi	70.85	—	61.28	—
Rajasthan	52.24	44.66	81.88	85.58
Uttar Pradesh	46.27	35.13	61.25	62.37
Bihar	28.47	28.17	59.67	79.19
Sikkim	63.04	67.14	75.48	114.23
Arunachal Pradesh	67.64	49.62	—	90.11
Nagaland	—	65.96	—	60.19
Manipur	72.32	65.85	111.30	108.34
Mizoram	89.20	89.34	—	101.45
Tripura	74.68	56.48	104.75	101.19
Meghalaya	56.27	61.34	90.46	87.62
Assam	66.78	62.52	67.08	75.10
West Bengal	59.04	43.40	110.75	67.33
Jharkhand	37.56	40.67	54.90	85.03
Orissa	55.53	37.37	88.50	89.66
Chhattisgarh	63.96	52.09	96.24	105.95
Madhya Pradesh	58.57	41.16	97.28	79.55
Gujarat	70.50	47.74	72.96	89.01
Daman & Diu	85.13	63.42	98.34	103.02
Dadra & Nagar Haveli	78.25	41.24	102.39	93.32
Maharashtra	71.90	55.21	100.86	98.15
Andhra Pradesh	53.52	37.04	91.57	78.76
Karnataka	52.87	48.27	100.67	93.91
Goa	71.92	55.88	101.83	—
Lakshadweep	—	86.14	—	102.91
Kerala	82.66	64.35	91.43	108.99
Tamil Nadu	63.19	41.53	105.63	108.16
Pondicherry	69.12	—	116.45	—
Andaman & Nicobar Islands	—	66.79	—	88.36

Education on the other hand refers to the process of schooling including every kind of training, vocational or general, one receives at a formal institutions. Following the Article 46 of the Constitution of India, there is obligation on the State to promote with special care, the educational and economic interests of the weaker sections of the people and in particular of the scheduled castes and the scheduled tribes and shall protect them from social injustice and all forms of exploitation. The Ministry of Education and the Ministry of Welfare have launched several educational plans and in every plan period sanctioned huge grants for the implementation of their plans related to programmes.

When we examine the educational developmental programmes in Sonbhadra, Chandauli, Mirzapur, Chitrakoot and tribal dominated areas of Allahabad districts, the survey data showed the very disappointing picture. How would it be possible for those tribal people of Sonbhadra, Chandauli and Mirzapur districts, who have regularly been displaced even from their temporary settlements also to think of sending children in schools. How their children would go to school if they are suffering from this phobia that when they would be displaced again from their temporary settlement is not at all certain.

As regards the tribal people of Chitrakoot and Allahabad it is naked truth that most of the tribals have been bonded labours since long. Their economic conditions cannot permit them to send their children in school. Table 5.33 shows an example of extreme degree of illiteracy in both the regions.

Table 5.33: Literacy Rate of Children of the Respondent Households

District	*Household*	*Literate*	*Literate*	*Illiterate*	*Illiterate*
Mirzapur	750	444	11.3	306	7.8
Sonbhadra	750	347	9.3	403	10.8
Chandauli	450	229	10.1	221	9.7
Naxalite area	1950	1020	10.3	930	9.4
Allahabad	600	373	11.0	227	6.7
Chitrakoot	450	166	36.9	284	63.1
Dacoit Area	1050	539	51.3	511	48.7
Total of five districts	3000	1559	52.0	1441	48.0

The above Table 5.33 shows 11.3 per cent literacy rate in Mirzapur, 9.3 per cent in Sonbhadra and 10.1 per cent literacy rate in Chandauli tribal children. In Naxal prone area the average literacy rate among the tribal children is only 10.3 per cent. In spite of all efforts like Right to Education, Sarva Shiksha Abhiyan, free facilities for schooling, etc., children in this region are helpless due to several reasons. One of them is repeatedly displacement of their families. Chronic poverty and temporary settlement of their parents do not allow them to go to school. As regards to Dacoit prone area the literacy rate in Allahabad tribal area is very poor, i.e., 11.0 per cent, but in Chitrakoot there is more than fifty per cent, i.e., 51.3 per cent literacy rate among tribal children has been recorded. There may be two reasons behind this rising tendency of literacy. One may be that the bonded labourhood tradition is almost over and the second reason may be that Chitrakoot district is now almost free from Dacoit terror.

Table 5.34 shows that only 22.5 per cent tribal respondents from Mirzapur, 15.6 per cent from Sonbhadra, 19.8 per cent from Chandauli, 7.3 per cent from Allahabad and 16.7 per cent from Chitrakoot could complete up to Primary level education. Average percentage of Naxal area tribal primary level education was 19.2 per cent and in the Dacoit area it was 11.3 per cent. The total literacy rate upto primary level of education in all the five districts was only 16.5 per cent.

The total percentage of middle school, high school, inter and Graduate level of all the five districts was 8.5 per cent, 5.9 per cent, 2.9 per cent and 0.1 per cent respectively. The conclusion can easily be drawn that in spite of implementation of Eleventh Five Year Plans and welfare programmes, a very little effort has been done for increasing literacy among the tribal people inhabiting in these five districts. The crores of rupees sanctioned by the Government of India and State Government in the name of educational development and welfare programme have met with loss.

The Government of India and the State Government has launched several programmes to enhance the education among all the children. Recently "the Right to Education" Act and Sarva Shiksha Compaign have been enforced and the grant has also been released to all the States. In Uttar Pradesh also these facilities are available to all the children. In spite of all sorts of facilitics, why a large number of children leave their schools after enrolment. This trend of dropout cases among tribal children is quite alarming. The difference of percentage of Gross Enrolment Ratio (GER) and Dropout Ratio is significant. In the following Table 5.35 the reasons have been analysed after enquiring 3,000 respondents of the households of all the five districts.

In the remote tribal areas the tribal people have suffered a lot on account of inadequate numbers of primary schools, teachers, absenteeism

Table 5.34: Educational Level of the Respondent of the Households, 3000 Sample

District	*House-hold*	*Primary*	*Primary %*	*Middle*	*Middle %*	*HS*	*HS %*	*Inter*	*Inter %*	*Graduate*	*Graduate %*
Mirzapur	750	169	22.5	60	8.0	18	2.4	4	0.5	0	0.0
Sonbhadra	750	117	15.6	59	7.9	37	4.9	24	3.2	2	0.3
Chandauli	450	89	19.8	34	7.6	41	9.1	9	2.0	0	0.0
Naxalite Area	1950	375	19.2	153	7.8	96	4.9	37	1.9	2	0.1
Allahabad	600	44	7.3	62	10.3	61	10.2	38	6.3	0	0.0
Chitrakoot	450	75	16.7	40	8.9	19	4.2	11	2.4	2	0.4
Dacoit Area	1050	119	11.3	102	9.7	80	7.6	49	4.7	2	0.2
Total of five districts	3000	494	16.5	255	8.5	176	5.9	86	2.9	4	0.1

Table 5.35: Reasons for Not Sending Children to School

Sl. No.	*Reasons*	*Number*	*Naxal Area Percentage*	*Number*	*Dacoit Area Percentage*
1.	School too far	273	14	126	12
2.	To supplement household income	546	28	168	16
3.	Education not considered necessary	234	12	84	8
4.	To attend domestic chores	741	38	630	60
5.	Others	156	8	42	4
	Total	1950	100	1050	100

of teachers, poor quality of learning inputs, parents apathy towards education, rural social milieu and lack of educational interest among children, due to child work culture and other factors.

In Table 5.35 the total areas of our study has been categorised in two parts Naxal area and Dacoit area. The first area covers the tribal areas of Sonbhadra, Chandauli and Mirzapur whereas the second area includes tribal areas of Allahabad and Chitrakoot. During interview with the respondents of households, the P.I. enquired about their opinion about the purpose and importance of educating their children. It was found that almost all the respondents were convinced of the need to educate their children. According to them after education their children would be able to get jobs and they would be informed citizens of the country. But despite recognising these benefits, nearly half of the respondents also believe that the opportunity will cost of sending their children to school, is very high; high enough, not to educate them. They would loose economic opportunity in the form of labour, grazing and taking care of siblings, etc.

It is evident from the above Table 5.35 that only 14 per cent respondents of Naxal area and 12 per cent of dacoit area were willing to send their children. For other reasons they said, that the schools were located far away from their home place. They did not have any transportation facilities so they can't send their children to the school. 28 per cent from Naxal Area and 16 per cent from Dacoit area express their views that their children were assets to their family income. When the respondents are out of their houses, their children take care of their houses, cattle and the small babies. Secondly, the children above the age of 10 support the family by earning as child labours in the crop fields and by offering their services in shops and to landlords houses as domestic servants. 12 per cent respondents from Naxal area and 8 per cent from Dacoit area were of the opinion that the education is luxury for them. Therefore, to educate their children is not of their prime importance in their life and, therefore, it is not at all necessary for them. 38 per cent respondents from Naxal area and 60 per cent from Dacoit area emphasised more importance on domestic chores rather educating their children. 8 per cent respondents from Naxal belt and 4 per cent from Dacoit area expressed several other reasons for not educating their children. For example, absenteeism of school teachers and irregular opening of schools. This is not surprising. Remoteness apart from provoking underdeveloped markets, rudimentary infrastructure and lack of opportunities, etc. also place high opportunity cost on child's education. Moreover, opportunities in remote areas are few. Any addition to family income, like child labour, like relieving an adult for employment if the child takes upto grazing or look after siblings, is welcome at the cost of child's education.

Table 5.36 shows the number and percentage of dropout cases in all the five districts from where the 3,000 tribals households respondents have been interviewed.

If we observe the percentage of dropout students at primary level of education, it is quite alarming. 40 per cent of dropout students in primary school level in Mirzapur, 43 per cent in Sonbhadra, 42 per cent in Chandauli, 55 per cent in Allahabad and 56 per cent in Chitrakoot tribal areas, clearly indicate that the tribal people, definitely passing their life under heavy pressure of economic and social problems. The attraction of Mid Day Meal facilities, free education, and several schemes of scholarship, etc., prove very little attraction to them. 14 per cent dropout cases in Naxal area and 13 per cent cases in Dacoit area at upper Basic education level, definitely show much less percentage in comparison to primary level education, but it does not mean that this is an encouraging indicator. Since the number of students in upper basic level was quite low, therefore, the percentage of dropout cases are also found accordingly. Dropout cases in high school level was 6 per cent, 3 per cent in intermediate level and 0.1 per cent in degree level virtually appear to be satisfactory but the question arises where are the tribal students in majority at these levels. A very few students reach at these levels. Their number is very very low.

Table 5.37 has been recorded from the statistical report 2001 (Sonbhadra) which shows the number of primary schools running in building and without building and the total number of male and female

Table 5.36: Dropout Cases at Different Level of Schooling in Tribal Areas of Sonbhadra, Chandauli, Mirzapur, Allahabad and Chitrakoot, Sample = 3000

District	*Total households*	*Primary*	*%*	*Middle*	*%*	*High School*	*%*	*Inter*	*%*	*Above inter*	*%*
Mirzapur	732	300	40.0	90	12.0	69	9.2	8	1.1	0	0.0
Sonbhadra	741	323	43.1	60	8.0	84	11.2	7	0.9	0	0.0
Chandauli	436	189	42.0	63	14.0	25	5.6	14	3.1	0	0.0
Naxal Total	1909	812	41.6	213	10.9	178	9.1	29	1.5	0	0.0
Allahabad	600	330	55.0	78	13.0	3	0.5	33	5.5	3	0.5
Chitrakoot	450	252	56.0	59	13.1	0	0.0	29	6.4	0	0.0
Dacoit Total	1050	582	55.4	137	13.0	3	0.3	62	5.9	3	0.3
Total of five Districts	2959	1394	46.5	350	11.7	181	6.0	91	3.0	3	0.1

tribal children enrolled in these primary schools run under the control of the Basic Shiksha Department, Sonbhadra.

Table 5.37: Number of Primary Schools and Number of Male and Female Tribal Children Enrolled in the School and Number of Teachers Male and Female, Sonbhadra—2001

Sl. No.	Development Block	Primary School		No. of male students		No. of female students		No. of teachers	
		Total	Without building	Total	SC/ST	Total	SC/ST	Total	Female
1.	Ghorawal	252	0	20456	9535	20885	9146	214	46
2.	Robertsganj	261	0	20207	7660	20092	7130	387	153
3.	Chhatra	122	0	8837	3098	8196	2966	94	24
4.	Nagwan	108	0	7594	4190	7249	3379	67	9
5.	Chopan	277	0	20707	11571	17160	9580	204	142
6.	Myorpur	216	0	21778	11359	18539	11317	180	91
7.	Dudhi	162	13	12328	7396	10968	6626	221	88
8.	Babhani	117	0	7127	4502	6520	4490	103	28
	Total	1596	13	135834	62947	122550	56002	1781	765
	Total %								

Sonbhadra district is worstly affected by the Naxalite activities and heavily affected by the displacement activities by the installation of several industries, Dams, Power plants and excavation of coal and other mines in comparison to Chandauli and Mirzapur districts. Therefore, the principal investigator selected Sonbhadra among the five districts as sample to show the number of students at primary level, teachers and the real situation of building and other minimum infrastructure facilities provided by the Basic Shiksha Department for at least the primary level of education.

Block-wise record shows that there are 252 primary schools in Ghorawal, 261 in Robertsganj, 122 in Chhatra, 108 in Nagwan, 277 in Chopan, 216 in Myorepur, 162 in Dudhi and 117 primary schools in Babhani Blocks are running. The total number of schools are 1,596. Out of 1,596, 13 schools are running without having any building. In these primary schools 62,947 scheduled castes and scheduled tribes male children are studying. And the female children number of SC/ST children is 56,002. In those primary schools the number of male teachers are 1,781 and female teachers 765 in number. Almost in all the schools non-tribal teachers are employed due to unavailable of SC/ST qualified persons.

As per Census 2001 record per school, out of total number of 161 children, 61 SC/ST children enrolled in primary schools. Out of total enrolled children (male) nearly 49 per cent SC/ST children were found enrolled. Nearly 51 per cent SC/ST female children were enrolled in 1,596 school. As regards, teachers, only an average 1.6 teachers were teaching in each school. The number of SC/ST children is quite high. These figures definitely show awareness towards education. But if we subtract the scheduled caste children, the number of tribal children will go down quite low. Thus, we can easily draw the conclusions that pressure of 161 students on one school and on 1.6 teachers are quite below the educational standard norms of the country.

Mid-Day meal planning has also been launched in rural and tribal areas as well. The main objective of this plan is to encourage and enhance those children who do not go to school due to the extreme poverty of their families. 1. Basic Shiksha Adhikari, 2. District Supply Officer and the District Manager of UPSFC (State Food Corporation) Department shoulder jointly to run this plan. On the basis of 80 per cent presence of children in a school, rice, pulse, dalia and other cereals total upto 3 kg per month is provided in cooked form to each child of the school. Through this kind of welfare programme the Government intends to eradicate the illiteracy from the village and tribal areas.

The following Table 5.38 shows the percentage of benefited children in Naxal prone and the Dacoit areas of the five districts.

Table 5.38: Benefited Tribal Children by Mid-Day Meal Scheme, 3,000 Samples

Facility Mid-Day Meal	*Naxal Area (Sonbhadra, Chandauli, Mirzapur)*		*Dacoit Area (Chitrakoot and Allahabad tribals)*	
	Number	*%*	*Number*	*%*
Benefited	758	38.87	412	39.24
Not Benefited	1192	61.13	638	60.76
Total	1950	100.00	1050	100.00

As per reply of the respondents 61.13 per cent children in Naxal prone area and 60.76 per cent children in Dacoit prone area have not been benefited by such lucrative plan for the children. It is quite natural poor children cannot tolerate their hunger. If there is any opportunity of availability of food they would run after it. The large percentage of children found deprived of their mid-day meal. Who are culprits of hungry children, is under the jurisdiction of Anti Corruption Department to enquire into.

However, the school staff including concerning departments are jointly held responsible for this crime. Thus, instead of eradicating iliteracy, they are making themselves richer and richer by stealing the food fund from starving poor children.

There is another welfare plan for *Dalit* and *Adivasi* children under Social Welfare Department. Under this plan the children belonging to scheduled caste, untouchable caste and tribes would be awarded scholarship in the following manner.

Class	*Scholarship in Rs.*	*Period in months*
From class I to V in school	Rs. 25/- per month	For 12 months
From VI to VIII in school	Rs 40/- per month	For 12 months
From IX to X class in school	Rs. 60/- per month	For 12 months
ITI students	Rs. 50/- per month	Till completion of the course

Children belonging to untouchable families will be awarded Rs. 500 per annum as additional award.

Children from III to VIII standard of class who are hostler will be awarded Rs. 200 month and Rs. 250 per month to children IX-X standard.

The investigator also wanted to know the reality of this plan by asking how many have been benefited. The following Table 5.39 depicts the following picture.

Table 5.39: Benefited Tribal Children by Scholarship Plan Run by the Social Welfare Department, Sample 3000.

Facility Scholarship	*Naxal Area tribals (Sonbhadra, Chandauli and Mirzapur)*		*Dacoit Area (Chitrakoot and Allahabad tribal)*	
	Number	*%age*	*Number*	*%age*
Benefited	410	21.03	171	16.29
Not benefited	1540	78.97	879	83.71
Total	1950	100.00	1050	100.00

It is evident from Table 5.39 that only 21.03 per cent respondents were benefited in Naxal prone area by the scholarships awarded by the social welfare department whereas only 16.29 per cent respondents from Dacoit prone area were benefited by this plan. The higher percentage 78.97 per cent and 83.71 per cent of non-benefited clearly challenges the Government welfare schemes. To what limit the scholarship grant is being embezzled by the involved officials and schools managements, is a matter of investigation. Often the print media flashes such type of news in newspapers. There may be several reasons behind this corrupt practices, but the ignorance, illiteracy, lack of political leadership and extreme poverty of the tribals are some important reasons.

If we analyse the concept of education, we may thus, understand in its four folds, (i) i.e., education and social values, (ii) education and economy, (iii) education and health and (iv) education and spiritual development. Education brings material changes and thereafter non-material changes in human lives. Formal education enriches formal informative knowledge and material prosperity whereas the informal education makes a man humane and it is full of conscience, over flooded with moral values and philanthropical values. Formal education, in the present educational system, certainly played a great role in economic development of the nation. We have to achieve self-sufficiency in food and agriculture to do much advancement in the fields of science, technology, medicines and making the life well equipped with all modern and material prosperity. But at the same time we are losing very very important part of our social humane, i.e., social/moral values; the role of which, in the social structure is like the cement in a concrete building. It helps in developing social relations between man and man and thus, causes the formation of social structure.

In its absence we develop in the society a sense of insecurity, dishonesty, insincerity, selfishness, disregards, anti community, anti national feeling. Only for material richness, we keep aside all values of morality, kindness, honesty, sincerity and feelings for down trodden poor class people. The tribals come in the same category spending their lives worst than animals.

Therefore, for development of all kinds of education, awareness, aspirations, capability of understanding and development of rationality in tribal people are very very essential. During survey and interview we realized their awareness and aspirations. They expressed their views that they were being tortured and exploited only because they were ignorant and illiterate. Now, they are very much ambitious to educate their children and also want to get adult education. During interview we wanted to know their opinion on this trend change in their family members. The

Table 5.40: Opinion of the Head of Households on Attitudinal and Aspiration Changing Trend in Education in their Family

District	*Total Households*	*Grand Father*	*%*	*Father*	*%*	*Self*	*%*	*Adult Son*	*%*	*No change*	*%*
Mirzapur	750	35	4.7	71	9.5	76	10.1	297	39.6	271	36.1
Sonbhadra	750	0	0.0	36	4.8	187	24.9	190	25.3	337	44.9
Chandauli	450	0	0.0	0	0.0	241	25.3	114	53.6	95	21.1
Naxal Total	1950	35	1.8	107	5.5	728	19.3	377	37.3	703	36.1
Allahabad	600	0	0.0	0	0.0	287	31.3	188	47.8	125	20.8
Chitrakoot	450	0	0.0	13	2.9	141	16.0	72	31.3	224	49.8
Dacoit Total	1050	0	0.0	13	1.2	428	24.8	260	40.8	349	33.2
Total of five Districts	3000	35	1.2	120	4.0	1156	21.2	637	38.5	1052	35.1

following table 5.40 shows the changing trend in educational standard in their family. Normally, the members of three generations reside under one roof as joint family.

36.1 per cent in Mirzapur, 44.9 per cent in Sonbhadra, 21.1 per cent in Chandauli respondent flatly refused that there was hardly any attitudinal change and aspirations for education emerging in their mind. Similarly 20.8 per cent in tribals of Allahabad and 49.8 per cent in Chitrakoot tribals were of the same views. 36.1 per cent in Naxal area and 35.1 per cent in Dacoit area almost were of the same views. This trend, however, may be out of their extreme and chronic poverty and frustration developing as an outcome of present critical situation.

On the other side, respondents of all the five districts agreed with the views that the trend of changes in awareness and aspirations were in upward and in rising direction. In Mirzapur 4.7 per cent grandfather's generation 9.5 per cent in father's generation, 10.1 per cent in self-generation and 39.6 per cent in son's generation, clearly indicate the rising trend in educational change. Same trends are also found in Sonbhadra. Chandauli, Allahabad and Chitrakoot tribal respondents. Thus, 50.4 per cent in Naxal prone area and 42.8 per cent in Dacoit prone area tribals, who are young and living in the present educational milieu are ambitious, aware and aspired for educational changes in their life.

Objective

To find of the difference of opinion of the head of the household on trend in Educational Standard. To prove statistically, is there any change in trend of educational standard in five tribal districts of U.P., i.e., Mirzapur, Sonbhadra, Chandauli, Allahabad and Chitrakoot.

The analysis of the data yields results in terms of mean, S.D. and Significance Value. The obtained results have been summarized in the Table 5.41.

Table 5.41: Statistical Analysis

Sl. No.	*Subject*	*N*	*Mean*	*S.D.*	*D.F.*	*Sig.*
1.	Mirzapur	750	3.61	1.191	4	0.00
2.	Sonbhadra	750	4.10	0.986		
3.	Chandauli	450	3.96	0.681		
4.	Allahabad	600	3.90	0.715		
5.	Chitrakoot	450	4.28	0.835		

Since, the significance value is less than the significant level at 0.05. Therefore, shows that there is no change in trend of educational standard. It proves that there is no significant difference in the five tribal districts of U.P., i.e., Mirzapur, Sonbhadra, Chandauli, Allahabad and Chitrakoot.

Comparison of level of awareness and Aspirations at least between father and son's generation has been analysed through statistical method by the following methods.

Table 5.42: Mean, S.D. and CR Value between Father Generation and Son Generation of Awareness and Aspirations

Sl. No.	*Subject*	*Mean*	*S.D.*	*DF*	*CR Value*
1.	Son's generation tribals	65.0300	7.822	998	–371*
2.	Father's generation tribals	63.0420	9.055		

* Significant at 0.01 level of confidence.

The objective was to find out the difference in awareness and aspirations level of father's generation and son's generation tribals. The hypothesis is that there is no significant difference in the level of aspiration between the two generations. The Table 5.42 shows that the obtained values of critical ratio is 3.71 which is highly significant and 0.01 level of confidence and, therefore, null hypothesis is rejected. This means that the tribals of father's generation do significantly differ from their son's generation. So, it is safe to interpret that there exists much difference in the level of aspiration of father's generation and son's generation tribals. The mean value in son's generation is higher than that of father's generation. The result leads to infer that the son's generation possesses significantly higher level of aspiration as compared to the father's generation. It may be because of their past and present socio-economic and political backgrounds which have quite different in both the generations. The father's generation has not been benefited by the modern socio-political awakening and efforts as compared to the present generation of sons.

III. HEALTH AND MEDICAL FACILITIES AS IMPORTANT INDICATOR FOR DEVELOPMENT

As per World Health Organisation (WHO), "Health is a state of complete physical, mental and social well-being and not merely the absence of diseases and infirmity. Sound health on one hand, is a by-product of socio-economic development and on the other hand, it is an important determinant of the quality of human resources of a country". Therefore, good health is a pre-requisite to human productivity and development process. In remote rural and tribal area people have suffered on account of factors like thin presence of medico and para-medico personnels, inadequate number of Primary Health Centres (PHC) and Sub-primary Health Centres (SHC) and negligence and insensitive approach of medico personnels.

The situation in all the five districts—Sonbhadra, Mirzapur, Chandauli, Allahabad and Chitrakoot tribal areas is still worst on account of several factors; health and medical care services are not easily accessible and affordable. Under these circumstances, the tribal population in remote tribal areas is left with no option but to turn either to traditional healers or untrained private quake practitioners located in markets nearby their villages and localities. Studies pertaining to health care and health practices among tribal groups are very few. These studies try to establish tribal health problems to factors such as morbidity and mortality, widespread poverty, illiteracy, malnutrition, hostile environment, insanitation living conditions, ignorance of causes of diseases, lack of health services and other several problems among the tribals living in remote forest areas.

The study of health status and health practices among tribals deserves special attention in the situation of poverty for any development plan. This is primarily for two reasons. Firstly, the majority of tribals are illiterate, ignorant and backward and living in the inaccessible and remote forest and hilly areas, where modern health facilities are not available, and tribal society is guided by traditionally laid down customs. The fate of an individual and the community depends on their relationship with unseen forces which intervene human affairs. It is blind faith that if man offend the mystical powers, they punish then by sickness, natural calamities and death. Secondly, there is rapid decline in growth rate of survival of the tribal population. This demands careful attention of socio-cultural habits and health practices of tribals.

The tribal communities have remained isolated from the rest of the society and their exposure to the modern world has been limited, the result being twofold. One; they had not contacted the diseases of the modern society, but may fall an easy prey to them once they come in more frequent contact with the members of modern society. Second, their physique is not used to allopathic system of medicine. Diseases are caused by bad spirits and the spirits are bad either because one has not properly propitiated them. Thus, to a tribal mind, the real enemy of human health and prosperity are gods and the dead.

The usual theory of disease in tribal society is that it is caused by the breach of some taboos or by hostile spirits, ghosts or the dead. Sickness is the routine punishment for every lapse and crime meted out to them by the spirits. Accordingly, they have taboos and prayers. The tribal village priest in addition to their religious functions acts as the mediator between the people and the mystical powers. By propitiations and prayers he tries for the good relationship between the people on one hand and maintains mystical powers on the other which intervene human affairs. In addition to the worship of the spirits, the tribal people have been very well acquainted with primitive medicines since beginning. That means the tribal people have pharmacopoeia of their manifold diseases like malaria, yaws, leprosy, scabies, venereal diseases, bowl complaints, influenza, ophthalmic, cholera, small pox, etc. Their selection of tribal medicines has never been scientifically proved as the right medicines and the right dose, but their blind faith is dominant fact in curing the diseases. Therefore, they prefer their own medicines in place of modern allopathic medicines and modern way of treatment.

During field survey the author met with several patients who had been suffering from different diseases like Anemia, Diarrhoea, T.B., Malaria, Fileria, Jaundice, Ulcer, Skin related diseases, deficiency of iodine, micro-nutrient deficiency, deficiency of dietary components, Arsenicosis, venereal diseases, AIDS, etc. During discussions with local leaders and Gram Pradhans we recorded the frequency of death in child birth and infancy, the ravages of diseases like T.B., epidemics like cholera, small pox, venereal diseases, the superstitious and the object fear of witchcraft and black magic of the spirits of evils, diseases and death. The diseases spread due to climatic conditions, due to change of seasons, due to bacteria, various insects and due to bad habits. But the main reasons are the ignorance, lack of rationality, illiteracy, poverty and inaccessibility of medical facilities. Therefore, any type of development cannot be achieved unless the poverty is removed, people are educated and their health condition is improved.

No doubt, the Union Government and the State Government as well have launched several health improvement programmes, special financial budget is allotted per year but the outcome of all such efforts are not at all worth appreciable. Most of these health projects have experienced implementation problems causing delays in disbursement and completion. Problems include delay in project mobilization and procurement. The direct beneficiaries are the big industrial houses, transnational corporations, political leaders like Gram Pradhan, Zila Panchayat Parishad, MLAs and M.P.s and local elite maphias.

The current example is NRHM embezzlement case in U.P. In the following Tables 5.43 and 5.44 it has shown the number of BPL card holders and smart card holders and has analysed that where the tribals utilized the medical facilities.

Table 5.43: Distribution of Smart Card, 3000 Sample Households

Area of Study	*Total Households*	*BPL*		*Smart Card Holders*	
		Listed	*%*	*Holders*	*%*
Naxal Prone Area	1950	1154	59.2	423	21.7
Dacoit Prone Area	1050	592	56.2	271	16.3
Total	3000	1746	58.2	570	19.0

Table 5.44: Places from where the Medical Facilities availed by the Respondent Households

District	*Total House-holds*	*Govt. Hospital*	*%*	*Private*	*%*	*Dhar-marth*	*%*
Mirzapur	750	178	23.7	250	33.3	0	0.0
Sonbhadra	750	45	6.0	205	27.3	0	0.0
Chandauli	450	44	9.8	82	18.2	0	0.0
Naxal Total	1950	267	13.7	537	27.5	0	0.0
Allahabad	600	57	9.5	349	58.2	0	0.0
Chitrakoot	450	58	12.9	118	26.2	0	0.0
Dacoit Total	1050	115	11.0	467	44.5	0	0.0
Total of five Districts	3000	382	12.7	1004	33.5	0	0.0

Table 5.44 shows that only 23.7 per cent respondents in Mirzapur, 6.0 per cent in Sonbhadra, 9.8 per cent in Chandauli, 9.5 per cent in Allahabad and 12.9 per cent respondent households of Chitrakoot availed medical facilities from Government hospitals like PHC, CHC and hospitals located at the district Headquarters. Only 13.7 per cent respondents households of Naxal prone area and 12.9 per cent respondent households from Dacoit prone area could avail medical facilities from Government hospitals.

Objective

To find out the difference of opinion of the head of the household on medical facilities available and availed by the household. To proves statistically about the medical facilities available and availed by the household in the five tribal districts of U.P., i.e. Mirzapur, Sonbhadra, Chandauli, Allahabad and Chitrakoot.

The analysis of the data yields results in terms of mean, S.D. and Significance Value. The obtained results have been summarized in the Table 5.45.

Table 5.45: Statistical Analysis

Sl. No.	*Subject*	*N*	*Mean*	*S.D.*	*D.F.*	*Sign.*
1.	Mirzapur	750	1.59	0.495	4	0.00
2.	Sonbhadra	750	1.93	0.254		
3.	Chandauli	450	1.78	0.412		
4.	Allahabad	600	1.83	0.377		
5.	Chitrakoot	450	1.85	0.361		

Since, the significance value is less than the significant level at 0.05. It proves statistically that the opinion of the head of household about the medical facility available and availed by the household are common, i.e., not up to the mark in the five tribal districts of U.P., i.e., Mirzapur, Sonbhadra, Chandauli, Allahabad and Chitrakoot. The medical facilities are not properly made available to the peoples of these areas.

Table 5.46: Benefited under National Maternity Benefit Yojana

Facility	*Naxal Area*	*%*	*Dacoit Area*	*%*
Benefited	665	34.1	434	41.3
Not Benefited	1285	65.9	616	58.7
Total	1950	100	1050	100

Under National Maternity Yojana all those pregnant women who come in the category of B.P.L. will be awarded Rs. 500 at the time of delivery with the condition that she has two children in total.

Table 5.46 shows that in Naxal prone area which covers Sonbhadra, Chandauli and Mirzapur only 34.1 per cent pregnant women could avail the opportunity of Rs. 500 award at the time of delivery. The percentage

41.3 of pregnant women were benefited in Dacoit prone area. It clearly indicates that more than 50 per cent tribal pregnant women are ignorant of this welfare Yojana. In other way it can be interpreted that their share has been embezzled by the concerning department.

Table 5.47: Balika Samriddhi Yojana

Facility	*Naxal Area*	*%*	*Dacoit Area*	*%*
Benefited	542	27.8	314	29.9
Not Benefited	1408	72.2	736	70.1
Total	1950	100	1050	100

Balika Samriddhi Yojana award is meant for those who have given birth a female baby. Table 5.47 shows that only 27.8 per cent in Naxal prone area and 29.9 per cent in Dacoit prone area have been benefited by this programme and the 72.2 per cent in Naxal prone area and 70.1 per cent in Dacoit prone area women's share has been embezzled by the hospital and the welfare department.

In spite of availability of free medical services and free medicines even tribal people did not utilize facilities of Government hospitals. The reasons are well known even to tribals also. Due to absence of doctors and hospital staffs and due to supply of duplicate medicines the percentage of patients are quite low in comparison to private medical practitioners, 27.5 per cent respondent households from Naxal prone area and 44.5 per cent from Dacoit prone area prefer to go to private doctors. The Principal Investigator personally visited these places and found that there were no doctor and only one or two Para-Medical staff were there on duty.

Table 5.48: Mortality Rate in Study Area

Mortality	*Total per thousand in India*	*SC and ST in all the five districts per thousand*
Post Natal	16.9	39.7
New Natal	54	63.5
Infant Child	104.8	109.7
Child	154	141.5
Life expectancy	57.1	54.8

Table 5.48 shows the post and neo natal mortality rate and infant child is higher among the surveyed tribal areas than that of the overall mortality rate of the State. But on the other side the child mortality rate is

lower. The life expectancy rate is also lower. Thus, the health indicators of tribal communities present a unique characteristic that why post-natal, neo-natal and infant child mortality rates are higher in comparison to the State, is explained in the following Table 5.49.

Table 5.49: Causes of Mortality Rate in the Study Area

Causes	*Child Marriage %*	*Adult Marriage %*
Marital Age	93%	7%
Medical care during Pregnancy	No medical care 98.6%	Medical care 1.4%
Cutting the umbilical cord and dressing	(unsterilized, blade, knife and thread by local untrained lady) 99.3%	0.7% Sterilized scissors, blade, knife and thread by local trained ANM
Place of delivery	Home delivery 96%	CHC or PHC or Hospital 4%

The early or child marriage leads to several major life threatening complications, like frequency of abortion, miscarriages and high blood pressure. This is one of the important causes of risen mortality rate of the child and mother mortality rate. Table 5.49 shows that 93 per cent girls were found married before the puberty age. The second cause of mortality is the medical care during pregnancy period. Due to advancement in medical science, every medical care is taken during total period of pregnancy of woman. The blood pressure rise, deficiency of iron, vitamin and calcium, jaundice and other problems arise during pregnancy. Therefore, the pregnant woman goes to qualified doctor for regular check-up. In addition to these normal problems, suddenly several other complications may also arise which could not be controlled without going to a qualified doctor. Due to complete ignorance of these complications and unavailability of medical facilities and unavailability of ANM and medical lady doctors, tribal women have to suffer pre-delivery and post-delivery problems a lot. Such women follow self-medication, herbal medicines and depend on elderly, experienced women for advice. 98.6 per cent women replied that they had not taken any medical care under the qualified doctors due to their poverty and easily availability of such facilities. Only 1.4 per cent women somehow could enjoy the medical facilities during pregnancy period.

The most dangerous and fatal action during delivery is cutting of the umbilical cord of newly born baby and, therefore, its dressing. Due to complete ignorance of the fatal consequences of this process elderly tribal women cut the umbilical cord with unsterilized scissors or blade or country made rusted knife. Unsterilized thread is used for tying the umbilical cord. Child and mother mortality rates rises due to unhygienic and tetanus diseases. During survey it was recorded that 99.3 per cent cutting of umbilical cord had been cut by unsterilized scissors, blade and knife and thread had been used. The negligible percentage 0.7 could seek help from ANM and qualified doctors. The same situation is applicable to place of delivery also. 96 per cent delivery has taken place in their thatched huts which are full of infections. Only 4 per cent pregnant women could manage to go to CHC, PHC and hospital for their delivery.

Under Women Welfare Programme the State Government provide vaccination facilities to the newly born children. Under this scheme essential medicines and vaccines are administered to pregnant women and newly born baby and mother as per instructions of the doctors. Facilities for regular health examination are also available by qualified doctors with the help of ANM.

Under medical facilities, care of Health and Implementation of Family planning programmes, following facilities are provided by the State Government.

> In order to control the birth rate, medical care and death rate following measures are being taken by the Government.
> Oral pills, Copper T, Permanent Step to Vasectomy of male and female, in the condition of removal of pregnancy the doctors have to observe seriously that the woman's health does not allow to conceive, the woman conceived due to rape, etc., and fear of defective birth of baby due to misuse of contraceptive devices.

In order to implement the population policy of the State government there are official instructions that the marriages of girls should not be performed before 19.5 years of age. Birth rate should be reduced from 4.3 to 2.1 before 2016. Mother's death rate should be reduced from 7.7 per year to 2.07 per year (Death rate is 7.7 per lakh mothers). The death rate of newly born baby should be reduced from 85 per thousand to 61 per thousand before 2016. And all men and women should be made acquainted about the consequences of AIDS and they should be taught precautions and to save them from this disease.

For safe motherhood, the women should be taught all sorts of precautions, necessary medicines and vitamins before and after delivery should be administered. For all such facilities ANM, Dais, Health workers and female doctors have been appointed and they have to shoulder the responsibility for their care and they have to take the patients through ANM to lady doctors for regular check-up at PHC. They have to administer iron, folic acid medicines (100) and two times TT vaccine in a gap of one month. Pregnant women should be encouraged and persuaded to be admitted in the hospital at the time of delivery for her and her baby's safety. In addition to regular medico staff one casual post has been created by the State Government. The name of the post is Asha Bahu who gets Rs. 3500 per month as honorarium and she will also get Rs. 700 per delivery case. Moreover, the BPL pregnant woman will also be awarded Rs. 1400 after delivery. The Ex-Chief Minister Ms Mayawati has also announced that Rs. 2500 amount will be fixed in the bank if female baby is born. The maturity amount of Rs. one lakh will be released to that girl at her marriage occasion.

The State Government has also issued instructions to the medical staff for taking care of babies. The weight of a baby should not be less than 2.5 kg at the time of delivery, to watch that the weight is increasing gradually. Special care should be taken if babies are twin. It should be ensured that the mother is capable of breast feeding. Babies should be administered TT, Pneumonia, Khasara, Malnutrition injections and for deficiency of water of the body. To ensure that the mother's feeding continue up to six months. In case it does not continue the dry milk should be provided to the babies. The babies should be given BCG vaccine within a year and DPT vaccine within six weeks to one year.

Tribals, living in Sonbhadra, Chandauli, Mirzapur, Allahabad and Chitrakoot districts are victims of drinking contaminated ground water and stagnant water accumulated during rainy season. They have no option except to use such polluted water for drinking purposes. Arsenic as water pollutant is very harmful for human health. All the power plants, chemical industries and coal mines installed in Sonbhadra, Chandauli and Mirzapur area regularly discharging very harmful chemicals and these pollutants are mixed with the soil and the Rihand, Son and other rivers making their water culminated. Tribals who have been displaced for the sake of these power plants and industries are rehabilitated around these plants. They have to consume such culminated water for drinking. Increasing number of handicapped children, peripheral vascular disorder, jaundice and hepatitis decreasing production of red and white blood cell, blood vessel damage, irritation of digestive tract, leading to pain, nausea, vomiting, diarrhorea, liver and kidney damages, impaired nerve functioning, foetus damage during pregnancy and so many water born diseases have been recorded in Naxal prone area. In Dacoit prone area which covers Allahabad and Chitrakoot, due to continuous draught many wells and tanks are dried. The source of drinking water only is accumulated by rain water in small ditches and ponds. They are highly infected. The tribals of Chitrakoot and Allahabad are helpless and they have no option except to utilize such water for drinking purposes. They are victims of several water borne diseases.

In order to deal with this acute problem and to provide clean drinking water, the Jal Nigam, the State Government department has installed India Mark II hand pumps everywhere in remote tribal villages. The State Government has also made the villagers aware of the water borne diseases. They are provided medicines and chemicals like cleaning powder, chlorine etc., for making the water safe for drinking purposes.

During survey it was found that in most of the villages of study area India Mark II hand pumps were in function and tribals were using this water for their drinking purposes. As regards to curing their water borne diseases, the efforts of the State Government was not at all appreciable. Again we come to the conclusion that due to ignorance, illiteracy, chronic poverty and lack of leadership their voices are unheard and consequently their overall conditions are quite pitiable. Thus, it may be concluded that the health and the medical facilities as an important indicator has met with the complete failure for development of the tribals residing in Naxal and Dacoit prone area of our study.

References

1. Sah, D.C., Bhatt, Ashish, 2008, *Trapped in Poverty; Chronic Poor in Remote Tribal Areas*, Rawat Publications, New Delhi.
2. Roy, Kanchan (ed). 2008, *Education and Health Problems in Tribal Development*. Concept Publishing Company (P) Ltd., New Delhi.
3. Pani, Niranjan, Sahoo, Jitendra, 2008, *Tribal Development*, Mahamaya Publishing House, New Delhi.
4. Damina Chaudhary, 2009, *Tribal Girls Aspiration, Achievement and Frustrction*. Pointer Publishers, Jaipur.

Chapter 6

Discontent: Issues and the Causes

Discontent is the manifestation of dissatisfaction of a person or a group of persons against what have been expected by them. It expresses the philosophical and psychological aspects of mind of a person who runs madly in search of material happiness in the world. But in case of tribal of India, the term discontent shows the extremity of their disappointment and frustrations against the lolly pop given by the Government in the name of their development welfare programmes. Now, they have started realizing that they have been befooled. Discontent arises in them when they lose their tolerance. For ages, the Indian tribals have lived a life of geographical isolation. They remained cut off from mainstream of national life resulting in their backwardness in the economic and social spheres when compared to other communities. They have continuously been exploited by the foreign rulers, landlords and moneylenders. Even after the expiry of the period of 68 years of our Independence about 85 per cent of the tribal families are still living below poverty line rather suffering from chronic poverty. They have been victimized by various exploitative means. Discontent is increasing in them day-by-day.

Tribal realize that they are being befooled and blackmailed in the name of development and welfare programmes. The achievements are generally assessed in terms of financial investments rather than the goods delivered. The discontent, among the tribal, surfaces time and again in one form or another; either in the form of a demand for a separate State, such as the agitation for separate State of Jharkhand and Chhattisgarh arose and these were created on the demand for better deal of development. Discontent, unrest and involvement in Naxal activities in tribal areas are the cumulative results of a number of contributory factors. They can be divided into the following heads. The tribal areas have been converted into sanctuaries for Naxalites and extremists.

Issues and Causes of Discontentment

Land Related Problems	Availability of insufficient fertile land.
	Less productivity
	Rocky and hilly land.
	Land Alienation
	Property Non-enforcible of Land Distribution and Forest Right Act. 2006
Unemployment	Main source of income has been forest produce—Tendu Leaf, Bamboos, Honey, Mahua, Wood, Fruits, Herbs and other things found in forest and agricultural land. Forest department has banned to collect the forest produce.
	Within their village and outside their village, they get a few opportunity to work as labourer. Due to low payment, their livelihood is very tuff.
	Forest department has banned to collect the forest produce. They are now treated as ambient and trespassers although they have been living in the forest from generation to generation as their fundamental right.
	Tribal youth is incapable of utilizing their constructive energy.
Corruption	The grant and funds granted by the Central and the State governments for tribals and for tribal areas development, have been embezzled by the government officials, maphias, contractors, local leaders and Gram Pradhan, and Netas. Several constructions and welfare programmes have been shown on papers, funds have been looted and misutilised.
	They are deprived of even minimum required infrastructural facilities.
	Roads, connecting roads, drinking water, Electricity primary health centres, medicines, food materials are scarcely available to them. Even for a small need and for medical treatment in any emergency and other requirements they have to travel 20 to 40 km distance from their places of living.
	Due to non-availability of emergency medical facilities, mostly patients die in the village or on the way.
	A very few sources of livelihood.
	Industries established on their own land do not employ them on priority basis.

Illiteracy	Rarely there is any school in tribal areas. If there is any, no teacher dare go to teach due to fear of wild animals, Dacoits and Naxalites. All the funds and facilities provided by the government has been shown on papers. The literacy rate in all the tribal region is very-very low. Due to illiteracy and absence of outer and rational knowledge, tribal have blind faith in ghost, devils and witches. Whatever happens in their lives, they think that they are all due to ghost and bad evils. They often come even to Police Station to lodge complaint against ghosts. Total no of primary schools in the study area was 1110 which are almost running on paper.
Adverse Geographical Conditions	Their residing places are surrounded by dense forest, Very few plain lands, It is hilly and rocky. It is the border places of Bihar, Jharkhand, Madhya Pradesh and Chhattisgarh to this geographical situation Naxalites take advantages for their anti social, anti national activities. They have safe shelter places and after committing any incident they cross the border and may enter into any other State. 54% land of study area is covered with dense forest where police force feels unable to enter into it. They do not have any road to march.
Exploitation and Torturing	Employees from revenue, forest and police departments often exploit and torture the Tribals. Moneylenders landlords and *dabangs*, maphias torture and exploit in fulfilling their ownselves interest. Honest and bold officers are rarely posted. If they are posted maphias, contractors, landlords and *dabang* persons get them transferred with the help of local and State level leaders.
Displacement	*Adivasis* have been displaced by installation of several dams, power plants, coal mines and industries.
Hunger	Thousands of *adivasis* can't afford their two times meal even today. Several deaths due to hunger have been recorded. Thousands of children dies due to malnutrition. Hunger youth is misguided by Naxalites. Women are sexually exploited for their livelihood.

Handicapped	Due to impure drinking water several children are born handicapped and no care is taken by the State.

In addition to the above mentioned causes, there are several other causes responsible for rising discontents among *dalit adivasis* of South-Eastern margins of Uttar Pradesh.

(i) *Social and Cultural Causes*: Tribal people are enriched with their own social and cultural traditions. They should not be underrated and not be treated inferior, uncivilized, illiterate and poor in comparison to other countrymen of India. But the fact is just reverse. They have very well understood the treatment they received from others who claim as civilized. That is why they are at all not satisfied with development process. In the eyes of law of the Constitution of India, they have full rights of the Indian citizenship. They should not be treated as untouchable and backward Hindus. Such an approach may save their culture, beliefs, tradition and life style. It should not be presumed that the tribals have no administrative capability, incapable of identifying their needs and managing their own affairs. The best cause of their survival and development is to follow the policies decided by them by keeping their social and cultural background not by others for them.

(ii) *Lack of Accountability*: The legislative powers of the Parliament and State legislatures are defined under Articles 245, 246 and 248. None of the three lists, i.e., the Union List, State List and Concurrent List includes in it the tribal affairs exclusively. Only the Parliament in exercise of its residual power under Art. 248(1) read with entry 57 in the list of the Scheduled Tribes. At the Government of India level, there are at least three agencies, *viz.*, 1. Ministry of Social Justice and Empowerment, 2. National Commission for Scheduled Castes and Scheduled Tribes, and 3. Planning Commission. Each Central Ministry is a Nodal Ministry for implementation of its scheme and programmes concerning the welfare of scheduled tribes.

Such multiplicity of agencies divides the responsibility and divided responsibility is often nobody's responsibility. The Seventh Schedule of the Constitution should be amended to incorporate clauses clearly defining the functional responsibility of the Union and the State Governments. Separate administrative apparatus must be evolved for execution of programmes.

(iii) *Denial of Participation in Development Process:* There has been no effective participation of the tribals in decision making of their own affairs. The policies and programmes have been formulated without consulting them. As a result, it has been resulted in fixation of wrong priorities and failure in achieving the desired results.

The expectation that mode of representation would ensure satisfactory tribal respresentation in the Panchayats in tribal majority areas, is belied in the absence of specific legislative stipulation in most of the States that only tribal candidates must be fielded. There is no provision that Panchayati Raj bodies in tribal majority areas should be headed by the tribals at all levels.

(iv) *Lack of Leadership*: Lack of leadership is an important cause of discontent. Leadership vacuum has adversely affected tribal development.

(v) *Inadequate Implementation of Constitutional Safegards*: The Constitution envisages a comprehensive and well designed scheme of action for tribal protection and development.

The Union Government's persuasive approach with the State Government regarding the measures to be taken for the protection and development of the tribals has not been very effective. The provisions contained in the Fifth Schedule have virtually remained non-operational.

(vi) The tribal Sub-Plan strategy launched in 17 States and 2 Union territories as new package for integrated development of tribal areas with specific focus on development of tribal communities has not been a success because of lack of orientation of the administrative machinery.

(vii) The economic assistance to family oriented programmes is inadequate to lift a family above poverty line. No specific data has been collected about the extent of impact of the programmes.

(viii) In recruitment of services and posts under the Government of India and the States, the scheduled tribes are still under representation.

Their representation in Central Government posts and services is below 2 per cent in Group "A" and "B" and below 5 per cent in group C and D as against 7.5 per cent prescribed for each of these categories.

(ix) There has been heavy influx of outsiders in the tribal areas; who have not only grabbed most of the resulting job opportunities,

> but also settled down in those areas and have increased pressure among others on the land resources. The power of imposing restrictions on the movement and settlement of outsiders in tribal areas are envisaged in clause 5 of Art. 19 of the Constitution has never been exercised. As a result the tribal population in certain tribal majority areas has been reduced to minority.

Causes and issues of discontent among *dalit adivasis* of Mirzapur, Sonbhadra, Chandauli, Allahabad and Chitrakoot districts are being mentioned point-wise in the following manner:

(a) *Economic*: (i) Extreme Poverty, (ii) Land alienation, (iii) Land grabbing, (iv) Deprived of forest rights 2006, (v) False distribution of Land *Patta*, (vi) Indebtedness, (vii) Bonded Labour, (viii) Unemployment, (ix) No Source of livelihood, (x) Hunger, and (xi) Embezzlement of BPL funds and facilities like PDS food materials;

(b) *Health and Sanitation*: (i) Poor Health conditions, (ii) Culminated drinking water, (iii) Consuming poisonous grass, mushrooms etc., in the absence of eatable food items, (iv) several chronic diseases, (v) malnutrition, (vi) Lack of medical care and facilities, and (vii) handicapped child birth;

(c) *Environmental Conditions:* (i) Polluted water to drink and polluted air to inhale due to excessive discharge of harmful chemicals, ashes, fumes and poisionous grabage accumulated near dam, industrial areas and near coal mines, and (ii) Drought and flood, dry well and ponds;

(d) *Social and Cultural*: (i) Social evils, (ii) Use of excessive liquor and intoxicant, (iii) gambling, (iv) Women sex exploitation, (v) Suicides, (vi) Rise in criminal activities, (vii) Torturing and exploitation by police, maphias, Feudal landlords and government officials, and (viii) Loss of cultural traits due to lack of any incentives to preserve them;

(e) *Educational*: (i) Illiteracy, (ii) Lack of Educational facilities and Institutions, (iii) Embezzlement of Midday Meal and Scholarship funds, and (iv) Absentees of children and teachers;

(f) *Infrastructural fracilities*: (i) No approach Roads, (ii) No proper housing, (iii) No electricity, and (iv) No drinking water supply;

(g) *Political and Administration*: (i) No political representation, (ii) No administrative representatives; and

(h) *Displacement*: (i) Multiple displacement, (ii) No proper compensation, and (iii) No proper rehabilitation.

Almost all the aspects of causes of discontent have been discussed and covered up during discussions in related chapters. Unemployment, Land alienation and displacement are the main causes of discontent, have been discussed in detail in the following chapters.

I. LAND ALIENATION

Among the total population of India, 72.8 per cent live in rural areas and 27.8 per cent live in urban areas (2001). Economy of the agro-based or pre-agro based society is very simple and they are tied up with land, forest and nature. The whole economic perspective is depending upon land and this is their prime property. Due to different reasons and in different ways numerous ethnic groups have lost their prime sources of income. This has made the people landless and resourceless which forced them to face all concern of hardship to maintain their daily livelihood. Their lands have been alienated into the hands of outsiders. According to the 2001 Census, there is a sharp decrease in the percentage of the tribal cultivators. It has gone down from 68.18 per cent in 1961 to 67.83 per cent in 2001. As a result of it, a large percentage of tribals are standing in the line of landless labourers. The agircultural labourers percentage have increased from 19.71 per cent in 1961 to 46.87 per cent in 2001. Decreasing in the number of cultivators and increasing in the landless labourers is indicative of the disturbing trend of land alienation.

The sample survey conducted by the Department of Rural Development 1988, showed that about 80 per cent land of the tribal people have been alienated to the non-tribals. Consequently, nearly 55 per cent tribal household have been affected by the land alienation in India. During survey it was also highlighted that in certain areas, although the tribals were the official owners of the land, the non-tribals have become its virtual owners. Opening of the tribal areas in the wake of the development process and setting up of various irrigation, power, mining projects and installation of several industries brought in the problem of land alienation. Grabbing of tribal land coupled with their exploitation by *zamindars*, contractors, maphias, middlemen and government officials like lekhpals caused widespread discontent among the tribals which manifested in a series of tribal revolts as consequence of their discontent. Due to unsatisfactory state of land records, tribals were not legally recognised as owners of their lands where they had been cultivating since beginning. Since, the new legal system gradually superseded the traditional system, the tribal, as an individual was unable to stand against the continuing pressure of outsiders. As a result of it, the concerned owner people have been displaced from their stable economic and surrounding environmental background.

The general methods of alienation has been through sale, mortgage, lease, benami transfers, collusive decrease and fraudulent methods of land grabbing. There have been many cases where the land has been taken *in lieu* of the money loaned. In many cases the tribals have not only been dispossessed of their land, but they are forced to work as agricultural labourers on their own land. In some other cases, the non-tribals created fictitious documents or manipulated the sale deed to show that the sale took place to protective provisions of the land laws became operative.

Today 86 per cent of *dalit* households (160 million) are landless. Those who do own land either own too little or lack adequate capital for purchasing resources for cultivation like seeds, fertilizers and or hiring farm implements. Laws and regulations prohibiting alienation of tribal and *dalits* lands, ceiling on single owners landholding and allocation of surplus land to ST have been ignored or manipulated by upper castes and local district administration.

During British Period: Since centuries the tribals had been the permanent occupants of dense forest of South-Eastern part of Uttar Pradesh which include Mirzapur, Sonbhadra and Chandauli, Allahabad and Chitrakoot districts. They had enjoyed full rights in the forest using forest produce for their livelihood. They were land owners of whatever they had occupied for their use.

Sonbhadra, Mirzapur and Chandauli districts are rich in minerals and other natural resources that contribute the maximum revenue for the State treasury every year. The land is extremely fertile with extremely good crop yield. But the tribal people enjoyed their rich heritage only till the resources were under the control of the community. Today the forest department is the biggest landlord and controls more than 40 per cent of land in these districts. It is understood that because of tough terrain, dense forest and fear of wild animals, the revenue records of this particular area were not prepared during the British rule, as had been undertaken for rest of the country.

In fact, whatever, land records were prepared, were done on the basis of visual measurement.

During late eighteenth century, Lord Cornwallis introduced the Permanent Settlement Act, in the area.

During British period, the extreme land was under possession of Raja (King) of Vijaygarh State. The tribals had been their subjects. The King often obliged these tribals especially Kol tribes by granting land against their services. Due to pressure of population several upper and middle caste people of other places started migrating and intended to settle in this area by offering *nazarana* to the King. In due course of time, the migrated people became landlords and started taking services from the tribes by employing them as bonded labour. That was the first stage of land alienation of the permanent residents, i.e., tribals.

After the abolition of the *zamindari* system and enactment of Land Reform Act in 1950, the Princely State had to relinquish their claim on entire land. In spite of land reform Act and Abolition of Landlordism, the control over the land and village commons got concentrated in the hands of the small section of landlords, as a consequence the benefits of all development schemes like irrigation, levelling of land, boundary construction of agricultural fields were reaped by this new class of *zamindars*. The *dalit* and *adivasis* who had toiled to clear the forest to make it cultivable and even tilled it, were denied any ownership and in fact driven away. The land on which these families are presently settled also belong to the forest Department. And every now and then the staff harasses them to vacate their land. Just around the huts they have sown some 20-30 plants of maize and the forest staffers often abuse them and threaten to destroy these alleging that they cannot cultivate the forest land.

The Second Stage of land alienation started after the enforcement of the Zamindari Abolition Act, the Zamindar Raja of Vijaypur State started disposing of his lands after receiving *nazarana* whosoever might be. The Kol and other tribes could not dare buying lands from Raja because they had no money for his *nazarana*. As result of it, they again remained landless although this Act was enforced in order to help them.

The main objective of Zamindari Abolition Act was to grant land to the tiller and remove all intermediaries. But in the case of Sonbhadra, Mirzapur and Chandauli the entire process was postponed for eighteen years. Due to feudal repression and lack of any alternative support structure, the *dalit* and tribal tillers were forced to clear the land in and around the forest to fend for their livelihood. Thus, in Sonbhadra, Chandauli and Mirzapur districts, the land was looted rather than redistributed. Which was diametrically opposite to the intention of the Zamindari Abolition Act.

The third stage of land alienation started when this part had experienced significant change with the construction of three Dams, named: (i) "Barundha Dam" on the river Belan, (ii) "Sirsi Dam" on the Sirsi river, and (iii) "Adva Dam" on the river Adva during 1950-70. During constructions of these dams, hundreds of well off people migrated to this area and purchased lands which was available in plenty and where the area was sparsely populated. Further, they started cutting and acquiring and denuding the forest by greasing palms of forest officials. That was the Fourth Stage of land alienation of tribal lands. They were completely at loss when they knew that the support and sustenance from the forest, their only means, was not theirs then.

The Fifth Stage of land alienation among tribals was worstly realized when the forest department under the provision of section 4 and section 20 of the forest Act started declaring that all the forest lands had been vested in the forest department by the order of the Union Government. The forest department declared the tribals as encroachers and trespassers. Consequently, the entire forest of south-eastern part of Uttar Pradesh (Mirzapur, Sonbhadra and Chandauli) came under its possession. The tribal population, *adivasi*, *banwasi*, scheduled castes and scheduled tribes. *dalit, adivasi, rahwasi*, etc., who had been cultivating the forest land, using the forest produce since decades, were declared trespassers. Today where Ghasia tribe are settled land has been declared as forest land under Indian Forest Act 1927 (IFA). In this area once again the law of the land has not been implemented without settling any dispute of these claims the land was declared as forest land and even today 500 villages are part of this dispute. Since 1997, the Forest Department has been trying to chase away these tribals using all kinds of the unscrupulous methods to evict them.

The sixth stage started around mid-1960s when there was a move on the part of the Government to increase the forest area in the State. Gram Samaj, particularly those located in the sparsely populated districts were asked to transfer Gram Sabha land to the Forest Department. Many Gram Sabha in these districts Sonbhadra, Chandauli and Mirzapur did so. It has been observed that many of the ceiling surplus land beneficiaries were later granted pattas on such lands and began to cultivate it. After many years, the Forest Department started uprooting them on the plea that the land belongs to the Forest Department. 1624 hectares of Gram Sabha land was transferred from one village namely Babura Raghunath. Around 100 persons were cultivating this land as allottees of ceiling surplus land.

The provision of Section 117 under the said Act was stayed as per notification No. 1768/IVX/695/1953 dated 10/10/1953 issued by the U.P. Government in reference to the letter No. 1932/35-12, September 9, 1953 of the Chief Conservator of Forest U.P. Nainital directing the Divisional Forest Officer of Dudhi and Sub-Divisional officer concerned, should of all, make out list of private forest and waste lands which will be managed by the forest department and these which will be given in the management of Gram Sabha for which certain guidelines were laid down in that said GO, the Government was under obligation to take steps to classify the entire land and to prepare a list as to which part of such land would vest in Gram Sabha, etc.

But it is surprising that the list was never prepared in spite of the standing orders of the U.P., instead, the forest department took the entire land in its possession. This action of the forest department caused displacement of nearly 10,000 families from their ancestral places.

The Seventh Stage of land alienation was badly experienced when thousands of tribal families had to vacate their houses for providing lands for construction of Rihand Dam 1954. The story of south of Kaimur, Singrauli of Sonbhadra district is even more startling. It is now known as the (Energy Capital of India), for its highest power generation capacity. One could recall that in 1954 it was with the construction of the "Rihand Dam" symbol of so called development that this entire process of displacement and alienation of *adivasis* was triggered off. As a result, the most fertile land was submerged under water and lakhs of tribal people lost their homes and livelihood. Establishment of HINDALCO (Renukut) 1962, Kanoria Chemicals 1965, establishment of Thermal Power unit in Obra 1968 and 1971, establishment of Thermal Power unit in Anpara 1980, National Thermal Power unit in Shakti Nagar 1984, Vindhyachal Power Plant unit in Bijapur 1987, establishment of cement factory in Dala 1971, Churk Cement Factory 1980, establishment of HITEC Carbon Plant, Sonbhadra 1988 and Singrauli Coal mines and other minor projects. Still there are several industries proposals in the process due to availability of several minerals here in this area. Thus, the continuing process of displacement of tribals of this place has not yet been stopped. The greatest tragedy is this that tribals have never been properly rehabilitated and no appropriate compensation had yet been granted to them.

The Eighth Stage of land alienation of tribals can be observed when Gram Sabha was authorised to distribute Gram Samaj land to landless families of oppressed class of people. There was standing order under the Acts that firstly a committee will be constituted called Land Management Committee (LMC) in which the Gram Pradhan will be Ex Officio President and the Lekhpal will be Secretary. It is a matter of great shocking that even after the expiry of 61 years of Zamindari Abolition Act and Land Reform Act (1950,1951), *Adivasis, Vanwasi*, Scheduled Castes and Scheduled Tribes based in area of Sonbhadra, Chandauli and Mirzapur, the southern part of Kaimur hill are deprived of constitutional and fundamental rights. Till date, 433 Gram Sabha of this region are being deprived of the constitutional rights and of Section 17 Zamindari Abolition Act by the authorities of the Forest Department. As per Government order the Land Management Committees must be constituted in 433 villages. Consequently, the question does not arise to allot the land to the landless tribals through the decision of the Gram Sabha, the constitutional institution. In spite of several orders passed by the Honb'le Courts, the Forest Department never bothered for the compliance of the court's orders. Forest Department never complied the Government Order No. 1768/XIV-695/1953 and its officers notified being all lands, *banjar* and *partis* of Forest Department under Section 4 of Indian Forest Act under Section 20 of Forest Act the habitats had to vacate. The Forest Department enjoyed the full right and advantage of 433 Gram Sabhas without having any legal and constitutional rights.

Thus, the said 433 Gram Sabhas and their members, tribals, *adivasis* and scheduled castes have been ignored from their fundamental rights by various non-constitutional procedures. They have restrained from the ownership of living life towards the flow of Development of the country. The social activist Sri Shyam Narayan Lal Srivastava, Advocate has been continuously fighting for this illegal actions of the forest department against the *adivasis* of Sonbhadra. He has lodged several complaints to the Uttar Pradesh Government and lodged writ petitions in the Honb'le High Court of Allahabad and the Hon'ble Supreme Court of India. In spite of orders passed in his favour, no orders have yet been complied by the Forest Department and the fate of 433 Gram Sabha and the Constitution of (LMC) Land Management Committee are still in the air. Under this democratic process no fair decision could be done and a very few landless tribals succeeded to acquire the land. The naked truth was that the Gram Pradhan with the collusion of Lekhpal (who maintains the revenue record) used to allot lands to his relatives and to those who greased his hands. The Lekhpal themselves grabbed the Gram Samaj lands by manipulating and changing the revenue records of the villages. Several cases of such type of fraudulent activities were described by the sufferers during the survey. Moreover, Lekhpal were found making huge money by assuring the needy people that this time Gram Samaj land would be allotted to them.

When they found that sufficient money was collected they got themselves transferred from that village to other village. The new lekhpals do the same thing. This was the general practice found among lekhpals who used to exploit the great land hunger of the tribal people.

The local dominant persons, maphias and musclemen were also found taking advantage of their economic, political and gunda power to capture and grab the Gram Samaj land which was to be allotted or already allotted to tribals, by terrorising the tribals, lekhpals and others. Due to their terror and political approach none of the persons from tribes was found lodging complaints in police or to SDM or DM for legal action against them.

Complaints against a great number of fictitious *pattas* of Gram Samaj land was somehow lodged in Uttar Pradesh government. The government constituted a committee known as 'Bhoomi Vyavastha Janch Samiti' in 1972 to look into the misappropriation of Gram Samaj land. After the enquiry that 'Janch Samiti' found that 7.9 million acres of Gram Samaj land allotted after the Zamindari Abolition and out of it 6.5 million acres of land was illegally distributed to undeserved persons and the rest of the land, i.e., only 1.4 million land was left in Gram Samaj by 1970. Out of 1.4 million acre land 5,65,000 acres were unfit for cultivation. The Gram Samaj land which was any how distributed, was infertile, worst land and far away from their harvest ends. A new phase in distribution of Gram Samaj land has appeared in recent years. Those lands which were left assuming as *banzar* completely unfertile, were distributed among the tribals. In this way the investigator could be aware of the real situations and of foul games of encroachment and grabbing activities of Gram Samaj land meant exclusively for tribals.

The Ninth Phase of land alienation of tribals was experienced when the land reform law and Land Ceiling Act 1960 came into effect. There was provision of allotment of *patta* from ceiling surplus land. Previously, there was no limit of possession of area of land. Landlords were maintaining unlimited area of land. But after the enforcement of ceiling Act, they had to spare the surplus land. That surplus land was to be distributed to landless people. But it was not so easy to acquire that type of land from the big landlords and *zamindars* who themselves have always been very powerful and dominant in their villages. No doubt, legal formalities were completed under the Ceiling Act and the surplus land was distributed among the tribals. But the real picture was entirely different. Tribals to whom surplus land was allotted, could not dare acquire their legal share of land due to fear and terror of landowners. Sometimes it also happened that the landowners got the land allotted in fictitious names or in their bonded labour's names. Ultimately, the land which was formally spared, was really in not their possession. In any case if some tribals revolted against their foul game, they were tortured and sometimes they were murdered of which no enquiry could start due to their terror. During survey, investigator found that in several villages *patta* of surplus land was distributed among the tribals through *patta*, but on spot not a single case was found who had possession in real sense. Such plenty cases have been recorded in 'Patha' region, i.e. in Allahabad and Chitrakoot districts.

Villages Makari Bari, Laua in Nagwa, Mathahwan, Silthem in Chatra, Basauli and Amauli in Robertsganj, Semara and Umbha in Ghorawal, Dewato and Machchigawan in Chopan, Bairkhar and Orukhand in Dudhi, Chaga Khudari and Arang Vani in Myorepur (displaced area from Rihand), Jura and Dhankhar in Babhni, Marihan in Mirzapur and some villages of Shankargarh, of Manikpur, Karvi were covered by the investigator. There, it was investigated that nearly 30 per cent land was their ancestral land, 24 per cent was allotted from Gram Samaj (though they did not have possession) and 6 per cent land was allotted under ceiling land, and 40 per cent tribals were landless (due to displacement from industrial places). The average holding size of land was recorded as 0.7 hectares. The land which was in their possession, was mostly barren due to rocky terrain and lacking irrigation facilities. Their average income from such types of land was quite low. Therefore, they have to work as landless labourers during sowing and cultivation seasons.

The problem of land alienation in Chitrakoot and Allahabad tribal people is different from Sonbhadra, Chandauli and Mirzapur.

In recent years the region of Mau, Manikpur and Karvi Blocks of Chitrakoot districts and Shankargarh Block of Allahabad have been appearing in national level newspapers for wrong reasons. Starvation deaths involving particularly the Sahariyar tribe, numerous cases of actual exploitation and land grabbing from Kol tribals and killings, abductions by the Dacoit gangs particularly the biggest in Chitrakoot, which enjoyed very good political connections despite killing dozens of persons, have often been highlighted in the newspapers.

In this region which is called "Patha" region, real land inequalities are greater than what is indicated by land records. A lot of land that is either supposed to be in the possession of weaker sections, i.e., of tribals, is shown as part of the village commons, has actually been encroached by big landowners. There are a large number of landless families who have been given land on paper, but due to several reasons, have not been able to occupy their lands.

Following the principle of social justice policy of the Constitution of India, Land Reform and Zamindari Abolition Acts were enforced in 1950. The main objective of these Acts, was to provide agricultural lands to the weaker section of the people so that they may earn their livelihood by doing farming on their lands. Before Independence tribals of this region enjoyed sovereignty of the forest land and its produce. They were the master of their own land. The 'Patha' region covers nearly 1,634 square kilometre of land. The forest area covers 37 per cent area of this region. Although there are several tribes found in the forest area but the Kol tribe is more popular. There are 233 Kol villages, 12,941 Kol families and total population was 46,098 of male and female Kol tribe. Out of total Kol families, only 3,011 families have their own land and others 2,883 are landless families. The total area of possession covered by the Kol families is almost 21,498 *bigha* and out of which 3,867 *bigha's* of land is unfertile and rocky. 7,229 *bigha's* of Kol's land has been illegally occupied by the landlords, other outsiders and maphias. In several instances where the landlords first allowed the new allottees adequate time to clear rocks from bad quality of land and then grabbed the land just when it was ready for cultivation. On paper, quite a lot of land has been distributed among the poor Kol tribe in this region, but in most cases the so called beneficiaries have not actually gained possession of the land. During the last century, the Kols have been treated very harshly by the dominant sections of the region. They suffer high level of exploitation, and marginalization at the hands of feudal landlords belonging to the upper Brahmin and Thakur castes; they find easy to victimise and exploit the Kols by disposing the tribals of their lands. They do this mainly through subterfuge and in collusion with local administration, whose members belong to the same social, economic and caste groups as themselves and when that failed, they used brute force by taking help from dacoits who have been the symbol of terror in this region. Often, the Dacoits attack on the villagers and to tribals and looted and murdered if there was any resistance against them.

The concept of private ownership and legal title of land is alien to tribal people. The Kols have been unable to establish legal ownership on the land that they have been cultivating for generations. In the face of relentless exploitation by the feudal interests, the Kols have had only two options of survival strategies available to them, i.e., retreating into the forest to eke out a living through their intimate knowledge of the forest and their wealth or becoming bonded labourers in the services of the very same feudal landlords or landowners. The first of the two options is becoming increasingly unavailable to them due to the extension of State control over forest and the recent tendency to close forest area for any kind of human activity in the name of environmental protection.

In the post-independence era the Kols have been displaced from the forests of Chitrakoot due to the establishment of Sanctuaries and Wildlife Parks in forest areas such as the Ranipur Wildlife Sanctuary that was created in 1978 and extended over 23,000 hectares of forest.

During survey of this area, the Principal Investigator alongwith his field workers managed with great difficulty to reach one Kol village namely "Girduha" which is located under the area of the Sanctuary. The construction of the road to reach to that village has not been allowed by the forest department. The habitats have to reach their village through overflowing canal.

Thousands of complaints from every State were sent to the Government of India against the forest department which has been uprooting the traditional habitats of forest regularly in the name of forest conservation. Several newspapers, electronic media and NGO's often drew the attention of the Central Government and State Government about how the tribal people had been tortured and forcibly made them landless and uprooted from the forest region by Forest Department. They are at the verge of starvation due to forest department. All the development programmes related to tribals and heavy budget allotted in the name of their development proved to be futile. The Central Government launched integrated tribal development programme, Multipurpose Tribal Programme, Tribal Development Blocks, Development of particularly Vulnerable Tribal groups, Special Central Assistance to tribal Sub-Plan and several others for the upliftment of thc tribals. But almost all the programmes could not meet with the success. Because landless, homeless and deprived of all sorts of livelihood tribals had no option except roaming hither and thither.

The National Sample Survey Organisation found that in 17 of India's most populous States, between the year 1972 and 1994 there was a marked decline in average calories intake. Since starvation is the direct consequence of food in security which in turn was directly to their land. Three-fourth of the scheduled castes and scheduled tribes live in rural and forest areas where land is the prime asset to determine their life conditions. Even today 86 per cent of *dalit adivasis* households are landless or near landless. For their miseries forest department's uprooting activities are mainly responsible.

After keeping all these problems related to the tribals in view, the Central Government passed a bill which was declared as "The Scheduled Tribes and other Traditional Forest Dwellers (Recognition of Forest Rights) Act 2006". This Act came into effect from 31 December 2007 in whole of the country. Right on natural resources, i.e., land, water and jungle for the cultivation of food and source of income is, therefore, highly relevant to the issue of survival. Possession of economically viable agricultural land for the cultivation of food crops to feed the family, accessibility of drinking water and access to grassland for grazing of animals and access to forest produce as source of income, will give the marginalized access to food and purchasing power. But it is again shocking that law and Regulations prohibiting alienation of dalit tribal land, ceiling on single owner's landholding and allocation of surplus Government land to scheduled castes and scheduled tribes, have been ignored or manipulated by the Forest Department for fulfilling its own interest and for muscles power persons, by saying the forest Rights Act gives legal holding to those who settled in forest before 2007.

On paper the role of the forest department in implementing the Act might be restricted, but in reality it is powerful. Under the Act 2007, a fifteen member Forest Rights Commission (FRC) is set up in every village. FRCs forward the applications claiming land rights to the committee at the SDM level. In the SDM Committee, the forest department is just a member. The committees and land approval are under the jurisdiction of the welfare department. Normally, the local administration and DM, SDMs rely heavily on the forest department for verification which could never be fair and honest. They can never go against their own vested interest.

During investigation in Sonbhadra, Mirzapur and Chandauli, several households expressed their grievances and injustice done to them by the forest department and the administration as well. Villagers told that it was the forest guards who perform the duty of verification in place of the administration. The forest guards have been secretly instructed and ordered by the forest department to give minimum possible land during verification. Households alleged that it was the forest guards who were responsible for a number of letters issued by SDMs refusing or reducing the land claimed. Of the 64,671 applications received by the SDMs in Sonbhadra, Chandauli and Mirzapur districts till end of May 2010, nearly 87 per cent (55,980) were announced rejected. What was the conspiracy behind this action was known only to the forest guards. One tribal woman complained that one day a forest guard came to inspect her land. He submitted false information to the SDM and as result, our land was reduced from 2 hectares to 20th part of a hectare. Similarly, the Forest Department rejected the claim of 3 hectares land of one Ram Bali and he was left nowhere. Only 9,725 applicants could, however, got land rights without satisfaction.

One Forest Rights Committee member explained the real situation of the distribution of land under FRA. FRC members say random allotment of land is an attempt to divide the tribals and turn them against FRCs. He further told that there were two options before him. Either he should quit the post or face the tribals' irk. The naked truth is this that practically the administration has given all powers to the Forest Department and practically there are no criteria for allotment of land. Thus, the FRC is toothless, Buddhi Narayan Toppoo, a member of the State level committee which monitored implementation of the Act had commented that the attitude and intention of the forest department appeared dictatorial; it never wanted to give land rights to forest dwellers. Toppoo has had several meetings with the district and forest officials on this issue. He then came to conclusion "Once land is allotted, the department would have to increase surveillance to check encroachment. Most crucial, the tribals will not allow illegal felling of trees. This will hamper illegal income of officials".

The Social Welfare Department has clarified that no forest workers or scheduled castes communities dependent on forests for their livelihood or living in forest for the past generations will be displaced. It is likely to clear the confusion arising after a recent statement reportedly issued by senior forest officials in Lakhimpur Kheri that communities living in forest can be displaced by giving Rs. 10 lakh compensation. The statement invited ire of forest workers, who threatened to launch an agitation against any move of displacement.

The National Forum of forest people and forest workers had lodged its protest against the statement of forest department officers. The forum said that no provision of displacement exists in the Forest Rights Act 2006. It said that the Act gives right to the tribals and forest workers on the forest land they are living and tilling since long. The Mayawati Government also gave ownership titles to over 3,000 tribals in Sonbhadra district. However, there were also reports that the scheduled castes in which majority of Kols comes, living in the forest were being asked to vacate the land by the forest officers. The forum was apprehensive that such a move will create a rift between the scheduled tribes and scheduled castes, who have been sharing forest land since long. It also expressed its concern that displacement of forest workers and scheduled castes could drive them to join the Naxalites who have always been in search of such type of opportunities.

On the complaint lodged by the forum, the social welfare department sought a clarification from the forest department officers, who denied having issuing any such statement of displacement of scheduled castes and forest workers. The State Government also asked the forest department to issue a statement to clarify the confusion. Mr. Prem Narayan, the Principal Secretary of Social Welfare also gave his clarification, told that the law was very clear. The tribals would get ownership titles on the land they were living. The other forest workers and scheduled castes who had been living for the last three generations. That is 75 years, would also get the same benefit, he further told. He further cleared that displacement clause was only applicable where forest had been declared a protected wild life sanctuary or a Park.

Uttar Pradesh has 14,127 sq. km. forest cover, which is 5.86 per cent of its geographical area and 8.203 sq. km tree cover, which is 3.4 per cent of its geographical area. Natural forests in U.P. are confined to Bundelkhand, Vindhya range and Tarai region. There are tribals and other dependents living for ages here, who would have nowhere to go if evicted. Therefore, the Uttar Pradesh Government put in efforts several times earlier to implement the Act 2006. The Government has identified 21 districts for the implementation of the Act and has constituted 707 Forest Rights Committees, 25 Sub-Divisional Committees and 21 District level committees (till November 2009). In order to sensitise inhabitants and departments involved in implementation copies of the Act 2006, pamphlets and posters have been distributed. Interactive meeting have been organised at various levels, viz., Gram Sabha, Sub-Division and district. Besides, an Expert Committee has also been set-up in order to identify critical wildlife habitat areas of 'National Park and Sanctuaries' on the basis of scientific objectives and criteria.

As a result, the distribution of titles started from December 2009 when more than 8,000 tribals in the U.P. State and over 3,000 tribals were handed over *pattas* in Sonbhadra till Feb., 2010. 500 more claims have been settled in Sonbhadra. Though claims have also been received from other divisions and districts like Mirzapur, Chandauli, Jhansi, Chitrakoot, Allahabad, Gonda, Bahraich, Lalitpur, Gorakhpur and others. The preamble of scheduled tribes and other traditional forest dwellers (Recognition of Forest Rights Act 2006, has a mandate of recognition of rights of forest dependent tribes and other traditional forest dwellers besides conservation of forest biodiversity and keeping a balance between recognition of rights ad conservation of forests along with its use on sustainable basis.

The tribals, who had been living on the forest land on or before December 13, 2005 will get the habitation rights on the land under the said Act. In case of other traditional forest dwellers, they are required to prove that they had three of their generations living on the same forest land as on December 13, 2005. Simply speaking other dwellers must have lived on the land for the past 75 years (December 13, 1930) in order to be claimant. The claimants would get the rights for the land they have been living on if the several committees set to look into the disposal of cases find the claims genuine. The maximum that a claimant could get is 4 hectares of land.

The figures of allotment of title and *pattas* have been provided by the forest department in a monthly in-house journal for a month of February 2010. A total of 8,171 individuals have been benefited till February 19, 2010. However, this is just a little over 10 per cent of 75,300 claimants who have laid their claims to land till date. But things are moving as the forest department expressed its views. When other majority claimants would get *patta* is still lurking in the hand of future. This slow tendency of disposal resulted in discontent, invites Naxalism in the regions.

Distribution of Land *Pattas*

The distribution of *pattas* was done according to the Sections 195 and 198 of the Zamindari Abolition and Land Reforms Act 1950. The impetus of this programme, as of the imposition of ceilings on landholdings during the 1960s and 1970s, came largely from political compulsions to keep the landless rural poor satisfied in order to prevent them from succumbing to radical ideas, including armed, that were being espoused by the extreme left groups in many parts of the country. The implementation of the ceiling law and the land *pattas* allotment programmes were almost completely frustrated by the feudal landlords of Patha region and by the land mafias of Sonbhadra, Chandauli and Mirzapur districts in Uttar Pradesh. In Patha region the feudal landlords, i.e., Dadus frequently appropriated loans that they persuaded the Kols to take from official agencies in their names (as ostensible owners of the land that had to be pledged as surety for the loan) by falsely promising to repay the loan on their behalf. But since the land was recorded in the name of Kol tribals, it was they who were held responsible for repayment of both the principal and interest thereon. When they failed to do this, they lost their not only their meagre possessions but also their freedom as they often ended up in jail. The land *patta* given to the tribals remained as entitlements on paper only. They were seldom given possession of the land. In many instances, they were not even aware that land had been allotted to them. In addition, much of the allotted land found of very poor quality, located on hill slopes, it was rocky merely difficult to irrigate and cultivate.

Further, large tracts of land allotted to them in 1960s came under litigation, with the Forest Department claiming ownership rights. For instance, a major part of the 2,300 hectares earmarked for the Ranipur Wildlife Sanctuary had belonged to the Kols for generations. But because they did not have documentary proof of ownership, they not only lost possession of this land, they received no compensation of it either. Local revenue officials, too, used wily tactics to ensure that several of the *pattas* given to the Kols were open to question. In some cases, more than one person was allotted the same piece of land, which inevitably led to dispute and even litigation.

During survey the Principal Investigator organised group discussions at several tribal villages of Allahabad and Chitrakoot districts. Their main grievances were narrated in following manner:

1. Allotted land has been grabbed by the landlords (*zamindars*).
2. *Zamindars* forced them to act as bonded labourers.
3. Bonded labourers were treated as slave from generation to generation.
4. *Zamindar* took loans from Banks in the name of their bonded labourers by pledging their lands as security.
5. The recovery of loan was to be realized from the bonded labourers land produced or by auctioning their lands.
6. Under land reform mission, the *zamindari* abolition and land ceiling acts were enforced. But the *zamindars* and dominant farmers somehow managed to occupy the land of the village in false names and in the name of bonded labourers. As a result of it, the cultivating land could not be occupied by the actual landless tribes.
7. Tribals like Kol have been occupant of their lands from generation to generation, but their lands have never been in written records and there were no official proofs. With the result,

their lands have been grabbed with the conspiracy of Lekhpal and other officials.

8. Their lands have been transferred to Gram Samaj under Sections 186, 222 by Lekhpal and other officials to benefit the local *zamindars*, dominants and Gram Pradhans.
9. Whenever they represented their claims of land before S.D.M., Tehsildars and Police Officers. They have been threatened by officials or by Dadus—the dominant persons. Several times Dacoits have been asked to terrorize to disown their claims on the lands.
10. In order to avoid exploitation cooperative farming, agricultural cooperative societies, etc., were encouraged by the Government. The land was allotted in the name of agricultural societies. This also could not continue for a long time because the local dominant persons started enjoying the total benefits of the produce of land although the names of tribal peoples were official registered in agricultural societies.

Table 6.1: Tribal Land Alienated and Restored (As of January 1990)

States	*Tribal Land Allienated*	*(In Acres) Restored*
Andhra Pradesh	2,79,419	1,06,315
Assam	5,174	448
Bihar	1,04,893	47,034
Gujarat	1,16,629	1,00,492
Karnataka	1,30,373	69,465
Madhya Pradesh	1,58,398	48,398
Orissa	95,015	53,245
Rajasthan	3,446	364
Uttar Pradesh	24,243	6,221

In Andhra Pradesh out of 2,79,419 acres of land only 1,06,315 acres of land was restored. In Uttar Pradesh out of 24,243 acres of land only 6,221 acres of land was restored in favour of SC/ST people. Due to unavailability of the latest figure we are quoting the statistical data of January 1990. This Table 6.1 is shown just to disclose the facts of the implementation of the Acts.

Land-Use Pattern

A survey on the land-use pattern in villages shows marked dissimilarities and there is major difference between the Dacoit prone area villages and Naxal prone area villages. The dissimilarities are in terms of the extent of forest area, barren land and land not available for cultivation. Forest constitute 23.6 per cent of the area occupies 39.3 per cent in Dacoit area and 1.6 per cent in Naxal prone area and 13.4 per cent of area not available for cultivation in Dacoit prone area and 7.4 per cent in Naxal prone area. The similarities are found in cultivable area. The dissimilarities are also seen in irrigated area as per cent of cultivated area.

Table 6.2: Land-Use Pattern in Sample Villages in Naxal and Dacoit Prone Area

Land-use category	*Dacoit Prone Area*				*Average*	*Naxal Prone Area*	
	Manikpur Block (12 villages)		*Mau Block (8 villages)*				
	Hectares	*% Share*	*Hectares*	*% Share*		*Hectares*	*% Share*
Total area	21536	100	5236	100	100	680961	100
Forest area	5729	26.6	1084	20.7	23.65	333609	49.0
Barren land	6773	31.4	1480	28.3	29.85	10907	1.6
Area not available for cultivation	4010	18.6	436	8.3	13.45	50458	7.4
Cultivated area	5022	23.3	2236	42.7	33	175631	25.8
Irrigated area as percentage of cultivated area		39.9		40.3	40.1	33229	18.9

As regards the fertility of land is concerned the Naxal prone area is more fertile in comparison to Dacoit prone area, but the basic difference between the two areas is that the tribals of Sonbhadra, Chandauli and Mirzapur are not settled permanently because of the establishment of industries and power plants. They have been displaced several times. Moreover, the forest department does not spare lands for them in spite of the Land Rights 2006.

There were standing orders of the Government around 1960 that the land *patta* should be done in the favour of landless tribals under Land Reformation Act. The Gram Sabha of villages will provide Gram Samaj land to the landless scheduled castes and scheduled tribes people. On paper about three-fourth of tribals of the South-Eastern region of Uttar Pradesh were benefited from this act. They received some land either from the Gram Samaj land or from ceiling surplus land. Usually, the Gram Samaj land and ceiling surplus land belonged to the most powerful

Table 6.3: Type of Landholding and Ownership

District	*House-hold*	*No Land*	*No Land %*	*Ancestral Land*	*Ancentral %*	*Land received from Gram Samaj*	*Land received from Gram Samaj %*	*Land under Ceiling Law*	*Land under Ceiling Law %*
Mirzapur	750	521	69.5	57	7.6	97	12.9	75	10.0
Sonbhadra	750	584	77.9	148	19.7	7	0.9	11	1.5
Chandauli	450	232	51.6	172	16.0	27	6.0	19	4.2
Naxalite area	1950	1337	68.6	377	19.3	131	6.7	105	5.4
Allahabad	600	305	50.8	100	16.7	42	7.0	153	05.5
Chitrakoot	450	309	68.7	43	9.6	36	8.0	62	03.8
Dacoit Area	1050	614	58.5	143	13.6	78	7.4	215	20.5
Total of five districts	3000	1951	65.0	520	17.3	209	7.0	320	10.7

Zamindar, feudal landlords, Raja and powerful persons in the village. They tried their best not to hand over the plot to allottees. The other problem was that the tribals who were dependent on landlords as bonded labour or on wage labour at their lord's farm, would hardly dare ask their master landlord to vacate their shares. As a result of it, still many of the ceiling surplus allotted plots of land remained in the hands of the very big landowners in Mirzapur, Sonbhadra, Chandauli, Allahabad and Chitrakoot.

During survey we could discover the real situation of the land holding and ownership of the land by the tribals. Table 6.3 shows that 69.5 per cent respondent households in Mirzapur, 77.9 per cent respondents in Sonbhadra, 51.6 per cent respondent households in Chandauli, 50.8 per cent in Allahabad and 68.7 per cent respondent households had no land.

Only 7.6 per cent respondent households in Mirzapur, 19.7 per cent respondent households in Sonbhadra, 16.0 per cent households in Chandauli, 16.7 per cent respondent households in Allahabad and 9.6 per cent respondent households in Chitrakoot were holding their ancestral lands and had their ownership of their lands, although this had been reduced in area for several reasons.

In real sense and practically only 12.9 per cent respondent households in Mirzapur, 0.9 per cent respondent households in Sonbhadra, 6.0 per cent respondent households in Chandauli, 7.0 per cent respondent households in Allahabad and 8.0 per cent respondent households in Chitrakoot are somehow holding and have ownership of Gram Samaj land.

As regards to land allotted under Ceiling Act and its ownership, 10.0 per cent respondent households in Mirzapur, 1.5 per cent respondent households in Sonbhadra, 4.2 per cent respondent households in Chandauli, 5.5 per cent respondent households in Allahabad, and 3.8 per cent households in Chitrakoot had ownership of the land allotted under ceiling act.

Table 6.4 shows the land particulars of the sample households. For tribals, agriculture is the main source of their livelihood. If there is any employment in the countryside, it is agriculture. The possession of agricultural land and production on that agricultural land, decide their socio-economic status in their society. In Table 6.4 the possession of agricultural land has been shown on three basis are: (i) Own land whether it is ancestral or purchased or allotted as *patta* in their favour; (ii) obtained agricultural land on lease from the landlords; and (iii) the land obtained from the forest department under forest land Right Act 2006.

It is evident from Table 6.4 that the average land owned by per

Table 6.4: Land Details of the Sample Households, (Total Land Owned, Leased and Forest Land) in hectares

District	*Total Households*	*Total land owned*	*Average Land/House-hold*	*Owned sown*	*Average Land/ Household*	*Leased*	*Average Land/ Household*	*Forest Land*	*Average Land/HH*
Mirzapur	750	676.62	90.20	260.71	34.80	19.13	2.60	1.50	0.20
Sonbhadra	750	1215.00	1.62	420.55	0.56	92.91	0.12	116.86	0.16
Chandauli	450	34.45	0.08	27.45	0.06	24.75	0.06	94.64	0.21
Naxal Area	1950	1926.07	0.99	708.71	0.36	136.79	0.07	213.00	0.11
Allahabad	600	659.88	1.10	537.63	0.90	347.50	0.58	42.00	0.07
Chitrakoot	450	561.10	1.25	415.41	0.92	91.88	0.20	9.88	0.02
Dacoit Area	1050	1220.98	1.16	953.04	0.91	439.38	0.42	51.88	0.05
Total of five Districts	3000	3147.04	1.05	1661.75	0.55	576.16	0.19	264.88	0.09

household was 0.90 hectares in Mirzapur, 1.62 hectares in Sonbhadra, 0.08 hectare in Chandauli, 1.10 hectares land in Allahabad and 1.25 hectares land in Chitrakoot. It clearly indicates that although the *patta* allotment process has been done by the State Government yet practically the tribals of all these five districts are deprived of their land rights. As consequent, most of the tribals come under small and marginal farmers. If we examine the total area used for agriculture production per household we find the area is small to fulfil their production requirement. In Naxal prone area 0.56 acre is on average land on which per household has used for agricultural production. In Dacoit prone area, the area is 0.47 hectares.

In order to enhance their agricultural output, the tribal households have also taken agricultural land from the landlords on lease. The land taken on lease in Naxal prone area was 0.07 hectare and 0.20 hectare was in the Dacoit prone area.

As regards the forest land released per household in Naxal prone area it was 0.11 hectare and 0.02 hectare in Dacoit prone area. Thus, it can be concluded that the implementation of land reformation Act, distribution of land and forest land right Act has not been implemented with full sincerity and done really in the welfare interest of the tribals of these five districts. Thus, it has resulted in chronic poverty and the food security has been significantly threatened to marginalized holders of land. As a result, the acute problems of malnutrition, starvation, deaths and suicides cases have often been by the print media and electronic media as well.

Table 6.5: Change in the Size of Landholding

District	*Household*	*Increase*	*increase*	*Decrease*	*Decrease*
Mirzapur	750	51	16.8	352	83.2
Sonbhadra	750	70	10.1	179	89.9
Chandauli	450	110	12.2	7	87.8
Naxalite area	1950	231	13.0	538	87.0
Allahabad	600	0	38.1	101	61.9
Chitrakoot	450	0	36.4	90	63.6
Dacoit Area	1050	0	37.3	191	62.8
Total of five districts	3000	231	25.1	729	74.9

Decrease in the number of cultivators and increase in the number of landless labourers is indicative of the disturbing trend of land alienation. The agricultural labourers have now increased from 19.71 per cent in 1961 to 43.67 per cent in 2011. It clearly shows that the tribals everywhere in India including south-eastern part of Uttar Pradesh also are gradually losing their land rights. With opening on the tribal areas particularly for development activities like construction of Rihand Dam, Several thermal plants, industries and mines activities, the tribals of this region have lost their ancestral lands and the pressure of migrant population on their lands increased. During survey we realized and observed that in several areas, although the tribals are the official owners of the lands, the non-tribals, maphias, contractors, *zamindars* and others have become its virtual owners. This problem is very acute in the Sonbhadra, Mirzapur, Chandauli, Allahabad and Chitrakoot districts.

During survey we also wanted to ascertain this continuous process of land alienation of the 3,000 sample respondents of all the five districts. 83.2 per cent respondents of Mirzapur, 89.0 per cent of Sonbhadra, 87.8 per cent of Chandauli, 61.9 per cent of Allahabad and 63.6 per cent respondents of Chitrakoot replied that their lands had been grabbed by the outsiders and by forest department and also by the Government in the name of development plans. Consequently, either the size of their lands had decreased or completely disappeared from the revenue record. At present most of them in Naxal prone areas are temporarily settled around the Rihand Dam, factories and mines areas. In Allahabad and Chitrakoot district the tribals are settled on their allotted lands although the areas of their lands have been reduced by the grabbers and dacoits.

II. DISPLACEMENT AND REHABILITATION

In a developing countries like India where overwhelming majority of the population lives in rural and tribal areas, is oppressed by chronic poverty, widespread unemployment, subsistence production and poor basic facilities. The execution of large development projects plays a vital role. The welfare of people belonging to tribal and other economically weaker sections, have been one of the major national concerns after Independence, for which the Constitution makes various specific provisions. Development in India as in the rest of the world is judged by number of Dams, Industries, Mining, Communication and other larger projects. While these projects are considered as symbol of national progress, what is hidden behind it, is the displacement of a large number of people from their habitats and traditional occupation. Majority of these oustees are often tribals and other economically weaker sections of the society.

The Five Year Plans and other public and private industrial activities have stressed the importance of establishing a number of development projects in backward tribal areas so as to accelerate the growth of national economy. There has, over several decades, been a steady exploitation of natural resources from tribal areas for the purpose of national building. Resource rich areas of the country, located largely in the traditional habitats of the scheduled tribes, have been looked upon as the resources of the entire country and have been exploited for the nation, unfortunately by extinguishing the rights of the local inhabitants by paying nominal monetary compensation only for land. Tribal communities quite often had their habitats and homeland fragmented, their cultures, disrupted, their communities shattered and have been converted from owners of the resources and well knit contented communities individual wage earners in urban agglomerated with uncertain future and their existence. One of the aims of our national planning has been ensuring the availability of these facilities to backward tribal areas through initiation of various development programmes. These programmes are poised for enabling the tribals and other local people to move faster and to attain the level of economic development close to that of advanced areas within a comparatively shorter period of time. The development projects have unquestionably became symbols of national progress and if properly executed, do have the potential of solving various socio-economic problems, such as generation of employment opportunities, formation of new skills, increase in income and consumption levels, improvements of infrastructural facilities, modifications in cultural patterns and changes in old social values and traditional organisations.

However, on the other side they have also resulted huge displacement of tribals and other local people from their ancestral habitats and caused large scale of loss of their traditional occupations. Though the development projects have been instrumental in the faster economic growth of the nation, they have often proved to be painful. The project authorities so far considered the rehabilitation primarily as an administrative problem and think their responsibility ends with the payment of compensation and transfer of people from project site to another location. Resettlement issues are usually governed by the State's revenue administration and funded by the firms, but there is a lack of awareness among officials about the living conditions of the poor. Post-project monitoring in India is very poor. And in many cases, the compensation does not reach people. Today, land is even more a burning issue as several big-ticket industrial projects face opposition from locals unwilling to give up their lands. Since, tribal land is generally non-transferable, the land markets are underdeveloped and the cost of acquiring land in tribal areas is extremely low. The subsequent value of the land after implementation of the project is enormous, but is never taken into account. This encourages the tendency to acquire land in excess of the requirement. Mining companies in particular, usually acquire land for in excess of requirements. The growing troubles have also forced the Union and State Government to address the problems faced by those displaced long ago. For the first time seriously, India still does not have a national rehabilitation and resettlement Act. Such a bill is now pending before a parliamentary panel, but many say it fails to address issues of those whose homes and livelihoods have already been devastated. Though new National Rehabilitation and Resettlement Policy (NRRP) 2007, notified by Ministry of Rural Development on 31-10-2007, endeavours to address many issues related with tribals including the compensation package and recognises the importance of consultations with Gram Sabha as per PESA Act 1996. Yet there are still some issues which have been left out. These issues have been considered by a Group of Ministers for incorporation in the Draft National Policy.

The following figures of displacement caused by the development programmes are some examples which would give an idea about the magnitude of displacement.

As many as 1,987 major dams have been constructed in India till date by investing huge sums of capital. Hundreds of Industrial and other major projects have also been launched. But gravity and magnitude of the problems can be realized when one examines that 5,422 villages mostly of tribals have lost their existence, 16.79 lakh people have been displaced as result of the execution of 33 projects and 9.85 lakh hectares of lands have been acquired for establishing 59 projects. A few largest dams and projects are being quoted here, Hirakud Dam displaced 20,000 people residing in 249 villages. The Srisailam Project completed in 1983, displaced a population of over one lakh. Tungabhadra project grabbed 90 villages and dislodged 55,000 people. Rourkela Steel Plant displaced 15,000 and Heavy Engineering Corporation Ranchi displaced 13,000 people from their native homes. The National Test range at Baliapada in Orissa displaced about 70,000 and grabbed 10,000 hectares of land. Narmada Project perhaps the largest river valley project in the world displaced about a million people. Tehri Dam displaced 35,000 population.

In addition to this widespread displacement of the population, these projects also caused loss of vast tracts of arable and forest lands. It has been estimated that the country is losing an average 3 million hectares of good land every year due to initiation of various projects. Irrigation projects have caused submergence of 14.01 lakh hectares of India's best deciduous forest land studded with teak, bamboos, etc. It was nearly 30,293 crores of wealth which was lost.

Displacement due to execution of various projects in Sonbhadra, Chandauli and Mirzapur have affected mostly the poorest sections of the society consisting of scheduled castes, scheduled tribes and other economically weaker sections less than 2 km south of the State run NTPC Ltd. Oldest 2000 MW plant in Shakti Nagar in Uttar Pradesh's Sonbhadra is the sprawling Chilka Tand colony, where many of the 2086 displaced people were shifted after their lands identified for the power complex in 1977. One Non-Governmental Organisation name "Sahyog" has calculated the actual figure of displaced people due to the power plants and coal mines, Sonbhadra district. It was 45,000 in number.

Mitihini and Khairi villages were acquired for construction of Rihand Thermal Power Corporation in 1986. In 1982, Bijpur, Dodhar, Sirsati, Adhaura villages were forcibly acquired for constructing Rihand Thermal Power Corporation employees colony. When the Rihand Thermal Plant started functioning and producing electricity 1,000 megawatt, another problem arose of fly ash accumulation. This huge deposition of fly ash was again needed for land. All the tribals who had been dislocated from Mitihini and Khairi villages, were somehow maintaining their lives in temporary huts just near to Thermal Power plant. But as soon as the fly ash problem arose, the authorities of NTPC again started displacing them through police and PAC force in 1994. As a consequence, there were several bloodshed conflicts between the inhabitants and NTPC authorities. Several complaints were lodged before the State Government and the World Bank authorities against these illegal activities of the authorities of the power plants. Several writ petitions were lodged in the Hon'ble High Court Allahabad. In spite of the favourable orders from the Hon'ble High Court, the action of dislodging the tribals could never be stopped. The district authorities have always been with the NTPC. On 3rd February, 1996 during operation of vacating their lands, ADM and Additional SP were very much present with the police force to guard the authorities. They warned the tribals that if they had not vacated the land, they would be put in jail in different false charges. Thousands of women and men had been demonstrating for their rights and rehabilitation. 10 tribal women and 23 tribal men were put behind the bar and tortured in the jail. Later, they were released from the jail after the order passed by the Hon'ble High Court to release them.

As the World Bank was the financer of these plants it came forward to settle the problems by offering rehabilitation and providing several facilities to the displaced tribals. They were as follows.

One nominated person of each land-displaced person/substantially affected person in each family will be offered employment, subject to vacancies being available. And then the nominee possessing the required qualifications/skill will be offered employment and further subject to the conditions that land displaced person will get the preference over substantially affected person.

The project would provide houses to all those who actually suffer from the loss of house and homestead land.

Each family displaced from their ancestral places, including the landless persons will be allotted three acres of reclaimed irrigated land.

If sufficient land is not available for allotted or if the allottees so desires that he is allotted less than 3 acres land, he shall be paid cash at the rate of Rs. 2,160 per acre *in lieu* of the extent of land not allotted to him. This cash amount may be required for fulfilment of his immediate needs like food, house construction, purchase of bullocks, agriculture implements and the like.

But practically the NTPC never abided by these rules. Instead of it the authorities again started displacing the tribals. As a result, several demonstrations, *dharana*, hunger strike were launched by the tribals at the gate of NTPC. The police administration which has always been with NTPC started arresting the agitators and put them in jail under Gunda Act on 15th January, 1998.

Another thermal power plant unit under NTPC was to be installed in Singrauli where the coal mines activities have been implemented since the British period. The World Bank sanctioned dollar 150 million in 1977 for running Singrauli Thermal Power Plant. This was a world record that the NTPC took loan worth dollars 400 billion for installing the Thermal Power plants at Vindhyachal and Rihand from the World Bank. The World Bank had already sanctioned loan for Duddhi Chua coal mines in 1985. As a result, the place Singrauli was declared as the 'Capital of power generation in India'. Several other small industries were installed due to easy availability of electricity at their place.

The Chilka Daad conflict between NTPC authorities and displaced tribals had been very alarming to the district administration. This incident was brought into notice to the World Bank authorities and this problem was raised for the first time in American Parliamentary Committee by Brush Rinch. As a result of it, a World Bank team was deputed for inspection on the spot and to report back to the World Bank authorities.

In Singrauli, when people were displaced by the Rihand Dam, they were literally thrown out without any compensation. People were not willing to take risks anymore when they have seen what had happened to others.

The fact behind this conflict was that the tribals who were displaced after installation of NTPC plant in Singrauli region, were rehabilitated in "Chilka Daad" village. The land was allotted in their favour. They were anyhow, accommodating with new settlement. But after some time they were again asked to vacate their rehabilitated area by the NCL authorities and by the NTPC. The reason behind this activity was that the plenty of coal storage was discovered under the new settlement area. Moreover, the coal mines at Kharia was just adjacent to this recently rehabilitated settlement namely Chilka Daad, officially 5,872 hectares of forest land from Singrauli Block had been allotted for non-forest use since forest conservation Act, came into force in 1980.

Another Super Thermal Power station, "Shakti Nagar was installed in 1997 for which 4,752 acres of tribal land was acquired by displacing them from their ancestral place of abode. Out of 4,752 acres 649 acres of land was transferred to NCL. As a consequence of it, 1,749 tribal families were forced to vacate their lands for getting all their belongings."

All the tribal families were again rehabilitated and accommodated in Chilka Daad and Parswar Roja villages. To what extent they had been tortured by these planners of different power plants and coal mines, can be easily realised by any human being after listening their pathetic story of multiple displacement activities. For the first time they were thrown out of their ancestral villages when the Rihand Dam was proposed to be constructed. Thereafter, they were rehabilitated in Kota, Bhantwari, Ranibashi and other villages. Immediately after some time they were dislodged again and rehabilitated in Chilka Daad and Parsawar as new settlements. Again, they were asked third time to vacate their new settlement in favour of Kharia coal mines.

The tribal communities as well as the other groups opposing further displacement and parties backing the agitators were congregated at one place and started campaign to unite tribal communities to fight against displacement and to protect their right to live peacefully on their ancestral lands. If this type of agitation had continued, there would have been another uprising over south-eastern region of UP against displacement and basically against all such types of development plans.

At this occasion, these tribals became very furious and violent and launched several *dharana*, demonstration, agitation and decided not to vacate their settlements. But the concerned authorities were adamant not to bow down before them. They took support of police, PAC, maphias and other criminals by greasing their palms. Entire area of the village was surrounded by the PAC force and forcibly the new settlement of tribals was dozered and converted into plain land. Several demonstrators including women were arrested and beaten brutally. Somehow, this inhuman behaviour was brought into notice of the then, Dr. Brahma Prakash, the Chairman of National Scheduled Castes and Scheduled Tribes Commission, New Delhi. Dr. Brahma Prakash along with the social activist Ms Medha Patekar personally visited the Chilka Daad and Navjeewan Vihar tribal settlements. They were very much aggrieved to see the worst and wretched pitiable conditions of tribal men. Dr. Brahma Prakash immediately after returning to Delhi, submitted his report to the Government of India and strongly recommended to take immediate actions against the NTPC and other industrial authorities for their inhuman activities. The World Bank team also visited that place and issued strict instructions to the NTPC and coal mines authorities to provide immediate relief to the sufferers. As a result, at the time the concerned authorities agreed to provide all the necessary and basic needs to these displaced tribals. Medical facilities, toilet, school, roads, drinking water, etc., would be available without imposing any conditions to the tribals. But later on nothing was done to the satisfaction of the displaced tribals.

But on the other side of this development is quite discouraging. Such planning and development brought a great chaos and miseries to the original inhabitants by heavy displacement. Water and air pollution, fly ash, industrial garbage, loss of farming land and deforestation etc. came as share in the tribals fate.

It is very shocking to learn that 90 per cent permanent inhabitants were displaced at least at one time and 34 per cent inhabitants were cursed by several times displacement in their present life. All the process of rehabilitation and providing them other facilities decided under the contract and the act, have met with complete failure.

The Investigator wanted to understand the depth of their grief and reaction about installation of all such establishment of electrical power plants, Dams, Industries and other projects. They were found very much disappointed with their present life.

It was a great shock to them that they had lost everything including their houses, villages, fields, culture and other heritage which were so near and dear to them. All their possessions have been submerged or taken away in the name of such development. In fact, the tribal and other indigenous people have a special attachment with the land they hold and to them the land is not simply a factor of production, but a source of spirituality, the repository of ancestral remains, clan origin sites and other sacred features important to their religious system.

Data regarding the first reactions to all the installation of development projects run either by Government or private showed that the degree of sensitivity varied among the affected people residing near the projects. It brought great shock to the people who were displaced. Among surveyed households about 45 per cent feared displacement from their habitat, while 18 per cent suspected displacement from the occupation, 38 per cent were found completely at loss when they came to know the reality of false assurance of their rehabilitation as was to be provided as per rule and contract. All of them were found in revolting mood against the Government and the project. Out of reaction they showed their favour, inclination with Naxalites.

The villages named Khadia, Mitihani, Khairi, Bijpur, Dadahar, Sirsati, Dibulganj, Adhura and Parswar and Chilka Daad of Sonbhadra and Chandauli districts, were the main places from where the tribals and villagers were forced to vacate their places for installation of Rihand Dam, Thermal Power, Singrauli, coal mines and other industrial units were installed. Thousands of families were displaced. All the rehabilitated huts and colonies were established and settled nearby these dams, power plants and industrial areas. The Principal Investigator Surveyed and took interview of the sufferers in order to investigate their problems. Out of these villages three villages named Bijpur, Dibulganj and Chilka Daad were selected for interview out of three villages. 265 households from Mitihini, 315 households from Dibulganj and 580 households were selected for interview.

Table 6.6: Distribution of Sample Households by Project Area

Category	*Rihand Dam*		*Anpara Thermal Power*		*Singrauli Thermal Power*	
	Mitihini Village	*Sample*	*Dibulganj Village*	*Sample*	*Chilka Daad Village*	*Sample*
Affected Villages	1	7 28.0	1	9 6.1	1	16 9.3
Affected Families	788	175 22.0	8514	225 2.6	9302	400 4.3
Families Residing Resettlement Places	375	90 24.0	419	90 21.5	794	180 22.0

It was a great shock to tribal people to hear that their houses, villages and fields which were so near and dear to them would either be submerged or taken away for public purposes. In fact, the tribals have a special attachments with the land they hold and to them the land is not simply a factor of production, but a source of spirituality, the reprository ancestral remains, clan-origin sites and other sacred features important to their religious system. The Table 6.7 the degree of sensitivity varied among the affected tribal people residing in the project areas.

Table 6.7 shows that 35.5 per cent in Mitihini, 45.2 per cent in Dibulganj and 40.7 per cent in Chilka Daad tribal respondents were reacted firstly that they had to be displaced from their ancestral places of houses, 16.3 per cent, 22.6 per cent, 19.7 per cent from the three village respondents were frightened that their traditional occupations would be destroyed. Since, several assurances like employment, change in better living standard and development of better infrastructural facilities, etc., were given by the Government officials, therefore, some of the tribals were much hopeful of such assurances.

Table 6.7: Reactions about the Projects

Reaction	*Rihand Dam*	*Anpara Thermal Power*	*Singrauli Thermal Power and Coal Mines*
	Mithihini	*Dibulganj*	*Chilka Daad*
Displacement from house	35.5%	45.2%	40.7%
Displacement from occupation	16.3%	22.6%	19.7%
Employment opportunities	23.7%	16.1%	19.7%
Better living standards	10.4%	8.4%	9.3%
Suspected Pollution Hazards	2.2%	0.6%	1.4%
Development of Infrastructure	8.9%	3.9%	6.2%
Others	3.0%	3.2%	3.1%
Total	100%	100%	100%
	265	315	580

That is why 23.7 per cent, 16.1 per cent and 19.7 per cent respectively from the villages were hopeful for employment opportunities; 10.4 per cent, 8.4 per cent, 9.3 per cent were hopeful for better living; and 8.9 per cent, 3.9 per cent, 6.2 per cent respondents of the three villages hoped that they would be benefited by better infrastructural facilities.

Table 6.8 shows that the displaced tribals gave first priority to built houses. 43.4 per cent, 50.8 per cent and 47.4 per cent tribals preferred to

Table 6.8: Opinion towards Compensation for loss of house and land

Compensation	*Rihand Dam*	*Anpara Thermal Power*	*Singrauli Thermal Power and Coal Mines*
	Mithihini	*Dibulganj*	*Chilka Daad*
House			
Cash	12.8%	11.1%	11.9%
Built house	43.4%	50.8%	47.4%
Plot and Cash	32.4%	29.2%	30.7%
Any of the above	11.3%	8.9%	10.0%
Land			
Land	27.9%	69.8%	50.7%
Cash	9.8%	7.6%	8.6%
Partly Land, Partly Cash	11.3%	11.1%	11.2%
Job	50.9%	11.4%	29.5%
Total	100%	100%	100%
Households	265	315	580

build houses. 27.9 per cent, 69.8 per cent and 50.7 per cent of the three villages of tribals preferred land in place of their ancestral land. 50.9 per cent, 11.4 per cent and 29.5 per cent of the Mitihini, Dibulganj and Chilka Daam village tribals gave preference for job in the projects. Thus, it is evident from the above percentage of opinions that built houses and partly plot and partly cash are considered as the most acceptable form of followed by job for land are taken as the most liked form of compensation for loss of agricultural land.

Table 6.9 shows 88.4 per cent, 90.2 per cent and 95.5 per cent of all the three villages displaced tribals were not at all satisfied with the compensation awarded by the authorities.

Table 6.9: Satisfaction with the Compensation Granted by the Authorities

Satisfaction	*Rihand Dam*	*Anpara Thermal Power*	*Singrauli Thermal Power and Coal Mines*
	Mithihini	*Dibulganj*	*Chilka Daad*
Satisfied	11.6%	9.8%	4.5%
Not Satisfied	88.4%	90.2%	95.5%
Total	100%	100%	100%
Households	265	315	580

Table 6.10: Inconveniences Faced during Displacement

If faced inconvenience	*Rihand Dam*	*Anpara Thermal Power*	*Singrauli Thermal Power and Coal Mines*
	Mithihini	*Dibulganj*	*Chilka Daad*
(a) If evacuation notice served			
Yes	18.9%	22.2%	18.7%
No	81.1%	77.8%	81.3%
(b) If Experienced Problems during shifting			
Yes	66.7%	64.0%	65.6%
No	33.3%	35.6%	34.4%
(c) If Provided transport for shifting			
Yes	14.4%	5.6%	10.0%
No	85.6%	94.4%	90.0%
Total	100%	100%	100%
Households	265	315	580

There is possibility that due to lack of proper means of communications, ignorance and illiteracy among tribal people the evacuation notice could not have reached in time to all the tribals of the villages. That is why the percentage of the reply received notice of evacuation (No) percentage 81.1 per cent, 77.7 per cent and 81.3 per cent in all the three villages are very high. As regards, facing problems during shifting, the percentage 66.7 per cent, 64.9 per cent and 65.6 per cent were very high. The high percentage of lack of transport facility is self-evident that the evacuating authorities did not bother for any convenience to the tribals. It appears they were forcibly evacuated their ancestral lands.

Table 6.11 shows that the displaced tribals are facing a lot of serious problems. These problems are scarcity of water, fuel wood, food items, disease, space in hut houses and other so many problems. The resettlers level of satisfaction with the conditions of living depends upon the extent of fulfilment of various promises made before displacement. It is quite disappointing that the resettlers tribals are facing a lot of problems like drinking water, sources of food, sources of fuel, extremely polluted environment, several diseases, born of pollution, lack of medicines and medical facilities, lack of space in a small hut. How in miserable conditions they are passing their lives is rearly beyond imagination for urban people.

Table 6.11: Most Serious Problems Faces at Arrival and at Present

Most serious Problems during arrival	*Rihand Dam*	*Anpara Thermal Power*	*Singrauli Thermal Power and Coal Mines*
	Mithihini	*Dibulganj*	*Chilka Daad*
Drinking Water	67.8%	62.2%	65.0%
Fuel Wood	16.7%	7.8%	12.2%
Food Items	15.5%	17.8%	16.7%
At Present			
Drinking Water	60.0%	71.1%	65.6%
Diseases	17.8%	18.3%	25.4%
Sources of livelihood	20.2%	18.0%	8.0%
Space in house	2.0%	1.6%	1.0%
Other	—	—	—
Total	100%	100%	100%
Households	265	315	580

Due to lack of sources of their livelihood, they are suffering from extreme poverty, malnutrition, starvation and serious diseases.

III. UNEMPLOYMENT

Unemployment is a concept that comes with development. In traditional set-up in the village or in forest nobody is unemployed. The term unemployed refers to a person who is unable to get the jobs he wants. *In lieu* of land alienation and displacement the original inhabitants were not provided the regular and permanent sources of the income through which they could manage their livelihood. Land, i.e., agricultural source of produce and all kinds of forest produces, cattle, milk, etc., were the main sources of the income of the *dalit adivasis* of this region. As a result, they did not have any concept of employment in their minds.

People in the Singrauli region were predominantly *dalit adivasis*. Primarily agriculturists, their dependence on forests was critical for their survival. The forests were an important source of fuel, fodder, food, timber and medicines. Agriculture was the mainstay, with cattle farming the backbone of the local economy. Artisans and other service class got paid in kind, which included land. Before the entry of the NTPC, people were more or less independent of the market economy and their lives after the first displacement continued to be under their control. After displacements the assets of the *dalit adivasis*, such as land, homestead, trees and wells were greatly under value and compensation rates for land were calculated on the basis of the average rates of land registered in government records in three years preceding the acquisition. Thus, the amounts received enabled the people to replace only up to 30 per cent of their lost assets. At the time of taking possession, permanent Class IV category jobs were promised to all. However, only one-third of the displaced people were actually given jobs. There was no written and publicly declared policy documents in 1980s during the initial round of displacement. There were many families to whom not a single permanent job was provided. Most of these people had to struggle for even contract labour or casual employment.

Why did the NTPC not provide permanent jobs to all affected persons? The answer provided is that there were not so many jobs and the people were not adequately trained. Both these arguments are myths as every power projects had at least 1,000 jobs of a perennial nature, which have been out on contract given to the displaced tribes. These include maintenance, both of the power plant and the township, housekeeping in the power plant. The skills required for these are basic, which the locals could easily master. But, if they were employed, the profit margin of the NTPC would diminish greatly. It is also not the true that the locals were not qualified for technical jobs. Even if they claim that the people were not qualified is allowed, NTPC had the responsibility of making sure that during the gestation period of at least five years before the project was commissioned, the locals acquired the necessary qualifications and received training for the jobs in the project.

Whatever jobs were given during the earlier phase and by the time people in later round of displacement were to be moved, NTPC flatly refused to give permanent jobs.

'It is grave injustice', said Shyam Lal Jaiswal, a clerk at the Anpara Power Plant and a Trade Union leader, "First they acquired out land and kept promising we will get jobs when they expand capacity. Then they gave the land away to another company and changed the rules for employment". He said many of the jobless belong to families evicted in the early 1960s by the Rihand Dam which created the Govind Ballabh Pant reservoir.

Ram Chandra Jaiswal resident of Kuldumri says, "Lanco and Anpara companies assured us in writing that they will give us employment by the 30th May, 2000, at the rate of 300 people every month. But nothing seems to move even now. How can we believe that the new projects will give us jobs when the previous project have just not delivered".

Unemployment, therefore, is a major issue. Unfortunately, this is compounded by the companies exploiting the region's resources. Acute unemployment is one of the biggest issues in Singrauli Area. As revealed by documents obtained under the RTI Act 2005 people were promised jobs by the Anpara Thermal Power Plant alone, but only 234 received employment in reality. Statements by villagers from Kuldumiri Panchayat in the Sonbhadra district corroborate the evidence gathered in these documents. About 90 per cent of the people are unemployed here.

But this is not the only way to get an employment with the growth of education. Many tribal youths are unemployed because the traditional economy does not provide a job communsurate with his educational level. By linking traditional economy with market oriented economy and by creating degree linked employment opportunity. The problem of unemployment in tribal areas of the south-eastern part of Uttar Pradesh including *patta* region has been created. The nexus between degree and jobs needs to be broken if unemployment in tribal society is to be removed. It can be done with specific vocational training and adoption of appropriate technology for the area concerned. Training could be given in such crafts as wood carving, carpentry, agriculture, bamboo handicrafts, lac cultivation, honey collection, fruit packing, vegetable growing, etc. Except a few voluntary organization, the Union as well as the State Government is not at all serious to think over the acute problem of unemployment in tribal people. This is one of the main causes of discontent among the *dalit adivasis* of south-eastern part of Uttar Pradesh. It may turn into another Nandigram if the people do not get their entitled compensation of land and employment.

References

1. Rath, Govind Chandra, (2006), *Tribal Development in India*, New Delhi, Sage Publication.
2. Pani, Niranjan, Sahoo, Jitendra, (2008). *Tribal Development*, New Delhi, Mahamaya Publishing House.
3. Somashekhar K. (2008), *Development Programmes and Social Change among the Tribals*, New Delhi, Serials Publications.
4. Census of India (2001) S.T. Atlas.
5. George, Jose and Kumar, S.S., (1993), 'Conceptual framework for Tribal Development', Social Change, *Journal of the Council for Social Development*, Vol. 23-79-82.
6. Mazumdar, D.N., (1961), *Raas and Cultures of India*, Bombay, Asia Publishing House.

7. Desai, A.R. (1966), *Rural Sociology in India*, Bombay, Population Prakashan.
8. Excerpts from Websites.
9. Census of India 2001
10. Census of India 2001, S.T. Atlas of India.
11. Ramana P.V. (ed.), *The Naxal Challenge; Causes, Linkages, and Policy Options*.
12. Roy, Arundhati, March 2010, '*Outlook*', *The Weekly News Magazine*.

Chapter 7
Manifestation of Discontent
Agitation, Demonstration, Revolt, and Naxal Activity

Normallly, tribals are peace loving people. But at the same time they have also at times reacted violently against their exploiters represented by money-lenders, middlemen, contractors, liquor vendors, *zamindars*, Government administrations, forest department officials, police and revenue officials. During British period, double edged policy was adopted by giving free rein to money lenders, contractors, *zamindars* and officials of excise, revenue, forest and police departments to exploit them. Thus, their exploitation resulted in their indebtedness and alienation of their fertile lands to the non-tribals. The tribals right in forests were substantially eroded by the Britishers. The British entry into the forest areas of the country resulted in a series of disturbances in 1789, 1801, 1807, 1808, 1831, 1855, 1862, 1856 and 1895. There are several examples of their revolts and uprisings in British period. Rajmal Hill revolt by martial tribe Paharyas, Kol Mutiny 1831, Santhal rebellion, Bisra movement, Revolts in Andhra Pradesh and Kandhar rising in Orissa are few examples of uprising and revolts recorded in the British history of India.

After Independence several welfare programmes for tribal people were launched and in every plan heavy budget was allotted for their total upliftment. The main object of the Government is to bring them into the main stream of the country by making themselves dependent and equal to other citizens of the country.

But in spite of the continuous efforts after Independence and providing all the required facilities, tribals resentment and degree of their discontentment have risen up. As a consequence, often the news are flashed by the print media and electronic media regarding their criminal activities as a result of their discontentment. Dantewada and Singur cases are recent examples of their reactions.

In south-eastern part of Uttar Pradesh which covers Sonbhadra, Mirzapur, Chandauli, Allahabad and Chitrakoot, the universe of our study has also shown in the main headings of the newspapers for their Naxal activities. The agitations and demonstrations are often organised and displayed before the administration at district headquarters. Few cases of revolts have also been recorded.

Reasons of their demonstration, agitation and revolts have been analysed from the newspapers which have flashed from time to time. There are several Non-Governmental Organisations (NGOs) which are dedicated to their welfare, have made them aware of their rights and their Government Welfare Programmes.

One of the biggest causes of their discontent is land alienation. Nearly 80 per cent of land has been alienated to the non-tribals in all the five districts. In this region land belonging to scheduled castes and scheduled tribes are under unauthorized occupation of the non-tribals and outsiders. Opening of the tribal areas in the wake of the development process and setting up of various irrigation, power plants, industrial and mining projects in this region especially in Sonbhadra, Chandauli and Mirzapur tribal areas, brought in the problem of land alienation.

As a result, problem of displacement, rehabilitation, livelihood, environmental pollution, chronic diseases, poverty, illiteracy, etc., arose among them.

The Forest Right Act 2006 is the bone of contention between the tribals and forest department. It has always resulted in clashes between them.

In order to minimize the poverty problems the Union Government launched Jawahar Rojgar Yojana, Pradhan Mantri Sadak Nirman Yojana and the most lucrative Yojana for employment guarantee is the 'Mahatma Gandhi National Rural Employment Guarantee Act (MNREGA)' through it every villager is entitled to get job for 100 days in a year.

Under Right to food, the rural/tribal people receive Rice, Wheat and other food materials on subsidized rate from the fair price shops (PDS) and several schemes under social welfare programmes have been launched by the Union as well as the State Government. Scholarship to handicapped, children, students, old age pension etc. are available to the deserving persons.

In order to eradicate all the infectious and contagious diseases, health programmes have also been launched and several PHC, CHC, ANM facilities are available for the very purpose.

Illiteracy is one of the biggest problems for which the Government has provided free education with scholarship and Mid-Day Meal facility by opening school in every village.

For infrastructural development like, approach road, drinking water and irrigation facilities, light, post office, telephone booth, police station, PHC, Gram Panchayat Bhawan and all other facilities are made available to tribal people.

For all the above mentioned projects and welfare schemes heavy budget is sanctioned every year. But really is this budget utilized with honest intention?

The clear reply comes in negative. Maximum work is done on paper in the name of development. Perhaps honesty has now become simply a foolish ideology for our countrymen. As a result, the economic corruption has reached at its extreme limit.

Due to extreme poverty the incidences of child labour, bonded labour and sex exploitation of tribal women are very frequent.

The other reasons of agitation, demonstration and incidences of revolts are the exploitation of tribals by the industrialists. The employees especially the labour class of after closure of Dala Cement, Churk Cement and Chunar Cement factories, reached at the level of starvation and resulted in deaths of five labourers.

The agitation, demonstration and the aggressive revolt activities were recorded when the villagers of the two villages named Mitihini and Khairi revolted against the NTPC which started forcing the villagers to vacate their villages. The World Bank played a very foul role with villagers. This renowned organization assured the villagers that they would get proper compensation *in lieu* of their lands. They would be properly rehabilitated as per world rehabilitation norms, but nothing was done. Inhabitants of these two villages were rehabilitated at the place named Chilka Dam. But after passing a few year of their settlement they were again forced to vacate that settlement area far excavation of coal mine.

It is worth to take in notice that the villagers of villages named Kota, Bhantwari, Ranibashi were forced again and again to vacate their lands. Thus, the multiple displacement ruined their whole life and economy. Due to all these inhuman acts of the industrialists and the World Bank Organisation came in the hit list of their aggressive revolts. In addition to all these serious problems, the tribals had to swallow all the pollutants produced by the plants, industries and coal mines resulting in victimisation of several air and water-borne diseases and handicapped childbirth. Several deaths have been recorded every year in this region due to the environment pollution.

The foundation stone laid by the Ex-Chief Minister Mayawati for the construction of 'Kanhar Dam' in Dudhi tehsil on Maoist affected area of Sonbhadra and Chandauli on January 15, 2010 has triggered a wave of revolt among the locals, mostly tribals, who are fearing a large scale displacement. They decided to launch a march of 100 km. Foot march from the construction site in Anwar village to the district headquarters at Robertsganj on March 10. About 5,000 people under the banner of 'Kanhar Bachao Andolan' reached the district headquarters on Monday the 20th. The People's Vigilance Committee on Human Rights also came forward in support of the tribals of affected areas. If a Dam is built, it would displace thousands of tribal families from their roots. In 1976 too the then Chief Minister N.D. Tiwari had laid the foundation stone of the 'Kanhar Dam', but the project was stopped due to opposition from the people. It was not the first when the local had opposed the construction of dam on the Kanhar river, tributary of Son river. Because, if it was constructed then 11 villages of Sonbhadra and Chandauli districts would have been submerged and 25 villages would have been partly affected causing displacement of about 8,000 families. Hundred of farmers and landless labourers belonging to Gond, Pannika, Kharwar, Pariha, Chero would have been displaced.

It is the tribal women who took leading part in this revolt.

In democratic set-up of society, agitation and demonstration are means of attracting the attention of the Government. Semi-Government or any employing institutions towards the resentment, problems, demands, non-fulfilment of requirements, violation of rules and exploitation hidden under the system of the public or employees or who are sufferers or who are being exploited within the system. Such group attempts and forces are applied when individual attempts fail. In such process the demonstrator do not violate the rules and regulations and do not open any confrontation with concerning authorities and they talk within the framework of the law. Even after understanding the genuinity and legal demands, if the authorities do not pay attention and do not find out the way and intentionally neglect their demands, then the agitators and demonstrators mobs knew no bounds and limitations of legality. As a results, they launch revolt against the authorities and try to damage at the worst.

The tribals in south-eastern part of U.P., as the whole has been victimized, tortured and exploited since, the British period. They have been treated as if they were not human beings. They were forced to remain in dense forest, hilly places and to those places where normal man cannot think of such inhuman and adverse conditions. Their living conditions are still worst than animals. They have never been allowed to join the main stream of the civilization of the society.

Table 7.1: Opinion of the Respondents on the Cause of Agitation, Demonstration and Revolt

District	*Total Respondents*	*Recognition*	*%*	*Livelihood*	*%*	*Harassment*	*%*	*No idea*	*%*
Mirzapur	750	55	7.3	604	80.5	48	6.4	43	5.7
Sonbhadra	750	103	13.7	263	35.1	79	10.5	305	40.7
Chandauli	450	2	0.4	14	3.1	152	33.8	282	62.7
Naxal Total	1950	160	8.2	881	45.2	279	14.3	630	32.3
Allahabad	600	0	0.0	412	68.7	63	10.5	125	20.8
Chitrakoot	450	0	0.0	273	60.7	91	20.2	86	19.1
Dacoit Total	1050	0	0.0	685	65.2	154	14.7	211	20.1
Total of five Districts	3000	160	5.3	1566	52.2	433	14.4	841	28.0

After Independence the Government of India launched several programmes for their educational and economic empowerment. A number of Centrally sponsored schemes have been implemented for socio-economic development of tribal communities. However, the financial support and development efforts in this direction could not make an effective dent on the poverty among the tribal population and enabled them to join the mainstream of development. Even larger tribal population has been victimized due to development induced displacement, modern economic forces and socio-cultural factors. The tribals face the problems related to land alienation, infiltration of non-tribals in the tribal regions, threatening to the cultural identity and involuntary migration and resettlement due to development projects. Tribals are also subject to and inextricable nexus of exploitation and are engaged in low yield agriculture. The single most important for their emancipation lies in raising agricultural productivity. In the wake of development process a large chunk of fertile tribal land has been acquired by the Government for industrial, irrigation, power, mining and other projects *in lieu* of meagre compensation which the tribals frittered away in no time. The unrestricted influx of outsiders into tribal majority areas also reduced the tribals to minority. Their traditional forestry rights have been reduced to more concessions.

Thus, extreme poverty, unemployment, ban on collection forest produce, land alienated by the feudal landlords and the Government, repeatedly displacement and no proper rehabilitation, exploitation by maphias and landlords, deprivation of forest rights, no proper payments to landless labourers and employees working in the industries, mines power plants, grabbing their welfare shares by the contractors, maphias and Government officials, facing all the time injustice and several other reasons have irritated them again and again. As result, the discontent among the SC/ST of these five districts surfaces time and again in one form or another. The situation is susceptible to exploitation by anti-national forces.

During discussion with the tribals we could realize that they had become very much reactionary with the present set-up of the system. Consequently, either they prefer to join Naxalites or organise their men to agitate, to demonstrate or revolt against the Government, police administration and industrial units. Therefore, in Table 7.1 we have tried to analyse their opinion on the causes of agitation, demonstration and revolt which have often been launched at the headquarters of all the five districts. 45.2 per cent respondents of Naxal prone areas and 65.2 per cent respondents of Dacoit prone areas replied that their existence and livelihood are at the stake, therefore, no option left except agitation, demonstration and revolt. 6.4 per cent respondents in Mirzapur, 10.5 per cent respondents in Sonbhadra, and 33.8 per cent respondents in Chandauli expressed their grievances that their voices were not heard by the concerning officials, police, administration and civil administration. Simply, they have been harassed without awarding any relief result to their personal and social problems. Only 5.3 per cent respondents in total five districts had feeling that agitation and demonstration are lodged by some local leaders to establish their identity in the eyes of administration. Instead of solving tribal problems, they exploit the administration for their own benefit.

During discussions, we could understand that many tribals believe that none is responsible for their present condition. It is predestined by the almighty God in their fate. Therefore, 32.3 per cent respondents in Naxal prone areas and 20.1 per cent in Dacoit prone areas respondents did not blame anybody. Due to ignorance and illiteracy they did not have any idea about causes of agitation, etc. Thus, it can be concluded that their problem of livelihood and harassment are the most dominating causes of discontent which is expressed into agitation, demonstration and revolt.

Objective

To find out of the difference of opinion on the causes of agitation, demonstration and revolt. The tribes do not have any cause of the agitation, demonstration and revolt in the five tribal districts of U.P., i.e., Mirzapur, Sonbhadra, Chandauli, Allahabad and Chitrakoot.

The analysis of the data yields results in terms of mean, S.D. and Significance Value. The obtained results have been summarized in Table 7.2.

Table 7.2: Statistical Analysis

Sl. No.	*Subject*	*N*	*Mean*	*S.D.*	*D.F.*	*Sig.*
1.	Mirzapur	750	2.00	0.352	4	0.000
2.	Sonbhadra	750	2.93	1.067		
3.	Chandauli	450	3.59	0.576		
4.	Allahabad	600	2.52	0.816		
5.	Chitrakoot	450	2.58	0.791		

Since, the significance value is less than the significant level at 0.05. Therefore, there are different causes in the five tribal districts of U.P., i.e., Mirzapur, Sonbhadra, Chandauli, Allahabad and Chitrakoot for agitation, demonstration and revolt (see Table 7.3).

Why the agitation, demonstration and revolt situation arose among the tribals can be explained by quoting some incidences which provoke to start and continue for the eradicating their problems.

Manti Naha, a widow of Sonbhadra tribal area did not have arable land at the time of displacement. She among others is not entitled to any compensation. Today she lives on alms. Five decades ago, farmers and forest dwellers mostly scheduled castes and scheduled tribes were uprooted to make way for industries, are still waiting for compensation, jobs and rehabilitation, even as employment pushes them deeper into poverty. Post project monitoring in south-eastern part of Uttar Pradesh is very poor. In many cases the compensation for displacement does not reach to people, land is even more burning issues for the tribals. Therefore, their resentment against the grabbers are quite natural. It may turn into another Nandigram if people do not get their entitled compensation land or jobs. Coal mines of Northern Coal Fields Ltd. evicted thousands and some 2,000 forest dwellers and 600 families are still owed jobs or money. The main cause of discontent is of their means of survival. There is a damning reason why tribals feel cheated. A resident named Ram Narayan explained, "We were given *pattas* (Title deeds) in 1995. We got only *Awasi Patta* (Right to live on the land) so, we can not sell this land, we do not get a loan against the *patta*. How can we survive without the means of livelihood."

The tribal women of over 500 villages in the range have taken around 20,000 hectares of land and were doing cooperative farming on it for the past two years, claiming ownership on grounds that they were original inhabitants of the forests. But the local landlords and a few companies in mining business in the area are conspiring with Government and forest officials to get the land back. A message was sent "It may lead to eruption of volcano brewing since long. Four months pregnant Lalita Devi coiled herself to escape the blows of heavy sticks. She was bewildered why each blow was directly at her belly. Police men were ruthless till she fell unconscious. She narrated that she was lying in a pool of blood; her seventh child was never born. She was among the 90 families demanding the right to land inside Margadaha forest and an end to corruption in logging. She said the forest officials along with police officers forcibly evicted them from the forest land in Sonbhadra on 16th March, 2010."

The cement factories in Dala, Churk and Chunnar were closed due to mismanagement and due to recurring loss of the income. As a result of it,

Table 7.3: Views of the Respondents on Continuation of the Agitation, Demonstration and Revolts

District	*Total Respondents*	*Increase*	*%*	*Spread*	*%*	*Stop*	*%*	*Leave it*	*%*	*No Comment*	*%*
Mirzapur	750	192	25.6	382	50.9	62	8.3	8	1.1	106	14.1
Sonbhadra	750	178	23.7	155	20.7	25	3.3	29	3.9	363	48.4
Chandauli	450	98	21.6	16	3.6	9	2.0	176	39.1	17	3.8
Naxal Area	1950	468	19.3	553	28.4	96	16.5	213	10.9	486	24.9
Allahabad	600	43	7.2	23	3.8	55	9.2	110	18.3	369	61.5
Chitrakoot	450	40	8.9	33	7.3	9	2.0	75	16.7	293	65.1
Dacoit Area	1050	83	7.9	56	5.3	64	6.1	185	17.6	662	63.0
Total of five Districts	3000	551	15.3	609	20.3	160	12.8	398	13.3	1148	38.3

the question of survival arose before the employees. On 24th September, 2004, 8 young men started hunger strike for their cause, five labours died of hunger.

Through some examples quoted above we can easily understand why are the tribals are so irritated and agitated to revolt. Now, they are under in this way that their problems would not be over unless they keep their agitation, demonstration and revolt alive. These actions may be converted into the form of a violence at any moment. They have their own history of uprising and revolution. Dantewada, Singrur and Nandigram are recent examples of tribal revolt against the existing situations.

The higher percentage of views of the respondents, i.e., in Naxal prone area and Dacoit prone area regarding increasing and spreading number of incidences clearly indicates their mental set-up of mind. They are now not so ignorant and innocent as they were before. Due to frequent social interaction with the outsiders, officials, NGOs and Maos and Naxalites, they have started realizing their problems and the way they would be solved. Their problems are not understood and no sincere efforts are being done in resolving their problems. They may adopt violent means by joining the hands of the Naxalites.

25.6 per cent respondents of Mirzapur, 23.7 per cent of Sonbhadra, 21.6 per cent of Chandauli, 17.2 per cent of Allahabad and 18.9 per cent respondents expressed their views that the agitation, demonstration, revolt should continue regularly. Consequently, its degree is showing the rising tendency.

50.9 per cent respondents of Mirzapur, 20.7 per cent of Sonbhadra, 33.6 per cent of Chandauli, 23.8 per cent of Allahabad, and 27.3 per cent respondents of Chitrakoot believed that their agitation activities are spreading very rapidly due to Envolvement of Naxalites. They favoured agitation, demonstration, etc.

8.3 per cent respondents of Mirzapur, 3.3 per cent of Sonbhadra, 2.0 per cent of Chandauli, 9.2 per cent of Allahabad and 2.1 per cent respondents of Chitrakoot were of the opinion that these agitation activities should be stopped because the Government administration instead of providing relief, tortured us.

To discourage the agitation, demonstration and revolt activities launched by the *dalit adivasis* and to save the vested interests of the district administration, Government officials, maphias and political leaders, police often take legal action by involving them in criminal cases. False charges are framed on the active participants and put them in Jail.

Table 7.4: Whether Respondent Families were Affected with Agitation, Demonstration and Revolt Activities

District	Total House-holds	Affected	%	Some affected	%	No com-ments	%
Mirzapur	750	499	66.5	174	23.2	77	10.3
Sonbhadra	750	559	74.5	148	19.7	43	5.7
Chandauli	450	378	84.0	54	12.0	18	4.0
Naxal Total	1950	1436	73.6	376	19.3	138	7.1
Allahabad	600	338	56.3	101	16.8	161	26.0
Chitrakoot	450	174	38.7	52	11.6	224	49.8
Dacoit Total	1050	512	48.8	153	14.6	385	36.7
Total of five Districts	3000	1948	64.9	529	17.6	523	17.4

On this issue, 73.6 per cent respondents of Naxal prone area and 48.8 per cent respondents in Dacoit prone area told that their families were worstly affected. The police involved them by framing false charges against them. 17.6 per cent respondents of all the five districts replied that their families were affected up to some extent. 17.4 per cent respondents refused to comment on this point.

Objective

To find out the difference of opinion of the head of the household on the effect of agitation, revolt and uprising launched in the region on the members of their families. To prove statistically about the effect of agitation, revolt and uprising launched in the five tribal districts of U.P., i.e., Mirzapur, Sonbhadra, Chandauli, Allahabad and Chitrakoot.

The analysis of the data yields results in terms of mean, S.D. and Significance Value. The obtained results have been summarized in Table 7.5.

Table 7.5: Statistical Analysis

Sl. No.	Subject	N	Mean	S.D.	D.F.	Sign.
1.	Mirzapur	750	1.99	0.239	4	0.00
2.	Sonbhadra	750	1.95	0.235		
3.	Chandauli	450	1.93	0.249		
4.	Allahabad	600	2.00	0.000		
5.	Chitrakoot	450	1.98	0.140		

Table 7.6: Information on Active Participation of the Respondents in Revolt, Agitation and Demonstration

District	*Total Households*	*Fully*	*%*	*Occasionally*	*%*	*Rearly*	*%*	*Never*	*%*
Mirzapur	750	426	56.8	119	15.9	155	20.7	50	6.7
Sonbhadra	750	352	46.9	165	22.0	150	20.0	83	11.1
Chandauli	450	319	70.9	61	13.6	27	6.0	43	9.6
Naxal Total	1950	1097	56.3	345	17.7	332	17.0	176	9.0
Allahabad	600	70	11.7	114	19.0	36	6.0	380	63.3
Chitrakoot	450	38	8.4	62	13.8	29	6.4	321	71.3
Dacoit Total	1050	108	10.3	176	16.8	65	6.2	701	66.8
Total of five Districts	3000	1205	40.2	521	17.4	397	13.2	877	29.2

Since, the significance value is less than the significant level at 0.05. Therefore, it proves that the respondents have common opinion about the effect of revolt, agitation and uprising in the five tribal districts of U.P., i.e., Mirzapur, Sonbhadra, Chandauli, Allahabad and Chitrakoot.

Table 7.6 shows that 56.8 per cent respondents of Mirzapur, 46.9 per cent of Sonbhadra, 70.9 per cent respondents of Chandauli, 11.7 per cent respondents of Allahabad, and 8.4 per cent respondents of Chitrakoot fully participated in all these activities.

15.9 per cent of Mirzapur, 22.0 per cent of Sonbhadra, 13.6 per cent of Chandauli, 19.0 per cent of Allahabad, and 13.8 per cent respondents of Chitrakoot shows their participation casually at certain occasions. 17.0 per cent respondents from Naxal area and 6.2 per cent respondents in Dacoit area have rarely participated in such activities.

9.6 per cent respondents from Naxal prone area and 66.8 per cent respondents from Dacoit prone area have shown their least interest in such activities.

Objective

To find out the difference of opinion on active participation of the respondents in revolt, agitation and demonstration activities. The tribes do not oppose the revolt, agitation and demonstration activities in five tribal districts of U.P., i.e., Mirzapur, Sonbhadra, Chandauli, Allahabad and Chitrakoot.

The analysis of the data yields results in terms of mean, S.D. and Significance Value. The obtained results have been summarized in the Table 7.7.

Table 7.7: Statistical Analysis

Sl. No.	*Subject*	*N*	*Mean*	*S.D.*	*D.F.*	*Sig.*
1.	Mirzapur	750	1.99	0.247	4	0.000
2.	Sonbhadra	750	2.00	0.097		
3.	Chandauli	450	1.95	0.225		
4.	Allahabad	600	2.00	0.000		
5.	Chitrakoot	450	1.99	0.115		

Since, the significance value is less than the significant level at 0.05. Therefore, it shows that there participation is common Mirzapur, Sonbhadra and Chandauli, Allahabad and Chitrakoot is common.

I. NAXAL ACTIVITIES IN SONBHADRA, MIRZAPUR AND CHANDAULI

The geneses of tribal districts which continue to be as real as it was at the time of Independence, is that the polity has failed to secure even drinking water, road or hospital to every tribal village. Right to food, shelter and education is still beyond the dreams of many who still wage a daily battle of survival. Whose desk—that of the politicians or bureaucrats—should be buck stop for this? Both have always parroted that "these huge socio-economic problems cannot be solved overnight" to ensure that the buck does not stop at anyone's desk.

Given the ground situation, the Supreme Court's 22 years old judgement in Maneka Gandhi case about "right to life" appears, even today, to be a myth. In 1978, the Supreme Court had said "The expression of life "in Article 21" does not connote merely physical or animal existence. Right to life includes right to life with human dignity".

When the life is so cheap in Naxalite infected areas, where is the question of the impoverished masses searching for elusive dignity?

It was not so in 1972 when the Naxalite movement was in its nascent state, in Joydeb Gorai *Vs* State of West Bengal [1972 SC (2) 4171]. The Supreme Court had taken a stern view of a Naxalite sympathiser for threatening a villager and forcing him to erase the anti-Naxalite slogan he had written on the wall of his hut. It had upheld the State's decision to take the aggressor into preventive custody for an indefinite period. So, when the Apex judiciary had mostly been supportive of the action against outlaws and almost has been acting as a catalyst for proper implementation of social welfare schemes that touched the prevailing situation in the Naxalite infected areas. Would Government know which desk the buck should stop for this?

For 68 years tribal people living in these areas have eagerly been waiting for the winds of development to touch their lives. But when the long await tears the fabric of the patience turns it into anger, they become willing pawns for exploitation by those armed groups who have no fear of law. The Government knows that since the 1970s Naxalites have been holding kangaroo courts and handing down death penalties to police informers and those who oppose their activities. The poor are caught in the middle of the neglect by the Government and ruthlessness of outlaws.

Uttar Pradesh has witnessed stirrings of Naxalite activities in the south-eastern belt in Sonbhadra, Chandauli and Mirzapur districts. On November 20, 2004, Naxalites blew up a police jeep in the forest of

Chandauli with a landmine killing 13 PAC and 4 police personnel. The factors, which gave rise to Naxalism in south-eastern part of Uttar Pradesh, are unfortunately, very much present today also. The extent of extreme poverty in these tribal areas continues to be abysmal. Land reforms remain a neglected area, unemployment figures are very high. Tribals have been getting a raw deal. Governance, particularly in remote areas are very poor.

Naxal movement reached Sonbhadra, Chandauli and Mirzapur in late 90s. Many youngsters joined it. But banned organisation could not establish a strong base because majority prefer peace. These ultra come from Jharkhand and Bihar take refuse in villages, execute violent acts and go back. But police catch innocent locals, level them as Naxals and put them in jail. Their families are harassed and women exploited. Such conditions make it easy for Naxals and Maoist groups to gain ground in the region housing around 8 lakh people. Further with the passage of time Naxalitie and Maoist groups are also turning into as regards to Naxal violence in these tribal areas, the police at times exaggerate the incidents to draw more money from the Government in the name of security. One social activist told during survey and cited an incident when a PAC truck was blown charging them as Naxalites, but later it was revealed that explosive was brought from a cement factory and was handed over to Naxals by a forest officer.

The Naxalites have kept Sonbhadra district under three 'U' zone. They accept Sonbhadra as a Gate of Entrance of Uttar Pradesh. Their prime aim has been to blast the Electrical Plants by this action they would succeed to put the whole country into darkness. For their mission they exploit levy from local contractors, industrialists and rich man by terrorizing them. In addition to it, they persuade the male/female tribal youths to understand the ideology of Naxalism and join them for their better future.

The Investigator met with some hardcore Naxal youths both male and female in jail and asked the reasons behind accepting this destructing ideology of Naxalism. Their reply was quite different from our understanding point of view. They were not at all followers of Maoists or Naxalites and they did not have any different ideology as the Naxalites claim. The prisoners who were locked in the jail, boldly told that their joining in this team, was only due to other reasons like land alienation, grabbing of their land, personal enmity, unemployment, poverty, exploitation, torture and displacement and no appropriate compensation and injustice given to us by the police administration and revenue department.

Incidents of Naxal activities which resulted in great damage and loss of lives and property in south-eastern part of Uttar Pradesh, i.e., Sonbhadra, Chandauli and Mirzapur are described.

Table 7.8: Incidents of Naxal Activities

Sl. No.	*Date*	*Police Station*	*Village*	*Naxal Activities and Loss*
1.	5/6/1997	Manchi	Papadhawa	Heap of Tendu leaves collected by tribals was set on fire.
2.	5/8/1997	Manchi	Papadhawa	One Rama Shankar Ayodhya Prasad was murdered.
3.	6/7/1997	Robertsganj	Cherui Merkudi	Heap of Tendu leaves collected by tribals was set on fire by Naxalites.
4.	7/6/1997	Manchi	Baijnath	Heap of Tendu leaves collected by tribals was set on fire.
5.	8/6/1997	Robertsganj	Magardah	Heap of Tendu leaves collected by tribals was set on fire.
6.	5/8/1997	Manchi	Ram Nathpur	Ramashankar Jaiswal was murdered by Naxalites.
7.	1/10/1997	Manchi	Ram Nathpur	Licenced arms possessed by Gulzar and Asgar were looted by Naxalites.
8.	19/10/1997	Pannuganj	Bhikhampur, Khogwa, Pahari	Two Tractors loaded with boulders were set on fire by Naxalites.
9.	2/4/2000	Manchi	Ram Nathpur	Bhola Dhangar was kidnapped and later on murdered by Naxalites.
10.	7/5/2000	Karma	Banardewa	Lal Bahadur was slaughtered by Naxalites.
11.	14/10/2000	Karma	Papi (Naugarh) Chandauli	During encounter between Police and Naxalite S.O. Naugarh and one police man were murdered by Naxalites.
12.	18/10/2011	Robertsganj		15 Naxalites wearing police uniform attacked on police team and PAC personnel were seriously injured.
13.	9/4/2001	Kon	Basuhari	Naxalite burn the house and grain heap of Balram Singh.
14.	4/05/2001	Manchi	Panaura	The Tractor of Slauddin was set on fire by Naxalite.

(*Contd.*)

Table 7.8 (*Contd.*)

Sl. No.	*Date*	*Police Station*	*Village*	*Naxal Activities and Loss*
15.	8/6/2001	Dudhi	Kaharai Tola, Dhanrawa	Rs 32,000 wage earned from the collection of Tendu leaves was looted by Naxalites.
16.	30/07/2001	Manchi	Padari	Bindeshwari and Munnate S/o Santoo were kidnapped and murdered by Naxalites.
17.	03/11/2001	Manchi	Baijnath	The house of Shankar Pannika was completely damaged by Naxalites.
18.	4/4/2002	Robertsganj	Parsauna	Theku S/o Jhuri was kidnapped and later on murdered by Naxalites.
19.	5/7/2002	Chopan	Pakari	The house and the tractor were burnt by unknown 35 Naxalites.
20.	5/7/2002	Chopan	Kanhara	Naxalites furiously attacked on Police team during combing.
21.	18/7/2002	Kon	Nakala	Prasant Kumar's house and tractor were burnt by Naxalites.
22.	18/2/2002	Manchi	Baijnath	Sri Shankar tiles house was destroyed by Naxalites and set on fire.
23	6/11/2002	Kon	Ranidih	Birbal Chero was threatened and thereafter, illegally, money was exploited from him by Naxalites.
24.	28/11/2002	Robertsganj	Parsaona	Ghanshyam S/o Bhaolu was murdered by Naxalites.
25.	29/11/2002	Kon	Karail	Smt. Dheeraji Devi W/o Rambriksh was terrorised and rupees Ten Thousand was realised.
26.	16/01/2003	Pannuganj	Pannuganj	Naxalites opposing for fishing contract at Dhadhraul dam, destroyed 17 boats, nets and thatched houses and killed the contractor.
27.	23/3/2003	Robertsganj	Samada	Naxalites blasted mines during Police combing in which Minhaj was killed.
28.	25/2/2003	Manchi	Rampur forest	Sharad Chandra Padam Bhushan Sharan Shah, The king of Vijaygarh was attacked by Naxalites and arms were looted after his murder and his assistance.

(*Contd.*)

Table 7.8 (*Contd.*)

Sl. No.	*Date*	*Police Station*	*Village*	*Naxal Activities and Loss*
29.	11/4/2003	Kon	Gadav	Naxalites fired on Rajkumar Singh S/o Damodar Singh for terrorising him. He was also threatened that his house would be blasted and tractor etc. would be burnt.
30.	5/1/2004	Robertsganj	Kusumha	Devendra Singh and Basant Singh aged 40 years of each were murdered by Naxalites for land dispute.
31.	5/1/2004	Robertsganj	Lakhanwara	Basant Chauhan S/o Haldhari Chauhan was murdered by Naxalites.
32.	26/2/2004	Chopan	Patbadh	In order to harm the police party, the road mines was blasted by Naxalites in which Jagdish Patel was killed.
33.	12/12/2004	Pannuganj	Ketar	Dhananjay Singh S/o Shiv Singh was murdered in house by Naxalites.
34.	26/02/2004	Chopan	Forest	Naxalites damaged 5 private trucks carrying bamboos of the forest department.
35.	14/12/2004	Chopan	Salkhan	Naxalites burnt two tractors and 4 dumpers of M/s R.B. Stone Industries.
36.	22/12/2004	Pannuganj	Ketar	Naxalites killed Shiv Singh in an attack at his residence.
37.	22/12/2004	Pannuganj	Chitvitraon	Naxalites murdered Nand Lal Giri.
38.	2/8/2005	Manchi	Khodiala	Armed Naxalites murdered Inder Kumar Gujar after charging his as informer of Police.
39.	3/7/2006	Chopan	Beach	Armed Naxalites murdered Radhey Shyam Jaiswal S/o Harish Chandra.
40.	9/7/2006	Manchi	Chichlick	Naxalites murdered Jai Ram Meth S/o Gulab.
41.	14/11/2006	Manchi	Mahuli	Naxalites murdered Bhola S/o Samtullah in Sonbhadra.
42.	26/2/2007	Kon	Ranidih	Naxalites murdered Udai Pratap Kamojiya S/o Bhola in Sonbhadra.

(*Contd.*)

Table 7.8 (*Contd.*)

Sl. No.	*Date*	*Police Station*	*Village*	*Naxal Activities and Loss*
43.	8/3/2007	Aorai	Banauli	Om Prakash Dube was murdered by Naxalites in Chargadha forest of Sonbhadra.
44.	11/07/2007	Manchi	Soma	Armed Naxalites murdered Shambhu Nai S/o Bachcha.
45.	24/1/2009	Chopan	Kanhaura	Armed Naxalites murdered Umesh Chaudhari S/o Deena Nath Chaudhari.

During field survey in Sonbhadra, Chandauli and Mirzapur, the Investigator tried to understand the views of local tribals regarding Naxalites. One woman who was literate, replied, "They are those people who kill innocent people and they punish only guilty government officials, Naxalites do not do fake encounters. At least they accept responsibility for killing they carry out. But violence cannot be the solution to a problem". She further expressed her grievances and told, "mostly tribals are extremely poor and without any education. They cannot even tell their age. Some are upset at Government neglect and apathy. Our people eat just three four days a week. Therefore, they get swayed by the Naxalites. Things will get better if our basic needs like food, education, employment needs are fulfilled. If we are allowed to live with dignity and respect, and if we are not cheated and looked down upon".

During survey it was found that the tribal women of over five hundred villages in the region had taken around 20,000 hectares of land and are doing cooperative farming on it for the past two years claiming ownership on grounds that they are original inhabitants of the forests. But local 'Landlords' and few companies in mining business in the area are conspiring with Government and forest officials to get the land back. But if any attempt to dislodge the inhabitants is done may lead to providing left ultras an opportunity to strengthen their bases in the region. Thus, tribal unrest over ancestral land is the most serious problems which provide fertile ground for the left wing extremists. No doubt, the factors which gave rise to Naxalism in the country are unfortunately very much present today also. The extent of poverty in the country continues to be abysmal. Land reform remains a neglected area. Unemployment figures are high.

Even as Naxal leader Kabad Ghany's arrest has kick-started a debate in the country on Justification of violence to oppose an oppressive State "tribals in the Naxal-infested Kaimoor range of Uttar Pradesh have launched an aggressive but peaceful struggle against both the oppressive State" and "Exploiting Ultras". After holding a series of protests in their areas, under the banner of 'Kaimoor Kshetra Mahila Mazdoor Kisan Sangharsh Samiti' and 'National Forum for Forest People and Forest Workers', these tribals have decided to write to the Ex-Chief Minister Mayawati about their plight. For long, tribals here have been exploited both by the Left Ultras and the local Police in the region. While Naxals and Maoists operating in the area force tribals to give shelter and food, local police allegedly support local mafias, landlords and companies which are exploiting natural resources spread over Robertsganj, Chandauli and Mirzapur and other forests in Uttar Pradesh bordering Bihar. A new dimension has been added in this oppression by criminal gangs who operate in the garb of Naxals. Tribals have been getting a raw deal Governance in remote areas of very poors.

These gangs mostly comprise those who have fallen out of Ultra groups and now running their own extortion racket and working for mafias. The latest incident which sparked the protest was the arrest of two innocent tribal men from Brahmori village under Kon police station in Sonbhadra. The village is in a dense forest bordering Bihar. The Pradhan is from Thakur caste and controls the public distribution shop.

Tribals complaint that they do not get foodgrains from PDS. Laxaman and Ram Lakhan from Brahmori came to the city on August 2003 to buy ration. They also lodged a complaint with the district administration about "unavailability of food". On August 4, 2009 when the two were returning home. Their ration cards were snatched by a group claiming to be Maoists. On August 11, the two youths were called again by the same group to supply food. On August 12, 2009 police arrested the two tribals men on charges of helping Naxals triggering protest in the area of tribals. Tribals claim that the group claiming to be Naxals is actually a criminal gang which thrived on extortion and works for local mafias and landowners. The members of the gangs are formal Naxals. Some of them were also said to be working as an informer of the police.

It also points towards a nexus of local police, landlords and criminals. The main grievance was that local lords, mafia and mining companies are conspiring with Government/forest officers to take over forest land. Therefore, any attempt to dislodge tribals, who so far have adopted peaceful measures to protest, may lead to violence and may strengthen ultras operating in naxal-infested districts.

The new type of trample has started when the tribals have started claiming their ancestral land under Forest Right Act notified in 2007.

Naxal Strategy

Armed violence cannot be tolerated in any true democracy challenge confronting the country's establishment system. It is naked truth that the original and the real owners of water, forest and land and other natural resources are not only deprived of their rights, but are having to fight for their social and cultural identity as also for the very basic needs of their daily existence. These are the areas, which almost 68 years after Independence are yet to feel the hand of development. Today, these are the areas of violence and bloodshed where we have failed to solve the problems of poverty, hunger, homelessness, illiteracy and above all, the social of discrimination in the name of tribal class. It is true, the Indian masses live in the throes of injustice and discrimination. That is the social condition prevailing today. There is the nexus of the politicians, the bureaucrats and sometimes even the mafias with their vice like grip on the tribal people, subjugating them to a life of miseries and hardships. In this backdrop, the advocates of violence, that Naxalites, argue that parliamentary democracy has disillusioned the masses and the only opinion left with the people is to violently confront the oppressors—the State, the bureaucrats, money lenders, landlords and mafias.

The Naxalites, who have always been active in Chhattisgarh, Andhra, Madhya Pradesh and Jharkhand, discovered that south-eastern part of Uttar Pradesh was the best region to launch their Naxal activities. Hence, they prepared Naxal strategy for this region and accordingly they tried their best to make them successful. They are the followings:

1. The Naxalites, where they select the area for their action, call as 'Liberated Areas'.
2. They always prefer the gorilla war policy in which they suddenly attack and if they find that their enemy is alert and in offensive mood, they themselves hide and do not prefer to face any confrontation.
3. In their opinion, police, forest officer, police informer, landlords and others are their enemies with whom they take revenge by damaging them.
4. Illiterate and poor tribals who believe that the Naxalites are fighting for their sake and cause, easily and willingly come in their control and they join them in their campaign.

5. Naxalites always try to impress the tribals as if they are dying for their causes. Consequently, the sufferers, unemployed youths, tortured and exploited youths including girls easily come in their grip.
6. They always preach the tribals that their real enemies are Government officials and their problems would not be solved unless they launch bloodshed revolt against them.
7. The Naxalites who are active in this part of Uttar Pradesh have declared from Sonbhadra to Ballia district as Naxal corridor. Since, Sonbhadra district is adjacent to Kaimoor forest area, therefore, they have accepted Sonbhadra as the gateway to enter into for their Naxal activities.
8. It has been reported by the intelligence department that in order to make their organization more powerful, they are trying to receive supports from Maoists, Litte and Lashkare Toiba terrorist organizations. It is quite alarming.
9. Their one of the missions is to exploit huge amount of money from all the industrial units functioning in Sonbhadra, Mirzapur and Chandauli by terrorizing techniques.
10. Their another antinational mission is to blast the Electric Power Plants producing 10 thousand Mega Watt electricity. If they succeed most parts of India will be without electricity.
11. To make them more strong and powerful, PWG and MCC have been merged each other and have declared a new Naxal Organisation namely CPI (Maoist).

Akhilendra Pratap Singh, the then State Secretary CPI (Male) U.P. and Ex-President of Allahabad University Students Union launched his first compaign in Sonbhadra district in 1996 and as such this was the beginning of Naxal activities in Sonbhadra district. And it spread all over the districts of Sonbhadra, Chandauli and Mirzapur. As per police record, 35 criminal incidents were recorded between 5-6-97 to 2-08-2005 only in Sonbhadra districts. The police stations named: (1) Karma, (2) Ghorawal, (3) Robertsganj, (4) Pannuganj, (5) Raipur, (6) Manchi, (7) Chopan, (8) Kon, (9) Dudhi, (10) Bijpur, (11) Vindhamganj and (12) Babhani and Police Chauki (1) Shahganj, (2) Churk, (3) Rampur Barkonia and Myorepur were declared as Naxal prone police stations and police chaukis, whereas (1) Pipari, (2) Obra, (3) Anpara, (4) Shaktinagar and Police Chauki (1) Robertsganj, (2) Renukoot, (3) Renusagar were declared Naxal free zone.

Out of 1,363 total villages of Sonbhadra district, 266 villages come under Naxal affected Zone.

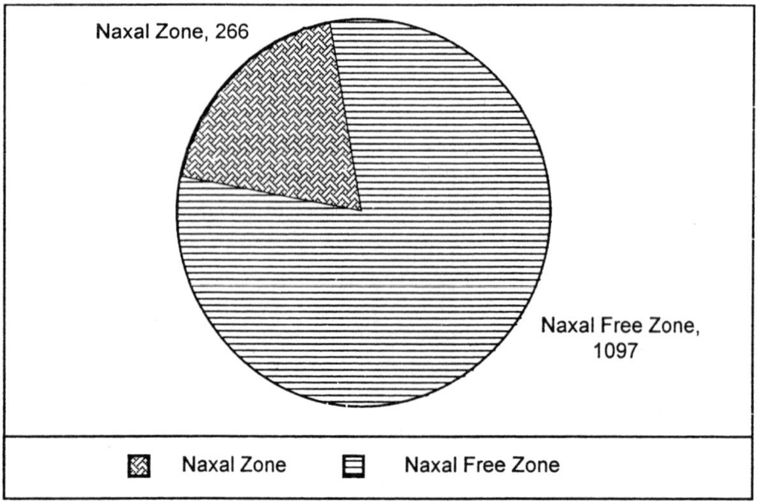

Fig. 7.1: Naxal Affected Zone

The U.P. Police Force and Central Reserve Police Force have always been vigilant and deployed for combing operation and for counter attack against Naxalites and their criminal activities in the district. During police operation several Naxals have been encountered and several were arrested. As per Police record following were encountered and arrested from 2001 to 2010 (see Table 7.9).

Table 7.9: Police Action against Naxalites in South-Eastern Part of U.P.

Year	*Arrested*	*Encountered*
2001	7	02
2002	17	05
2003	32	07
2004	15	02
2005	48	0
2006	24	03
2007	07	02
2008	26	01
2009	18	02
2010	06	0

Year: 2005

Naxal Operation	01
Police Operation	
Arrested	48
Surrendered	01
Encounter	03

The significant achievement of the police force during this operation was to recover—Riffle, Guns, 90 bullets in the village Hinhat, district Chandauli. These arms were looted by killing 34 PAC battalion force on 20th November, 2004.

The Police Force could feel relaxed when Kameshwar Baitha, the PWG Zonal Commander was arrested and surrendered before Police officers, Chandrabhan, the hardcore Naxalite was killed during operation and the other hardcore Naxalite named Meva Lal was arrested.

All those naxals, who were arrested, were interviewed by the police force, the prime media news correspondents and by other social activists for knowing the reasons and the conditions of joining the Naxalites.

The statements uttered by these arrested Naxalites have been categorized into three broad reasons. First one was that, our poverty would be removed by Naxalite ideology. The second was that we were hypnotized by the ideology of Naxalites; and the third one was that we would get relief from all sorts of torturing and exploitation from all the exploiters by joining Naxal group.

However, the Uttar Pradesh Government giving top priority, has also prepared its own strategy to control the Naxal activities in other States. It is very shocking that during the period of 2008-2009, this State lost 107 U.P. Police men and 82 CRPF jawans during operation against Naxalites. All of them were posted in those States where Naxalites were very active. Hence, with full determination, the State has prepared the following strategy:

1. In order to counter the attack of Naxalites, the strategy of Police force combing would have to be made purposeful and offensive.
2. During combing, the force has to survey the tribal villages and they should try at the best to solve the problems of the tribes at the spot also.
3. The police force should have to be watchful for those who provide shelter to the Naxalites and who conspire against the police force by instigating Naxalites.

4. The police force had to show its presence regularly at those places which are not easily approachable. Such activities would alarm the Naxalites and they would be helpless to get safe places to hide in the forest.
5. In order to encourage, the State Government has declared 30 per cent extra allowance for those who have been posted in Naxal affected areas.
6. All those police forces, who are being posted at these sensitive areas, would be given special training for how to operate the newly and highly sophisticated weapons.
7. In addition to civil police force, 13 companies of para-military forces would be posted for quick operation.
8. The Government would organise several awareness programmes in tribal areas in order to change the mind of the misguided tribal youths, so that, they may join the mainstream of development.
9. There would be regular campaign in tribal areas to provide the food, medicine, tuition fee and to fulfil all their basic needs.
10. The Police has to make itself as the helpers and friends to the tribal people. The false terrorism existing in the mind of tribals has to be removed through the Police community activities.

The Central Government has also declared the following projects for controlling the Naxal activities.

1. Grant of Rs. 17.5 lakh has been released to meet out the expenditure on SRI (Security Related Expenditure).
2. Rs. 5 lakh grant has been released for the community development in this region.
3. The Government order has been issued to constitute 'India Reserve Vahini' in addition to the regular force.
4. Helicopter facilities will immediately be provided to the Police during operation on its demand.
5. All the Central Government social and economic welfare programmes will equally be enforced in tribal areas. With this declaration the tribals would join the mission of Sarva Shiksha Abhiyan, MNREGA, Grains for Work, Rajeev Gandhi Electricity Yojana and they would be equally benefited.
6. After creation of the post of SPO, the funds were demanded by the State. The Central Government has released the fund as it was demanded.

The State Government has introduced a new Community Policing Method through which the Police as well as civil administration would personally visit and meet the tribal people to understand their real problems and root causes of their discontent by developing rapport position. In order to make this compaign successful the District Magistrate, Superintendent of Police and several other district officers in Sonbhadra personally met the tribal people in their villages by campaigning. Under this campaign then got success to maximum extent. During campaign tribal problems have been heard and solved on the spot. The tribal youth have been trained in different branches of profession to make them capable to earn their livelihood through self-employment. The tribals have been supported by providing several domestic articles to fulfil their minimum needs. All the district officers regularly visited the tribal areas and participated in all social and religious function and provided and encouraged them by providing fund. For example, group Marriages have been organised by the administration and necessary gifts and expenses on such ceremonies have been borne by the administration. Sewing machines, blankets, bicycles, wheel chairs, wheel bicycles, rickshaws, etc., have been distributed among the handicapped persons. All schooling facilities have been provided to tribal children. In this way this experiment of Community Policing method has met with great success in discouraging Naxalites in this region.

II. SOME PATHETIC INSTANCES

The researcher personally visited several tribal villages of Sonbhadra, Mirzapur, Chandauli, Allahabad and Chitrakoot and tried to record their economic and social conditions of their families. It was seen that there was no source of food, no source of water, no source of income for fulfilling the bare needs and needs like clothes, no medicines and other essential needs of their lives. No approachable roads, no light and no other means of communications. Right on natural resources, i.e., land, water and jungle for the agriculture, are highly relevant to their lives. Possession of economically viable agricultural land for the cultivation of food crops to feed the family, accessibility of drinking water and water for irrigation, access to grassland for grazing of animals and access to forest produces as a source of income give the marginalised access to food and purchasing power, but they are deprived of all the resources.

During survey the researcher met some Kol families in Girduha, Khekarra, Tedhwa and Sakroha tribal villages of Manikpur tehsil of

Chitrakoot district, where the families light their Chulha once a day, in the evening and live on one meal. The families were found waiting for the meals on the only earning members to return with daily wages. Many families have no land. All the members have to depend only on Rs. 10-25 per day.

They describe their hunger as 'burning pit' in the abdomen. Most of the children below six were found suffering from malnutrition. Tuberculosis and rheumatic fever which are very common there.

The death of 8 children between July and September, 2003 allegedly due to lack of food, has sparked concerns about growing starvation in a landless indigenous community in a remote village in Sonbhadra. The truth was confirmed when we observed the pathetic and malnourished conditions of several children of Manikpur, Mau Blocks and Makari Bari, Laua of Nagaon Blocks and Semara, Umbla villages of Ghorawal Block and children of Shankargarh tribal children. We found that most of the children were mere skeleton, as if their bodies and flesh had been sapped away. They were suffering from the extreme limit of poverty. There was one Ghasia tribe living in Sonbhadra district tribal areas. They are living in a settlement area declared as a forest area by the Government. Decades ago, the tribe made the forest their home, after fleeing their ancestral villages to escape the tyranny of the regions of feudal landlords. Their families were surviving on poisonous grass and wild mushrooms for many years. The children were unable to tolerate the poison and succumbed to death.

Since, Sonbhadra, Chandauli and Mirzapur tribal areas have turned into the hub of several power plants, industries and mines, the tribals have been repeatedly displaced several times. They have been forced to live in very-very wretched conditions of housing. Mostly, their houses were made of grass and garbage.

Under land reform and distribution of Land to Landless Act to tribals, 398 villages were taken into consideration by the S.D.M., Karvi Tehsil on 31st December, 1991. In that programme 2,528 tribal men were to be allotted *patta* for agricultural purpose. Total area of land 887607 hectares barren land was located for allotment of *patta* for agriculture purpose. Officially, it was claimed that the allotment of *patta* of land was completed as per declaration. But practically nothing was done.

The cases mentioned here are only the proverbial tip of iceberg as these and other villages of Patha region are simply too many stories of extreme distress caused by injustice and repression.

Mohan Kol describe that 10 *bighas* of land was awarded to him as *patta* in Kihunia village but he never received its possession due to pressure of mafia landlords. Similarly Chandrama, Hari, Meena, Sarita, Amar, Ram Khelawan and others' lands have been graobed by the upper castes *dabang* landlords.

57 *bighas* of land of Vishesar, Lallo, Budhua, Gopal, Khelawan and Shankar, all from Kol tribe of Chcherihakhurd have never been demarcated and shown by the Lekhpal due to the terror of landlords. This land since it was very fertile and very near to canal had been grabbed by Dadus of Kihunia and Markundi villages, Chitrakoot.

Shiva, Ramashre, Pitambar, Mahadev and other 35 tribals of Jaromaphi village were never told the exact location of their *patta* land.

100 *bigha* of land was distributed as *patta* among 135 tribals in Nihi village, but they never dared claim due to terror of landlords. Mahesh, Krishna, Durga and other Kol tribe showed their claim on 25 *bigha* of land which was allotted as *patta* long-long ago. When they started claiming their land, they were forcibly displaced from their village.

57 claimants of Gobarhi village whose area of land had been entered into land record, i.e., Khatauni, could never dare for their claim. The extremity of terror can be understood after this narration that the Brahmin landlords of this village forced the Lekhpal to record the land of 5 Kol Pattedars in their names by showing all the claimants Kol as dead although they were alive, but had no courage to protest against such false records.

Widow women Ramratia and Gurja of Hela village were allotted 19 *bigha* land as *patta*, but they could not get possession, one local leader had illegally occupied on gun point. These widow women were tortured, beaten and thrown out of their village.

One woman namely Bitto, Paras Kol Haddiha Calon village could never get possession on her 29 *bigha* of land. Another women Sorsati w/o Rameshar Kol submitted application in the Court of S.D.M. Manikpur for measurement of her 8 *bigha* land allotted in her name. The Lekhpal measured her plot, but even then the powerful landlord did not spare her land ever after the expiry of 25 years, in spite of High Court orders in his favour.

Phoolan S/o Balak of Gram Sabha Saraiya could not get possession on his land. One local political leader has occupied a plot of 5 *bigha* of land of a widow lady named Sikaria. She was found very much disappointed because there was no support for her livelihood.

Intikara village, one old man named Vinod of 70 years old, narrated his problem. "The one local landlord had taken loan from the Bank by mortgaging my land. The Gram Pradhan of his village forcibly constructed Panchayat Ghar and Indira Awas on my possessed land".

One Kaloa Chamar of Chcheriha Khurd was given 5 *bigha* of land as *patta*, but one day some *dabang* landlords came to his hut and forced him to put his thumb impression on loan paper. They took loan for purchasing pumping set for their own purpose. When he showed his resentment for this illegal action, he was severely beaten by them. Thereafter he left his village forever.

The kind of land-grabbing that has been taking place in 'Patha' region may appear incredible to many people. There are several instances when influential and big landlords colluded with lower level Government functionaries to get the land records changed in such a way that living persons (tribals) were shown as dead. Then they went one step further and got themselves registered as the legal heirs. Such incidents have been reported recently from Nili and Chamrauha villages. When such victims protest, they faced repression. In Terva village a landlord who was a terror in nearby villages, had his eyes on the fertile land of a Kol tribal namely Sugia. When she resisted efforts to grab the land, she was murdered. The next step was to get rid of her husband Dinesh. He was falsely implicated in the murder of his own wife.

As though all these injustice were not enough to break the back of the poor, the rich landlords even resort to the shameful tactic of borrowing in the name of the poor or diverting loans meant for poor families to themselves. With tears in their eyes, several Kol tribals told moving stories of how many they toiled for several months to make rocky land productive and that land was taken away by the powerful landlords of the region.

The stories of the repression of woman are even worse. Ramia was forced by a policeman to live as his mistress. She had to undergo three abortions. Meena of Sarhat village first experienced distress when she was raped, but later when she reported it. She had to face even more distress at the hands of the same person. The culprit got her husband arrested after implicating him in false legal cases and destroyed the standing crop in their field.

Exploitation of the poor tribal by making them bonded labour has been very common in Patha region. Debt bondage is commonly referred to as 'forced labour' or 'Bonded labour', terms that can be classified as euphemisms for slavery. A report in 2003 by Human Rights watch proposed that there are between 20 and 65 million bonded labours in India. Agricultural debt bondage slavery is directly related to land possession. In Indian families who were once free (typically landless) farmers fell upon hardship and saw no other choice but to take out a loan from a local landlords in order to keep working on the land. Without any form of assets or belongings the debtors (and their families, if applicable) pledge their own lives and labour as collateral against the debt to the landlord. Once a contract was established with a landlord it was nearly impossible to break it. Technically, a slave is free once he pays his debt, but landlords do not allow the debtors to accrue any capital. Any wages earned from daily labour are applied towards the interest on the interest on the debt, which is certainly an inaccurate figure concocted by the landlord. All bonded labourers work under the threat of imminent violence. Debts are passed to the wives and children of slaves in the event of death, escape, imprisonment, etc. The conditions of agricultural debt bondage are so inhumane that thousands of farmers, when faced with possibilities of a lifetime in bondage, have chosen to commit suicide instead. A recent article reported that over 180,000 Indian farmers have committed suicide since 1997 because of their formidable debts. In Indian children most often fall into debt bondage of the actions of their parents. Debt inheritance is a common way for children to become indebted to a landlord. In rural areas the landlords expect the debt to be worked off by any means.

There are some examples of pathetic stories of bonded labours, narrated here. One Shiv Pujan a Kol youth of Ooncha Dih village of Chitrakoot narrated, "His father Ravindar had been a bonded labour of a Brahmin landlord who grabbed our land. At the time of mother's death, my father took loan from the landlord by mortgaging mother's jewellery for performing her last rites. The jewellery was never returned to my father. As my father was a T.B. patient he was not able to work in the landlord's family. For that he was beaten severely, so to spare his father's beatings, I started going in his place although I was too young for this work. I as bonded labour had to work hard from 5 AM to late night every day".

A landlord of Terva village, was involved in beating badly his worker Manbharan who had tried to resist conditions of bondage. He was later implicated in a false case and sent to jail where he died. His land was grabbed by the landlord while his wife and 2 years old child had to starve. Manik Kol of Dandi village resisted conditions of bondage and insisted on having some rest and food after toiling very hard. For this, he was beaten up very badly and whipped with a rope. Five days after this beating Manik died. In Helagaon the master of two bonded labourers Chchotoo and Mannu Kol, took loan in their names. He used the money, but the recovery notice came in the name of his bonded labourer. They were locked and subjected to a lot of ill treatment. Their harassment and the resulting tension increased so much that both of them committed suicide. Later, the master grabbed whatever land was left behind by them.

In recent decades a small number of rich and influential families have managed to cover a major share of the earnings from the forests and mines of course a significant part of the loot was shared with politicians and officials, but in many parts of Chitrakoot and Shankargarh tribal areas of Allahabad district, a part of the booty also goes regularly to dacoit gangs. Senior politicians go to attend social celebrations in the families of leading dacoits and of course seek their blessings to win elections in return for offering them protection. No mean achievement, going by Patha's history of violence and terror over recent years. There are several examples of incidents of dacoit actions in Chitrakoot and Shankargarh region.

A dacoit gang invaded Ramu Purva because they suspected the people of this hamlet had helped in arrest of one of their colleagues. In a matter of minutes, nine persons were shot dead. In Singwa village, two brothers working in their fields, were suddenly descended upon by dacoits. Accused of helping the police, both were shot dead. In Babatalab village, some villagers were asked for directions by a gang of dacoits. When they hesitated, there was a scuffle. One of the dacoits was injured and the gang fled. But they returned, killing three villagers and set some huts ablaze. Some women of Harijanpur village who had gone to collect wood from the forest were set upon by dacoits and raped. The brother of Vishwanath Pratap Singh the then Chief Minister of Uttar Pradesh have gone hunting in a forest area when he was taken unaware by a gang of dacoits. He was killed and a spate of developments followed which culminated in the C.M.'s resignation. Near Manikpur town of Chitrakoot district, three railway employees were abducted by dacoits. Subsequently, staff and members of their families, numbering about 1000 had to be shifted elsewhere.

Thus, there are few examples of incidents in Patha region over recent years that have made the headlines and occasionally influenced political developments in Uttar Pradesh.

One lady named Lalita Devi of Chero tribe of Magardha village (Sonbhadra) narrated her pathetic incident which happened with her, "I was lying in a pool of blood. My seventh child was never born because of severe blow of police stick on my belly. The police arrested my family with 90 families who were demanding the right to land inside Magadaha forest and an end to corruption in logging. The forest officials alongwith nearby villagers and some police officers, forcibly evicted us from the forest on March 16, 2010 by charging and imposing several allegations upon us.

Nakdu was a boy child belonging to the Mushahar *dalit adivasis* in Sonbhadra. He alongwith his parents and other children of his family were working as bonded labourers in a brick kiln factory. Like other families of their community they have been working as bonded labourers for more than 20 years. The small amount paid to them as wages was just enough for one wholesome meal for one day. As a result of it, children were suffering from malnutrition. The huts they live in hardly protects them from heavy rain or the severe winter.

Poonam, a *dalit adivasi* girl child of 2 years old of a village nearby Rihand Dam was suffering from tuberculosis, chronic and acute malnutrition and retardation of growth. Her parents were too poor to meet her medical expenses.

The news of several starvation deaths of Kol *dalit adivasis* of Kubradhi village in Nawgarh Block of Chandauli were flashed in 2010. During survey it was found that Red Card meant for BPL families was not issued to them. Their livelihood was totally depended on collection of *tendu* leaves. The contractors had not paid any amount as their wage.

Kaulasha Devi, Munna, Vishawambhar and so many *dalit adivasi* women and men were found living in a pathetic condition.

Nandu Lal a Harijan of Basauli village said that the population of the village was about 2,500. More than 40 per cent of these have no land. He said that agricultural labourer did not get work for more than 15 days in the month of July. The prevalent wage rate was rupees 23 per day and 5 kilograms of rice. They were paid rice, but not the money. No one can get work without paying bribe of 10 per cent. Only 28 persons in the village have Red Cards. No one has received Blue Card. The Blue Card is given under Annapurna Programme. The Village Pradhan has given this to his known and moneyed families. Most of the people have received the Yellow Card. They get oil on this card.

One Bachcha Lal of this village, told that during President's Rule many people of this village were members of MCC (a banned organization) and were arrested. This was oppression of the *dalit adivasis*. When Raj Nath Singh was the Chief Minister, this operation also continued in his period. Such operations still continue. The police believes that the *dalit adivasis* are generally in the MCC and, therefore, they terrorise them. Fact is this that the MCC members have really helped us in getting wages for *tendu* leaves. The police still terrorise us if we demand wages for *tendu* leaves.

One Gupt of Mushahar *adivasi* of Vinayakpur village Chandauli, told that everyone was given White Card, but they had not been provided any relief from the Government or from any source. They were paid only 5 kg of rice as wage along with water to drink. They earn a very little amount by making '*donna*' (bowl) of leaves. Bachaoo, Ramlakhan, Bachchan (Mushahar) Samundari, Munnu, etc., told that they were given a White Card, except Samundari who was given a white card on which they could get kerosene oil at the rate of rupees 2 per litre.

Maddar told that they worked as labourers as they were landless. They were happy if they could eat once in a day. There was no succour from any source. No one has been able to transplant. If this situation continued they would be reduced to beggary. He revealed that he had reported this to Gram Pradhan. The Gram Pradhan and the secretary conducted search of his house to see if he had hidden some foodgrains in his house. When nothing was found, they abused him and went away. But did not provide help.

Fauzdar told that he had a plot on which he was cultivating for the last 50 years and on which he had planted *arhar* pulse. It was cordoned off by the Ranger of the forest department. The Ranger had cordoned off about 150 *bighas* of land belonging to 100 households and the villagers have been evicted. Ashok Narayan Singh, of Lalitpur Basoli, Muraahum of Amdahaan village and many *adivasis* peasants of Vinayakpur, Samera, Sadhopur and Deori Galann told that the Forest Department had evicted them by force from their agricultural land on which they had been doing farming for the last 50 years. At present they had no means of their livelihood. As a result they had reached at the starvation.

Hundreds of thousands of residents of Mitihini and Singrauli villages had been forcely displaced for installation of National Thermal Power Corporation and Singrauli Coal mines and unjustly improvershed as a result of World Bank's financial activities.

2,086 displaced *dalit adivasis* living in Chilka Tand Colony after displacement were shifted again after their lands were identified for the power complex in 1977. They were pushed to the edge of the Khadia Coal mine a ravaged landscape of dugout mountain side stripped of any vegetation; and residents daily battle against dust and disease. In the dozen resettlement colonies for the displaced, there was no clean water or proper health care. Nearly 30 per cent of the people who live near the power plants suffered bronchial asthama and TB.

Naha a frail widow with a wizened face from Dibulganj in U.P. A displaced woman lived on alms from passers by of the Anpara station, gathering rice and *dal* from different homes.

2000 forest dwellers were evicted for the coal mines of Northern Coal Fields Ltd., a subsidiary of Coal India, are still owe money or jobs. They have not yet been rehabilitated.

In continuation of the above mentioned pathetic stories of exploitation of tribals we are narrating the pathetic stories of two hard core Naxals. Information was gathered from their family members. Why did they join the Naxal group in Sonbhadra, has been explained as under:

1. Mewa Lal – Hardcore Naxalite, S/o Khajoor Baiga, Case-Kharwar, Resident of Gram and Post Baki, Police Station Manchi, Tehsil Robertsganj, Sonbhadra.
   Like others he was innocent and unaware of fraudulent tricks of dealing with the public and the government officials. He was dedicated to his studies and successfully completed his High School course in 1990. Thereafter, he started working as teacher in one NGO named 'Janjati Vikas Samiti'. His father Khajoor Baiga, alongwith his family members used to work on his own allotted *patta* land. One member of his village, named Rudra Yadav, having malafide intention conspired to grab his land. His father was insulted and beaten severely by them and thereafter, he was involved in criminal offence. Mewalal approached the police administration repeatedly, but due to the political power and the bribe money, his complaint were thrown into waste paper basket. Mewalal was very much depressed and did not prefer to spend life in such an insulted situation. Thereafter, he made up his mind to join Naxal group in 1997-98. There he was appointed as Area Commander of Hardcore Naxalite. Due to his terror, Rudra Yadav vacated his land. The administration contacted his family members to make him surrendered before the administration with assurance that full justice would be done in releasing his land and other facilities would be provided also. However, Mewa Lal surrendered before the administration but soon after he was arrested and put in jail in Patna (Bihar). Till date his land is under dispute and no justice has been given in his favour.
2. Sanjay Kol, Area Commander Hardcore Naxalite, Resident of Village Majgaon, Police Station Naugarh, Tehsil Chakiya, Chandauli district.

His father purchased one piece of fertile land in Gangapur by selling anscestral land. But the registration formalities were not completed in Registrar Office. In the mean time, one man named Chulhai Yadav bought this piece of land by paying Rs. two lakh and got registered. Due to this reason the dispute arose. Sanjay Kol complained in police administration and the matter was discussed in Gram Panchayat also. But Chulhai Yadav was adamant not to release the land.

Due to this great loss of land Sanjay's family were put in hardship and in starving condition. Consequently, Sanjay Kol decided to join Naxal group. He was also appointed as Area Commander of Hardcore Naxalite. Firstly, Sanjay Kol made conspiracy and murdered Chulahi Yadav and Babunder Yadav. After few years he was very active in committing crime but later on he was killed during police operation.

There is another pathetic story of one Naim Akhatar, Gram and Post Rampur, Police Station Manchi, Sonbhadra district. He narrated how he was falsely and forcibly involved by the police administration through false charges imposed on him.

References

1. Ramana, P.V. (ed.), 2008, *The Naxal Challenge; Causes, Linkages and Policy Options*, Dorling Kinderslay (India) Pvt. Ltd., Delhi.
2. Reddy, I.U.B., 1992, *Displacement and Rehabilitation*, Mittal Publications, New Delhi.
3. Roy, Arundhati, 2010, *'Outlook' the Weekly Magazines.*
4. 'पहरूआ पहल' अंक 5, अक्टूबर-दिसम्बर, 2006.

Summary, Conclusions and Suggestions

The Study under the title "Betwixt Development and Discontent" its sociological analysis of the root causes of discontent among the *dalit adivasis* on the south-eastern periphery of Uttar Pradesh, even after all sorts of development programmes and social welfare programmes, launched by the Union and as well as State Government under Five Year Plan periods, and an explanation for the continuing tribal unrest, revolt and violence have been analysed and explained.

The following have been the main objectives of the study:

1. To examine the prevailing socio-economic conditions among the *dalit adivasis*.
2. To analyze the awareness and impact of the various development welfare projects and schemes on the basis of the Economic growth, Education growth and the improvement in health conditions and medical facilities growth in the area of study.
3. To analyze the discontent among the *dalit adivasis* related to Land Alienation, Forest Land Right Act 2006, distribution of Land (allotment of *patta*) under Land Reformation Act 1950, displacement due to construction of several dams, installation of power plants and coal mines and finally the exploitation and torturing nature of feudal landlords, maphias, contractors and also that caused by power and industrial units.
4. To know the perception of the community/group leaders regarding causes of unrest and violent protest action, in specific term the so called 'Naxalite Movement' and its legitimacy as well as direct relevance to the perceived causes of unrest.

The universe of the study at the first stage, Mirzapur, Sonbhadra and Chandauli districts were chosen because they rank first in terms of Naxal prone tribal population. At the second stage Allahabad and Chitrakoot districts were chosen because the tribal populations living in dense forest have continuously been exploited by the landlords of higher castes and victimized by dacoits. At the next stage, the Blocks of all the five districts were selected on the intensity index. Lalganj, Hallia, Marihan, Rajgarh and Kon Blocks from Mirzapur districts, Robertsganj Babhani, Chopan, Dudhi, Nagwan from Blocks from Sonbhadra, Naugarh, Sahebganj and Chandauli from Chandauli district, Jasra, Shankargarh, Meja, Koraon Blocks from Allahabad Karvi, Mau and Manikpur Blocks from Chitrakoot district were selected on the intensity index. 150 households from each Block were randomly selected. The number of households from Mirzapur and Sonbhadra were 750 from each district, 450 households were selected each from Chandauli and Chitrakoot district. 600 households were selected from Allahabad district. Thus, the total number of sample households from all the five districts were 3,000.

To know the practices, beliefs and attitudes in the area and other recent informative, a normative survey was made.

This was done with the help of (a) Library study and Documentation, (2) PRAs (Participatory Rural Appraisal) Groups, Focus Group Discussions and Participation Observation, and (3) Survey-Community and household and the case study method.

The *adivasi* have been the oldest ethnic groups of India's national population. They are called original inhabitants of the country. Marlin, A.B. Thakkar, Herberty Risley, Lele and others have used the term 'aborigines' for them. M.K. Gandhi called them *adimjati*. The tribes living in dense forest of this region are almost cut off from the so-called modernity and civilization, are still maintaining their original tribal cultural traditions and tribal economy. Hence, the term '*adivasi*' has been thought appropriate and used in the study.

The term, 'Development' in this study, has been considered as 'change in the desired direction within stipulated time. When we talk about as sensitive an issue as tribal development, the question that automatically comes is: whose desires—those of the planners or of implementers or of tribals are themselves. The question becomes more relevant when we realize that in the name of tribal development, others have tried and have imposed their wills on tribes. In the present study, the concept and programmes of development have been examined in the context of *dalit adivasi*. Issues, diversions and strategies pertaining to tribal development have been examined sociologically speaking functional and dysfunctional from the point of view of fulfilment of their (i) basic needs, (ii) restoration of their human rights, (iii) Attainment of the state of improvement, and (iv) to examine the functioning of tribal development project.

As regards the term 'Discontent', it is the manifestation of dissatisfaction of a person or a group of persons against what have been expected by them. It exposes the philosophical and psychological aspects of mind of a person who runs madly in search of material happiness in the world. But in case of tribals, the term discontent shows the extremity of their disappointment and frustration against the lollipop given by the Government in the name of their development and welfare programmes. They have continuously been exploited by the foreign rulers, by the henchmen of the alien rule, and lords, moneylenders. In spite of all sorts of development and welfare programmes since Independence, 85 per cent of the tribal families are still living below poverty line rather suffering from chronic poverty. The gap between the targets and the physical achievements of various tribal development schemes is widening beyond control.

The Naxalite movement is essentially an ideological movement and not an ethnic movement or religious movement. It gets its sustenance from social evils. Such as poverty, unemployment, exploitation of the poor classes. In 1960s, a kind of revolt erupted in Naxal Bari village of north Bengal and caught on, giving birth to the term 'Naxal Bari' movement. The Naxal movement could be termed as 'Left Wing Communism'. It is a concomitant growth of the communist movement. The south-eastern region of Uttar Pradesh is rich in forest produce and mineral resource. Whatever be the scale of development, it has been market oriented and not people oriented. The tribals living scattered here and there are still in the State of chronic poverty, many of them are landless, indebted and deprived of all necessary amenities. Due to their land problem and rehabilitation problem they are easily being trapped and exploited by the Naxalites who blackmail and involve them in Naxal activities in the name of relief from all sorts of miseries.

The Naxal prone areas as the first part of the universe of the study—Mirzapur, Sonbhadra and Chandauli—have been the main hub of all sorts of development due to the natural richness, several industries, mines and power plants. On the one side they were accepted as indication of developments of this part of region, but on the other side, this development resulted in extreme exploitation of original tribal inhabitants. As a result, several problems came up like displacement, alienation and denial of forest rights. Naxalites are always in search of such type of situations where their ideologies can flourish. Consequently, they got the place

Sonbhadra, Mirzapur and Chandauli forest as the safest shelter and tribals as their best carriers.

The other part of the universe of study is the Dacoit prone area, includes Allahabad and Chitrakoot districts. In this part tribal particularly Kol tribes have occasionally been looted, tortured, exploited murdered and forced to commit suicide by the upper castes feudal landlords, Dadus with the help of dacoits hidden in the forest. Rocky agricultural land, shortage of water, drought grabbing of land, indebtedness, bonded labourhood, prohibition of forest produce, hunger, poverty, death suicide and rape with their women are allotted in their faith.

As regards to the socio-economic characteristics of the sample houses:

1. It was found that the majority of villages, i.e. 87 out of total 94 villages were quite remote from the district Headquarters. Most of the facilities, essential for villages, e.g., Hospital, Child Care Centres, Primary Schools, Post Office, Telephone Office, PCOs, Bus Station, Commercial Banks and other necessary infrastructural facilities were not available even at the shorter distances. Mostly the villages were found ill equipped as regards infrastructural facilities like transportation and communication. Most of them were not located on the road sides. Approach roads to the tribal villages in forest areas were not plain.
2. 81.3 per cent in Mirzapur, 79.3 per cent in Sonbhadra, 61.1 per cent in Chandauli, 80.0 per cent in Allahabad and 87.8 per cent in Chitrakoot had thatched walls and thatched roofs of the tribal houses, clearly indicate their extreme conditions of poverty and backwardness. (Table 3.23) Mostly respondents were found residing in their own constructed houses. Thus, even after multiple displacements especially in Naxal Prone Areas, they had not been rehabilitated in constructed houses by the concerning authorities.
3. They had also been repeatedly displaced and migrated which was evident from the fact that the highest percentages of acquisition of houses were found 79.3 per cent in Mirzapur, 72.7 per cent in Sonbhadra, 74.4 per cent in Chandauli, 68.3 per cent in Allahabad and 66.4 per cent in Chitrakoot, within a period of 1-3 years.
4. The majority of household respondents told that they could acquire their houses only out of savings from their agricultural income. The housing facilities provided under Indira Awas

Yojana, ITDP and IRDP schemes had rarely reached to the *dalit adivasis* of the study area.

5. As regards the basic facilities 100 per cent multiuse covered area was having only one room in all the houses of the sample households. Talking of a separate kitchen, bathroom, toilet, private bore-well, etc., are out of question. Open fields were available for toilet and bathroom. Small ponds, rivers and some waterfalls were the sources of drinking water. At very few common places, hand pumps were found bored with the help of Jal Nigam. As a result of drinking culminated water most of the respondents were found victims of several water-borne diseases.
6. Most of the families, i.e., (77% in Naxal Prone area 86.0% in Dacoit Prone area) were found of nuclear nature. It clearly indicates that the *dalit adivasis* had lost their agrarian functions because of alienation of their land. Multiple displacements, due to the installation of industries and repeated migration in search of livelihood were also the other factors for maintaining nuclear family in place of joint family.
7. The marriages either of male or female in these areas had never been a social or economic problem. Early childhood marriage was found prevalent in the *dalit adivasis*. Remarriage and widow marriages were not found prohibited.
8. More than 59 per cent of the respondents in Naxal prone area were found migrated for some other places, whereas in Dacoit prone areas most of the respondents were found residing at permanent places. This shows that in Naxal prone area the maximum percentage of respondents and their families were forced to vacate their permanent places of abode due to installation of industrial units and coal mines, etc.
9. The respondents; Table 3.29 shows that the maximum percentage of Chamar and Kol concentration was found in Naxal prone area, the Gonds and the Cheros also: The percentage of Ghasia, Kharwar, Bhuiya, Agaria, Mushahar, Waiga, Pathari and Danger were negligible in number. In the Dacoit prone area the Kol *adivasis* though not included in Scheduled Tribes list, were found in maximum percentage.

Most of the respondents in all the five districts were found engaged as agricultural labour. (69.3% in Mirzapur, 57.2% in Sonbhadra, 60.2% in Chandauli, 80.7% in Allahabad and 66.7% in Chitrakoot). In Patha region (Allahabad and Chitrakoot) most of the agricultural labourers were found as bonded labourers. More than18 per cent respondents in Mirzapur, 31.6 per cent in Sonbhadra, 25.8 per cent in Chandauli, 17.8 per cent in Allahabad and 31.1 per cent in Chitrakoot were found engaged in their own agricultural field. This low percentage clearly indicates that they had been deprived of their own agricultural field, i.e., land ownership. The employment percentage in service sector and business sector, was extremely low.

The majority of respondents (66.0% in Naxal Prone area and 66.5% in Dacoit prone area) were found illiterate. The inaccessibility to schools, their poverty and ignorance of importance of schooling might be the dominant reasons behind this.

On the basis of the analysis with regard to development during Five Year Plans and social welfare Yojana and benefits, opinions and participation of the sample households, have revealed the following facts

1. It is very pertinent point to make at the very outset that officially the Union Government and the State of Uttar Pradesh have not yet located south-eastern region of Uttar Pradesh as "Scheduled Tribes Area", and also one of the largest groups of *adivasis*, 'Kol' has not yet been included in the list of 'Scheduled Tribes', though they are recognised as Scheduled Tribes in the adjacent districts of Madhya Pradesh. Therefore, the constitutional provisions, benefits and all special packages issued during Plan periods from time to time for development and upliftment of Scheduled Tribes Area and Scheduled Tribes could not help much the *adivasis* of this region. The most of the tribes of this region have been categorized in Scheduled Castes. Although the fact is that the inhabitants of this region have been the original tribes since beginning.
2. Villages of forested south-eastern region of Uttar Pradesh (Mirzapur, Sonbhadra, Chandauli, Allahabad and Chitrakoot) have changed to some extent and inhabitants embraced some of the modern amenities like electricity, radio, telephone, primary schools and PHC, etc. However, their mindset and state of living are unchanged or to some extent changed to the worst in the name of tribal development. For example approach roads were constructed and those 'roads of development' turned out to be 'road of exploitation'. Through these roads mostly money lenders, forest contractors, Government Officials and non-tribals

forcibly entered into the tribal world to snatch their share, claiming as if they were realizing their own legal share from tribal resources.

3. The framers of the Constitution while taking note of the centuries old injustice perpetrated against the tribal communities, have adopted two pronged strategy of tribal development which sought to (i) Protect them from exploitation; and (ii) to assist them in their economic development. Both the Union as well as the State Government have tried to develop the tribals in two ways. Under one way which many industrial projects, dams and mines, etc., were installed in order to make them acquainted with modern ways of productions and to provide tribals opportunities to work as technical and non-technical workers. The other way was to implement welfare programmes like fulfilling their basic needs, economic development, educational development, improvement of health and medical facilities and infrastructural development, etc.
4. The study revealed that centuries old injustice against tribal communities has not yet been stopped, rather has been aggravated through snatching their ancestral land, forest produce and right to live in the forest. In the name of 'Indirect way of development' several Dams like Rihand Dam, Barundha Dam, Sirsi Dam, National Thermal Power Corporation Power Plants, Renu Sagar Power Plants, Kanoria Chemical industries, Cement factories and coal mines like Singrauli, etc., were established in this region. But they have displaced them from their permanent places of establishment and deprived them from their century old means of livelihood.
5. Under Five Year Plans various strategies were adopted for tribal development through increasing their economic and employment potential and through provision of adequate social facilities like education, health, housing, communications, developing infrastructure, etc. However, the south-eastern region of Uttar Pradesh presents a picture that proves the hollowness of the claims of progress in the task of tribal development include housing, land development, agriculture development, cattle development, construction of link roads installation of non-conventional sources of energy for lighting purposes, social security including Janshree Beema Yojana or any other innovative activity meant for the comprehensive socio-economic

development of PTGs more particularly for the PTGs who are nomadic in nature. The south-eastern region of Uttar Pradesh tribals were not covered under this sort of scheme.

6. To tackle the problem of Naxals in Uttar Pradesh, the State Government had started to focus on a comprehensive development for these districts of south-eastern region. The State Social Welfare Department decided to introduce Integral Tribal Development Programme (ITDP) in the Naxal hit Mirzapur, Sonbhadra, Chandauli and Dacoit hit Allahabad and Chitrakoot districts. Within this programme, the focus was on creating infrastructure like roads, drinking water supply, schools, Anganbari centres for children, mini primary health centres in all the villages and community health centres at Block level. The welfare department claimed to ensure employment generation through various Government sponsored welfare schemes like MNREGA and Swarnajayanti Gram Swarojgar Yojana (SGSY). However, the development programmes implemented so far have not led to any significant improvement on the quality of life of *dalit adivasis* of south-eastern region of Uttar Pradesh.

What is the accessibility of development to all the tribal communities? To what extent the development programmes are responsive to the needs of tribal people and what is the nature and extent of participation of *dalit adivasis* in development programmes? What discontents are developing in the minds of *dalit adivasis* as result of development programmes and in what direction they are going ahead? Attempt has been made to examine these questions and analyse the facts in greater details in order to properly assess the success and effectiveness both in positive and reverse directions of the tribal development programmes. Findings are as follows:

1. As per Table 4.6 the BDO and the Gram Pradhan had not thought of their legal duty to inform the tribals of the development programmes. The maximum percentage of respondents could know it through their friends and relatives. It can be assumed that the Gram Pradhans with the collusion of BDO and other Government officials tried to conceal the programmes so that they may make foul money out of the grants meant for the development of the region.
2. More than 24.1 per cent of respondents of Naxal prone area and

61.1 per cent of Dacoit prone area believed that no benefits of welfare programmes could be received unless the palms were greased. In addition to this, bungling and black marketing of their legal share were also reported by most of the respondents. A very few percentage of respondents having relation with the Gram Pradhan were satisfied. (Table 4.7).

3. Similarly, 59.8 per cent in Naxal prone area and 56.38 per cent in dacoit prone area respondents were not benefited by the government facilities. This may be the indicator of the fact that major portion of the welfare funds were embezzled by the concerning officials.
4. More than 88 per cent respondents in Naxal prone area and 89.05 per cent in dacoit area expressed their resentment informing that the fund for handicapped had also been embezzled by the concerning officials. The number of handicapped persons is quite high in this region.
5. Similarly, that maximum percentage of aged persons (86.15% in Naxal prone area and 68.67% in dacoit prone area) showed their resentments about the sort of such fund for them.
6. Another important concern is the poor housing conditions in this region. Only huts made of thatched/mud walls and thatched roofs were found everywhere. Under Indira Awas Yojana and Pradhan Mantri Gramodaya Awas Yojana Rs. 20,000 is released to construct one living room alongwith toilet and kitchen room. Every *adivasi* family is entitled to have a house under these schemes. However, as Table 4.12 shows only 34.51 per cent *adivasi* in Naxal prone area and 24.00 per cent that in Dacoit prone area could avail this benefit.
7. Today a considerable number of the *adivasis* are aware of their rights and they do not hesitate to contact the concerning officials with their problems. According to Table 4.14, about 26 per cent respondents were not much satisfied and 31.4 per cent of them were fully disappointed in all the five districts. This is the another cause of discontent, growing in their minds.
8. As regards the experiences of the respondents about attitudes of the government officers when they meet them regarding their problems, 41.1 per cent of the respondents felt that their attitude towards problems were full of partiality and discouraging, while 16.8 per cent of them felt neglected by the officers (Table 4.16). The twenty two per cent respondents reported that they would

have to face financial exploitation problem if they wished to be solved.

9. When the respondents were asked their opinion on the operation of the Government's work. More than 45 per cent of them were of the view that the development work was only on paper, and 40.0 per cent of them reported that the process of completing the work was full of economic corruption.
10. In order to develop the awareness and interest of the tribals, all the community development and welfare programmes are officially recognised as Participatory programmes. Effective participation in development process and welfare process under the Act, is essential. Participation is must in educational and skill development programmes, in environmental concern, trading practices, legal and land rights, agricultural practices, land and water management, agro-medical matters, etc., are essential. But, Table 4.20 revealed that 70.5 per cent respondents of this region had never been asked for such type of participation while 16.4 per cent of them told that they rarely had been taken into confidence. It can clearly be assumed that in the absence of their participation, the misappropriation and embezzlement of the fund would be easy for the Gram Pradhan and the officials. Thus, programmes might not be beneficial as per their priority requirements.
11. In the absence of their active participation how the Government could succeed in completing the work, had also been studied. More than 71 per cent of the respondents had opinion that no actual work on the spot had been done, while 12.7 per cent of them remained dissatisfied with the Government work. Thus, only paper formalities seem to have been done in the name of development in tribal places. It is creating a suspicion leading to the embezzlement of the allotted fund.
12. Due to absence of tribal participation and also not considering their social and cultural background, all aspects of their development have suffered a lot. More than 61 per cent respondents of this region showed their negative attitude towards the Government policies regarding their development activities.
13. As regards the actual benefits received by the 3000 sample households in different heads, it was found that 22.9 per cent respondent households were benefited by agricultural land, 30.8 per cent by Indira Awas Yojana, 19.4 per cent by Scholarship,

20.0 per cent Old Age/Widow pension and 2.7 per cent Jobs. No one had recorded residential land or any business benefits. About 18 per cent respondents believed that political persons grab their shares, 48.9 per cent of them had the opinion that politically powerful, elected ruling party leaders grab their shares, 18.4 per cent respondents charged the contractors, 7.3 per cent respondents blamed to mediators and about 6 per cent respondents believed that powerful selected mediators and persons having relations with officers grabbed their shares. Thus, it leads us to the presumption that the ruling party leaders seem to have grab the lion's share of the development and welfare funds allotted in the name of tribal development and this could have happened with collusion of senior district officials with other related officers.

14. The three-tier system of Indian democracy, shoulders all types of responsibilities regarding the village development. The Gram Panchayat happens to be the most responsible Constitutional Institution both the Union as well as State Government provide funds to the Gram Pradhan through which all sorts of development work is done. In this context the people (villagers) participation is very essential in checking out the rural development programmes and making budget in order of priority.

    During discussions with PRI groups and the *dalit adivasis*, it was found that there were serious mismatch between the needs of the community and the programmes undertaken by the Gram Panchayat. Principal causes for this mismatch, were the poor representation of *adivasis* in the PRI, their lack of participation in decision-making and the lack of accountability of elected representatives. More than half of the respondents of 3,000 sample households expressed no faith in the role of Gram Panchayat. It clearly indicates that due to the absence of *adivasi* member and *adivasi* Gram Pradhan, his members took decision against the interest of the *dalit adivasis*. All the funds received in the name of tribal welfare seem to have embezzled by the Gram Pradhan and his members.

15. In addition to the Government, there are other agencies and NGOs that work for their development and welfare parallel to the Government. It was found that one social activist namely Gopal Bhai had done a lot for the removal of bonded labourhood, and due to his efforts 4,000 acres of land had been released

from the feudal landlords in favour of Kol *adivasis* through his Akhil Bhartiya Samaj Sewak Sansthan (ABSSS) in Patha region. The other social activist Sri Shyam Narayan Lal Srivastava, Advocate and the editor of a newspaper *Mahakal Samachar Vivaran*, had been fighting several court cases of *adivasis* of Sonbhadra, Chandauli and Mirzapur districts up to the Supreme Court. Mostly cases were related to land alienation, displacement and environmental pollution due to installation of several industrial units.

With regard to the proposed indicators of development, the following are the important findings:

I. Economic Growth as an Indicator of Development

Economic growth is an important indicator of development. It is true that the *advisis* are completely unfamiliar with the money economy, but they do understand that ownership and control on the basic resources of land is the solution to the problems of their livelihood. Agriculture has been the main source of livelihood of people and it was the mainstay with cattle farming as the back-bone of the local economy. The next, forest has been an important source of fuel, fodder, food, timber, medicines of them. The collection of minor forest produces such as mahua, chiraunjee, tendu leaf, amla, lakh, etc. which allow them to earn some money seasonally.

The tribal belt of Sonbhadra, Mirzapur, Chandauli, Allahabad and Chitrakoot is characterized by resource poor, technologically stagnant and remote from State and the market, where depletion of resources like land, forest and water has a history. In this situation, the livelihood struggles end up creating a vicious circle of multidimensional, unframed livelihood struggles, under shocks prompt as social process of mortgage and asset losses, borrowing and inability to service, debt, hunger and migrations. These aspects have not been given adequate attention while planning for economic development of these tribals. It has been the corruption and inefficiency siphons off a larger amount of resources, which have kept them where they were, the eastern Uttar Pradesh comes under high poverty region and southern Uttar Pradesh comes under very high poverty region. Thus, the south-eastern region of U.P. which includes the *adivasi* also are the most poor region of the country.

As regards, the economic development, several provisions have been made for the tribals under Articles 275 (1) first provision and 339 (2).

These provisions assign special responsibility to the government not only for drawing of special schemes of development but also for providing them financial assistance. The framers of the Constitution while taking note of the centuries old injustice, perpetrated against the tribal communities, adopted strategy of tribal development by assisting them in their economic development. But practically, what, where the results? Why are they suffering from chronic poverty? The answers have been tried to obtain throughout the study. It was noticed that more than 61 per cent respondents opined that the Government had failed in eradicating poverty from their region. It seems to have been because of the nexus of political elite, bureaucracy and contractors, who disconnected the poor from developmental affairs.

2. It would not be wrong to comment that 100 per cent *dalit adivasis* are below poverty line. Practically our findings show that the average per month income of an *adivasi* was found only Rs. 322 whereas the National Poverty level has been Rs. 368 per month per individual. It was found that only Rs. 1,610 per month per household income was found in all the five districts of our study.

3. As a consequence of this chronic poverty they were not in a position to meet out their two times meal everyday. Table 5.6 reveals that out of 3,000 sample households, only 29.7 per cent. respondents households could manage regularly two times meal for their survival. It clearly indicates that their most of the resources and job opportunity, e.g., land, forest produce, cattle, had been taken away by the mafia, contractors, feudal landlords, forest department and the Government officials. Due to unavailability of eatable food items, they were forced to eat wild mushrooms, grass, mouse and other wild animals which resulted in malnutrition, starvation, diseases and deaths. As there is no guarantee of regular sources of income, they often take loan which could never be refunded.

4. *Adivasis* who took loan from moneylenders and landlords, has to serve as slave according to the terms and conditions of the loan. That endless slavery often converted into bonded labourhood. Table 5.9 reveals the fact that 38 per cent bonded labours in Naxal prone area and 88 per cent in dacoit prone area, were found as bonded labours. According to the programme evaluation organization of the Planning Commission about 83 per cent of the total number of bonded labours belonged to scheduled castes and tribes in India and these bonded labour remain bonded from generation to generation. During survey and personal interview they told that they have been tortured, had not been given sufficient meal for their family, their women were often raped, and if they showed any resentment

they had been ousted from village or beaten severely by the moneylenders and by feudal lords.

5. In Naxal prone area mostly *adivasis* had been repeatedly displaced from one place to another by the industrialists, NTPC and by other power plants and by coal mines authorities. This has resulted in great loss of the sources of their livelihood. Frequent displacement, land alienation and deprived from collection of forest produce had forced them to remain in chronic condition of poverty. Owing to failing monsoon and indifferent agricultural performance, in dacoit prone area the *adivasi* has been marginalized and are forced to live in extreme poverty. Table 5.10 revealed that in their average days of work in Naxal prone area was 107.6 days in a year and 148.1 days in a year in Dacoit prone area. Average days of work to females were 61.9 and 81.6 in Naxal and Dacoit prone areas respectively. Average monthly income per family was Rs. 1,729 and 1,491 respectively in both the areas. While the same per member were Rs. 288.16 and Rs. 248.5 in both the areas. The average monthly income from all sources were only Rs. 349.32 and Rs. 335.97 respectively in Naxal prone area and Dacoit prone area. The average annual income from crop come to Rs. 5,350 per household (Table 5.11).

6. The Government scheme under PDS for the welfare of the BPL listed *adivasis*, appeared to be completely failed when the actual conditions prevailing among them were investigated. It was found that none of the tribal families had Antyodaya Ration Card meant for BPL families. Even those having the card never got the due ration. Those who got the ration got only one-third of their rightful amount and that too at higher cost after giving their thumb print against full ration. It was found that only 24.51 per cent households in Naxal prone area and 39.43 per cent in Dacoit prone area could be benefited by the PDS shops, while 68 per cent sample households were found deprived of this welfare facility.

7. Under Mahatma Gandhi National Rural Employment Guarantee Act 2005, the Gram Panchayat after registration issues a 'Job Card' to each applicant household, the job is provided up to the limit of 100 days to each household. The labourers are paid Rs. 100 per day and this is to be paid weekly.

Really it has proved as "Renaissanse" in the history of Independent India in which 100 per cent employment guarantee has been assured to downtrodden people including *dalit adivasis*. But ironically, the embezzlement of crores of money by the concerned officials has also been unveiled at several places. The south-eastern region of Uttar Pradesh is also not untouched with this epidemic. Therefore, this employment guarantee scheme has been failed. As per Table 5.13 more than 80 per cent households had been the recipients of job cards and got jobs accordingly. But what was hidden under this programme has also been revealed through investigation. It was found that about 72 per cent sample households were victimized by the economic corruption of Government officials and Gram Pradhan. During group discussions *adivasis* expressed their several problems relating to the MNREGA scheme. Firstly, maximum number of persons did not get work for more than 40 days in a year; secondly in their job cards 100 days' work had falsely been shown; thirdly, the excess amount or false day's work amount had been embezzled by the Gram Pradhan and the Government officials; fourthly, whatever actual amount was to be paid had not been paid by the Gram Pradhan. Thus, *dalit adivasis* had been exploited and forced to remain in the worst conditions, of extreme poverty, can be realized. As has been reported, this process of exploitation is continuously going on.

8. During our survey in *adivasis* villages we experienced that people were worstly suffering from extreme limit of poverty. They had nothing to eat, nothing to wear and having no shelter. All were victims of malnutrition, diseases and several types of day to day problems. In such conditions every household has to be enlisted in BPL list. But only 58.2 per cent sample households were found enlisted for Government welfare grants and facilities. The remaining 41.8 per cent households were deprived of being included. When enquired from these *Adivasis*, more than 60 per cent respondents boldly told that since they were not able to pay the bribe, their names were not included. About 22 per cent of them blamed the Gram Pradhan, who due to personal enmity and local politics, did not bother for their inclusion in the BPL list. In this adverse situation no option was left, except to accept slavery in the form of bonded labour. More than 73 per cent respondents in Naxal prone area and 81.9 per cent those in the Dacoit prone area were found working as bonded labour in money lenders house and at their agricultural fields (Table 5.20).

9. As regards the average days of work obtained by male workers during different seasons and schemes, it was noticed that they got work for 20.3 days in *Kharif* season, 16.2 days during *Rabi*, 17.3 days in other work, 2.4 days in Government construction work, 39.9 days in MNREGA and 12.1 days at the contractors place. Thus, having only 107.6 days of employment their pitiable conditions in the rest of these days can easily be imagined. The situation of female workers were even worst than their male counterparts.

10. The income of agricultural family was also assessed by the

number and quantity of crops produced. More than 72 per cent respondents in all the five districts clearly indicated that their income from crops was nominal and they were not able to afford their livelihood. The average production of paddy in all the five districts was 7.6 quintals per household, maize 0.7 quintal, Bazri 0.1 quintal, Pulses 0.4 quintal wheat 6.5 quintals, sarso 0.5 quintal and others 0.5 quintal. The average crop production per annum comes only 16.3 quintals per households and 3.2 quintals per head per annum at the maximum. The income obtained from this minimal production, apart from their livelihood, is utilized in repaying loan, and we can imagin that to what extent the fulfilling secondary needs like clothes, medicines, etc.

11. When the crop production is not sufficient to meet out their basic needs they look for some other means. As Table 5.26 shows 40.6 per cent of them worked as labour, 26.1 per cent took loan on credit, 8.3 per cent depended on forest produce, 11.1 per cent adopted beggary, and 13.9 per cent earned money by displaying some cultural activities.

12. No doubt, Government has been spending heavy amount on economic development programmes for the tribals and by its statistical magic, the degree of economic development has continuously gone higher and higher in the country. In order to assure whether economic development in terms of living standard has any upward change for the *dalit adivasis*, an investigation has also been made. As exhibited in Table 5.27, they not only remained where they were, but had gone worst in every walk of their life. In fact they and their lives continued to be untouched and uncovered by all the overwhelming forces of change that were making everything into new. Majority of them told that their grand-fathers' period was much better than the present one. Those were the days when there was no such scarcity of food, milk, and meat, forest produce, fodder and fuel, etc. However, the Kol *adivasis* in the dacoit prone area were pained to remember the grand-parents days when they had severely been tortured by the feudal landlords.

Thus, the positive intentional efforts for the economic growth have actually put the *dalit adivasis* of this area to the extreme poverty. The *dalit adivasis* used their franchise in deciding as to who would govern them freely. However, this process created fissures in a homogeneous community with social, political and economic interests. Once the political leaders took over their responsibility, the process of decentralized governance instead of becoming participatory, become highly centralized. The gains of the decentralized governance had been to few and high iniquitous. *Dalit adivasis* expectations in their economic growth as indicator of their development remained unfulfilled.

II. The Educational Growth as an Indicator of Development

No doubt, education which is a prime fact in literacy development is a key ingredient in sustainable tribal development. The Constitution ensures equality of opportunity for education at all levels and also guarantees the educational advancement of the scheduled castes and scheduled tribes because of their backwardness in education, therefore, it is one of the most important indicators for the development of society.

While examining the educational growth programmes in the Naxal area and the dacoit prone area there appeared a very disappointing picture. The literacy rate among 3,000 sample households was 16.5 per cent at primary level, 5.9 per cent at high school level and 2.9 per cent at intermediate level.

Inspite of implementation of Right to Education and Sarwa Shiksha Campaign and all the facilities including financial support, it is very surprising that why a large number of children of this south-eastern region leave their school after enrolment. This dropout case among the *adivasis* of this region is alarming. As depicted in Table 5.35 the reasons of dropout tendency among the *dalit adivasis* were: (i) School being situated to far from their homes; (ii) Children being supportive to their income by assisting them in domestic and some other small works; (iii) their ignorance about the priority of education; and (iv) viewing domestic work as more important and compulsory than the education to the children.

As regards the dropout case of the 3,000 sample households at different level of schooling, 46.5 per cent dropout cases were found at primary level, 11.7 per cent at middle class, 6.0 at high school, 3.0 at intermediate level (Table 5.36).

As Sonbhadra is the most affected district from all point of view by Naxal activities and the multiple displacements, it was selected as sample among all the five districts to find a trend of establishment of primary schools, the number of male and female children enrolment and the number of teachers appointed. There were 1,596 primary schools, out of which 13 schools were having no building. The total number of school children (male) were 1,35,834, out of which 62,947 children belonged to the SC/ST. Among 1,22,550 enrolled female children 56,002 came from SC/ST. The total number of teachers was 1,781 out of which 765 were females. There was no SC/ST school teacher's in these schools. The pressure of

161 students on 1.6 teachers is quite high than the educational standard norms.

In order to encourage the downtrodden *adivasi* children, the Government has launched mid-day meal scheme. With the joint efforts of Basic Shiksha Adhikari, District Supply Officer and the District Manager of UPSFC (UP State Food Corporation), total up to 3 kg cooked rice, pulse, *dalia* and other cereals per child per month is provided on the basis of 80 per cent presence of children in school. Through such an incentive the Government intends to eradicate the illiteracy from the villagers and tribals. But this programme seems to have not been successful. Only 39.24 per cent of children in Dacoit prone area and 38.87 per cent in Naxal prone area were benefited by the programme. The share of remaining children has reportedly been misappropriated jointly by concerning departments and the school staff.

There has been another lucrative incentive in terms of financial assistance to students of all standard of schooling. Under this scheme students from Ist class to Vth class were proposed to be given Rs. 25 per month, from class VI to VIII, Rs. 40 per month, from class IX to X Rs. 60 per month, to ITI students Rs. 50 per month for the whole year. The children belonging to the untouchable castes were to be awarded Rs. 500 per annum as an additional award. But practically more than 78 per cent students in Naxal prone area and 83 per cent in Dacoit prone area had not enjoyed and benefited by this scheme (Table 5.39). The major portion of the scholarship amount seems to have been embezzled by the school manager in collusion with Social Welfare Department.

The educational growth does not mean only the rising of the literacy rate. As an indication of development it has to be made more and more humane loaded with all social and moral values. But the corrupt models, presented by the so called highly educated and technically qualified and the dominant powerful leaders before the *adivasis* seem to have failed in making them educated in real sense and thereby affected the desired development of the *adivasis*.

III. Health and Medical Facilities

Health care is not only everyone's right, but also everyone's responsibility. Therefore, health is by-product of socioeconomic developments and also an important determinant of the quality of human resources of a country. Good health is a prerequisite to human productivity and development. In all the Five Year Plans for development the tribal health has been highlighted particularly in sections of the documents devoted to development of scheduled castes and scheduled tribes. Tribal health problems are acute due to poverty, illiteracy, no regular availability of foods, polluted water, adverse environmental conditions. Morbidity, mortality, malnutrition starvation, insanitation, poor living conditions, ignorance of causes of diseases, lack of medical facilities, etc., are the common features of the tribal society. Keeping all these facts in mind health and the availability of medical facilities were taken up as indicator of tribal development.

2. During survey, researcher visited all the five selected districts. It was noticed that several persons were suffering from different type of diseases like anaemia, chronic diarrhoea, TB, Malaria, Filaria, jaundice ulcer, skin related diseases, deficiency of iodine, micro-nutrient deficiency, deficiency of dietary components, arsenicosis, venereal disease, AIDS, leprosy, etc. During discussions with local persons and Gram Pradhan, frequency of deaths in child birth and in infancy, the ravages of diseases like TB, epidemics like cholera, small pox, venereal diseases, etc. were recorded. The superstitions witchcraft and black magic of spirits of evils, etc., were also reported. A complete gap of availability of modern medical facilities were found and the Government claims in terms of development and welfare programmes appeared to be false.

3. Regarding the availability of medical facilities during illness, it was noticed that only 12.7 per cent of the sample households availed the Government medical facilities whereas 33.5 per cent patients preferred to private practitioners (Table 5.44). It was found that PHCs and CHCs of these areas were not having sufficient medical and para-medical staff. Moreover, the medicines and other medical facilities were not available. Available medical staff too were not found giving sufficient care whereas the private Doctors, though taking their medical fees, used to attend the patients and administer the right medicines. As regards National Maternity Benefits it was found that 31.0 per cent in Naxal prone areas and 41.3 per cent that in Dacoit prone area, pregnant women were benefited by this *yojana* (Table 5.46). The same was the case with Balika Samriddhi Yojana. Table 5.47 shows only 27.8 per cent in Naxal prone areas and 29.9 per cent in disease prone areas sample households were benefited. The amount sanctioned under these schemes seems to have been embezzled by the concerned department.

4. The high mortality in all the five districts of our study was indicative of the gross negligence from the government medical department side. It was found that among the sample household of all the five districts it was

39.7, 63.5, 109.7, 141.5 and 54.8 mortality per thousand of children which was quite high in comparison to Government of India statistical data. The causes of high mortality rate in the study area seem to be the early child marriage, negligence and absence of medical care during pregnancy, cutting the umbilical cord by unsterilized blades, knife and threads and infectious delivery places. As Table 5.49 shows the child marriage percentage in the study area was 93 per cent, during pregnancy 98.6 per cent of women were having no medical care, in 99.3 per cent cases, Umbilical cord of infant babies were not cut by sterilized blades, knife and thread by the domestic women in 99 per cent cases the child delivery were found in house having 100 per cent chances of infections. Only in a few cases deliveries were performed by trained ANM or at CHCs, PHCs and Government hospitals. Thus, the health improvement and medical facilities available in the area did not bring positive results to *dalit adivasis*.

Causes of Discontent

The following are the important findings with regard to discontent, developing among the *dalit adivasis* sample households even after the implementation of development programmes:

1. The causes of discontent arisen among the *dalit adivasis* of the 3000 sample households are related to following main problems:
   (A) *Economic*: (i) Extreme poverty, (ii) land alienation, (iii) land grabbing, (iv) Ban to collect forest produce, (v) Being deprived of forest right 2006, (vi) False distribution of land *patta*, (vii) Indebtedness, (viii) Bonded labourhood, (ix) unemployment, (x) no source of livelihood, (xi) hunger and hunger death, and (xii) embezzlement of BPL funds and facilities like PDS food materials.
   (B) *Health and Sanitation*: (i) Poor health conditions; (ii) culminated drinking water, (iii) consuming poisonous mushroom and grass in the absence of eatable food items, (iv) suffering from several infections, chronic and vulnerable diseases, (v) Malnutrition; (vi) lack of medical care and facilities; and (viii) handicapped childbirth.
   (C) *Environmental Conditions*: (i) Polluted drinking water and polluted air due to excessive discharge of harmful chemicals, flash, fumes and poisonous garbage accumulated near Dams,

surrounding industrial areas and coal mines, (ii) Drought and flood, and (iii) deforestation, drying of wells and ponds.

(D) *Social and Administrative*: (i) exploitation of female sex, (ii) suicides, (iii) Inactiveness of revenue department and police administration, (iv) exploitation by police, maphias, feudal landlords and government officials.

(E) *Educational*: (i) Illiteracy, (ii) lack of educational facilities and institutions, (iii) dropout of children and absenteeism of teaching staff.

(F) *Infrastructural*: (i) Lack of approach roads, (ii) lack of housing facilities, (iii) lack of electrical supply, (iv) no supply of clean drinking water, (v) lack of transport and communication facilities.

(G) *Political and Administrative*: (i) Lack of political representation, and (ii) lack of selection in administrative parts.

(H) *Displacement*: (i) Multiple displacement, (ii) lack of proper compensation and (iii) lack of proper rehabilitation.

(I) *Economic Corruption*: (i) No attention from the Government officials without greasing their palms; and (ii) embezzlement of all funds relating their development and welfare programmes.

2. The survival and livelihood of all the forest dwellers, scheduled castes and scheduled tribes of this south-eastern part of Uttar Pradesh have been totally dependent on forest land, forest produce and water since beginning. However, in the name of development of these habitats their main livelihood resources were encroached, banned and they were ousted by treating them as trespassers. Thus, the main causes of their discontent were the land alienation, Right of Forest Act 2006, Ban to collect and use forest produce, dispute of claim between forest department and their own, false distribution of land allotment (Land *Patta*), forcibly multiple displacement from their ancestral forest land in the name of construction of Dams, installation of several power plants industries and excavation of coal mines without providing appropriate compensation, proper rehabilitation and security of the means of their livelihood and continuous exploitation, torturing and grabbing of land by maphias, contractors, non-tribal feudal landlords, Government officials and dacoits especially in Patha region.

3. Sharp disease decrease in the percentage of cultivators causing sharp increase in the landless labourers from 19.71 per cent in 1961 to 46.87 in 2001, is the indicative of the disturbing trend of land alienation. As per sample survey of the department of Rural Development, 1988, about 80 per cent of land of the tribal people had been alienated to non-tribal. In the present study area 86 per cent of *dalit adivasis* were found landless.
4. The general methods of land alienation have been through sale, mortgage, lease, benami transfers, collusive decrees and fraudulent methods of land grabbing. A sizeable area of the *dalit adivasis* of the study area had been alienated on account of the indebtedness, lacunae in the land laws and its acquisition for public purposes by the Government and other institutions.
5. Since, centuries the tribal had been the permanent occupants of dense forest of south-eastern region of Uttar Pradesh, had enjoyed full rights in the forest using forest produce for their livelihood and were the land owners of whatever they had occupied for their use. But at present they are deprived of all.

The land alienation was badly experienced when thousands of *dalit adivasis* families had to vacate their original habitats for providing lands for construction of Rihand Dam (1954) of NTPC, Obra (1968-71) HINDALCO Renukut (1962) Kanoria Chemicals (1965), Thermal Power Unit, Shakti Nagar (1984), Vindhyachal power plant unit, Prijpur (1987-2000) establishment of cement factory in Dala (1971), Churk Cement Factory (1980), establishment of HITCE Carbon Plant, Sonbhadra (1988), and Singrauli coal mines and others. This sorts of development activities of the Government made the *dalit adivasis* completely pauper and landless.

The land alienation was also observed when Gram Sabha was authorized to distribute the Gram Samaj land to landless families of oppressed class of people. This was also observed when the *dalit adivasis* could not dare occupy in their possession of allotted *patta* land from maphias, landlords, economically and politically powerful persons.

During survey it was found that out of 12,941 Kol families in Patha region only 3,011 had their own land and the rest were found landless due to reportedly corruption practices in revenue department. The total area of possession by the Kol families was 21,498 *bighas* and out of which 3,867 *bighas* of land was unfertile and rocky. 7,229 *bigha* of Kol's land was found illegally occupied by landlords, outsiders and maphias. However, as per revenue records every Kol family was found in possession of land. Thus, the Kol *adivasis* suffered high level of exploitation, miserisation and marginalization at the hands of feudal landlords belonging to upper Brahmin and Thakur castes. Earlier the Kols had also been made landless by the forest department in the name of Rampur wild-life sanctuaries for which over 23,000 hectares of land had forcibly been vacated from the Kol tribes.

As a result of arbitrary decisions and anarchism tribals had been tortured, exploited and forcibly made them landless and uprooted from the forest region. They were left at the verge of starvation. All the development programmes related to tribal having heavy budget allotted in the name of their development proved to be futile. After receiving several complaints against the forest department activities the Central Government ultimately posed 'Forest Right Act 2006, which came into effect on 11 December, 2007. Under this act traditional forest dwellers have to prove that they had three of generation living on the same forest land as on December 13, 2005. But in spite of this act the forest department of the south-eastern region of Uttar Pradesh was adamant not to provide land to the *adivasis*. Thereafter, the U.P. Government identified 21 districts for implementation of the Act and after constituting several committees and sub-committees till November 2009 more than 8,000 tribals in UP and over 3,000 tribals were handed over *pattas* in the study area till February 2010.

It is evident from the figures in Table 6.3 that 65.0 per cent of the respondent households were not found having land, only 17.3 per cent sample households were inhabited on their ancestral land. 7.0 per cent respondent households received land from Gram Samaj and only 10.7 sample households could manage to receive land under ceiling act. Thus, 65.0 per cent *dalit adivasis* are roaming here and there because of the gross injustice is being done to them in this region.

Thus, the average landholding by a sample household was only 1.05 hectares. 0.55 hectare of land was sown by per household, 0.19 hectare land was sown on the lease land by per household. As regards forest land available for household, it was only 0-09 hectares per household. This clearly indicates that implementation of land reformation Act, distribution of land Act. and the forest right Act, have not benefited the downtrodden *dalit adivasis* of this region.

As per the data revealed in Table 6.5, the size of landholding has decreased in comparison to their ancestral generation. This is the real situation of the consequence of the land alienation for which the

Government proved be completely failure in its claim of development of the tribals.

IV. The Following are Manifestations of the Discontent Developing among the Sample Dalit Adivasis

During discussion with the *dalit adivasis* we felt that they were much dissatisfied, discontented, disappointed and frustrated with all the development and welfare programmes, which have been launched in the name of their upliftment. Now, they are very much reactionary and say 'We cannot bear it any more'. There is a long history of their exploitation which still is going on. There are hundreds of reasons for their discontent, which is manifested into agitation, demonstration and revolt (may be bloodshed).

The daily newspapers often flashed the news that the *dalit adivasis* of Naxal prone area and Dacoit prone area have often been raising their demands before the District Magistrate on different issues of their problems related to land *patta*, PDS NREGA, NRHM, economic corruption among all the welfare programmes etc.

Recent example of 500 *dalit adivasis* of Sonbhadra and Chandauli was 100 kms. on foot march on January 15, 2010 against the construction of Kanhar Dam. That march triggered a wave of revolt among the *adivasis* who were fearing of a large scale of displacement. In spite of the foundation stone laid down by Ms Mayawati, the Ex-Chief Minister of UP, the construction work could not start due to the *adivasis* revolt.

The second most important example of agitation demonstration and revolt was launched against the Dala, Churk and Chunar Cement Corporation which took decision to close the factories. As a result, hundreds of *dalit adivasis* reached at the verge of starvation. During their agitation 8 labourers died due to hunger strike on 24th September, 2004.

The third revolt cannot be forgotten when all the *adivasis* women revolted against the privatization of cement factories in Dala on June 1991. In that revolt more than nine persons were killed during firing by the police.

The agitation, demonstration and revolt started in HINDALCO, against their displacement from their native villages Mitihani, Khauji, Chilka Dadd and other tribal villages, when the construction of Rihand Dam, NTPC, Rihand Power Plants, Anpara Power Plant, HINDALCO, Singrauli coal mines were proposed to install.

The other most important factors of their agitation, demonstration and revolt had been the dispossession and encroachment of their ancestral forest land. The environmental problems and the land alienation problems had been the major causes of bone of contention.

During discussion with the *dalit adivasis* we could realize that they had become very much aggressive with the present set-up of the system. Consequently, either they had option either to agitate, demonstrate and revolt against the Government administration or to join the Naxalites. They expressed their opinion on certain causes which provoked them to do so. More than 45 per cent respondents in Naxal prone area and 62 per cent in Dacoit prone area focused on this point that their livelihood and existence were at stake, 14 per cent respondents were found reactionary because of their harassment during expedience of their work. Nearly 36 per cent respondents gave emphasis on this point that such agitation, demonstration and revolt activities should continue because there was no other way to attract the attention of the Government towards their demands and problems.

Due to the vested interests of the district administration the Government officials, maphias, political leaders, etc., tried their best to crush the *dalit advasis* by evolving them in criminal cases and often false charges were framed on the active participation. Nearly 74 per cent respondents told that their families had been tortured through false allegations imposed by the administration.

More than 67 per cent respondents accepted that they were in favour of active participation in such activities because they had no other options except to revolt.

V. Manifestation of Discontent in the Form of Naxalism

During discussion with the *dalit adivasis* of Sonbhadra, Mirzapur and Chandauli we drew conclusion that they were very much aggressive against the present set-up and the socio-economic and political conditions of their places. They expressed their mind that only one option is left before them and that is to join Naxalite. That would set them free from endless exploitation and poverty.

During field survey, one *adivasi* woman admiring Naxalites, told; 'They are those people who do not kill innocent people but they punish only guilty government officials. Naxalites do not do fake encounters. At least they accept responsibility for killing they carry out'.

Some of the Naxals who were arrested, explained the reasons behind joining Naxalites. First one was that their poverty would be removed through Naxal ideology, the second was that they would get relief from all sorts of torturing activities and exploitation and the third one was that they had been misguided and persuaded by the ideology of Naxalism.

Naxal movement reached Mirzapur, Sonbhadra and Chandauli in late 90s and the ultra came from Jharkhand and Bihar, took refuse in villages, executed violent acts and went back. Naxalites kept Sonbhadra under three 'U' zones and accepted Sonbhadra as gate of Entrance of Uttar Pradesh. Their prime aim had been to blast all the power plants and other industrial units which caused exploitation of tribals of this region

Starting from 5th June, 1997 the Naxali destructive activities continued till 24th January, 2009 and 45 incidents of murder, loot, fire and attack on police forces were officially recorded at different police stations. During police operation 12 Naxals were encountered and 118 Naxals were put behind the bar after arrest.

Villages under the Police Stations, Manchi, Robertsganj, Kon, Chopan and Babhani were very worstly affected Naxalite areas. In addition to them, two hundred villages of these districts were also extremely Naxal affected villages. Out of 1,363 total villages of Sonbhadra district, 266 villages were under Naxal affected zone.

Thus, violence cannot be tolerated in any true democracy, but it has to be accepted for what it is a real, basic and significant challenge confronting the country's established system. Thus, face of the Naxalites is reflected in a montage of those areas of the three districts which are impoverished and hungary, face suicidal debts, unemployment, illiteracy and shortage of potable water. The original and real owners of water, forests, land and other natural resources were not only deprived of their rights, but also are having to fight for their social, economic and cultural identity as also for the very basic needs of their daily existence. These *dalit adivasis* are allowed to vote, ours, being a democracy, but the same democracy seemed to have not given them the right to protect themselves from exploitation and even from threats to their lives.

Highlighting all these sensitive aspects of manifestation of the discontent among the *dalit adivasis* of south-eastern region of Uttar Pradesh we can conclude that this region, almost after 68 years of our Independence, are yet to feel the hands of development. Today, these are the fertile areas of unrest and violence only because the development, instead of happiness, has brought total chaos in their lives. In the task of *dalit adivasis* development of this tribal region, the planners seemed to have nothing at stake.

Their vision of this is not only myopic, but reflects their apathy. Those involved in the implementation, have plenty at stake but not in the duties assigned to them, but in terms of squaring the benefits and playing with the statistics, At the last, the moral degeneration, and the extremity of economic corruption, has grabbed all the fruits of development and has left only residues in the share of downtrodden *dalit adivasis* of this region of Uttar Pradesh.

In the last part of this chapter some pathetic situations of the *dalit adivasis* have been narrated which were recorded through case study method. In short, few of them are mentioned here in the following manner:

1. There was no proper approachable roads, no light, and no other means of communications available in tribal villages.
2. *Dalit adivasis* were found suffering from extreme chronic poverty because there was no regular sources of food, water and no regular sources of income for fulfilling their bare needs.
3. They described their hunger as 'burning pit in the abdomen'. Most of the children below six were found suffering from malnutrition and starvation.
4. The death of eight children between July and September, 2003 allegedly due to lack of food, had sparked concerns about growing starvation in a landless indigenous community in a remote village in Sonbhadra. The truth was confirmed when the principal investigator personally saw the pathetic and malnourished conditions of other several children of Manikpur (Chitrakoot), Makari Bari, Laua of Nagaon Block and Semara, Umla villages of Ghorawal Block and children of Shankargarh (Allahabad) *dalit adivasi*, children. Most of the children were mere skeleton as if their bodies and flesh had been sapped away.
5. There was one Ghasia *adivasi* tribe in Sonbhadra, which families were found surviving only on poisonous grass and wild mushrooms. Their children were unable to tolerate the poison and succumbed to death.
6. All the *dalit adivasi* families, who were settled temporarily in huts around the Rihand Dam, NTPC coal mines in Singrauli cement factories and other industrial plants, after displacement, had been found facing the excessive air and water pollution problems. As a result of this environmental pollution, they have been victimized by several chronic diseases. Many of the born babies were found handicapped.
7. Under land reform and distribution of land to landless Act to *dalit adivasis*, allotment of land *patta* for agricultural and

settlement purpose were found officially completed with the collusion of revenue officials and landlords. The legal entry into Khasra and Khatauni was also found on official records but practically, most of them were found completely false and fictitious.

8. Some cases of this nature of false allotment of *patta*, can be exemplified by quoting the name of Mohan Kol, Chandram, Hari, Savita Amar, Ram Khelawan, Visheshar, Lallo, Buddwa, Gopal, Shankar, Shiva and others whose allotted lands were either grabbed by the feudal landlords or they were terrorized not to claim their lands. Such cases were mostly in Chitrakoot and Shankargarh Tribal villages.
9. The stories of repression and rape of *dalit adivasis* women were found in the worst situation. They had been treated as kept and concubines of feudal landlords for their sexual enjoyment.
10. Exploitation of the poor *dalit adivasis* by making them bonded labour had been very common in Patha region of Uttar Pradesh. Hundreds of cases of debt bondage or forced labour or bonded labour were observed in most of the villages of all the five districts of our study. It was found that the landlords never set them free even after the payment of their total debts. They remained slaves from generation to generation.
11. It was also found that a small number of rich and influential families had managed to cover major share of the forest produce earnings of the *dalit adivasis* and a significant part of the loot was shared with dacoits and politicians in Chitrakoot and Allahabad.
12. It was also found that dacoits in Chitrakoot and Allahabad and Naxalites in Sonbhadra, Mirzapur and Chandauli districts killed several *dalit adivasis* only on the suspicions that they had been informers to the police administration. They were mostly not true.
13. It was also found that the forest department in all the five districts have not yet vacated tribal land even after the enforcement of Forest Right Act 2006 and the orders of the Hon'ble Courts. For example one lady named Lalita Devi of Chero tribal of Magardaha village of Sonbhadra can be quoted, who was severely beaten by the police and ninety families were arrested and tortured only on the instigation of the forest officials. The

reason was only that they had been demanding the right to land inside Magardaha forest under Forest Act 2006.

14. Several starvation deaths of Kol *dalit adivasis* of Kubradhi village in Nawgarh Block of Chandauli were flashed in 2010. During survey it was found that Red Cards meant for BPL families were not issued to them. Their livelihood was totally dependent on collection of *tendu* leaves, but the contractors had not paid any amount as their wages.
15. Thousands of inhabitants of Mitihini and Singrauli villages had been displaced for power plants, dams and coal mines, but still they had not been properly rehabilitated.
16. 2,086 displaced *dalit adivasis* living in Chilka Dam colony had to face multiple displacements. It has completely shattered their social-economic and cultural traits and their traditional set-up.

In continuation to the above mentioned pathetic instances of exploitation, we are narrating the pathetic stories of two of the so-called hard core Naxalites. Information was gathered from the members of their families.

1. Mewa Lal a hard core Naxalite, S/o Khajoor Baiga, Caste: Kharwar, resident of Gram and Post Baki, Police Station: Manchi, Robertsganj, Sonbhadra.
   Thus, the above mentioned descriptions have been presented to unveil the real situations prevailing among the *dalit adivasis* in the south-eastern region of Uttar Pradesh. This would surely help in judging the extent of development and welfare schemes and the object of the Government to bring the *adivasis* into the mainstream of national development.
2. Sanjay Kol, Area Commander Hardcore Naxalite, resident of Village Majgaon, Police Station Naugarh, Tehsil Chakiya, Chandauli district.

His father purchased one piece of fertile land in Gangapur by selling anscestral land. But the registration formalities were not completed in Registrar Office. In the mean time, one man named Chulhai Yadav bought this piece of land by paying Rs. two lakh and got registered. Due to this reason the dispute arose. Sanjay Kol complained in Police administration and the matter was discussed in Gram Panchayat also. But Chulhai Yadav was adamant not to release the land.

Some Suggestions

1. First of all 'the south-eastern Margins of Uttar Pradesh' should officially be recognised and declared as the 'Tribal Area', to be authorized and entitled to receive all the benefits of the Government schemes.
2. The second most populated tribes in all the five districts, is Kol who have been the original inhabitants since pre-historic period. Surprisingly, it has not yet been included in the list of Scheduled Tribes. As soon as possible, the Union Government as well as the State Government of Uttar Pradesh should constitutionally recognise 'Kol tribe' and provide the status of 'Scheduled Tribe', so that, they may be in a position to receive all the benefits of the Government schemes.
3. Strong National character and public morality have to be built up if any development programme including tribal development programme is launched.
4. Before outburst of any sort of revolt, rebel and uprising and mutiny initiated by tribals like hungry lion, the present prevalent corrupt practices of scams, practices of percentage of commission, bribe and economic corruption forcibly and strictly have to be stopped by the strict laws of the Government.
5. *Dalit adivasis* had been enjoying the full rights over water, forest and land since pre-historic period. After Independence they have been deprived of all their three properties by the forest department. They have been treated as trespassers. Consequently, they have become pauper, landless and resourceless for their livelihood. They have reached at the verge of starvation and death.

   Thus, keeping their critical conditions in view, the Government should take strict action to implement the Forest Right Act 2006 in their favour and strict instructions should be issued not to interfere in their possession and in the right of their livelihood.
6. There should not at all be ban in collecting forest produce which is the main source of their livelihood.
7. Tribals ancestral agricultural land which had been vacated for power plants, dams, coal mines and other industrial units, should properly be compensated by providing agricultural land along with the monetary assistance.
8. Displacement of *dalit adivasis* started with the construction of

Rihand Dam and still it is continuing due to discovery of coal, lime, gold and other minerals. *Dalit adivasis* have already suffered from multiple displacements. Therefore, it is very necessary on humanitarian ground that the displacement should be stopped right now and as per national norms, all the displaced *adivasis* should be rehabilitated with all the essential facilities and they should be provided proper opportunities to earn their livelihood and make their family and generation happy and prosperous.

9. Due to excessive discharge of industrial garbages, gas, fly ashes, etc., the surrounding areas of all the industrial power plants, coal mines and Rihand Dam, have been completely over polluted. With this result, the *adivasis* living around these places in huts, have been victimised by several types of diseases. As a result of it, the coming generation is becoming physically disabled and handicapped. Therefore, the Government has to take immediate action against these serious problems and the *dalit adivasis* should be rehabilitated at different places which are free from all sorts of pollution.
10. All the lands which had been grabbed by the maphias, contractors and feudal landlords, should be returned to them to make them free from all sorts of phobia and make them psychologically normal.
11. A special campaign should be started to make the *dalit adivasis* free from the clutches of the feudal landlords and moneylenders who had been exploiting and torturing by keeping them bonded labourers.
12. The Government should provide special financial assistance so that they may be free from indebtedness for ever.
13. Before launching any development and welfare programme, the infrastructural developments should be given top priority. Construction of inter-connecting roads, easy availability of means of communications, PHC and CHC, Post Offices, Schools, PDS Centres and other Welfare facilities should be easily accessible and available at shorter distance.
14. Bridges, culverts, electrification, irrigation, drinking water, seed and fertilizer shops and shops of utmost necessities should easily be available near their villages.
15. In order to make them aware of their rights and duties, Government facilities and all their welfare schemes, Gram

Pradhan, BDO, ADO and Other Government Officials should frequently visit in tribal areas and in their groups, everything should be made aware to them. In return, their personal problems and community problems should be heard attentively and should be solved at the earliest. Government officials have to achieve rapport position with the *dalit adivasis*.

16. The tribal psychology is very-very conservative and it is full of blind superstitions, totems and taboos. They have blind faith in spirits witches and devils. For them, whatever happens in their life, all because of these gods and evil spirits. Therefore, it is most essential to change and transform their conservative psychology and blind superstitions. It could be done only through awareness, literacy, education and through visual media.
17. In this mission, schools and colleges should be opened along with free hostel facilities. Only those teachers should be appointed who are dedicated by heart to serve the tribals in real sense. Tribal children and their guardians as well should all the time be encouraged for their interest in educational development. The financial hindrances should not come on their way.
18. To make the education financially fruitful, professional and occupational training institutes should be provided at the nearest places from their villages and that should be free. Vocational training should be given to the tribal youths in different areas of profession.
19. Top priority should be given to female education and adult education.
20. 'Adivasis Forest Produce Corporation' should be established for marketing different forest products collected by the tribals.
21. Production of tribal handicrafts should be encouraged and it should be commercialized.
22. Tribal dance, music and other cultural activities should be encouraged by displaying in other societies.
23. The local administration, the Revenue Department and the Welfare Department have always to be watchful and be assured that each and every facility like White, Red and Blue Ration Cards, Job Cards. Smart Cards have been distributed among all the BPL listed *dalit adivasis*. It is to be assured that financial assistance and scholarship and mid-day meal facilities are easily and certainly available to all the children, pregnant women, newly born babies, old men and women and widow financial assistance

and facilities are reaching to them in true sense. Food items available at PDS shops are properly distributed to the BPL listed and other tribals.

24. Alongwith allopathic, homoeopathic, Unani and Aurvedic medicines, the tribal herbal and traditional type of treatment should also be encouraged in order to satisfy them psychologically.
25. Gram Panchayat is the smallest unit of the democratic system of our country. Therefore, in order to make them aware and to change their views, majority of the members in Gram Panchayat of tribal villages, should be from *adivasis* and it must be headed by *adivasis* Gram Pradhan.
26. The constitution of Land Management Committee in 433 villages of Sonbhadra district has not yet been constituted by forest department due to its illegal interference for a long time. This should be done at the earliest in order to provide land to the landless tribals.
27. The physical and financial linkages should be assessed and active participation must be ensured in the local administration and in development programmes. Therefore, the active tribal community participation is highly essential.
28. All the plans of development should be framed by keeping the priority of the requirement of that particular area. The *adivasis* of that area will be proved the best guide.
29. A simple and adequate personnel system should be evolved for getting right persons for right work in tribal areas.
30. A cadre of motivated work force in tribal areas should be placed, so that, persons having desire to work with tribal people and having a social achievement motivation, should get the chance to serve in tribal areas and perform the difficult task of tribal development.
31. In order to assure better services as well as for creating awareness about these schemes and services among the tribal folk, "mutual co-operation, voluntary support service", is the need of time.
32. More and more awareness and conscientisation drives should be undertaken in *adivasi* areas so that the *dalit adivasis* masses may generate an urge for growth and development amongst them. This task can well be performed by trained social work professionals.
33. All the tribal development schemes should be implemented in

such a way that they may contribute to a common objective of tribal development. All the departments should prepare a coordinated strategy in this connection. Inter and intra departmental connectivity through e-governance is a right step in this direction.

34. Mirzapur, Sonbhadra and Chandauli tribal areas are now recognised as Naxal activities zone and Allahabad and Chitrakoot tribal areas are dacoit activities zone. Both the zones have provided sufficient opportunities to flourish the Naxalism and dacoitism. Oppressed and tortured *adivasis* were forced to search other alternatives and that was to see towards Naxalites and dacoits. In order to make both the zone free from Naxalism and dacoitism and other isms it is most essential to stop their land alienation, displacement, harassment and exploitation of the *dalit adivasis* from the hands of moneylenders, feudal landlords, contractors mafias, middlemen, police, rural elites, Government officials and forest department. 'Community Policing Experiment in Sonbhadra' experiment has recently met with success in removing police phobia among the tribals.

In the end, 'Humanitarian and Philanthropical Cooperative Outlook and Changed Attitude' are very much essential with full honesty for changed facilities towards *dalit adivasis* development. All the clouds of discontent have to be removed for the rising sun of development.

Bibliography

Alok Kumar – *Tribal Cultures and Economy.*

Ambasht, N.K. and Rath, K.B. (1995), *Effects of household, community and School factors on the enrolment, retention and achievement by scheduled tribes children at Primary level, In school effectiveness and learning achievement at primary stage. International Perspective* NCERT.

Ambastha, N.K. (1993), "Status of Tribal women in India: Educational Implications," *Social Change,* 23(4):60-65.

Aram, M. (1974), *Peace in Nagaland, Eight Years Story of 1964-72,* New Delhi, Arnold Heineman.

Atal, Yogesh (1968), *The Changing Frontiers of Castes,* National Publishing House, New Delhi.

Aurora, G.S. (1972), *Tribe, Caste, Class Encounter,* Administrative Staff College of India, Hyderabad.

Awasthi, B.P. (1987), *"A study of the Inter-relationship between education of the scheduled tribes and their socio-economic mobility,"* Independent Study NCERT.

Baily, F.G. (1957), *Caste and the Economic Frontier.* Bombay: Oxford University Press 1960, Tribe, Caste and Nation: A study of political activity and political change in highland, Orissa, Manchester University Press.

Banerjee, Sukumar (1981), *Impact of Industrialization on Tribal Population of Jharia – Ranigunj Coal Field Areas,* Culcutta: Anthropological Survey of India.

Banjujari, H.K., (1970), *Problem of the Hill Tribes of North East Frontier 1822-42,* Gauhati Laer's Book Stall.

Bardhan, A.B. (1973), *The Unsolved Tribal Problems,* Communist Party Publication, New Delhi.

Bardhan, A.B. (1977), *Ansuljhi Janjati Samasya,* Delhi. Communist Party of India.

Barkatki, S. (1969), *Tribes of Assam (India)—The Land and People,* New Delhi, National Book Trust.

Basu, S.K. (1993), "Health Status of Tribal Women in India", *Social Change,* 23(4):19-39.

Beteille, Andre and T.N. Madan (1975), *Encounter and Experience, Personal Accounts of Field Work*, Delhi, Vikas Publishing House.

Bhagat, L.N. and Verma, (2000), U.K., *Tribal Area Development: Need for Alternative Strategy.*

Bhandarkar, A. (1980), "Science Instruction Strategies of Tribal Development", In *Problem Development of Tribal Areas* by Deogankar S.G., Leela Publication, Delhi.

Bhowmick, K.K. (ed) (1971), *Tribal India: A Profile of Indian Ethnology*, The World Press, Calcutta.

Boas, Franz (1963), *The Mind of Primitive Man,* New York, Free Press.

Boddley, John H. (1982), *Victims of Progress, California:* The Benjamin Cummings Publishing Co.

Bose, (N.K.), *Some Indian Tribes,* National Book Trust, New Delhi.

Bose, N.K. (1971), *Tribal Life in India*, New Delhi: National Book Trust.

Bose, N.K. (1967), *Culture and Society in India,* Calcutta.

Brdly, Brit, F.B. (1905), *The Story of an Indian Upward.*

Census of India (2001), Series I New Delhi, 2001.

Chakrabarty, M. and Mukherjee, D. (1971), '*Indian Tribes,* Saraswati Library, Calcutta.

Chakrabarty, B. and Malakar, C.R. (1962), *Demographic Data—An Imperative Need for the Welfare of the Tribal Population in India* (*Mimeo*) Indian Statistical Institute, Calcutta.

Chandrashekhar, S. (1954), *Hungary People and Empty Land,* George Allen & Unwin Ltd., London.

Chaturvedi, Vijay Shankar (2010), 'A Flame of Hope', *Community Policing in Sonbhadra*, Press Club, Sonbhadra (UP)

Chaudhari, Budhadev (ed.) (1982), *Tribal Development in India,* Inter-India Publications, New Delhi.

Chaudhari, C. (ed.), *Tribal Development in India: Problems and Prospects,* Inter-India Publications, New Delhi.

Chaudhari, G.N., (1978), *Impact of Industrialization on Tribal Villages*, Department of Anthropology, Ranchi University, Ranchi.

Chaudhary, B. (ed.) (1982), *Tribal Development in India: Problems and Prospects*, Inter-India Publications, Delhi.

Chaudhary, Damina (2009), '*Tribal Girls' Aspirations, Achievement and Frustration,* Pointer Publishers, Jaipur.

Chaudhary, S.N. (2009), *Tribal Development since Independence,* Concept Publishing Company (P) Ltd., New Delhi.

Chauhan, Abha, (1990), *Tribal Women and Social Change in India,* Etawah: A.C. Brothers.

Chauhan, B.R. (1970), *Towns in the Tribal Settings,* Delhi, National Publishing House.

Chowdhry, Prem (ed.) (2009), *Gender Discrimination in Land Ownership*, Sage Publication, New Delhi.

Chocko Pariyaram, M. (2005), *Tribal Communities and Social Change*.

Chop-Chaudhari, Buddhadeb (1981), *Tribal Development in India*, Delhi, Inter-India Publications..

Christopher, Von, Furer Haimandorf, (1985), *Tribes of India the Struggle for Survival*, Oxford University Press, Delhi.

Cohen, Gaynor (ed.), *Social Change and the Life Course*, Tavistock Publications, London.

Crook, William, (1975), *The Tribes and Castes of the North Western India*, Cosmo Publications, Delhi.

Danda, A.K., (1973), *Tribal Economics and their Transformation*, ICSSR.

Das, Amal Kumar (1966), *Hand Book on Scheduled Castes and Scheduled Tribes of West Bengal*, Tribal Welfare Department, Government of West Bengal.

Das, Ashish Kumar (2009), *Contemporary Issues and Social Movement in India*, Sarup Book Publishers Pvt. Ltd., New Delhi.

Das Gupta, N.K. (1963), *Problems of Tribal Education and the Santhals*, Bhartiya Adimjati Sewak Samaj, New Delhi.

Das, N.K. (2009), *Tribes, Cultural-Adaptations and Belief Systems, Conceptual and Methodological Perspective*, Serial Publications, New Delhi.

Das, R.K., (1971), *The Problems of Tribal Identity in Manipur*, The Eastern Anthropologist, Vol. 24, No. 2.

Datta, Kalikinkar (1940), *The Santhal Insurrection*, Calcutta University, Calcutta.

Deogaonkar, S.G., (1980), *Problems of Development of Tribal Areas*, Inter-India Publications, New Delhi.

Dogra, Bharat (1997), '*Struggle for Land Reforms and Social Justice*', A voluntary organisation's effort in Patha Region of Uttar Pradesh'; Chitrakoot.

Dogra, Bharat (2006), '*Alternative Planning for Sustainable Livelihoods in Bundelkhand Region, Uttar Pradesh*', ABSSS, Chitrakoot.

Dogra, Bharat (2000), '*Fighting Terror, Protecting Dignity*', Report on a voluntary organizations (ABSSS) work in Chitrakoot Region' New Delhi

Dube, S.C. (1977), *Tribal Heritage of India (4 Vols)*, Vikas Publishing House Pvt. Ltd., New Delhi.

Dutta, Kalikinkar (1940), *The Santhal Insurrection*. Calcutta University.

Fernandes, Walter, Geeta Menan and Philip Viegas (1988), *Forest Environment and Tribal Economy*, Indian Social Institute, New Delhi.

Ghurye, G.S. (1963), *The Scheduled Tribes*, Bombay, Popular Prakashan.

Government of India (2001), *Report of the Steering Committee on Empowering the Scheduled Tribes*, New Delhi: Planning Commission.

Tribes, in Budhadev Chaudhary (ed.), *Tribal Development in India, Problems and Prospects*, Inter-India Publications, New Delhi.

Reddy, I.U.B. (1993), *Displacement and Rehabilitation*, Mittal Publications, New Delhi.

Reddy, T. Prabhakar (1989), 'Tribal Land Alienation in Andhra Pradesh', *Economic and Political Weekly*, Vol. XXV, No. 28, 15 July.

Roy Burman, B.K. (1982), "Transfer and Alienation of Tribal Land", in Budhadev Chaudhary (ed.) *Tribal Development in India, Problems Prospects*, Inter-India Publications, New Delhi.

Roy, Kanchan (ed.) (2008), *Education and Health Problems in Tribal Development*, Concept Publishing Co., New Delhi.

Sadanandam, P. (2008), *Art and Culture of Marginalised Nomadic Tribes in Andhra Pradesh*, Gyan Publishing House, New Delhi.

Sadangi, Himansu Charan (2008), '*Dalit*' *The Downtrodden of India*, ISHA Books, Delhi.

Sah, D.C. and Ashish Bhatt (2008), *Trapped in Poverty, Chronic Poor in Remote Tribal Areas*, Rawat Publications, Jaipur.

Satya, Narayan M. (1990), *Tribal Development in India: A Trend Report*, Inter-India Publications, New Delhi.

Shah, Ghanshyam (2009), *Social Movements in India*, Sage Publications, New Delhi.

Shah, Ghanshyam, (1982), 'Tribal Issues: Problems and Perspectives' in B. Chaudhari (ed.). *Tribal Transformation in India*, Vol. 2, pp. 113-141 Delhi: Inter-India Publications.

Sharma, B.D. (1977), 'Administration of Tribal Development' *India Journal of Public Administration*, Vol. XXIII, No. 3, July-Sept.

Sharma, K.L.; (1976), 'Jharkhand Movement in Bihar', *Economic and Political Weekly*. Jan.10, II, 1-20, pp. 37-43.

Shilu, A.O.P. (1969), *Report of the Study Team on Tribal Development Programme*; New Delhi.

Singh, Amar Kumar, M.K. Jabbi and C. Rajya Laxmi (1991), '*Status of Tribals in India; Health, Education and Employment*' *Status of Tribals in India*, (ed.), Amar Kumar Singh and M.K. Jabbi, Har Anand Publications, New Delhi.

Singh, Awadhesh Kumar (2008), *Tribal Development in India*, Serial Publications, New Delhi.

Singh, Bhupendra (1977), *Tribal Development At Cross Roads*, A Critique and a Plea '*Man in India*', Vol. 57, No. 3.

Singh, Ekta (2009), '*Caste System in India: A Historical Perspective*. Kalpaz Publications, Delhi.

Singh, K.S. (1985), *Tribal Society in India*, New Delhi.

Singh, Suresh K. (1972), *Tribal Situation in India,* Indian Institute of Anthropology, Simla.

Singh, B. (1984), *The Saora Highlanders; Leadership and Development,* Bombay, Somaiya Publication.

Sinha, A.K. (1992), *Tribal Development in India:* Issues and Strategies in a Book.

Sinha, S.P. (1986), '*Tribal Development Administration*' in L.P. Vidyarthi (ed.), *Tribal Development its Administration.* Concept Publishing Company, New Delhi.

Sinha, Sachidanand (1954), Bisra: An Adivasi Fighter for Freedom, *Vanyajati* Vol. 4.

Somashekhar, K. (2008), *Developmental Programmes and Social Change Among the Tribals.*

Sriniwas, M.N. (1965), *Social Change in Modern India,* Allied Publications, Bombay.

Thakur, Devendra (ed.), Thakur D.N. (1964), *Tribal Life in India,* Vol. 3 (Tribal Life and Forest) Deep & Deep Publications, New Delhi, 1994.

Thakur, Devendra and Thakur, D.N., *Tribal Development and Planning.*

Tribal Cultural Research and Training Institute (1971), *Absenteeism, Stagnation and Wastage the Primary Schools of Tribal Areas of Andhra Pradesh,* Hyderabad.

Tribal Research Institute, Maharashtra (1970), *Report on Wastage in Primary and Secondary Education of the Scheduled Tribes of Nasik District,* Puna.

Tripathi, S.N. (1998), *Tribals of India,* Discovery Publishing House, New Delhi.

UNESCO (1981), *Transfer and Utilization of Information for Development in the 1980s; Main Problems and Strategies for the Solution.*

UNO: *Rural Development Administration in India, UNO.*

Upreti H.C., *Indian Tribes, Then and Now,* Pointer Publishers, Jaipur.

Verma, Mahendra Mohan, *Tribal Development in India: Programme and Perspectives.* Published by Mittal Publications, New Delhi.

Verma, R.C. (2002), *Indian Tribes Through the Ages,* Publications Division, Ministry of Information and Broadcasting, Government of India.

Vidyarthi, L.P. (1964), *An Appraisal of Leadership Pattern among the Tribes of Bihar. Tribal Situation in India,* ed. by K. Suresh Singh, Shimla, Indian Institute of Advanced Study. The Historic March of Jharkhand Party; A Study of Adivasi Leadership in Tribal Bihar, *Indian Sociological Bulletin.* 1(2).

Vilayuthan, K. Shanmuga (1979), A sub-plan approach to tribal development. *The Indian Journal of Social Work,* Vol. XI, No.2, July.

Zafur, M. (1975), *Policy for Planning and Development in Tribal Areas,* NICD, Hyderabad.

अखिल भारतीय समाज सेवा संस्थान गोपाल भाई (1999), *मानवाधिकार हनन विशेषांक।*

अखिल भारतीय समाज सेवा संस्थान गोपाल भाई (2005), *सफलता एक अनुकरणीय अभियान।*

अखिल भारतीय समाज सेवा संस्थान (2006), *उ०प्र० जोत चकबन्दी अधिनियम* 1953-1955, चित्रकूट।

उ०प्र० ग्रामीण एवं खेतिहर मजदूर यूनियन (2006), *अनुसूचित जनजाति एवं अन्य आदिवासी* (वन अधिकारों को मान्यता) अधिनियम 2006।

केसरी, डॉ. अर्जुनदास (1994), *यह सोनभद्र है,* लोकरुचि प्रकाशन, सोनभद्र।

केसरी, डॉ. अर्जुनदास (2004), *विन्ध्य क्षेत्र का सांस्कृतिक वैभव,* उत्तर-मध्य क्षेत्र सांस्कृतिक केन्द्र, इलाहाबाद।

खंडेला, मानचन्द्र (2008), '*दलित अधिकार एवं व्यवहार*' पोइन्टर पब्लिकेशनस, जयपुर।

चतुर्वेदी, डॉ. संजय (2002), '*करमा*', हिन्डालको इन्डस्ट्रीज लिमिटेड, रेनूकूट, सोनभद्र।

चतुर्वेदी, विजय शंकर (2004), '*नक्सली आतंक और सोनभद्र*', प्रेस क्लब, सोनभद्र।

चतुर्वेदी, विजय शंकर सम्पादक (2004), '*सोन वैभव स्मारिका 2009*', दुर्गा कम्प्यूटर रानिक्स, इलाहाबाद।

चौधरी, नैना, शशी भूषण, जगदीश गिरी (2010), '*रोज़गार गारन्टी योजना*', फैजाबाद।

डोगरा, भरत (1991), '*पाठा*' *सूखे खेत प्यासे दिल,* रक्षा कुंज, नई दिल्ली।

नारायण, बद्री (2008), '*दलित वैचारिकी की दिशायें*', राधाकृष्ण प्रकाशन, नई दिल्ली।

भूषण, लोक शांडिल्य राजेश्वरी (2006), '*दलित पुरुषार्थ कुछ सूत्र*', प्रिन्स प्रिन्टर्स, लखनऊ।

शर्मा, के.एल. (2006), *भारतीय सामाजिक संरचना एवं परिवर्तन,* रावत पब्लिकेशन, जयपुर।

शिवेन्द्र, राम नाथ (2005), '*सोनभद्र प्राचीन*', आनन्दकानन प्रेस, वाराणसी।

श्रीवास्तव, अ.र.न. (1956), '*भारत की जनजातियाँ*', ज्ञानदीप प्रकाशन, इलाहाबाद।

श्रीवास्तव, श्याम नारायण लाल (2007), '*मूलाधिकार और आदिवासी*', *जल, जंगल, जमीन,* महाक़ाल समाचार विवरण, सोनभद्र।

श्रीवास्तव, श्याम नारायण लाल (2010), '*मूलाधिकार और प्रदूषण*', महाकाल समाचार विवरण, सोनभद्र।

श्रीवास्तव, श्याम नारायण लाल (2010), '*संवैधानिक और आदिवासियों की उत्तरजीविता*', महाकाल समाचार विवरण, सोनभद्र।

Journals

A Case Inter Specification of the Development of Tribal Areas, A.3 *Aijappan*, Vol. VII, No. 1, 1965-66.

Academy of Tribal Dialects and Culture, Orissa, Review 2003, '*Adivasi*'

Tribal Welfare and Some Social Aspects of Development Blocks, Tribal Research Bureau, Orissa, 1965.

Approaching the Tribal People for Wefare, Kulamain Mohapatra, Vol. V, No. 3, 1963-64.

Area Approach to the Socio-Economic Development of Tribal Communities, B.K. Roy Burman, Vol. IX, No. 2, 1967-68.

Forest Policy and Tribal Development, Bhupindar Singh, Vol. XXVII, No. 1, 1987.

Forestry and Tribal Development, N. Pathak, Vol. XXXII, No. 2, 1992.

Health Problems of Primitive Tribal Groups/Communities of Orissa, Allnas Ali, Vol. XXIII, No. 2, 1983.

Indicator of Tribal Development, Vinay Kumar Mathur, Vol. VII, No. 4, 1966-67.

On Significance of Tribal Economic Institutions in Development Programmes, A.R.N. Srivastava, Vol. XX, No. 1-4, 1980-81.

Planning Process Vs. *Poorest Among the Poor:* A Review of Planning for Tribal Development, *Sharma*, Vol. XXVI, No. 2, 1986.

Problem of Integration of the Tribals in Indian Society. B.K. Roy Burman, Vol. III, Nos. 3-4, 1958-59.

Some Aspects of Development Infrastructure in Tribal Areas, P. Venkata Rao, Vol. XXXIV, No. 1-2, 1994.

Training for Tribal Development, Vijay Kumar Mathur, Vol. IX, No. 3, 1967-68.

Tribal Development: The Strategy, B.D. Sharma, Vol. XVI, No. 2, 1972.

Index